Praise for *Chick Flicks: Theories and Memories of the Feminist Film Movement*

"B. Ruby Rich reinvents both herself and her approach to film criticism in a fascinating book that alternates autobiography and theory. She is wise and funny at the same time, never dogmatic, always allowing her discovery process to remain in clear view."—**ROGER EBERT**

"This collection of writings by B. Ruby Rich is sure to become a classic. She has proven herself to be a courageous guide into uncharted aesthetic and political territory and, in describing so eloquently what she finds there, she does what critics aspire to but rarely achieve: she both educates and entertains."
—**SALLY POTTER**, director of the films *Orlando* and *The Tango*

"This is a remarkable book. B. Ruby Rich has written a memoir that encourages the reader not only to see the original essays in a new context but also and especially to understand the development of an intellectual and political moment with all of its complications and personal investments."—**JUDITH MAYNE**, author of *Cinema and Spectatorship*

"Memoir and manifesto, Rich's incisive collection chronicles how she found it at the movies: 'It' being self, feminism, and the contours of a feminine aesthetic and politics. With essays on filmmakers Leni Riefenstahl and Leontine Sagan and her considerations of actress Julie Christie and director Chantal Akerman, *Chick Flicks* connects filmgoing to feminism to fortitude."—**CARRIE RICKEY**, *PHILADELPHIA INQUIRER*

"A longtime film curator and critic . . . [Rich] is in the rare position of having freely crossed usually impermeable boundaries: between mainstream filmmaking and the avant garde, between the academic and the popular press, between lesbian and heterosexual feminists. . . . She loves film and believes in its power to change lives—and in her own power to educate audiences about the films she loves."—**LINDA DELIBERO**, *IN THESE TIMES*

"B. Ruby Rich, cultural critic extraordinaire, ties her nonsequential chapters together as a 'cinefeminism' manifesto. Go with Rich to Cuba to understand the impact of the late director Sarah Gomez (*One Way or Another*); to Belgium in 1974 for the stunning Knokke-Heist EXPMNTL Film Festival; and to Michigan to learn about Adrienne Rich's 'euphoric' fans and the beginnings of lesbian cinema. Whatever you do, don't go without her."—*GIRLFRIENDS*

D1603133

"Like the feminist and female-authored films that Rich has championed throughout her professional career as a critic, professor, exhibitor, film festival judge, and grantmaker, *Chick Flicks* is an experimental, documentary-style narrative about what it means to bring women's interests into filmmaking. . . . It is not just another book of feminist film criticism: it is one woman's account of how feminism changed her life both intellectually and personally."—**ANNALEE NEWITZ**, *CINEASTE*

"*Advocate* columnist B. Ruby Rich re-creates the days when feminism met film and hatched a new movement whose sexiness and cool are now only dimly remembered. Samples of her own film writings from the '70s and '80s alternate with juicy dish on the doings (in and out of bed) of a generation of wild women and their pals."—**ANNE STOCKWELL**, *ADVOCATE*

"A rare and momentous book. . . . Not simply a tome of the collected works of one of the fiercest minds of feminist film. It is, in the end, a lexicon for the new vernaculars of the future, a feminist film manual for the new millennium."
—**PATRICIA R. ZIMMERMAN**, *AFTERIMAGE*

"Required reading. . . . Rich has written on virtually everything and everyone in feminist film culture worth writing on."—**AMY VILLAREJO**, *GLQ: A JOURNAL OF LESBIAN AND GAY STUDIES*

"Perhaps *Chick Flicks*'s greatest strength is the number of ways in which it can be read: as a professional retrospective strewn with delicious gossip, a personal diary of hindsight recollections and revisions, a copious document of '70s and '80s feminist film culture, a historical memoir and a memoir of history. . . . *Chick Flicks* is a model of politically rooted, socially conscious, intellectually challenging—but not intellectually alienating—cultural criticism."
—**JOSH KUN**, *SAN FRANCISCO BAY GUARDIAN*

"Working first as a critic, exhibitor, and curator, Rich gradually became involved with academic film theory and gained a reputation as a passionate, original film scholar whose sophisticated theoretical commentary was matched by her lively and down-to-earth perspective and prose. . . . Although her topic is cinema, Rich's larger concern is women as artists and subjects of visual media. . . . *Chick Flicks*, with its multiple contexts and locations, Sundance to Cuba to Edinburgh, demonstrates how widely spaces of theory can be imagined and how inclusive its visions can be."—**LINDA MIZEJEWSKI**, *WOMEN'S REVIEW OF BOOKS*

NEW QUEER CINEMA

B. RUBY RICH

NEW QUEER CINEMA

THE DIRECTOR'S CUT

DUKE UNIVERSITY PRESS DURHAM AND LONDON 2013

© 2013 Duke University Press

All rights reserved

Printed in the United States of America on

acid-free paper ∞ Designed by Amy Ruth Buchanan

Typeset in Minion Pro by Copperline Book Services, Inc.

Library of Congress Cataloging-in-Publication Data

Rich, B. Ruby.

New queer cinema : the director's cut / B. Ruby Rich.

pages cm

Includes bibliographical references and index.

ISBN 978-0-8223-5411-6 (cloth : alk. paper)

ISBN 978-0-8223-5428-4 (pbk. : alk. paper)

1. Homosexuality in motion pictures.

2. Gays in motion pictures. I. Title.

PN1995.9.H55R53 2013

791.43'653—dc23   2012048672

for

Mary

the love

of my life

CONTENTS

ACKNOWLEDGMENTS

This book has been in process for so many years that the many friends, colleagues, and editors who have supported, assisted, cheered, and resurrected this manuscript are too numerous to name here. I'm very lucky to be the recipient of their generosity. One thing is certain: this volume would not have materialized in your hands without them. And without the filmmakers, of course, none of this writing would exist; thanks to them, mine and so many other lives have been transformed. Their imagination and bravery have helped to transform the world in my lifetime.

There are so many people whose impact on my ideas, my life, and my access to and knowledge of films have shaped this volume. I've been lucky to have old friends and comrades-in-arms stick around, to have new voices join in, and to be the beneficiary of so much inspiration and good energy for so long a time. My deepest thanks, then, to Sheila McLaughlin, Kate Horsfield, Faye Ginsburg, Carrie Rickey, Carol Becker, Isaac Julien, Mark Nash, Tony Safford, Marti Wilson-Taylor, Richard Dyer, Catherine Zimmer, Claire Aguilar, Sharon Thompson, Fred Myers, Christine Vachon, Joan Braderman, Michelle Erai, Bill Horrigan, Judith Mayne, and Jeremy Podeswa.

No writing transpires in a vacuum; for their scholarship and intellectual engagement, in addition to those thanked above or below, my deepest thanks to Linda Williams, Patricia White, Patricia Zimmerman, Jackie Stacey, Michele Aaron, Monica B. Pearl, George Chauncey, Ron Gregg, Pat Aufderheide, and Michael Renov. Special thanks go to Lisbeth Haas for the sustenance of West Cliff walks, her historian's eye on these pages, and her companionship in writing. To M. Paloma Pavel, thanks for courage and strategies: her wisdom has been essential.

In San Francisco, thanks for time well spent in good company go to Connie Wolf, Catherine Wagner, Loretta Gargan, Terry Castle, Blakey Vermuele, Clara Basile, Emiko Omori, Toni Mirosevich, Shotsy Faust, Susan Gerhard, Charles Wilmoth, Kathy McNicholas, Lisa Van Cleef, Mark Gunson, Nancy Stoller, and my old pals Jewelle Gomez and Diane Sabin. I've also benefited mightily from the ministrations of the Russian Hill film gang: Marcus Hu and Ross Nakasone, Lynn Hershman-Leeson and George Leeson, and indispensable part-timer John Waters. In Paris, thanks to Marie-Pierre Macia, Juliette Lepoutre, Joan Dupont, and Nathalie Magnon. In Toronto, thanks to Susan Feldman, Helga Stephenson, Kass Banning, Warren Crichlow, Elle Flanders, Lynne Fernie, John Greyson, Richard Fung, and Kay Armatage. At NYU, thanks to Lisa Duggan, and Catharine R. Stimpson for conversations over the years, and to José Muñoz, Ann Pelegrini, and Eric Zinner for early encouragement of this project.

In Scotland, thanks to the great Tilda Swinton. She occupies no dedicated chapter, but her presence limns the New Queer Cinema's evolution all the way back to her performances with and for Derek Jarman and her incarnation as Orlando, and on through her many gender-transgressive roles. Thanks to Tilda, then, for spirit, work, and friendship.

Thanks too to my film festival friends, who have had as deep an impact on my thinking as anyone over the years: John Cooper, Paul Louis Maillard, Anne Thompson, Lesli Klainberg, Alberto Garcia, Noah Cowan, Michael Lumpkin, K. C. Price, Shannon Kelley, Jenni Olson, Jennifer Morris, Marion Masone, Jytte Jensen, Connie White, Gabby Hanna, Andrew Peterson, Peter Knegt, Shari Frilot, Caroline Libresco, Trevor Groth, Norman Wang, Maxine Bailey, Alison Baine, Laura Thielen, Piers Handling, Jane Schoettle, Gabrielle Free, Alberto Garcia, Laura Kim, Tom Luddy, Meredith Brody, and the dear departeds, Mark Finch and Jay Scott.

In Santa Cruz, thanks to my dear friends and colleagues Renee Tajima-Peña and John Jota Leaños, with whom I've taught in the UC Santa Cruz Social Documentation Program, alongside Marcia Ochoa and Spencer Nakasako and Leo Chiang, and to my friends and colleagues across the campus: Lisa Rofel, L. S. Kim, Lourdes Martinez-Echazabal, Karen Yamashita, Carla Freccero, Emily Honig, David Brundage, Herman Gray, Rosa-Linda Fregoso, Sharon Daniel, Shelley Stamp, and Marilyn Chapin; and to the fantastic students and alumni of the SocDoc graduate program for their commitment to making documentaries in the service of social justice. Thanks too to the colleagues and staff of my new home there, the Arts Division and the Film and Digital Media Department, with special thanks to Robert Valiente-Neighbours and Tristan Carkeet. Thanks to Dean David Yager for his key support.

The two heroines who read this manuscript for Duke were revealed to me only after the fact. For assistance beyond the bounds of friendship or professional obligation, thanks to Linda Williams for her substantive advice on the manuscript and intellectual clarity, her characteristic generosity, years of support, and example of scholarly excellence, undaunted and ever-hopeful; and to Amy Villarejo, thanks for her typically incisive reading of the manuscript and for her own contributions to this field, a model of scholarship in the service of ideas without borders.

For their research assistance and manuscript reading over the past several years, I owe great thanks to Charles Wilmoth for his astute and patient oversight; to Jason Alley, for his research and sagacious input; to Onnesha Roychoudhuri, for her editing; to Cheryl VanDeVeer and Nhu Tien Lu, for contributions to its completion; to April Anthony, for key conversations; and to Ann Martin for early suggestions.

For material and intellectual support, thanks to the Camargo Foundation and its residency fellowship in Cassis, France, where in 2007 the chapter on Ozon, cinema, and French sexual politics was written and vetted. My Francophile cohort provided research tips and cultural clarifications, as well as conviviality and parties that made our time together a pleasure. Special thanks to then-directors Jean-Pierre and Mary Dautricourt for their vision for Camargo and the spirit of community they fostered there. Above all, I'm grateful to the University of California, Santa Cruz, for the sabbatical leave that allowed me to accept the fellowship.

For any writer, editors are unseen but crucial; for journalists, even more so. Major thanks are due to the editors who put their faith in me, prodded me, and got me to write: Susan Gerhard at the *San Francisco Bay Guardian* and *sf360*; Andrew Pulver at *The Guardian* (London); Lisa Kennedy and Dennis Lim at the *Village Voice*; Philip Dodd, Pam Cook, and Nick James at *Sight and Sound*; Art Winslow at *The Nation*; Rob White at *Film Quarterly*; and Anne Stockwell, Alonso Duralde, and Bruce C. Steele at *The Advocate*. Thanks to Eugene Hernandez and the gang for the NQC forums on indiewire. Thanks to Patricia White, Chris Straayer, and Thomas Waugh at GLQ: *Journal of Lesbian and Gay Studies*, and to Carolyn Dinshaw for conscripting me into its pages in the first place. Thanks to Julien Mustin at the *Revue Poli-Politique de l'Image* (Paris) for a stimulating interview.

Finally, I owe tremendous thanks, for the indispensable last stage, to my editors at Duke who bring you this volume: to the peripatetic Ken Wissoker for all his expert support and belief and to the energetic Jade Brooks for invaluable assistance and morale-boosting. Their enthusiasm for this project was indispensible to its completion.

Thanks to my family, my bio-anchor on this earth, for a lifetime of support: my sister Susan Rich, sister and brother-in-law Cheryl and Doug Koeber, and my saxophonist nephew, Zachary Koeber. Thanks too to my other family, Richard and Esther Ross, Allyn Peelen, and my sister- and brothers-in-law in Michigan, Connecticut, and Florida.

Finally, deepest thanks to Mary Peelen, my one and only, who has been along for so much of this New Queer Cinema ride. She has made me think harder, feel more deeply, and always give my very best in the service of history, reflection, inspiration, and interpretation. Our life together underlies it all. For her faith in me and this project, for disbelieving my endless declarations of its impossibility, for her rigor and her own bravura display of what dedication to writing and knowledge looks like, for all that, I cannot thank her enough. Without Mary, my work would be the poorer, as would my life. This book is all the better because of her.

■

This volume has been made possible in part by Yale University's James Brudner Award for Outstanding LGBT Scholarship, which sustained research and writing of the manuscript; the Camargo Foundation for a writing residency in Cassis, France; the Social Sciences Division of the University of California, Santa Cruz, for sabbatical support that made the Camargo residency possible; and by the Rockefeller Foundation in the Humanities Fellowship at New York University's Center for Media, Culture, and History that nurtured the early stages of this project.

INTRODUCTION

This volume is a record of a time, the 1990s, and a subject, the New Queer
Cinema, and the decades and lineages of representation to which they gave
rise. It was then and there that a new class of films and videos found a home
and defined an era. These videos and films, so fresh and powerful, decisively
shifted modes of representation, exhibition, and reception in ways that continue to evolve today. This book traces their arrival and evolution. In the
process, it also records my own participation in that founding moment, for I
had the privilege of christening the New Queer Cinema way back in 1992 and
have been along for the ride ever since.

Definitions and descriptions of the New Queer Cinema (NQC) fill these
pages, for it was a kind of filmmaking characterized by a melding of style and
subject in its moments of origin. I once called it, in passing, Homo Pomo in a
nod to the postmodern theories then current. It was a style favoring pastiche
and appropriation, influenced by art, activism, and such new entities as music
video (MTV had just started). It was an approach in search of new languages
and mediums that could accommodate new materials, subjects, and modes of
production. Emanating from a (mostly) new generation, the NQC embodied
an evolution in thinking. It reinterpreted the link between the personal and
the political envisioned by feminism, restaged the defiant activism pioneered
at Stonewall, and recoded aesthetics to link the independent feature movement with the avant-garde and start afresh.

What made the New Queer Cinema possible? It's a question that has re-
curred over the years, one that I can answer only with hindsight. Four ele-

ments converged to result in the NQC: the arrival of AIDS, Reagan, camcorders, and cheap rent. Plus the emergence of "queer" as a concept and a community. Outrage and opportunity merged into a historic artistic response to insufferable political repression: that simple, yes, and that complex.

Illness and death, contagion and indifference, made a generation desperate. AIDS was first reported as a mysterious "gay cancer" in 1981. That year, six friends founded GMHC, the Gay Men's Health Crisis, with nothing but an answering machine—and got more than a hundred calls the first night.[1] HIV was diagnosed as the cause of AIDS in 1984. ACT UP formed in 1986 to fight the government, rescue LGBT pride and dignity, and take on the pharmaceutical establishment; it demonstrated for the creation and release of new AIDS drugs as well as to stop "war profiteering" on the backs of the dying. In 1987 the drug AZT was released with record speed in response to such activism. Ever since, ACT UP has been a model—or should be—for how to act politically to gain empowerment in the face of overwhelming repression.

Reagan's eight years as president rubbed salt in the wounds as he played spokesman for a new conservative Christian version of the Republican Party devoid of compassion, moral compass, or love of New York City, queers, or the arts. Bowing to that influence, his administration directed policies that ignored the dying and stigmatized the ill. Reagan's speechwriters never let him utter the word AIDS, apart from a few demands for testing or quarantine. Construing AIDS as God's retribution for the sin of homosexuality, he and his neocon cronies set the tone for the country. On a plane trip in the mid-1980s, I was upgraded to business class and was soon in a heated argument with a fellow Yale alum who, between drinks, insisted anyone with AIDS should be tattooed. And he wasn't even the worst of them.

In 1986 the Supreme Court's *Bowers v. Hardwick* decision, a pivotal moment in LGBT history of the 1980s, gave legal cover to homophobia by ruling as legal a Texas police raid at gunpoint on a gay couple's bedroom.[2] That decision led hundreds of us to occupy Seventh Avenue for a sitdown in the center of Greenwich Village in protest (and for a bunch of us to go dancing afterward at the Girl Bar on St. Mark's Place). The combination of presidential muteness and judicial malfeasance set the stage for more pointed, amped-up public activism. In 1987 the SILENCE=DEATH poster was designed and displayed in the window of the New Museum. On White Street, on the edge of what would soon be Tribeca, the Collective for Living Cinema was showing the imaginative new short films and videos that made visible the human cost of the AIDS epidemic, claiming the right to speech and self-definition.

Gay men became the new lepers, a status that Todd Haynes's *Poison* would soon make explicit, as everywhere young men were dying (as well as people of color of both genders, needle drug users, and others for whom it would take much longer to get help). Indeed *Poison* would be released to a firestorm on Capitol Hill, one of a series of scapegoats (the "NEA Four," Mapplethorpe, etc.) attacked by the forces of the Right in an ongoing attempt to do away with the National Endowment for the Arts and its chair, John E. Frohnmayer. The Mississippi hit man Donald Wildmon, head of the American Family Association, attacked *Poison* for its (nonexistent) "explicit porno scenes of homosexuals involved in anal sex."[3] He later admitted he never saw the film.

Though Frohnmayer valiantly defended the film as neither prurient nor obscene, that wasn't really the point: the forces of the Right were in their tenth year of the Reagan-Bush regime and very much wanted to destroy the imaginary Homosexual Agenda as well as stop all governmental funding for the arts; Haynes had received a $25,000 grant. When screenings were arranged in Washington, D.C., for members of Congress (true story), one congressman's wife said she needed to bathe in Clorox to cleanse herself of it.[4] Frohnmayer resigned the following year.

If a powerful combination of interests, corporate and governmental, appeared to build an impregnable shield against change, a little device called the camcorder called its bluff and made all the difference. Thank you, Sony. Corporate power, caught in a contradiction between marketplace and ideology, can sometimes contravene its own interests. Newly invented camcorders enabled easy production of electronic media at the personal level for the first time in history. A new generation emerging from art school seized the new tools to reimagine cinema with a video eye, revising the medium thrillingly from the bottom up. In the streets, the camcorder enabled the reversal of surveillance: police could now be recorded by the crowds. And in Los Angeles in 1987, my friend Bill Horrigan and I co-curated *Only Human: Sex, Gender, and Other Misrepresentations* for the annual American Film Institute national video festival. There we presented the first-ever public showing of an AIDS video to a shocked public, earning a visceral response and a profound sense of importance.

The 1980s was also the decade in which cable television arrived, providing an instant outlet in the form of the municipal public-access cable channels, where the work could be seen and come of age.[5] The invention of VCR machines and VHS tapes, now obsolete, was a revolution in distribution, putting film and video for the first time on a par with books for ease of use. Then as now, technological changes could lead to social and political transformation too.

And there was cheap rent. As tough as times were then, economically they were nothing like what a young generation faces today. New York City in the 1980s was a very different place from today.[6] Condos were just being invented and starting to remove rentals from the marketplace by pushing out long-time tenants. The artists whose live-work lofts made SoHo and Tribeca safe for financiers and chain stores had not yet been bought out, fled, or been evicted. The neglect of New York City (and other cities across the United States), increase in crime and drugs, and political castigation of its residents and governments, all created a no-fly zone for wealthy residents and corporate interests. Wall Street endured, but its henchmen commuted from Connecticut.

The city was ours. Property values were low, apartments had rent control, clubs were everywhere, and the streets were locations of congregation, invention, and celebration. New York City wasn't yet the post-Giuliani, Bloomberg-forever, Disneyland-Vegas tourist attraction of today, trademarked and policed to protect the visitors and tourism industry. It was still a place of diversity, where people of color lived their lives in vibrant communities with intact cultures. Young people could still move to New York City after or instead of high school or college and invent an identity, an art, a life. Times Square was still a bustling center of excitement, with sex work, "adult" movies, a variety of sins on sale, ways to make money for those down on their luck. The benign economics and easy density enabled the continuation and even growth of a widespread community united by issues, sexualities, politics, aesthetics.

The city still had the requisite level of danger too, to preserve it as the domain of the adventurous: simultaneous with AIDS, the crack epidemic arrived in the 1980s. One day my friend Linda announced that she had to move immediately out of her Upper West Side rent-controlled apartment, a sublime space that was the envy of us all. The day before, she had looked out her window and spotted the security guard of the building across the street crawling along an outside ledge, twelve stories above the street. Even the security guards were high on crack.

I lived in the East Village, known to earlier arrivals as Alphabet City. It was the place to score heroin in the old days, then the place to score crack. On East Seventh Street, the ruling drug dealer magnanimously hung Christmas lights from abandoned buildings every winter.[7] Today the vacant lot is gone; there's a doorman there instead. Across town, the West Side piers where gay men cruised and trysted were still in full swing; so were bathhouses and bars with back rooms. Lesbians mostly held meetings, true, but we still had bars of our own and a distinct, more romantic sense of sexual adventure.

The notion of "queer" surfaced at the turn of the decade. A conference held in 1990 at the University of California, Santa Cruz, was titled "Queer Theory" in a radical gesture. To be sure, the word *queer* was already circulating and mating with other terms: Queer Nation, the group that outed celebrities, was also founded in 1990. Teresa de Lauretis, one of the UCSC conference organizers, is credited with coining *queer theory*, though she herself soon disavowed it; she had been a keynote speaker at the conference "How Do I Look?" in 1989 in New York City, where queer cinema first got its public voice.[8]

Against all odds, film and video work began to emerge. The need was intense for work that could make sense of what was going on, take stock, and reformulate our imaginings, to grieve the dead, yes, but also to reinvigorate life and love and possibility. For gay men, it was a matter of life or death, a question of mortality or immortality. For lesbians, it was a matter of empathy, a horror at what was happening to our/their gay brothers and outrage at society's response. There also was a need to preserve a visible presence, some scrap of identity, and create a new lesbian role, sensibility, and vision. It was in 1992 that the Lesbian Avengers group was first founded, in part to address this continuing lack of a public presence.

A renaissance of film and video arrived, just when the passionate energy that had characterized AIDS activism was flagging. Made by some of the same people, it was a fiercely serious cinema, intent on rewriting both past and future, providing inspiration for whatever and whoever was going to come next. As urgency and rage began to collapse into despair and frustration for the ACT UP generation, the New Queer Cinema created a space of reflection, nourishment, and renewed engagement. The NQC quickly grew—embryonically at first, with its first steps in the years 1985–91, then bursting into full view in 1992–97 with formidable force. Its arrival was accompanied by the thrill of having enough queer videos and films to reach critical mass and tip over into visibility. An invention. A brand. A niche market.

I played the role of baptismal preacher to the movement, creating a category with a widely circulated report of my transformative experiences on the film festival trail of fall 1991 and winter 1992, the "New Queer Cinema," and speaking about it as the headliner of a symposium that autumn at London's Institute of Contemporary Art. Remember, before the Internet, print publications had power: publication in the *Village Voice* and *Sight and Sound* propelled my ideas into the spotlight for use, debate, and disavowal.

Still, the identification of a New Queer Cinema would never have happened without the revolutionary films and videos that thrilled me into writing in the first place, or the press of forces both positive and negative that sparked them into being. That synergy of creative and critical impulses is one of the lessons of the NQC, or so I hope: the power that comes with inhabiting historical time, writing in sync with a moment of palpable importance, a synchrony that endows anyone lucky enough to be in the right place at the right time with powers of prescience that might otherwise fall by the wayside. Of course, the birth of a movement is never unilateral, never a solitary affair; it's an impulse aimed at creating community and made *by* community. With the handy NQC tagline, films released over the next few years were able to get production financing, festival play, distribution, and, above all, a connection to their proper and even improper audiences. They were unprecedented films and videos, crossing new borders in search of an updated queer vernacular.

My own life was paralleling these stages of development. Between 1991 and 1992 I'd moved from the East Village to San Francisco. As I struggled with geographic displacement, the New Queer Cinema became my virtual home, the place I felt whole, nurtured, and secure with my comrades-in-arms, battling for a place at the table and a place in history, happy to have all my worlds of films and festivals, journalism and friendship united under one grand nomadic tent. Little wonder, then, that from the first moment—when I flew from my first class at the University of California at Berkeley to Park City in January 1992 for a "Barbed Wire Kisses" panel at Sundance—I remained the NQC's steadfast chronicler.

This volume has been shaped by distinct circumstances of creation as I have occupied successive positions in relation to queer filmmaking: as funder, critic, curator, pundit, publicist, scholar, champion. I've written for weeklies, dailies, and glossies, jotted lecture notes on airplanes, and wrote for academic journals. Ideas take shape differently in each of these sectors, so these chapters have different lengths, idioms, and anticipated audiences. Each publishing sector enforces its own values, even when an article manages to migrate across categories or jump the limits of its niche.

In this volume, some chapters have endnotes, others have attitude. Some were rushed into print to stake out a claim or were sequentially rewritten, while still others show the benefit of historical perspective. Variety dominates: wit here, depth there, in answer to editors demanding one or the other unapologetically. There are multiple ellipses, some shameful, in these pages, but it would be dishonest to rewrite history to my advantage. In both academic and popular language, breathless or analytic, the essays track my evolutions of thought, allowing the reader a sense of the ups and downs that go into chronicling the emergence of a movement, on and off screen.

The name New Queer Cinema was so quickly adopted as shorthand by the media that the concept fossilized almost before it could be properly identified. This volume tries to make sense of the movement from its inception to its flowering, seeming collapse, successive comebacks, and unexpectedly mainstream renewals. The film scholars Richard Dyer and Julianne Pidduck understand such circumlocutions, for they once issued a formidable explication of its inner workings: "The many gyrations of lesbian/gay film are part of the ceaseless process of construction, reconstruction and deconstruction of identities and cultures, ceaseless because experience always outstrips constructions so that they are never quite satisfactory, never quite get it, and yet also ceaseless because we need construction in order to make sense of experience at all." Lest all that ceaselessness deter a reader from even trying, they significantly added a bit of a pep talk: "This and the simple need to express in order to survive, to be seen to be believed, is why lesbians and gay men have to go on making lesbian and gay films which all the while may betray the folly of the enterprise."[9] Ah, folly. In that spirit, this volume dares present itself. It is divided into sections that seek to make sense of my engagement as a writer with the New Queer Cinema throughout its various manifestations. While there's something of a nod to chronology, issues and formats and throughlines interrupt and rearrange it.

Part I, "Origins, Festivals, Audiences," gathers the foundational essays in which I claimed the New Queer Cinema category and sought to set out its parameters. From the very first moment, this writing argued for the importance of the NQC as a cultural response to troubled times as well as a breakthrough aesthetic movement that deserved praise, emulation, and analysis.

In "Before the Beginning," I acknowledge antecedents and early stirrings, placing the NQC in context, both before and after Stonewall. Deliberately not encyclopedic, this chapter sketches the contours of a world in which no queer cinema could be taken for granted. At the same time, it reclaims the contributions of the American avant-garde, European art cinema, and the "affirmation" documentaries of the preceding era. Recalling the late 1980s, I also recall early short works that carried out the experiments without which the NQC could not have been built. I also seek to place into this prehistory a key set of gay and lesbian features made in the United States in the mid-1980s which began to point the way stylistically to the NQC and to grapple with the same sort of exciting and disturbing subjects.

The second chapter presents my original "New Queer Cinema" article of 1992 in an expanded version that restores portions originally deleted in the editorial process. Offered here in the present tense, as do all chapters that were originally published in the moment, it conveys the excitable atmosphere of the times and the thrill of discovery that I was experiencing from the inside. While all of this volume is located in my particular perspectives and experiences of the epoch, this essay in particular shows me entirely immersed. I'm clearly there, in the red-hot center of it all, an on-the-ground participant-observer of what felt very much like my own history. It's still vivid.

"Collision, Catastrophe, Celebration: The Relationship between Gay and Lesbian Film Festivals and Their Publics" is different. As NQC films were being released onto the festival circuit to be embraced or rejected by their desired publics, I was troubled by a pronounced audience tendency: the desire for something predictable and familiar up there on screen, a sort of Classic Coke for the queer generation, not the boundary-busting work that I cared about and wanted to proliferate. This essay was prompted by that feeling of a gulf opening between my taste as a critic and the demands of the communities to which I was a party. It addresses an issue that continues to concern me: the narrow limits of tolerance demonstrated by audiences at LGBT film festivals when confronted with uncomfortable ideas, stories, and representations.

In "What's a Good Gay Film?" I continue this inquiry into community standards, poke fun at the rules erupting all around me, and argue for the importance of two taboo-breaking films in particular, Lisa Cholodenko's debut *High Art* and, less predictably, the Hong Kong star director Wong Kar-Wai's *Happy Together*. My informal survey of movie wishes reveals that Mary wants a new *Sound of Music* while Gus Van Sant wants queer McDonald's Happy Meals characters.

Part II, "Bulletins from the Front," takes the reader into the heart of journalism. Unlike features or essays for academic journals, these shorter pieces for the popular press are all devoted to particular films or filmmakers who commanded my attention, or my editor's, at that moment.

As the NQC got and lost a reputation, as producers, awards, and distributors came and went and returned, I charted its progress. Here I've collected some high points of its past and future, but in truth it had begun to shape-shift during the mid- to late 1990s into a launching pad for temporarily bankable movies to usher into the multiplexes. Instead I threw myself into rustling up audiences for the work I cared about. Derek Jarman's *Edward II* was such a film. At Sundance, I ran into Jarman and his companion Keith skipping through the snow as they left the gay party to which I was headed. Was it over? No, Jarman shouted with a grin: "We're lesbian boys! It's all men in there." His insouciance and political incorrectness informed all his work. *Edward II* starred Tilda Swinton, whom I'd first met when she was preparing to work on the great proto–queer film, Sally Potter's *Orlando*, which premiered just after "New Queer Cinema" was published. Swinton would become a sort of presiding deity for the New Queer Cinema in the decades that followed. I loved seeing her chew up the scenery, and the royals, in Jarman's film, just as she would later in the films of John Maybury, Susan Streitfeld, and so many other LGBT filmmakers. She's an eternal friend to the tribe and, a guiding spirit to this volume.

My journalistic pieces often sought to bring something like equal attention to the lesbian work that had finally started to appear: *Forbidden Love*, *Go Fish*, *Watermelon Woman*. I loved those films, each so different from the other, and as I wrote about them and the filmmakers I was intent on expanding their influence. I traveled to Columbus, Ohio, to see a remarkable installation, *Domestic Violence*, that coequal co-creators Todd Haynes and Christine Vachon installed at the Wexner Center for the Arts to challenge assumptions about violent movies, deploying babies and pets instead of humans. Throughout the decades, whenever I was stopped in my tracks by a film or event, I wrote about it in order to figure out what was going on. *Tarnation* and *I.K.U.* were two such films; the more that the queer audience tilted toward normativity, the more I sought to balance the scales for the films I identified as worthy of the NQC birthright. As the first generation of NQC filmmakers came into new maturity, I was delighted: I got to write about Gregg Araki's *Mysterious Skin*. (Sadly, I somehow never had the chance to write about Todd Haynes after *Poison* made him famous, and have simply watched and admired him and his evolving corpus of work from afar.)

In the mid-1990s, when much of the NQC took a detour into the commercial world of happy-ending popcorn movies, the trend was anointed with a new name by the *New York Times* critic Stephen Holden, "Giddy Gay Lite."[10] There followed a disparaged pseudo-genre packed full of cheesecake gay male romances and chocolate-box lesbian confections. I tried for a while to justify the transformation. Hey, I would argue, why shouldn't queer audiences be entitled to the same date-night mediocrity that heterosexual audiences can buy every Saturday at the multiplex? I always got a laugh, but I was increasingly unhappy with the new careerism that led filmmakers without commitment or community to claim a market where the New Queer Cinema pioneers had worked for a broader good, for a deeper purpose than a mini-major acquisition or a two-picture deal. The NQC set out to save souls or lives or movies, or something, with all the requisite passion that entailed. So I kept my eyes on the prize and shone the spotlight on those that still cared.

Kicking films while they're down has never been my style. Kicking them while they're up, of course, is a different matter. I busied myself in the late 1990s with such diversions as attacking Kevin Smith for *Chasing Amy* (1997), not included in these pages, which I felt unfairly drew attention away from two of my favorite films of the time, both by lesbian directors: Alex Sichel's *All over Me* (1997), a teen girl's gritty coming-of-age tale unfolding over one hot New York summer (as Alison Folland falls for Leisha Haley) and the Australian director Ana Kokkinos's *Head On* (1998), which seared the eye with its up-close vision of how homosexuality plays out in the life of a Greek immigrant community's favorite son. And for a film that turned its back on the box office in favor of crucially needed discomfort, there was Ira Sachs's *The Delta* (1997), charting the tragic consequence of a pleasure-boat ride by a rich white boy and the half-black, half-Vietnamese hustler he's picked up and misused.

In the first decade of the twenty-first century, just as the burdens of answering for what the NQC was becoming in the United States had grown too heavy to bear, I was thrilled to find a brand-new NQC with new names coming to the fore in other parts of the globe. Julián Hernández and Apichatpong Weerasethakul were busily revisiting myths, remapping cities, reinventing rural habitats, and renavigating desire.[11] The films from Latin America and Asia looked different from their Anglo-American counterparts, but they were fresh and sassy and nonstop in surprises. There seemed a way out of the boxes that divided the world into multiplex, festival, and art house: a path straight through the urban jungles and the tropical forests, past animalistic humans and all-too-human animals, into a new NQC universe that departed from earlier iterations.

I frequently had to spin on a dime to see a new film or video, figure out its position in the NQC constellation, and get those ideas into print in a very short timeframe, sometimes even overnight. That's nothing heroic: it's what working journalists do all the time. But the drama of the NQC upped the ante for me as its chronicler: where to expand it, where it contracted, whether a film was in or out, in for trouble or out of bounds, worth taking seriously or not. These articles weren't just a way to pay the rent, though of course they did that too at a crucial time; they were my contribution to keeping the NQC flag in the air and getting enough bodies to the box office to ensure its survival. These bulletins are included to provide a snapshot of the multiple fronts on which NQC was advancing, with a feel of the excitement each new film would bring to the ongoing collective conversation, one that's still going on.

In part III, "Genre Meets Gender," intersections of conflicting agendas and intents come to the fore as I audition a range of rules and categories and ideas to try to make sense of what I was seeing, this time importing popular culture into the mix. One considers the new documentary biopic and speculates on whether emerging queer ones repeat the sins of the past: hero worship, idealism, whitewashing. In another, I spot *Boys Don't Cry* at its Toronto premiere, try to assess its relationship to the NQC, and notice the year's only lesbian happy ending involves a portal into John Malkovich's brain. The most capacious essay, "Lethal Lesbians," is an examination of a suddenly popular type of film, almost entirely made by heterosexual men, in which pairs of maybe-lesbians team up to commit murder as a way of sealing their bond. I became fascinated with the ever-widening subtexts of this mini-genre and returned to some of the early feminist texts to sort intention from reception. Films always exist in relationship to their societies and moments in time, and the NQC is no exception.

Part IV is my contribution to the queering of Latin American cinema, taking past and present into account through the arc of my own works, trips, and intersections. Latin America's film industry and LGBT movements have intersected to produce interesting new examples of a revised NQC, tailored not only to the continent but to the very different social and sexual tropes found in its range of countries.

Tracking the current cinemas back to their own origins, "Queering a New Latin American Cinema" is an ambitious, kaleidoscopic tour through decades, nations, and cinematic histories. Kidnapping, inchoate lust, rural transgressions, bourgeois accommodations, and even street hustling figure in these new films as strongly as the shadow figure of *la reina* (the queen) and the limits of social norms so haunted an earlier generation. In Brazil the past is fertile ground; in Argentina it's the North. Everywhere I looked in those days, queerness was invading Latin American cinemas. Lucrecia Martel became my special focus as she became a greater and greater filmmaker, with queerness always haunting the scene. Assessing the Cuban situation, I conscript my own trips to the island into the record to illuminate the contradictions of a society famed for homophobia yet home to a rich LGBT subculture.

Every time I thought the NQC was over, finished, shorn of its particulars, relegated to academic histories, I was surprised again. The latest stage of the New Queer Cinema came into view during the early twenty-first century and was characterized by an evolution that was explosive, scattering ideas and images into dozens of genres and countries and thousands of screens large and small. It was the time of the NQC blockbuster, the crossover movie that escaped subcultural status while trying to sort out new problems and issues. Some filmmakers were able to negotiate a trade-off with new theatrical expectations: Todd Haynes, Gus Van Sant, and Lisa Cholodenko, for example, became crossover successes. Others revived the old-school radicalism of an earlier, pre-AIDS-cocktail cinematic era, to my equal delight.

Part V, "Expansions and Reversals," introduces the LGBT megahit. It's hard to know whether to call *Brokeback Mountain* and *Milk* queer or gay, postqueer or simply our movies. Two essays explore how they built a new beachhead for gay male representations, not only for huge LGBT audiences but also into the middle of the country, small towns, and the DVD shelves of families, neighbors, and coworkers, a population that had never experienced this sort of film. Both films opened up history for discussion, relating contemporary identities back to the struggles that made them possible.

Lesbian film, though, lagged far behind in terms of capitalization and theatrical release. Then another film came along that returned to the early roots of New Queer Cinema as well as of feminist film, 16mm, and the start of indie film itself. Jamie Babbit jumped into a time machine to produce *Itty Bitty Titty Committee*, her fanciful tale of lesbians, collectivity, generation gaps, and tongue-in-cheek media intervention. Packed with some of the community's most beloved actresses, it's also a shout-out to the first ladies of the NQC.

The essay "Queer *Nouveau*" is the result of a residency fellowship in the south of France, where I was fascinated by French sexual politics and how they shaped the films of François Ozon and his predecessors. Films then newly in release became an invitation to rethink on-screen and off-screen politics and track the links between coming out and wearing the veil, between gay mayors and queer cinema, and ultimately between the past and the present. The essay argues that the French notion of *Républicanisme* has considerable relevance for the NQC in its current state. In part IV, "Expansions and Reversals," the options of DIY, European art cinema, and open-wide U.S. box-office releases all get a fair hearing.

Finally, a conclusion extends the New Queer Cinema onto the television and web and into the gallery, reconsiders the place of gender, and pays a final moment of attention to a new generation with new stories to tell and new ways to tell them. Meanwhile webisodes, interactive websites, and installations have begun to tell queer stories across new platforms. And it's become clear that trans is the new queer, where energies are building and discoveries happening, reminiscent of the NQC's long-ago emergence on the world stage. The conclusion also tracks trans film's development and seeks to understand the new templates for its representation on screen, in both outsider fictions and insider documentaries and hybrids.

New incarnations of Web 3.0 and the transient, quickly extinct technologies of consumer cameras (iPhone? webcam? DSLR?) continue to tantalize with the prospect of future identities etched in digital images. As civil society crumbles under privatizing tech advances and as new, cheaper, faster, and more far-reaching machines hit consumer shelves and websites, it's impossible to guess what form of representation is lurking around the corner or the cloud for the next edition of representation. It's hard to imagine a queer 3D culture, but I don't dare dismiss the possibility.

Yet technology, however advanced and advancing, has not fully supplanted the yearning for community nor succeeded entirely in mediating its fulfillment. The identificatory attractions of LGBT and NQC films continue to exert a magnetic force on audiences for premieres on screen and directors in person, and for the ever-renewed eye candy in lines winding around the block, animated and flirty and full of expectation, still worth leaving the house (and home entertainment system) to see.

Indeed, this volume's final moments, 2011–12, produced yet another renaissance, one that transpired right there in the festivals and theaters that are under threat. Yet again, stories of the past and present from the United States and around the world exploded into view, as urgent and captivating as ever before. This is a movement that just won't accept an obituary. New documentaries brought histories and crises into view, while new dramatic films have opened up a new generation of debate and redemption. And where better then the festivals to see them?

A desire to bear witness is still intense: the need to sit in an audience with others of one's kind for the shared experience of those stories and characters on the screen, marked by the unmistakable sensibility of a thousand kindred spirits holding their breath in the dark. The director's cut is not the only standard: the audience cut has long been my favorite version of a movie, shaped by a call-and-response pattern of group acceptance and disavowal of whatever dares to parade by on screen. Authority is never the sole prerogative of the writer who writes the history. All views are partial and ephemeral. Can the shape of a movement ever entirely be known, even by those credited with launching it?

The New Queer Cinema continues to be a perpetual-motion machine stoked by helium and history. Somehow the NQC has become an ever more attractive tagline the more it appears to fade, lasting way past any long-ago expiration date yet somehow never out of style. It has evolved dramatically since 1992, expanded way beyond its roots in the queer activism scene of the 1980s and 1990s. Early fights for visibility and acceptance are long over; queer cultures have evolved, and the very shape of legal battles has shifted enormously; choice is just another downloadable app. Original sets of options are no longer fraught with peril in most places where this text will be read, but new options have inherited even greater risks (Brandon Teena, Gwen Araujo, Tyler Clementi).

This volume aims to revive a time when a tiny band, flush with passion and filled with mission, convinced by that old saying that "an army of lovers can't be wrong," seduced an audience and eventually an industry. It lays claim to a past, assesses the histories, and memorializes the establishment of a queer cinematic voice that dared to speak its name, a vision that dared to show its bodies and dreams. The New Queer Cinema deserves a future, to be sure, but it also deserves a recognizable past, at least as can be conjured by this survivor's recollections of a glorious time.

Recently perusing some photos taken at the Grubsteak Restaurant in Park City at the lunch following the "Barbed Wire Kisses" panel in 1992, I was shocked to spot a baby-faced John Cameron Mitchell sitting happily among the gang.[12] I never knew he was there. Two decades later, at the Provincetown Film Festival, during another lunch, I had the chance to ask him about it. "Oh yes, it was a huge inspiration," Mitchell confessed. He was a newbie with no idea of how to do things, admitting his humiliation when Christine Vachon reminded him years later, "You handed me your head shot!" Mitchell, with three features under his belt, including the queerest musical ever, *Hedwig and the Angry Inch* (2001) and his follow-up films *Shortbus* (2006) and *Rabbit Hole* (2011), then in postproduction, blushed at the memory. Vachon, sitting nearby with her partner, Marlene, and their daughter, Guthrie, in the glorious Provincetown sun, overheard the story and laughed. That was then, this was now. But surely Mitchell's presence at that table helped to make him who he is today. And thus who we are as well.

I can only wonder what other bodies were in that room at the Prospector

Square theater as the panel transpired, or there in the Grubsteak, observing, as the Mormons visibly winced at seating and serving us. Were those other festival-goers similarly inspired, transformed, bound for greatness? Perhaps you were one.

In the early 1990s a fellow movie critic once took me to task. "We're just supposed to review the films and rate them good or bad," she scolded, complaining that I was "championing my favorites" instead, a scofflaw. I still am. For that reason, no doubt, I've rarely been trusted to do the yeoman's work of issuing stars for box-office results, though twice I did get to vote with my thumb on television thanks to Roger Ebert. Instead I've always tracked ideas and worked hard to link films to social concerns. I'm never happier than in those rare times when my own interests, the films I love, the interests of a community to which I belong, and the larger society's attention all converge. I live for those moments still.

Notes

1. See the GMHC website, http://www.gmhc.org/about-us. For a restorative history and analysis of the entire period and process, see Gould, *Moving Politics*.

2. Gould, *Moving Politics*.

3. Barbara Gamarekian, "Frohnmayer Defends Grant for Prize Film," *New York Times*, March 30, 1991.

4. Todd Haynes, personal communication, Los Angeles, May 12, 2012.

5. Gregg Bordowitz's *Fast Trip, Long Drop* (1993) contains one of the best send-ups of the cable-access aesthetic ever. It was an affectionate send-up: he and Jean Carlomusto produced the *Living with AIDS* cable show for the Gay Men's Health Alliance from 1988 to 1993. For his interview regarding these years and his subsequent career, see Robert Atkins, "Fast Trip, Long View: Talking to Gregg Bordowitz," Artist in the Archives, http://www.artistswithaids.org/artery/artist/artist2.html.

6. In 1975 New York City was on the verge of bankruptcy when the Municipal Assistance Corporation was made its financial caretaker. The city was also decimated by racial tensions, underfunding by state and federal governments, and the infamous Blackout of 1977 that resulted in the acceleration of "white flight" to the suburbs. See Greenberg, *Branding New York*; Markham, *A Financial History of the United States*, 47–48.

7. The filmmaker Sheila McLaughlin and the composer and musician John Zorn both lived on that block of East Seventh Street between B and C and still do.

8. See de Lauretis, "Queer Theory." Other foundational texts include Sedgwick, *Epistemology of the Closet*; Butler, *Gender Trouble*; Bad Object-Choices Collective, *How Do I Look?*; Fuss, *Inside Out*; Warner, *Fear of a Queer Planet*; Gever, Parmar, and

Greyson, *Queer Looks*. See too my own contribution, "Reflections on a Queer Screen."

9. Dyer and Pidduck, *Now You See It*.

10. Stephen Holden, "Opposite of Gloom: Time to Be Gaily Gay," *New York Times*, June 4, 1999.

11. For an excellent analysis of Asian queer cinema, which I am not able to tackle here despite its importance, see Leung, "New Queer Cinema and Third Cinema."

12. My poor-quality VHS videocassette dub of a long-lost Sundance original recording of that panel has been loaned to two films already: Isaac Julien's *Derek* (as the only footage he could find of Derek Jarman discussing reaction to his public announcement that he was HIV-positive) and Walter McIntosh's *Projecting the Body* (as the only evidence of the late Stephen Cummins's participation in Sundance 1992 with *Resonance*). A quick plea to each of you reading these words: please record everything you can, on whatever device or technology you have, high or low. The present becomes the past in the blink of an eye, and I know the future will be hungry for your glimpses of today.

PART I

ORIGINS, FESTIVALS, AUDIENCES

BEFORE THE BEGINNING

Lineages and Preconceptions

1 Nothing starts at the beginning, not really. The first chapter of every book already has a backstory, every birth its conception myth, every decade the shadow of the one before it. The New Queer Cinema is no exception. The first generation of NQC filmmakers, and many that followed, were well versed in the works and lives of their predecessors, the pioneers who'd lost their wagon wheels on the road to a different way of being. They were all watching films long before they made their own, and the traces of their cinematic education are coded in their own work, explicitly or implicitly.

Memory in the United States is short-lived, and cultural memory is no different. With every new technology that debuts, eons of earlier films, videos, and writings disappear into the mists of old technology, unreachable across the borders of phased-out formats, out-of-print books, defunct journals. If the markers of the 1980s live on a little longer in the flowerings of the New Queer Cinema, we're all the better for remembering. Movements of history and cinephilia demand acknowledgment. The NQC didn't come from nowhere: it came from (almost) everywhere.

Hints and Glimpses

Consider the state of "gay and lesbian" theatrical movies in the United States before 1969. Arguably there was no such thing, just a scattering of gay and lesbian directors, often closeted, making films that were masquerading as mass-market heterosexual fare, albeit with the occasional gay or lesbian actor or subtle wink. If characters were openly identified as gay or lesbian on screen, it was most often for a punch line or tragic demise. George Cukor, Dorothy Arzner, James Whale: they were about fitting in, not standing "out." There were instead gay and lesbian audiences that adopted certain films as their own, celebrated subtexts and coded language, knew enough gossip to be able to identify gay and lesbian actors and actresses, and prided themselves at being adept enough to read their own desires into the plots. The category was a relational one, constituted by the interaction of viewers with films.

Gay and lesbian stories, aesthetics, and filmmakers were found elsewhere in the avant-garde cinema of the time. The New York filmmakers James Sibley Watson and Melville Webber were some of the first, with *The Fall of the House of Usher* (1928) and *Lot in Sodom* (1933). The American expatriate poet H.D. and her lover Bryher were in Switzerland, where they published the film journal *Close Up* and made *Borderline* (1930), a feature starring H.D. and Paul Robeson, with Kenneth MacPherson, H.D.'s lover and Bryher's husband back then, before he became "gay" (or gayer).

The postwar avant-garde cinema that developed in the United States has been written about at length in terms of its experimentation, aesthetic invention, and modernist sensibility. What's rarely noted is that this early avant-garde is manifestly a gay cinema (though not lesbian), where artists shut out of other worlds could find expression. Starting in 1947 with Kenneth Anger's *Fireworks*, the "underground" cinema would grow to include Jack Smith, Gregory Markopoulos, Taylor Mead, George Kuchar, James Broughton, Nathaniel Dorsky, José Rodriguez-Soltero, and the most famous and successful of them all, Andy Warhol.[1] The official histories of the New American Cinema as recorded by heterosexual chroniclers don't take note of the sexuality of so many of its practitioners or link their aesthetics back to the subcultures and traditions to which they paid tribute.[2] Today it is impossible to show Anger's *Scorpio Rising* (1964) or Markopoulos's *Twice a Man* (1963) without facing disbelief from audiences over how they could have ever *not* be considered gay films. The American avant-garde was a very queer place indeed, hiding in plain sight for years until it was safe to come out.

In France too a new cinema was under construction. The most enduring gay film of this period was Jean Genet's *Un Chant d'Amour* (1950). Based on memories of prison and its erotic regimes, it would be a major influence on Todd Haynes and others. More mainstream audiences could turn to the European art cinema, with its long tradition of openly gay filmmakers and films. Luchino Visconti's *The Leopard* (1963) and *Death in Venice* (1971) and Pier Paolo Pasolini's *Teorema* (1968) influenced a generation. Lesbianism was still a fillip for voyeuristic tastes—Claude Chabrol's *Les Biches* (1968) or Bernardo Bertolucci's *The Conformist* (1970)—yet films were eagerly adapted by image-starved lesbian viewers. If hints and glimpses were the currency of the time, well, gay and lesbian audiences were used to reading between the frames.

After Stonewall

When Gay Liberation arrived, it came hand in hand with the movies. The legendary Stonewall Riots started on the night of June 27, 1969. It was the day of Judy Garland's funeral at the Frank E. Campbell Funeral Home uptown, which had stayed open the previous night to accommodate the crush of weeping mourners in lines around the block waiting to view the casket and bid their idol goodbye. Garland was a gay icon too, and it's easy to imagine that on Judy's night, butch dykes, nelly queens, and fierce trannies were not going to take any bullying by the police who routinely raided gay bars. For Judy, they fought back. And in that moment, and the day of street fighting that followed, a new era was born.[3] And with it, a new cinema.

In the United States the gay and lesbian cinema that emerged in the 1970s emphasized documentary and experimental work.[4] On the West Coast in 1971, Milton Miron's documentary *Tricia's Wedding* (1971) captured the The Cockettes for posterity, and Jim Bidgood's *Pink Narcissus* (1971) updated experimental cinema for the new era.[5] Jan Oxenberg's *A Comedy in Six Unnatural Acts* (1975) became a classic of lesbian cinema. In the Bay Area, the filmmakers Curt McDowell (a friend and disciple of George Kuchar) and Barbara Hammer created an aesthetic for the gay and lesbian scene exploding around them in *Thundercrack!* (1975) and *Dyketactics* (1974).[6] In 1977 the landmark documentary *Word Is Out: Stories of Some of Our Lives* was (collectively) released. It was made while Harvey Milk was still alive and the Castro district's baths were still steaming.

Despite such West Coast classics, gay cinema would become most firmly based in New York City, the storied metropolis, where it flourished amid other subcultural arts and figures of its time, from Allen Ginsberg to Frank O'Hara, from Langston Hughes to Djuna Barnes. In fact the history of New York City ought to be viewed in terms of its gay and lesbian history as much as its Italian or Puerto Rican or Irish or Jewish history; gay men and lesbians too were immigrants, part of the great domestic migration that left the heartland for the coasts in search of a better life.

Audiences had long looked to European cinema for sexual sophistication, and that continued to be the case even after Stonewall, as a gay and lesbian cinema developed there. In 1971 *Sunday Bloody Sunday* was John Schlesinger's coming out; in 1978 Ron Peck's *Night Hawks* uncovered gay London. Stephen Frears's gutsy gay films *My Beautiful Laundrette* (1985) and *Prick Up Your Ears* (1987) opened an era of frankness barely rivaled since. In Germany, R. W. Fassbinder, Ulrike Ottinger, and Frank Ripploh (*Taxi Zum Klo*, 1980) were all in their prime. In 1981, when Vito Russo published *Celluloid Closet*, the field was already changing: an independent American cinema was about to end the binarism of U.S. filmmaking.

When Christine Vachon started out, she said, "there were extremely experimental films and there were Hollywood films, but there wasn't a whole lot in between."[7] Not a lot, no, but there was one. At Sundance in 1988 I was escorted up a rickety staircase to the Egyptian Theater and settled into a folding chair next to the projection booth by the festival's director Tony Safford. It was there I saw the world premiere of John Waters's *Hairspray*, the film that brought his radically outré sensibility to a mainstream audience. The crowd went crazy, and *Hairspray* won the jury's grand prize. Waters predates the New Queer Cinema by decades; he's a creature of the hippie past, the countercultural revolution, a pre-Stonewall era of shock and awe. He's an indelible part of NQC prehistory, a patron saint presiding over its doings, chuckling at its follies, applauding its successes.

John Waters was there first. He and his films were formed by the nutty, exuberant prelapsarian days of the 1970s, after gay liberation, before AIDS. The trademark Waters style, with its camp sensibility and impatience with both heteronormativity and homonormativity, is well reflected in the New Queer Cinema, as if its traits were lying in wait all that time like a recessive gene. A shout-out, then, to the ever-young daddy of us all, the one with the Maybelline moustache, Mr. Waters.

Queering the American Independent Film

If the emergence of an American independent cinema is the fertile ground from which the New Queer Cinema will soon leap, then the year 1985 is as close to its defining moment as any. It was in that year that Susan Seidelman's *Desperately Seeking Susan* and Donna Deitch's *Desert Hearts* thrilled a new generation of lesbian audiences and filmmakers and showed it was possible to make a sexy movie that could be empowering to women and even lesbians, and actually play in theaters, something not taken for granted at the time.

Four other American independent features, all released in the mid-1980s, stand out as precursors to the early New Queer Cinema: Lizzie Borden's *Born in Flames* (1983), Gus Van Sant's *Mala Noche* (1985), Bill Sherwood's *Parting Glances* (1986), and Sheila McLaughlin's *She Must Be Seeing Things* (1987).[8] All four blazed a trail of formal innovation, queer sexuality, and eccentric narrative that deeply informed the early NQC filmmakers. All four were low-budget broadsides issued to the world by communities of outsiders, laying claim to a new and authentically queer way of being: sexual, a/political, courageous, and, not incidentally, urban.

Lizzie Borden was part of a downtown radical art world that included Adele Bertei, Cookie Mueller, Kathryn Bigelow, and a host of others. Her *Born in Flames* was an exercise in utopian imagining, set in the near future with women battling an indifferent state. The women of Radio Ragazza and Radio Phoenix swing into action, fight the powers that be, form bike brigades, and even blow up the transmission tower on the roof of the World Trade Center.[9] Conceived during the heyday of feminism, it starred Honey, the African American leader of Radio Phoenix and Borden's partner at the time. Honey's face dominated the posters for the film, plastered all over the plywood construction walls of lower Manhattan, beaming out at passersby with a defiant, irresistible gaze.[10] Released when Ronald and Nancy Reagan inhabited the White House, *Born in Flames* offered a vision of a different world.[11] The soundtrack came straight out of punk, bands like the Red Crayons and Honey's own music. With a stirring vision of political organizing and militancy, it was a vicarious experience of battling power in some alternative— and sexy—universe.

At the same time, across the country, Gus Van Sant was back in Portland after trying to break into the film industry in L.A. He turned to low-budget filmmaking instead, with his debut feature *Mala Noche*, based on the autobiographical novel by Portland's native son Walt Curtis.[12] Filmed in atmospheric black-and-white, it focuses on a skid-row universe populated by the eponymous Walt, a down-and-out Anglo store clerk, and the desperate young Mexican workers he meets, lusts after, and tries to get into his bed with $15 offers. One of the few films to look at the erotic economics of gay cross-race, cross-class desire, it had a creative intensity at least as powerful as its sexual charge. A gritty style and a loopy nonlinear narrative defied the bland viewer-friendly movies of the time, appealing instead to a band of subcultural adventurers. By example, *Mala Noche* announced how tame gay representations had been and suggested the potential of the medium to capture life as lived, off-screen, if only filmmakers would dare.

More conventional in form but no less radical in subjects and themes, Bill Sherwood's *Parting Glances* constructed a very different slice-of-life piece of evidence. Steve Buscemi was Nick, an acerbic no-illusions gay man living with AIDS in a tiny New York City apartment, tended to by his ex-lover. It was Buscemi's first starring role, and Sherwood was the first to bring the quotidian realities of AIDS to the screen, presenting the horrors of the illness with a matter-of-fact clarity that was the exact opposite of the hysterical demonizing in the newspaper headlines, television news, and government propaganda of the time.[13] It was a hugely important film for the city's gay community, shot in 1984 and released in 1986, one year prior to the founding of the AIDS Coalition to Unleash Power (ACT UP). Its qualities were those of early independent film: unrepresented communities, low-budget rough-hewn production, characters who appeared in daily life but never yet in movies. A gay man with AIDS certainly fit the bill, especially one who was full of opinions on New York's bars and relationships and hangers-on. He was full of catty cynicism and wary romanticism, with dreams and despair to match. Just like us.

Equally revelatory was the representation of lesbian desire drawn by Sheila McLaughlin's *She Must Be Seeing Things*, which drew its themes from her own life and from the seventeenth-century legend of Catalina de Erauso (the "Lieutenant Nun"), its style from the taboo-breaking work of performances in a storefront theater in the East Village, near where McLaughlin herself lived. The WOW Café's Lois Weaver starred as Jo, a filmmaker having trouble keeping her girlfriend happy, her life on track, and her cash-strapped film in production.[14] Sheila Dabney, a member of the repertory company founded by the famed Cuban lesbian playwright Irene Fornes, played her paranoid girlfriend Agatha, convinced that Jo is cheating on her with a man in her crew.

Remarkably for a film that today appears so innocent, *She Must Be Seeing Things* endured the kinds of fights that erupted in the NQC years. It was denounced by a cadre of antiporn feminists, including Sheila Jeffreys of Great Britain. In the United States it divided the crowd by ideology, for it arrived at the height of the feminist "Sex Wars." McLaughlin's film became a case in point for both sides and helped lead the way to the new queer representations that lurked just around the corner.[15]

All four films were shot in 16mm, a sign of their predigital era. All made on a shoestring budget, they departed from established aesthetics by going for a rough urban look, using friends as actors, using borrowed apartments or lofts for locations, even borrowing passersby for demonstrations and rallies. All four struck a blow for the outcasts, the subcultural heroes and heroines who'd been waiting so long in the wings.

Life goes on. Bill Sherwood died in 1990 of complications from AIDS without ever getting to make another film. Sheila McLaughlin stopped making films; she lives in the same East Village apartment where she shot her film, but today she's one of New York's best acupuncturists and a terrific photographer. Lizzie Borden made two more films and now lives in L.A., but Honey, her star and lifelong friend, died of congestive heart failure in the spring of 2010.[16]

Breakthroughs

Harbingers of the NQC had bubbled up throughout the 1980s, as filmmakers struggled to make sense of the time. Or to make fun of it. In 1987 a little film titled *Superstar: The Karen Carpenter Story* made such a brilliant satire of Nixonian pop culture that the filmmaker Todd Haynes became an immediate sensation, though he was just two years out of college. In the same year, Isaac Julien's *This Is Not an AIDS Advertisement* and John Greyson's *The ADS Epidemic* struck back at the fear-mongering official campaigns against AIDS, using the new language of music video. Greyson's humor and parody used lyrics as manifesto: "This is not a death in Venice, it's a clear unholy menace, acquired dread of sex." Julien's take was elegiac, a subdued outrage leaking desire and soliciting dignity.

With *Looking for Langston* in 1989, Julien moved to a syncretic, meditative rewriting of history, queering Langston Hughes only to be censored by an unhappy Hughes estate, which denied copyright and forced the New York Film Festival to screen it with parts of the soundtrack muted (figs. 1.1–1.3). *Looking* sought to fuse a range of cinematic strategies (a return to black-and-white film, incorporation of still photographs and archival footage, a post-Brechtian embrace of theatricality and artificiality) with his love of pop culture (Jimmy Sommerville, resonances of Robert Mapplethorpe, Andy Warhol) to reclaim history for the queer black kids written out of it. Its status as a brilliant work was perhaps confirmed by the attacks it engendered for being too beautiful for its own good.[17] Today it's such a classic that it's hard to recall the controversies set off in the 1980s or the bravery that produced it.

And there are so many more that came out of the fertile soil of the mid-

1.1 Isaac Julien directs *Looking for Langston* (1989) with
Sunil Gupta. Looking for Langston Series (No. 6), Auteur
Mise en Scène No. 2. Courtesy of the filmmaker.

1980s and built the energies and dreams from which the NQC would arrive
in force in 1992. While not part of this argument, they are key works that
merit serious attention: in Canada, Richard Fung's *Orientations: Lesbian and
Gay Asians* (1984) and *Chinese Characters* (1986) and John Greyson's *Moscow Doesn't Believe in Queers* (1986) and *Urinal* (1988); in the United Kingdom, Stuart Marshall's *Bright Eyes* (1986); in the United States, Su Friedrich's
Damned If You Don't (1987), Marlon Riggs's *Tongues Untied* (1989), and Jenny
Livingston's *Paris Is Burning* (1991).[18] Chicago's Video Data Bank engaged Bill
Horrigan and John Greyson to compile a three-part program, *Video against
AIDS* (1989), for video was where the most experimental work and the most
urgent outcries could be found. Video artist Gregg Bordowitz, who worked
with DIVATV, *Testing and Limits*, and GMHC's *Living with AIDS* (1984–86),
made *Fast Trip, Long Drop* (1993), a hybrid meditation on his life and the
irony of community-approved AIDS messages. In 1990 the renowned dancer,
choreographer, and filmmaker Yvonne Rainer announced, "I am out. small
o."[19] She began living openly as a lesbian around that time, and declared that
MURDER and murder (1996) was "about three unholy groups—lesbians, old
ladies and cancer survivors. The deviant the damned and the desperate."[20]

1.2–1.3 Screen grabs from *Looking for Langston* (1989).

1.4–1.5 Screen grabs from Ira Sachs's *Last Address* (2010).

Against the odds and the forces arraigned against them, filmmakers were creating a new queer film and video vernacular. A generation poured its heart and soul, shock and anger into modes of representation capable of spinning new styles out of old and new genres out of those that had worn out. Before the NQC emerged, lots of people would die, some that made films, some that acted in them, some that watched them.

In Martin Scorsese's *Public Speaking* (2010), Fran Lebowitz says something I've never heard anyone say before: AIDS didn't just kill the best artists of a generation, but also the best audiences.[21] It's an obvious truth and one that haunts me as I think about a lost generation and its voices. Revisiting the old hood, I'm stalked by ghosts. Avenue A, my old street, was the heart of a cultural scene that's long gone, many of its denizens dead, and those who followed long since decamped for Dumbo, Williamsburg, Fort Green, Bushwick, wherever artists can still afford the rent.

In 2010 Ira Sachs created *Last Address*, an elegiac testimony to the final residences of numerous beloved New York City artists who died of AIDS.[22] At first, he gives us only street noise and exterior shots of buildings, urban streetscapes divulging nothing—until a title quietly appears on screen: a name, an address (figs. 1.4, 1.5). It's a work that matches the present geography of the city with the lives of those who are gone. Here in these scenes of (mostly) Lower Manhattan are the traces of what transpired in the 1980s, the fabulous contributions and artists remembered even when the streets have obliterated their traces. *Last Address* does the kind of work to which I aspire, the work of not merely mourning but remembering and carrying on, holding the door open all the while to the new neighbors who continue to arrive, drawn by the siren calls and sirens of the past and the hopes and dreams of the future.

Notes

1. Suárez, "The Puerto Rican Lower East Side and the Queer Underground." Thanks to George Chauncey and Ron Gregg for all their work on New York City's early queer cinema. For a visceral immersion in Warhol's world from the perspective of Valerie Solanas, see Mary Harron's *I Shot Andy Warhol* (1996).

2. P. Adams Sitney's *Visionary Film* defined a terrain that Jonas Mekas and Annette Michelson canonized.

3. For a full history, see Duberman, *Stonewall*.

4. For the most comprehensive history and analysis of this period and others, see Dyer and Pidduck, *Now You See It*.

5. See David Weissman's *The Cockettes* (2002) for the definitive history, with clips.

6. See Hammer, *HAMMER!*

7. Christine Vachon, speech at the San Francisco International Film Festival, 2011.

8. Deeply relevant are the earlier films of Derek Jarman and the shorts and first feature of Isaac Julien, but they are both discussed elsewhere. I'd also mention Arthur Bresson's *Buddies* (1985) which, like *Parting Glances*, was an insider look at the AIDS devastation through a pair of men, one who is dying and one who is a volunteer helper; Bresson himself died of AIDS in 1987. For a broad collection of favorite, mostly early LGBT films, see Chuck Wilson, "Playing Favorites: Queer and/or Peculiar Films That Have Mattered," *LA Weekly*, July 10, 2002, http://www.laweekly .com/2002–07–18/news/playing-favorites.

9. It's chilling to see today. But prior to September 11, 2001, the World Trade Center was extremely unpopular with the downtown crowd, who regarded it as an architectural outrage and a blemish on the landscape. I remember living in its shadow on Warren Street in 1981, in the loft of Kate Horsfield and the late Lyn Blumenthal. We resented its brute scale and sheer ugliness as an intrusion onto the more village-like scale of a neighborhood then beginning its transformation into Tribeca.

10. At that time New York City was covered in plywood, its sidewalks transformed into dark tunnels of wood to protect pedestrians from chunks of crumbling stone facades falling off buildings and to protect landlords wary of liability and lawsuits. As a result, artists, filmmakers, and musicians had free access to the best billboards in town, and culture thrived.

11. See Betsy Sussler's interview, "Lizzie Borden."

12. *Mala Noche* was first published in 1977 as a chapbook and later included in his collection *Mala Noche: And Other "Illegal" Adventures* (1997) with a foreword by Van Sant.

13. John Greyson's *Zero Patience* (1993) would extend this impulse into a radical counter-history of disease, contagion, and panic.

14. Weaver's then-partner and constant costar Peggy Shaw has a cameo as the clerk in the sex toys shop who demonstrates the choices of dildos.

15. Jeffreys created a "porn-free zone" outside the conference venue where the film was screening, where women could escape; when it was shown theatrically, suspicious bomb threats were phoned in to disrupt screenings. *She Must Be Seeing Things* is discussed positively later in 1989 at the How Do I Look? conference in New York City, where Teresa de Lauretis delivered a talk that became her essay "Film and the Visible" focused on McLaughlin's film. See Bad Object-Choices Collective, *How Do I Look?* for the essay. Its cover features a scene from the film.

16. Lizzie Borden, personal communication, July 2010.

17. Paradoxically, Julien was attacked by both the *New York Times* critic Caryn James and his fellow queer filmmaker Marlon Riggs.

18. For more on Canadian queer work in this epoch, which was extremely important and is woefully neglected in this volume, see, among others, Beard and White, *North of Everything*; Gittings, "*Zero Patience*, Genre, Difference, and Ideology" Goldie, *In a Queer Country*; Muñoz, "The Autoethnographic Performance." and the new forty-two-chapter anthology, Longfellow, MacKenzie, and Waugh, *The Perils of Pedagogy: The Works of John Greyson*, For the definitive essay on Marshall, see Gever, "Pictures of Sickness."

19. Rainer, *A Woman Who*, 109.

20. After-the-fact conversation between Yvonne Rainer and Cecilia Dougherty, July 1997, Bard College.

21. Thanks to my friend Meg Wolitzer for this.

22. See it online at http://www.youtube.com/watch?v=YKKeWsMyDXQ.

THE NEW QUEER CINEMA

Director's Cut

2 Anyone who has been following the news at film festivals over the past few months knows that 1992 has become a watershed year for independent gay and lesbian film and video. Early last spring, on the very same day, Paul Verhoeven's *Basic Instinct* (1992) and Derek Jarman's *Edward II* (1991) opened in New York City. Within days, the prestigious New Directors / New Films Festival had premiered four new "queer" films: Christopher Munch's *The Hours and Times* (1991), Tom Kalin's *Swoon* (1992), Gregg Araki's *The Living End* (1992), and Laurie Lynd's *R.S.V.P.* (1991).

Had so much ink ever before been spilled in the mainstream press for such a cause? *Basic Instinct* was picketed by the self-righteous wing of the queer community (until dykes began to discover how much fun it was), while mainstream critics were busily impressed by the so-called queer new wave and set to work making stars of the new boys on the block. Not that the moment isn't contradictory: this summer's San Francisco Gay and Lesbian Film Festival had its most successful year in its sixteen-year history, doubling attendance from 1991, but the National Endowment for the Arts pulled its funding anyway, courtesy of the resurgent right wing in the Republican Party that saw votes wherever there were "family values" to be defended.

The queer film phenomenon was introduced in fall 1991 at Toronto's Festival of Festivals, the best spot in North America for tracking new cinematic trends.[1] There, suddenly, was a flock of films that were doing something new, renegotiating subjectivities, annexing whole genres, revising histories in their image. All through the winter, spring, and summer, the message was loud and clear: queer is hot. My itinerary accelerated my rate of discovery, as I went from festival to festival and took time out for the Fifth Annual Lesbian and Gay Studies Conference at Rutgers University. I checked out the international circuit from Park City to Berlin to London. Awards were won, parties held. At Sundance, in the heart of Mormon country, there was even a panel dedicated to the queer subject, hosted by yours truly.

"Barbed Wire Kisses" put eight panelists on stage, with so many queer filmmakers in the audience that a roll call had to be read. Filmmakers stood, one by one, to applause from the matinee crowd. "Sundance is where you see what the industry can bear," said Todd Haynes, there to talk about *Poison*'s previous year on the firing line. He stayed to be impressed by an earnest eighteen-year-old *wunderkind*, Sadie Benning, whose bargain-basement videos, shot with a Fisher-Price Pixelvision toy camera and produced for less than $20 apiece, had already received a retrospective at the Museum of Modern Art in New York.

Isaac Julien was unexpectedly cast in the role of the older generation. Summarizing the dilemmas of marketing queer product to general audiences, he described a Miramax Prestige advertising campaign for his *Young Soul Rebels* (1991) that used a bland image of guys and gals hanging out, like a Newport ad gone Benetton.[2] The film wasn't doing well until Julien got them to change the ad to an image of the black and white boyfriends, Caz and Billibud, kissing on a bed. The box office immediately improved.

Tom Kalin struggled to reconcile his support for the queer community's disruptions of *Basic Instinct*'s shoot last spring with his film *Swoon*'s choice of queer murderers as subjects. And to explain how his passion for queer transgression related to his earlier participation in Gran Fury, the arts wing of ACT UP, responsible for many of the most memorable graphics of the era in New York. The Australian filmmakers Stephen Cummins and Simon Hunt, who were there with their short dance film, *Resonance*, regaled the audience with a story of censorship Australian-style, involving one episode of *The Simpsons* in which a scene of Homer kissing a swish fellow at the plant ended up on the (censor's) cutting-room floor.[3]

When time came to open up the session to the audience, the panel turned surprisingly participatory. One Disney executive identified himself as gay and then excoriated the homophobia of the industry. A filmmaker called for a campaign to demand that Oliver Stone not direct the announced biopic of Harvey Milk (later rumored to be readied for direction by Gus Van Sant in

1992, with Stone as coproducer).[4] Meanwhile Derek Jarman, the grand old man in his fourth decade of queer activity, beamed. He announced that he'd never been on a panel of queers at a mainstream festival before.

Try to imagine the scene in Park City. Robert Redford held a press conference and was asked, on camera, why there are all these gay films at his festival. Redford finessed: it is all part of the spectrum of independent film that Sundance is meant to serve. He even allowed that the best-feature and best-documentary awards last year to *Poison* (1991) and Jennie Livingston's *Paris Is Burning* (1991) might have made the festival seem more welcoming to gays and lesbians. He could just as easily have said, These are simply the best films being made.

Of course, the new queer films and videos aren't all the same and don't share a single aesthetic vocabulary, strategy, or concern. Nonetheless they are united by a common style: call it "Homo Pomo." In all of them, there are traces of appropriation, pastiche, and irony, as well as a reworking of history with social constructionism very much in mind. Definitively breaking with older humanist approaches and the films and tapes that accompanied identity politics, these works are irreverent, energetic, alternately minimalist, and excessive. Above all, they're full of pleasure. They're here, they're queer, get hip to them.

All the same, success breeds discontent, and 1992 is no different from any other year. When the ghetto goes mainstream, malaise and paranoia set in. It can be ideological, generational, or genderational.[5] Consider the issues that might disturb the peace. What will happen to the lesbian and gay filmmakers who have been making independent films, often in avant-garde traditions, for decades already? Surprise, all the new movies being snatched up by distributors, shown in mainstream festivals, and booked into theaters are by the boys. Surprise, the amazing new lesbian videos that are redefining the whole dyke relationship to popular culture remain hard to find and marginalized.

Amsterdam's Gay and Lesbian Film Festival made these discrepancies plain as day (fig. 2.1). The festival was staged in November 1991, wedged between Toronto and Sundance. It should have been the most exciting place to be, but wasn't, not at all. And yet that's where the girls were. Where the videos were. Where the films by people of color and ex–Iron Curtain denizens were. Only the power brokers were missing.

Christine Vachon, the coproducer of *Swoon* and *Poison*, is sure that the heat this year has been produced by money: "Suddenly there's a spotlight that says these films can be commercially viable." Still, everyone tries to guess how

2.1 T-shirt created for the Amsterdam Gay and Lesbian Film Festival '91. Collection of the author.

long this moment of fascination will last. After all, none of this is taking place in a vacuum: what is celebrated in the festivals is despised in the streets. Review the statistics on gay-bashing. Glance at would-be presidential candidate Pat Buchanan's demonizing of Marlon Riggs's *Tongues Untied* (1989), which was attacked on its own and as a proxy for defunding the National Endowment for the Arts. Check out U.S. immigration policy. Add the usual quota of internecine battles: girls against boys, narrative versus experimental work, white boys versus everyone else, elitism against populism, expansion of sights versus patrolling of borders. There's bound to be trouble in paradise, even when the party's just getting going.

Dateline: Toronto, 1991

Music was in the air in Toronto in September 1991, where the reputation of queer film and video started to build up. Or maybe I just loved Laurie Lynd's *R.S.V.P.* because it made my elevator ride with Jessye Norman possible. Lynd's film used Norman's aria from Berlioz's *Les Nuits d'Eté* as its Madeleine;

supposedly Lynd sent Norman the finished film as a belated form of asking permission, and she loved it so much that she offered to attend the world premiere at Toronto. With red carpet in place and a packed house going wild, Norman sat through the screening holding Lynd's hand. *R.S.V.P.* suggests that the tragedy and trauma of AIDS have led to a new kind of film and video practice, one that takes up the aesthetic strategies that directors have already learned and applies them to a greater need than art for its own sake. This time, it's art for our sake, and it's powerful: no one can stay dry-eyed through this witty elegy.

Lynd was there as a producer too, having worked on fellow Canadian John Greyson's *The Making of "Monsters."* In Greyson's wonderfully fevered imagination, Georg Lukács comes out of retirement to produce a television movie and hires Bertolt Brecht to direct it. Along with Greyson's signature comedy and lingering shots of boys in briefs, there's a restaging of the central aesthetic argument of the Frankfurt School as it might apply to the crises of representation engendered by today's antigay backlash, violence, and television treatments of the AIDS era.

Both low-budget and high-end filmmaking showed up in Toronto. Not surprisingly, the guys were high end, the gals low. Not that I'd begrudge Gus Van Sant one penny or remove a single frame from *My Own Private Idaho*, a film that securely positions him as heir apparent to Fassbinder. So what if it didn't get a single Oscar nomination? At the other end of the spectrum was the veteran avant-gardist Su Friedrich, whose latest film, *First Comes Love*, provoked catcalls from its largely queer audience. Was it because its subject was marriage, a topic on which the film is healthily ambivalent, mingling resentment with envy, anger with yearning? Or was it an aesthetic reaction, since Friedrich returns to a quasi-structuralist mode for her indictment of institutionalized heterosexuality, and thus possibly alienated audiences accustomed to an easier queer fix? Was it because the director was a woman, since the only other lesbian on hand was Monika Treut, who by now should probably be classified as postqueer given the expansion of her filmic characters and interests. Whatever the reason, Friedrich's elegant short stuck out, a warning-of-storms-ahead barometer in a pack of audience pleasers.

The epiphanic moment, if there was one, was the screening of Jarman's *Edward II*, which reinscribed the homosexuality so integral to its sixteenth-century source. Christopher Marlowe's lifestyle actually prohibited his corpse from being buried in the hallowed Poets' Corner of Westminster Abbey a full three centuries after his rough-trade death in a tavern fight, per Jarman. No wonder he was drawn to the man's finest creation. To honor it, Jarman applied a syncretic style that mixed past and present in a manner so arch that the film easily fits its tag, no doubt scripted by Jarman himself: the "QE2." Think anachronistic pastiche, as OutRage demos and gay-boy calisthenics mix with minimalist period drama. Homophobia is stripped bare as a timeless occupation, tracked across centuries but never lacking in historical specificity. Obsessive love, meanwhile, is enlarged to include queer desire as a legitimate source of tragedy, entitled to inhabit center stage.

For women, *Edward II* is a bit more complicated. Since the heroes are men and the main villain is a woman, some critics have mistakenly condemned it as misogynist. Indeed Tilda Swinton's brilliance as an actor—and full co-creator of her role—invests her character with more weight, and thus more evil, than anyone else on screen. Further, the film is a critique of both heterosexuality and conservative governance: in a world ruled by Royals and Tories, Isabella seems more inspired by a hatred of Margaret Thatcher than by any generalized misogyny. Annie Lennox is clearly meant to be on the side of the girls, and the angels. Her solo song "Every Time We Say Goodbye" accompanies King Edward II and his lover Galveston's last dance, bringing grandeur, modernity, even postmodernity to their tragedy. The song was first recorded on the landmark *Red Hot and Blue* CD, the first of the AIDS benefit collections, and was released as a video too, which Jarman was actually supposed to have directed for Lennox. Instead, ill with AIDS-related blindness, seemingly near death, he was unable to do it; Lennox went ahead with the video as scheduled but inscribed images of Jarman's childhood into it, his home movies literally projected onto her face, in a tribute to his life, his activism, and HIV-positive status. By casting Lennox and this song into the stone castle of *Edward II*, he imported not only the singer but his own personal history. By such means does Jarman's time-traveling cinema insist on carrying the royal court of yore into today's queer world and vice versa.

Dateline: Amsterdam, 1991

The official car showed up at the airport with the festival's steamy poster of girls in heat and boys in lust plastered all over it. Amsterdam, city of lights for faggots and dykes, offered the promise of an event purely one's own in the city celebrated for queerness. The city with the best laws. The place where "gay liberation" has been most institutionalized. The home of Cinemien, the oldest distributor of women's films in the world. Opening night had front rows reserved for heterosexual dignitaries and speeches by local politicos eager to claim a queer constituency; the speeches by deputy mayors and cultural ministers went on seemingly forever. But little concession was made to their presence: a 35mm trailer was projected, filled with naked couples of queers of both genders, getting it on right there on screen, heating up the beds, then abruptly surrendering the pleasures of the flesh to roll onto the floor, transfixed by the nun on the television set, presumably a nod to the festival co-organizer Annette Forster's favorite theme of lesbian nuns.

The opening ceremony's official and subcultural discourses merged in the set of lifetime achievement awards presented to the directors Ulrike Ottinger and Derek Jarman. Typical plaques, they were less typical in whom they commemorated: the Bob Angelo awards. Named for a famed Dutch antifascist and Resistance fighter whose nom de guerre was Angelo, the awards point to his equally prominent identity as a queer. He founded the first Dutch "homosexual liberation" organization in 1945, immediately after the war, and went on to establish the precursor to the Netherlands' major gay rights group. I usually find awards ceremonies pretty dull, but there was something sincerely moving about this one. When Derek Jarman used the occasion to call for the decriminalization of Oscar Wilde in an official pardon in time for the centennial of his conviction in 1995 and vowed to spearhead a commission to place a statue of Wilde in the London streets, queer past and present seemed to be firmly in dialogue with one another.

The festival had two directors, one male and one female, and two sets of T-shirts, one with guys, one with gals. My Brit pal Mark Nash caused an uproar by demanding one with the women on it for himself. There were two theaters too, and the festival tended to screen the guys' movies in the bigger house. One international guest hazarded the guess that the girls got the smaller house because its snack bar was the only one with hot chocolate, clearly a lesbian necessity.

Expectations were running high, but in fact the festival showed all the precious advantages and irritating problems that life in the ghetto entails. Amsterdam was a crucible for queer work, all right: some got celebrated, some got burned, some could have skipped it completely. How does this event fit into the big picture set by the big festivals? Well, it doesn't. The identity that elsewhere becomes a badge of honor here became a straitjacket. But could "elsewhere" exist without the "here"?

Amsterdam was an exercise in dialectics in action, with both pleasures and dangers. For dialectics in tourism, the video maker Cecilia Dougherty and the video distributor Kate Horsfield took me on a field trip to the city's gay monument, a tripartite structure of triangles set in stone to commemorate the genocide of homosexuals under the Nazi occupancy. I thought it was tacky; Cecilia found it subtle; Kate said it was enough just that it was *there*. She taped it with her ubiquitous Video-8 camera, state-of-the-art technology. Sadie Benning was there too, in Amsterdam if not on this tour; it was her first time ever out of the United States. She had different adventures. One day she bought a stolen bicycle at the flea market; a few nights later she was surprised to leave the festival and find her bike still there, only her lock missing. Undaunted, off she went to look for rad fourteen-year-old girls (and, of course, found them).

The filmmaker Nick Deocampo from the Philippines was planning his country's first gay festival and hoping that the War of the Widows wouldn't forestall it.[6] Events suggested he might have some problems. For instance, the planned Amsterdam revival of Ishmael Bernal's *Manila by Night* (1980) never came off: banned under the Marcos regime, the print ironically wasn't allowed to leave Aquino's Philippines either. A tribute to Thai queer cinema never happened either: the trilogy of Thai films never arrived, detained at the airport in Bangkok, prohibited from exiting the country.

Race, status, romance, gender, even the necessity of the Amsterdam festival came up for attack and negotiation on those few occasions when the public got to talk back. Pratibha Parmar affirmed the importance of a queer circuit, "my lifeline," and was sure that it is key to the work she brought, most produced for Channel Four (which gets a lot of credit for the Brit queer revival). Fellow Brit Jarman disagreed: "Perhaps their time is up." Maybe life in the ghetto now offers diminished returns. Jarman expressed a hope that the days of "ghetto" festivals were over.

Not that there weren't good films at Amsterdam. But the best work seemed to come from long ago or far away, like the great archival shows of German cross-dressing movies which included Asta Nielsen in Urban Gad's *Zapata's Band* (1914), an early Ernst Lubitsch, *Ich Mochte Kein Mann Sein* (*I Don't Want to Be a Man*, 1918), and even Reinhold Schünzel's *Viktor und Viktoria* (1933) with nary a Julie Andrews in sight. The detective novelist Mary Wings paid tribute to "Greta Garbo's lesbian past." For me, though, the most extraordinary revival was a more recent one but no less unseen: Toshio Matsumoto's *Funeral of Roses* (1969), a gay fantasy from Japan. A mad underground rant that came off as a cross between Jean-Luc Godard and the late great Lino

Brocka, it included an oedipal narrative turned upside down, intrigue, sexual liberation, drugs, cross-dressing, protest politics, full color gone haywire, and an aesthetic manifesto quoting Jonas Mekas. It had audiences screaming with pleasure and disbelief.

There were two terrific new lesbian films too, both deserving of instant cult status. Direct from Frankfurt, the former Oberhausen director Karola Gramann's fine-tuned show "Cerebral Ecstasy" unearthed a Swiss film that was instantly captivating. Cleo Uebelmann's *Mano Destra* (1986) delivered bondage and domination straight to the viewer, serving up knot fetishism and the thrills of specular anticipation with an uncanny understanding of cinema's own powers. It knit the viewer directly into a visceral experience of bondage and domination.

From a trio of Viennese filmmakers—Angela Hans Scheirl, Dietmar Schipek, Ursula Puerrer—came *Flaming Ears* (1991), a surreal fable that drew on comics and sci-fi traditions for a post-human love story visualized in an atmosphere of cabaret, rubble, and revenge.[7] The fresh cyber-dyke style reflected Austrian sources as diverse as Valie Export and Otto Muehle, shot through with Super-8 visual rawness and a script that could have been written by J. G. Ballard himself. Shunning narrative, it embraced junkyard surrealism as a plausible substitute and became the lesbian hit of the festival.

Oddly enough, Amsterdam suffered from a curious lack of a public sphere: it was a local event gone global, an identity festival without an identity. The Dutch press, which I expected to be fully in evidence and engaged, was missing in action. It was a shame that they marginalized the festival, because the kind of scoop that the *New York Times* and *Newsweek* would later find in Utah and trumpet as a discovery could have been theirs right at home.

On those rare occasions when a public dialogue did take place, the levels of contestation and divergence of agendas became painfully apparent. The film theorist Teresa de Lauretis, who was in residence at the University of Utrecht that fall, had organized a panel, "Lesbian Cinema: After the Love Story." It was a great idea, an attempt to move the thinking forward beyond the first, girl-meets-girl phase. Think again. The Dutch women didn't want to move on past the love story; incensed, they resisted what they mistook for a scholarly plot to take away their pleasure.

At the panel on race, meanwhile, the conflict that took place was between the conference's success in finding a great deal of work by lesbians and gay men of color to screen, and foreigners to invite, while failing utterly to find or include those filmmakers of color who resided in Amsterdam itself. Pratibha

Parmar, Marlon Riggs, and Felix de Rooy (the Dutch Curacao filmmaker of *Ava and Gabriel*, 1990) all addressed the issue only to be shouted down by the festival codirector Paul Verstraeten, who counterattacked with gusto, taking on the whole room at times, and the devil take the consequences. Only the levelheadedness of one panelist, a Dutch Guyanese lesbian activist, salvaged the situation. As it was, the Dutch came away accusing the non-Dutch of ignorance and of exploiting a misunderstood situation, while the North American and European delegates departed with a revised view of Dutch "tolerance."

The festival had an undertone of a world feeding on itself, with race only the most predictable manifestation of the tensions. Another was the uprising by some of the lesbian film and video makers, who felt mistreated in comparison to the male feature filmmakers. Yet another was the frequency of half-empty theaters due to the paucity of local press. Nevertheless a new kind of lesbian video surfaced here, and with it emerged a contemporary lesbian sensibility. Like the gay male films now in the limelight, this video has everything to do with a new historiography. But where the boys are archaeologists, the girls have to be alchemists. Their style is unlike almost anything that's come before. I would call it lesbian camp, but the species is, after all, better known for the kind of camping that takes place in a tent. And historical revisionism is not a catchy term. So I'll borrow from Hollywood and think of it as the Great Dyke Rewrite.

Here's a taste of the new genre: in Cecilia Dougherty's *Grapefruit* (1989), loosely based on Yoko Ono's original book, some white San Francisco dykes (including Susie Bright in an early incarnation) unapologetically impersonate John, Yoko, and the Beatles, proving that appropriation and gender-fuck make a great combination. Did I say impersonate? They *are* the Beatles for the brief period of this video, finally compensating every dyke who ever wanted to be something more than a fan in the rock scene of the early 1960s.

Sometimes the dyke fan wants her idols just the way they first appeared on screen—but, well, different. Cecilia Barriga clearly felt that way too and did something about it. Barriga's *The Meeting of Two Queens* (*Encuentro entre dos Reinas*, 1991) reedits Dietrich and Garbo movies to construct a dream narrative: get the girls together, help them meet, let them get it on. It's a form of idolatry that takes the feminist lit-crit practice of "reading against the grain" into new image territory, blasting the results onto the screen (or monitor, to be exact).

In one episode of Kaucylia Brooke and Jane Cottis's *Dry Kisses Only*

(1990), Anne Baxter's back-stage meeting with Bette Davis in *All About Eve* is altered, inserting in place of Baxter a dyke who speaks in direct address to the camera about her tragic life, growing up on a farm, moving to San Francisco to work in a lesbian bar and meet the girls in the Forces, her true love lost to World War II combat. She's cross-cut with Bette's original reaction shots, culminating with Davis taking her arm (and taking her home). The cross-cutting attached heterosexual grief and admiration to lesbian grief and courage. Brooke and Cottis not only provided a happy ending for lesbian viewers but actually offered a logical explanation for the original film's narrative.

Apart from the videos, festival lesbians pinned all voyeuristic hopes on the "Wet" Party, where they would finally get to the baths. Well, sort of. Everyone certainly tried. Outfits ranged from the campiness of childhood-at-the-beach to show-your-leather seriousness. Women bobbed in the pool, playing with rubber rafts and inflated black and white fuck-me dolls. (Parmar would later note that there were more inflatables of color in attendance than actual women of color.) The San Francisco sex stars Shelly Mars and Susie Bright both performed, though the grand moment in which Bright seemed to be lecturing us on "oedipal underwear" turned out to be a cruel acoustical joke: she was actually extolling the virtue of edible underwear. But the back rooms were used for heart-to-hearts, not action. Caught between the states of dress-up and undress, everyone waited for someone else to do something.

Other parties offered other pleasures. At one, Jimmy Somerville, unscheduled, performed an homage to Sylvester, San Francisco's late and much missed disco diva. At another, Marilyn Monroe appeared, frosted on a giant cake, clutching her skirt, only to be carved up by a gaggle of male chefs. In the end, somehow, Amsterdam was the festival you loved to hate, the place where everyone wanted the world and wouldn't settle for less, where dirty laundry could be washed in public and anyone in authority taken to task, where audiences were resistant to experimental and nonnarrative work, and where criticisms were bestowed more bountifully than praise. And yet . . . while the marketplace might be seductive, it's not democratic. Amsterdam was the place where a Wet Party could at least be staged, where new works by women and people of color were accorded pride of place, where video was fully integrated into the programming. Amsterdam was a ritual gathering of the tribe and, like a class reunion, filled with cliques, tensions, and ambivalence alongside the celebration.

Everything came together at the Sundance Film Festival in Park City. Everything. The excitement that had started building in Toronto in the autumn picked up speed. The sense of a historical moment, however contested, that began in Amsterdam now burst into full view. Something was happening, and this time, finally, everyone noticed.

Christopher Munch's *The Hours and Times* is a good example. Audiences fell in love with this imaginary chronicle of Brian Epstein and John Lennon's last tango in Barcelona. Munch's camera style and script were a reprise of cinéma vérité, as though some dusty reels had been found in a closet in Liverpool and expertly edited, as though Leacock or Pennebaker had turned gay-positive retroactively. Epstein tries to get Lennon into bed, using old-world angst, homo-alienation, Jewish charm. Lennon tries to sort out his life, balancing wife Cynthia against groupie against Epstein, trying to have it all and to figure out whatever will come next. Just a simple view of history with the veil of homophobia pulled back. It was rumored that the dramatic jury at Sundance loved it so much they wanted to give it the Grand Prize—but since it wasn't feature length, they had to settle on a special jury award.

"Puts the Homo back in Homicide" is the teaser for Tom Kalin's first feature, *Swoon*, but it could easily apply to Gregg Araki's newest, *The Living End*, as well (fig. 2.2). Where Kalin's film was an interrogation of the past, Araki's is set resolutely in the present. Or is it? Cinematically, it restages the celluloid of the 1960s and 1970s: early Godard, *Bonnie and Clyde*, or *Badlands*—every pair-on-the-run movie that ever penetrated Araki's consciousness. Here, though, the couple are both guys and they are HIV-positive, one bored and one full of rage, both of them with nothing to lose. They could be characters out of a porn flick, the stud and the john, in a renegotiated terrain. Earlier Araki films were often too garage-band, too cheesecake, too far into visual noise for my taste, but this one was different. Camera style and palette updated the New Wave. Araki's stylistic end runs paid off, and this time he captured a queers-on-the-lam portrait deserving of a place in movie history: an existential film for a postporn age, one that puts queers on the map as legitimate genre subjects. It's quintessentially a film of its time.

And so was *Swoon*, though it might have seemed otherwise, what with the mock-period settings, the footage purloined from the 1920s, and the courtroom-accurate script based on the trial in Chicago in 1924 of Leopold and Loeb, the pair of rich Jewish boys who bonded, planned capers, and finally killed a boy. In the wake of the Jeffrey Dahmer case, it would be easy to think of this as a film about horrific acts.[8] *Swoon*, however, deals in different stakes: it's the history of discourses that is under Kalin's microscope, as he demonstrates how easily mainstream society of the 1920s could unite discrete communities of outsiders (Jews, queers, blacks, murderers) into a commonality of perversion. The whole look of the film—director of photography Ellen Kuras won a Sundance prize for cinematography—emphasized this point of view with the graphic quality of its antirealism, showing how much Kalin, Kuras, and coproducer Vachon tailored its look to its implicit arguments.[9]

As part of a new generation of directors, Kalin isn't satisfied to live in the past, even a postmodern past. No, *Swoon* takes on the whole enterprise of "positive images" for queers, definitively rejecting any such project and turning the system on its head.[10] I doubt that anyone who damned Jonathan Demme's *The Silence of the Lambs* for toxic homophobia will swallow *Swoon* easily, but hopefully the film will force a rethinking of such positions. Claim the heroes, claim the villains, and don't mistake any of it for realness.

Throughout Sundance, a comment Richard Dyer made in Amsterdam

2.2 British advertisement for *The Living End* (1992), directed by Gregg Araki. Courtesy of Craig Gilmore.

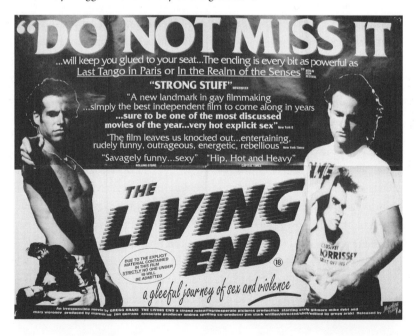

2.3 Sundance 1992, "Barbed Wire Kisses" panelists. Front row:
Stephen Cummins, Simon Hunt, Derek Jarman; back row:
Todd Haynes, Ruby, Isaac Julien, Tom Kalin, Sadie Benning, Lisa
Kennedy. Photo © Brook Dillon. Courtesy of the photographer.

echoed in my memory. There are two ways to dismiss gay film, he pronounced: one is to say, "Oh, it's just a gay film," while the other is to proclaim,
"Oh, it's a great film, it just happens to be gay." He was speaking of Jarman's
and Ottinger's films at the time, arguing that they were both great precisely
because of the ways in which they were gay. But his standard held at Sundance
as well, as queer film after queer film captured my imagination, audience applause, press attention. No, their queerness was no more arbitrary than their
aesthetics, no more than their individual preoccupations with interrogating
history. On celluloid and magnetic tape, just as in life and culture off-screen,
the queer present negotiates with the past, knowing full well that the queer
future is at stake.

Video is an even greater harbinger of that future, yet Sundance, like most
film festivals, showed none. To make a point about the dearth of lesbian work
in feature film and to confront the industry with its own exclusions, our
"Barbed Wire Kisses" panel opened with a projected screening of Sadie Benning's video *Jollies*, which brought down the house (fig. 2.3). With an absolute
economy of means, Benning constructed a Portrait of the Artist as a Young

Dyke such as we'd never seen before. "I had a crush. It was 1978, and I was in kindergarten." The lines are spoken face-front to the camera, black-and-white images floating into the frame alongside the words enlisted by Benning to spell out her emotions on screen, associative edits calling settled assumptions into question. Yes, a genre was born.

The festival ended, of course. Isaac Julien returned to London to finish *Black and White in Color*, his documentary on the history of blacks in British television. The high school dropout Sadie Benning left to show her tapes at Princeton and to make another one, *It Wasn't Love*, that proved she's no fluke. Derek Jarman and Jimmy Somerville were arrested back in London for demonstrating outside Parliament.[11] Christopher Munch and Tom Kalin picked up prizes in Berlin. Gregg Araki found himself a distributor. New work kept getting produced: Frameline's San Francisco gay and lesbian film festival reported that its submissions were up by 50 percent in June. The Queer New Wave had come full circle: the boys and their movies have arrived.

But will lesbians ever get the attention for their work that men get for theirs? Will queers of color ever get equal time? Or video achieve the status reserved for film? Take, for example, Cheryl Dunye, a young video artist whose *She Don't Fade* and *Vanilla Sex* put a sharp, satiric spin on black romance and cross-race illusions.[12] Or keep an eye out for Jean Carlomusto's *L Is for the Way You Look* for the episode in which friends at a Reno performance notice Fran Lebowitz in the audience, then gradually realize that the person with Fran is none other than Dolly Parton. It's a definitive take on dyke fandom, the importance of subject position, and the frailty of friendship when celebrity is at stake.

Questions may still have remained, dreams stoked, disappointments ahead, but let it be known that on one magical Saturday afternoon in Park City, there was a panel that traced a history: Derek Jarman at one end on the eve of his fiftieth birthday, and Sadie Benning at the other, just joining the age of consent. The world had changed enough that both of them could be there, with a host of cohorts in between. All were engaged in the beginnings of a new queer historiography, capable of transforming the decade, if only the door would stay open long enough. For him, for her, for all of us.

Notes

This article was first published in the *Village Voice* of March 24, 1992, under the headline "A Queer Sensation." It was reprinted as the lead article in a special section of *Sight and Sound* 2.5 (1992), 30–34, with the headline "The New Queer Cinema." The phrase originated in a conversation I had with Philip Dodd, then the editor in chief, about how I viewed developments since the *Voice* piece had been published. It is to that conversation that I owe the serendipity of my term's immortalization as a title and, later, movement. In the journal's special section, Dodd and coeditor Pamela Cook commissioned responses to my "manifesto" from Derek Jarman, Isaac Julien, Pratibha Parmar, and Constantine Giannaris, plus additional articles by Amy Taubin and Andy Medhurst. See the following anthologies, which include the original 1992 article and expand significantly beyond it: Aaron, *The New Queer Cinema: A Critical Reader*; Benshoff and Griffin, *Queer Cinema: The Film Reader*. More recently, it was reprinted in the context of the field of critical theories in general: Corrigan, White, and Mazaj, *Critical Visions in Film Theory*.

When this essay was originally published in 1992, it was cut by the *Voice* for considerations of space and newsworthiness. Since all prior reprints used the same text, this marks the first publication of the essay in its entirety, as written.

1. The Toronto Festival of Festivals (today the Toronto International Film Festival, or TIFF) was always a queer-friendly event, whatever that means today, thanks to its former director Helga Stephenson, the late Jay Scott in the press, and programmers Kay Armatage, Noah Cowan, and the late David Overby.

2. Miramax was an upstart company in 1992, Prestige its short-lived, art film label.

3. Stephen Cummins died two years later, in 1994, of AIDS-related causes. Simon Hunt has a long and continuing career as a writer, satirist, even would-be politician, performing under the name Pauline Pantsdown. He interviewed me in Sydney in 1999.

4. Only fourteen years later, it finally happened—with Van Sant, without Stone.

5. This wasn't a theoretical aside. I had already been attacked by filmmakers who felt left out of the discussion. As always, Sundance staff selected the panelists out of the pool of filmmakers whose work was being shown at the festival (plus Todd Haynes, the prior year's laureate). After refusing to moderate an all-male panel, I was able to add the video artist Sadie Benning and my *Village Voice* editor Lisa Kennedy, but no filmmakers. Su Friedrich sent me a single-spaced diatribe accusing me of betrayal and treachery. I was attacked in the letters column of the *Voice* by Jennie Livingston for leaving her out of the article, though she'd had no role in the events I described. Even the admired Teresa de Lauretis sent me a letter of complaint, though a much more supportive one, phrased in terms of disappointment rather than anger: why did I have to describe such a bleak gender imbalance?

6. That was the term for the events surrounding Imelda Marcos's return to Manila in defiance of Corazon Aquino's government, a reversal of the time when Aquino's

martyred husband sought to return under Imelda's husband's dictatorship and was assassinated. For more details, see Sandra Burton and Nelly Sindayen, "The Philippines: The War of the Widows," *Time*, November 18, 1991.

7. Its provisional title at the festival was *Red Ears Hunt through Ash*.

8. Jeffrey Dahmer was the notorious serial killer and cannibal who murdered seventeen men and boys in Milwaukee. He was captured in the summer of 1991 when his intended eighteenth victim managed to escape while still handcuffed and led police back to the apartment. Dahmer was tried in 1992, sent to prison, and murdered two years later by another inmate. His crimes were being widely reported in the media at the time of the Sundance premiere of *Swoon*.

9. This effect is even more pronounced in the Strand release of *Swoon* on DVD, for the cinematographer Ellen Kuras oversaw the digital mastering that bestowed a clarity impossible to see in the original 16mm print. Strand's dedication to bringing back many of the films of the early 1990s in high-quality DVD formats is key to preserving NQC history, just as Strand's founding was key to the initial flowering of the NQC.

10. Nobody uttered the name of Vito Russo, but he might have been turning in his grave if *Celluloid Closet* (the book) is a reliable guide to his map of positive and negative images; Rob Epstein and Jeffrey Freedman's *The Celluloid Closet* and Jeffrey Schwartz's new documentary *Vito* are excellent sources for Russo's activist views.

11. Jarman would die of AIDS complications on February 19, 1994.

12. Dunye went on to make *The Watermelon Woman* and other films. In Chicago a young lesbian couple named Rose Troche and Guinevere Turner would read this very article in *Sight and Sound* in the fall of 1992 and decide to contact Christine Vachon about a little film they had started working on together: *Go Fish*.

COLLISION, CATASTROPHE, CELEBRATION

The Relationship between Gay and Lesbian

Film Festivals and Their Publics

3 The past two decades have witnessed a phenomenal growth in the size and number of film festivals focused on gay, lesbian, bisexual, and transgender work and representation. The model of festivals as political interventions playing to small self-selected audiences that predominated in the 1970s and 1980s has morphed into the large events of the 1990s, complete with corporate sponsors and huge audiences that return annually and grow exponentially. I'm interested not in the success stories or myths of progress but rather in a particular point of stress: What happens when audiences reject programmers' choices? Why does this occur? And what are the implications and consequences of such dissonance?

A few examples might help to describe the territory. My own first experience of the phenomenon transpired in 1982, when I viewed the film *Immacolata e Concetta* (1981) at the Gay and Lesbian Film Festival in New York City. I had already seen the film at that spring's New Directors / New Films Film Festival. In that heterosexual crowd, the film was nonetheless so devastatingly sexy and tragic that my friend Joan grabbed me when the lights came up and whispered, "We have to kill them all now, because they know too much." I could hardly wait to see it again with the lesbian crowd at the festival—until I got there. Snickering began early on, escalating whenever the plot turns moved out of acceptable territory into rawer emotions (jealousy, bisexuality, pregnancy) and turning to anger with the murder at film's end. The starkly convincing realism of the film was repudiated. Laughter took the place of empathy for this audience. Outside in the street after the screening, furious,

I stopped members of the audience to ask them why they had laughed. "Because it was a prick movie," spat one butch at me. "I came out here with my girlfriend to have a good time."

Throughout the 1980s and 1990s, other films have taken a turn at playing lightning rod for the festivals' gay and lesbian audiences. Sheila McLaughlin's *She Must Be Seeing Things* showed at the San Francisco Gay and Lesbian Film Festival in 1987 right after its premiere at the International Women's Film Festival in Créteil. A breakthrough film for lesbian representation, it was informed by the sex controversies of the early 1980s, in which pitched battles were fought over the acceptability of any practices involving dildos, bondage, sadomasochism, butch/femme roles, pornography, even heterosexual penetrative sex. The film pushed buttons for a Bay Area audience unwilling to have its borders expanded by McLaughlin's free-ranging fiction. The fact that its tale of a lesbian relationship in crisis was centered on one lover's nightmare paranoia of heterosexual betrayal by her girlfriend didn't help; fantasy and action became conflated and the audience objected in no uncertain terms. In San Francisco, that took the form of grumbling; in London, in a workshop scene reported by Sue O'Sullivan, the antiporn lesbian audience turned militant and tried to rip the film out of the projector.[1] The film's representation of lesbian sex play, betrayal, and insecurity was too much for them to bear, but the response was cloaked in ideological rectitude.

The Canadian filmmaker Midi Onodera's *Ten Cents a Dance* (1985) also stirred up some surprising lesbian resistance. In part, this was due to its tripartite structure: a lesbian scene, in which the women talk and talk but barely touch; a gay scene, in which the men fuck and fuck but barely speak; and a heterosexual scene, which turns out to be phone sex. The beginning didn't raise their ire, but the absence of any further lesbianism angered the audience, which, as usual, came to the festival in the expectation of 100 percent lesbian content. The whimsy of the lesbian filmmaker's satire was lost on its public, which additionally took exception to the avant-garde split-screen strategy.[2]

In Amsterdam in 1991 I'd eagerly awaited the Dutch lesbian reaction to screenings of Su Friedrich's *First Comes Love* and Sadie Benning's *Jollies,* happy that the United States was showing off two of its best lesbian visions. To my amazement, the Dutch women reacted with scorn. "So badly made," they complained. Their verdict ignored the aesthetic importance of the avant-garde and obliterated a breakthrough moment for video, as they condemned both Friedrich and Benning for failing to deliver the glossy marquee-movie products that they wanted. They felt that gay men were getting these pictures and insisted that the pioneering avant-garde works by lesbians were consigning them to second-best, aesthetically inferior, and less entertaining "movies." Categories were severely regulated in Amsterdam, on all fronts. The fags flocked to the guy movies, the girls to the dyke shows. There were even separate festival T-shirts: Rock Hudson hugging John Wayne, Marilyn Monroe with Brigitte Bardot.

This same parochialism would go on to doom festival screenings of *First Comes Love* elsewhere as well. Friedrich had used footage shot at heterosexual weddings to make a point about the need to legalize gay and lesbian marriage around the globe. Alas, by the time the rolling title at the end revealed the filmmaker's strategy (a long, scrolling list of the countries where gay and lesbian marriage is illegal), lesbian audiences at the mainstream Toronto International Film Festival were in a fury over being forced to sit through these heterosexual ceremonies. There was little room for modulation with this crowd.

Eventually trouble crossed the gender aisle and set up camp with festivals' male audiences too. Leave it to the New Queer Cinema to start pushing buttons. In the early years, there was some leeway. Tom Kalin got away with *Swoon* in 1992. By the late 1990s, though, the gay male audiences had caught up to lesbian feminism of the 1970s and wanted positive images from their movies. When the late Mark Finch programmed Steve McLean's *Postcards from America* as part of a posh benefit tribute to producer Christine Vachon in 1994, it turned into his darkest hour. The lesbians in the house were mad at the exclusively male focus, while the gay men emerged furious at the "negative" representations: hustling, drugs, and alienation were not the image of gayness they wanted projected to America. Vocal opposition ensued.

The following year, *Frisk* upped the ante. Gay men nearly rioted when the film was featured at a tribute to the Strand distributor and *Frisk*'s producer Marcus Hu, who actually feared for his life in view of the violent reaction against the film. Based on Dennis Cooper's novel of the same name, *Frisk* had the nerve to explore fantasies of murder in the context of anonymous sexual encounters. As in the book, the status of the murders as fantasy or reality is left ambiguous, but that play of ambiguity was rejected by the audience, which objected to the film as if it advocated serial killing. Similar objections surfaced to Ira Sachs's film *The Delta* (1996), which had the courage to look at the race and class conflicts at the heart of the gay male sex-for-hire world. Once again audiences rebelled against the film's grittily authentic presentation of an encounter between a rich white boy from Memphis society and the mixed-race Vietnamese hustler he picks up and who falls in love with him. As with *Immacolata e Concetta* a decade and a half earlier, a murder at film's end tipped the scales and set off a conflagration of audience opposition. Yet in a matter of weeks, the real-life crime spree of Andrew Cunanan riveted the nation and should have made these audiences reconsider their rejection of films that went far to explain just such boy-toy behavior.[3]

No doubt these examples will continue as the New Queer Cinema continues to mature and audiences continue to elaborate their own agendas. Were this all simply a matter of conflicting "taste," as sometimes happens with mass-media assessments of mainstream festivals that don't claim any particular agenda apart from the specious one of "quality," there wouldn't be much point in my tracking the history of these incidents. But if viewed in the context of similar tensions that rise to the surface of other specialty festivals— whether Asian American, Jewish, Native American, or Latino—these points of conflict may actually have something to tell us about how gay and lesbian communities define and construct themselves and what part culture has to play in those self-descriptions.

The unique position of gay and lesbian film festivals within their communities is due to their simultaneous deployment of sacred notions of both sexuality and oppression as key to identity—an insistence that proves as powerful as it is volatile. Audiences come with particular expectations. One survey conducted by the San Francisco festival a few years ago uncovered a surprising statistic: 80 percent of the audience didn't go to movie theaters the rest of the year. Were they all lesbian coparents with VCR habits? At the same time, it was discovered that 80 to 90 percent of the work shown at gay and lesbian film festivals never plays elsewhere.[4] These figures suggest a world apart from the mainstream, one with its own particular communities, markets, and customs. What position exactly do film festivals occupy, then? Is a gay/lesbian/bi/ trans film festival comparable to a bar? a gym? a club? a community center? a softball game? a queer conference? a magazine? a daytime talk show?

What we do know about film festivals in general is that they are frequently symbols of sociopolitical ambition. Most often cited is the story of the Venice Film Festival's claim to being the very first film festival in the world, founded under the aegis of Mussolini. Ferdinand Marcos started a film festival in Manila, the shah of Iran started one in Tehran. After independence, the joke once ran, a country had to do three things: design a flag, launch an airline, and start a film festival.

Gay and lesbian film festivals, which grew exponentially in the 1990s just as film festivals have in general, pose slightly different problems due to their function in constituting community within a larger society. They offer a space where diverse queer publics can come and frame their attendance as community. In this, they may well be comparable to such traditional populist gatherings as the circus, the carnival, the courtroom, or even sporting events. Perhaps they're properly comparable to opera in its older proletarian stage, or Shakespeare (ditto). Perhaps they are indeed festivals, in the oldest sense of the word, and serve an important function in terms of instilling faith and inspiring agency. Perhaps attendance at these festivals should be viewed as a form of pilgrimage for the faithful.

This shared communion has its effects: it reinforces the faith of the faithful, assures supplicants of their worthiness, creates a bond to carry individually into the larger world, and puts audiences back in touch with shared experiences and values. However, this very same dynamic creates a version of community that can be quite prescribed and excluding. Audiences don't want disruption or "difference." There is instead a hunger for sameness, replication, reflection. What do queers want on their night on the town? To feel good. To feel breezy and cheesy, commercial and acceptable, stylish and desirable. A six-pack and *Jeffrey*. A six-pack and *Bound*. They just wanna have fun. And if it's serious, then it had better be predictable: the AIDS quilt or lesbian adoption rights.

Of course, this is a desire that drives mainstream audiences as well: my late father would go to movies only if assured of a comedy. But what happens when a community that is politically constituted engages in this sort of expectation deployment? It's particularly troubling given the festivals' histories of commitment to the exploration of new representations (across gender, race, class) and new systems of representation. Their mandate, after all, is not to show the same matinee of *In and Out* (1997) that could be seen at any multiplex within the same season. As the festivals try to stay true to their aesthetic and ideological agenda and as their audiences grow ever larger, the opportunities for conflict just keep expanding.

To be sure, there have always been contradictions and battles within the lesbian and gay community: gender splits, confrontations between the academic and activist populations, fights between yuppie and on-the-dole contingents, disdain between strategies of respectability and radical rebellion. Cinematically such conflicts have played out both over aesthetic categories (avant-garde versus mainstream) and the nature of characters or plots (the "Is it good for the Jews?" yardstick).

In this regard, 1998 was a particularly interesting year because of two films that challenged people's expectations and crossed over into theatrical release on the art house circuit: Lisa Cholodenko's *High Art* and John Maybury's *Love Is the Devil*. Both films upset utopian views of gay and lesbian relations as inherently more equitable than, or superior to, their heterosexual counterparts. Both push the envelope of queer consumer expectation and force viewers to move beyond comfortable boundaries to confront the less visible and less savory aspects of our most intimate interactions with those we claim to love.

Both films aired some seriously dirty laundry. *High Art* catalogued lesbian infidelity, bisexuality, drug use, social climbing, ambition, and opportunism. *Love Is the Devil* picked up issues of exploitation, physical abuse, ugly class relations, cruelty, and appropriation. Both films peer at our treatment of one another with the rose-tinted glasses completely removed. Both bring Fassbinder to mind, notably *The Bitter Tears of Petra Von Kant* (1972) and *Fox and His Friends* (1975). As they wend their way through exhibition and distribution channels, the responses from lesbian and gay audiences will indicate the current level of maturity found there. These films' uncompromising, unblinking views of lesbian and gay life are badly needed today, when, too often, idealized images take the place of authentic ones.

I would argue, finally, that these responses are inflected by something far more specific and complex than the usually subjective taste governing mainstream movie choices. Queer audiences see themselves as complicit in these representations, as if they are compromised or validated by them. Queer audiences are cathected to that screen and those characters to a degree that surpasses other audiences' investments. But there is usually no polymorphous dimension to these audience reactions; instead films and videotapes are accepted or rejected based on the narrow acceptability of the representations on offer.

It's as though these works are considered tests: not, alas, tests of the audience's resilience, imaginative power, or daring, but rather tests of the filmmakers themselves—their obedience to community standards, their effort to comply, the degree to which approval has been earned.

I continue to enter the darkened halls of the movie theaters and festivals in search of new experiences. And I continue to hope that my status as a critic will not separate me forever from the community with which I watch these movies. I'm ready to give up the game of "smart critic, stupid audience" if only they (you?) will give it up too. Then film festivals can finally own their spirit of adventure and we, as audiences, may finally get the films we deserve.

Notes

This chapter originally appeared as "Collision, Catastrophe, Celebration: The Relationship between Gay and Lesbian Film Festivals and Their Publics," GLQ: *A Journal of Lesbian and Gay Studies* 5.1 (1999), 79–84.

1. Ardill and O'Sullivan, "Sex in the Summer of '88."

2. In San Francisco folklore, this incident has come to be known, somewhat misleadingly, as the Lesbian Riot. The audience's incomprehension led to an aggressive reaction against the film, in part because it was featured as part of a Lesbian Shorts program. For a thoughtful discussion of the incident and her perspective as a Canadian Japanese lesbian filmmaker, see Onodera, "Camera Obscura for Dreams."

3. Andrew Cunanan was a hustler and boy-toy who turned serial killer. On a spree, he murdered four men before killing the fashion designer Gianni Versace outside Versace's Miami home on July 15, 1997. After avoiding an increasingly frantic manhunt for over a week, Cunanan committed suicide. For contrary renderings of his life and tale, see Orth, *Vulgar Favors*, and Indiana, *Three-Month Fever*.

4. Frameline staff, personal communication, 1997.

WHAT'S A GOOD GAY FILM?

 Every year, when gay and lesbian film festival season strikes, I watch this buoyant community turn out in public to celebrate itself. Marquee madness rules, celluloid obsessions alternating with the hope of celebrity spotting and the guaranteed satisfaction of in-line cruising. Queer audiences want to be entertained. But many still scan the offerings for positive values, fret over lesbians who die on screen ("Not that old stereotype again!"), and lament the predictability of mainstream script fashion ("Not another faggot best friend!"). They prefer the girl-gets-girl and boy-gets-boy movies, where heart meets heart and flesh meets flesh. Yet more and more I feel isolated there in the dark, the dyke done in by the critic in my cerebellum. I wait, dreading another bad movie that the body in the next seat will cheer, fearing that mediocrity has come to roost now that the barricades have come down.[1]

Mostly I shut my mouth. Grumbling about commercialization, selling out, or going mainstream are the defenses of leftover radicals intent on remarginalizing our community in the face of success, right? Wasn't it only a short while ago that no such images could be found on movie screens at all? Not so long ago, the major problem was invisibility and its consequence: a sad vacuum of the imagination and the marketplace both. But I'm not sure I like this current moment, when we have the marketplace without the imagination. Hasn't anyone noticed that some distinctions need to be made between films that pander and films that inspire, between our highest common denominator and our lowest? Where are our cultural standards? And what are they, anyway?

In the fabled 1970s, when the first gay and lesbian film festivals started and the first round of self-consciously up-front homopolitico films began playing to audiences whose very act of identification was deeply ideological, a model was established. Everything took place on the fringe, disconnected from mainstream popular culture both by choice and by exclusion. This oppositional culture was deeply tied to the political debates of the time, aiming to eradicate "prejudice" and instill "pride." The emphasis was on documentary, the agenda was civil rights, and status depended on claiming an identity as an oppressed class. True, it was also the era of celebration and sexuality, whether Olivia Records or backroom sex, whether cruising the piers or cruising womyn's events, but the contradictions remained off-screen.

Moments of origin always cast a long shadow. Today queer film and video still bear a birthright linked to the umbilical cord of post-Stonewall gestation. There's a generation of elders that expects film and video to toe an eternally prescribed line of righteousness and legitimacy, while ever new and needy generations recycle the old and add their own requirements. These queer publics want films of validation and a culture of affirmation: work that can reinforce identity, visualize respectability, combat injustice, and bolster social status. They want a little something new, but not too new; sexy, sure, but with the emphasis on romance; stylish, but reliably realistic and not too demanding; nothing downbeat or too revelatory; and happy endings, of course. It's an audience that wants, not difference or challenge, but rather a reflection up there on the screen of its collective best foot forward. Part of the audience also wants higher production values than the independents can deliver: a queer Hollywood, popcorn movies for a fun Saturday night out.

But I'm an old-time outlaw girl. I love the films that push the edge, upset convention, defy expectation, speak the unspeakable, grab me by the throat and surprise me with something I've never seen before. "That's not what we want!" cry the feet leaving the theater during my favorite films. And who can blame them? Why should I expect more of queer audiences than I expect of any good-time heterosexual crowd at the multiplex? But I do. Alas, nowadays, if the world portrayed by a film is alien or unwanted, if the view is dark instead of light, if there's tragedy at the end of the tunnel instead of an embrace or a coming out, then the queer audience reneges on its half of the contract and refuses acquiescence. "No, that's not me!" they silently scream as they exit the theater in anger. And the film suffers the hostile word of mouth that's poison at the box office.

Of course, the problem can't be blamed simply on gay and lesbian audiences. Hollywood studio execs hardly envision producing any ground-breaking movies to warm my heart either. At the Outfest in L.A. in 1994, I moderated a panel of lesbian studio execs and producers, whose blonde girlfriends sat in the audience applauding. The she-execs predicted the next wave of crossover movies: lesbian romantic comedies, which they were busily optioning. Not a single one made it out of development hell. I'd insisted on titling the panel "The Lesbian Minute Comes to Hollywood" because I figured that was about how long it would last.[2] Sadly, I was right. The filmmaker Elaine Holliman told me she remembered going from studio to studio with an actress dressed in a bridal gown, pitching a romantic comedy based on her short documentary *Chicks in White Satin* (1994). The result? No green light, but "I gave them the idea for *My Best Friend's Wedding.*"[3] In Hollywood even the lesbian romantic comedy that's pablum to me evidently pushes the proverbial envelope too far and can't be made.

I don't want to make the mistake of falling into that comfortable old victim box, complaining of absence in the midst of presence. We're not invisible anymore. We can now write a queer cinematic history that stretches way back. I can even celebrate a shining lineage of films that combine the creative spark that I crave with the groundbreaking stories that audiences have loved. In the indie boom years of the 1990s, I could hardly keep up with the U.S. films alone: *Poison, Paris Is Burning, Swoon, The Incredibly True Adventure of Two Girls in Love, Go Fish, All over Me, The Delta, The Watermelon Woman, Safe.* And, yeah, I'm still waiting along with the rest of you to see the long-promised crossover movie that pleases "us" as well as "them" and makes a bundle of money.[4]

The cranky critic in me remains unsatisfied. Why are filmic representations so often out of date, stuck in the past, tied to outmoded ideas about representation? Is complication so terrifying? I like edgier films and I always have, all the way back to my adolescence, when I escaped curfew to see *Scorpio Rising* (1964) or felt racy watching *Emmanuelle* (1974). When I think of lesbian and gay films that I love, they are always films that go beyond identification, oppression, or coming-out stories to tap into larger issues or deeper emotions. And if their aesthetics take advantage of the opportunity to depart from realist norms, so much the better.

I examine my own favorites, looking for clues. In Diane Kurys's delicious *Entre Nous* (1983), it was the clothes. That's what got me: two sexy women, admiring each other in the mirror, designing clothing for each other and luxuriating in fabrics and colors to satiate their senses. The tease didn't hurt either, never does. In Stephen Frears's *Prick Up Your Ears* (1987), I loved not only its tragic ending but especially its dissection of Joe Orton's life with his lover: the jealousy, the fame, and the price people were willing to pay for celebrity. And when the New Queer Cinema came along, I was thrilled with filmmakers like Rose Troche and Todd Haynes for breaking aesthetic barriers and taking the queer audience along for the ride.

And in 1997? My favorite film in years, of any kind, from any place, was *Happy Together* by the genius Hong Kong filmmaker Wong Kar-Wai. In this male melodrama, two lovers leave Hong Kong for Argentina with dubious results. After the hot sex of the first five minutes, it all goes wrong and they fight like bats out of hell for the rest of the movie. But oh, how familiar is the way they fight! "We were just like them," said one friend to me, explaining why he and his boyfriend split. "Oh, my god, he's just like me," said my ex-girlfriend halfway through the screening. "Hmmm," said Wong Kar-Wai to the outraged Asian fans incensed by the gay content. "Just come in five minutes late. They're brothers."[5]

Happy Together is a poem to frustrated desire, grief, longing, exile, cultural displacement, and sexual commerce, all timed to a brilliant tango beat. Wong's cameraman, Chris Doyle, finds a visual register for every chord of emotion. And Wong's longtime collaborator William Chang—editor, art director, and the only gay member of the triumvirate—has a genius for the emotional weight of location, planting all the right trappings to snag our hearts. It's an ode to love that shows us what happens when love rots and vanishes, leaving tragedy in its wake.[6]

And what a deep wellspring of emotion is tapped with this tale of two guys who just, well . . . can't live with him, can't live without him. It's very much a gay story—and one that no gay director has dared to show us. Why is that? Why are we still covering up the realities of our lives in order to present a respectable image in public? "Why are the women in these awful lesbian movies completely unlike any lesbian I've ever known?" wrote a straight filmmaker to me, seeking my supposed expertise. No easy answer. Hmmm. Rent *Happy Together*, I am tempted to say, and pretend they're women.

Then I was captivated by the summer release of *High Art*, the indie film hailed as Ally Sheedy's comeback and writer and director Lisa Cholodenko's breakthrough. Sure, it's a love story in which girl kinda gets girl, or at least is on her way to it until death interrupts the plan. But it is equally a cold-eyed view of other emotions entirely: ambition, greed, emotional blackmail. Lesbian characters move within a sophisticated milieu that exceeds yet includes them. At the same time, the film offered a sexy read of a triangulated lesbian relationship such as we've never seen before on screen.

Why doesn't anyone ever want to tell the truth about lesbian relationships? Behind every "life partner" granola couple, there are twenty kinds of dysfunctional pairs with details that would make your hair curl. I want to see the power-tripping girlfriend, the suicidal boyfriend, the adulterous neighbor, the abusive partner . . . the whole cast of characters currently being swept under the carpet.

Here's a game to play: try to imagine what movies with gay and lesbian characters and plots would look like if someone pulled out all the stops and then financed the visions. What if, just for one glorious minute, we tried to imagine the absolutely fabulous film we could see if "they" let us. What would it be? Isaac Julien, the British filmmaker honored in 1998 by the Center for Lesbian and Gay Studies at the City University of New York's Graduate Center, says it would be "something cheesy about the family. Cheesy because that's what it takes to get the queer audience to come out to see it. And about the family, because that is the great unspoken subject in queer culture, the site of trauma that no one has talked about."[7] John Waters, devilish as usual, elaborates a fantasy: "All nude heterosexual Hollywood movie stars trying to win the Oscar by playing gay parts and failing miserably." And Donna Deitch, still worshipped for her classic, *Desert Hearts* (1985), admits her own preference up front: whatever the subject, "it better be hot."

Gus Van Sant, holed up on the set of *Psycho* and already planning his film about gay cowboys, says he's never had to cut any shots from any of his films due to their being gay. But his wish list? "In fantasy, it would be great to have a full-budget Disney animated feature with gay leads: *The Prince and the Stableboy,* or *Peter Pan: Love in Never-Never Land,* or *The Little Mermaid 2: Ariel and Samantha.* All with full promotions, y'know, McDonald's Happy Meals with the characters. And love songs between the two. It would be great."

Closer to home, Mary, raised in the 1960s, wants an old-fashioned musical with tap-dancing nuns and Cheryl Ladd (*Charlie's Angels*) as a novitiate. My friend Catherine, raised in the 1970s, thinks differently: "Forget gay pride for a while. I want to bring back gay shame." And me? I have lots of ideas, from the mundane to the epic. I want a post-coming-out, post-get-it-together kind of movie, something full of sex, romance, tragedy, and life outside The Relationship. I want to see the evil girlfriend manipulating some sweet thing into that special dyke circle of hell. I want to see the gold-digging boy-toy out trolling for a new daddy. I want the curtain raised on all the dirty lesbian secrets: the power plays, the naked lust, the sick transference, the poaching of friends. And I want the intimate familiarity of daily life reinvented aesthetically, remodeled for us. I want clues, signposts, prophecies, playfulness, and revelations.

Is your heart beating fast? What kind of movies and videos do you want? Does it matter? Yes, it does. In the world of desire and evolution, we can only get from here to there over the bridge of our imaginations. If we limit ourselves to what we see in the mirror, we're lost. If we're scared of anything new or different, or made uneasy by films and videos that challenge our notions of the homonatural universe, we'll be stuck with the status quo. If queer audiences stay away from controversial groundbreaking work, then the distributors and studios, those who watch the box office like a seismologist watches the Richter needle, will pull out completely. And the queer community will be abandoned, condemned to a static universe, comforted only by the sure knowledge that the earth, alas, won't move under our feet.

Notes

This chapter originally appeared as "What's a Good Gay Film?," OUT 60 (November 1998), 58.

1. This article is dedicated to the memory of Sarah Pettit, for her work as an editor and for her life as an exemplary homo girl. I was commissioned to write it for *Out* magazine when she was still its editor in chief; her subsequent firing marked a low point in gay and lesbian journalism. Pettit, who had started her career at the feisty *OutWeek*, went on to become *Newsweek*'s senior arts and entertainment editor, then died of non-Hodgkin's lymphoma in 2003 at the age of thirty-six. There's a fellowship in her name at Yale, her alma mater.

2. Thanks to Sande Zeig, who organized the panel, invited me to moderate, and kindly let me have my title.

3. Elaine Holliman, personal communication, 1997.

4. No, I didn't see *Brokeback Mountain* coming, even though Van Sant mentions his idea of making a cowboy movie toward the end of this very article.

5. Wong Kar-Wai, personal communication, 1997.

6. I should also note that the film has been widely interpreted as an allegory for the handover of Hong Kong back to China in 1997 (the passports at the beginning, the film's ninety-seven-minute running time, the shot of a television screen announcing Deng Xiaoping's death in 1997), in which case homosexuality is merely a stand-in. But what a stand-in.

7. This and all other quotations in this section were personal communications, gathered in person or via telephone or email, specifically for this piece.

PART II

BULLETINS FROM THE FRONT

THE KING OF QUEER

Derek Jarman

There's an astonishing renaissance under way in gay cinema, though you might not think so, given the single-minded focus on *Basic Instinct*. Derek Jarman's *Edward II* (1991) is playing at the same time as Paul Verhoeven's movie, and the contrast is instructive.

Jarman has taken Christopher Marlowe's four-hundred-year-old play and fashioned it into a modern (dare I say postmodern) masterpiece. The tragic love of King Edward for the handsome Gaveston is once again the centerpiece of the play, while its court intrigues and a spurned queen's revenge are recontextualized in Jarman's staging as a battle between queer desire and heterosexual condemnation. Precisely because of the anachronistic manner with which he combines seventeenth-century art direction with motorcycle jackets and OutRage-style protest demonstrations, *Edward II* succeeds in bringing past and present into fruitful consort.

For those who have never before encountered Derek Jarman, imagine a cross between Andy Warhol and Keith Haring, but somebody alive and kicking, warm and generous, irreverent and uncompromising. As an artist and activist, Jarman has a life history that seems to encompass the very development of modern gay culture.

When he revealed his HIV status publicly, Jarman became at once a beleaguered spokesperson for AIDS activism in Great Britain and a favorite focus for the British tabloids. Now, in 1992, he finds himself complaining, on the one hand, about being scapegoated and, on the other, about enduring saint-hood. "There's an element of worship at work now in people's treatment of me that I really don't want."[1]

Jarman started out as a London art student in the Swinging Sixties. It was there, painting and partying, that he first got swept into film, as the art director on Ken Russell's *The Devils* (1971). Despite the era, he found the British film industry to be a "violently heterosexual" milieu. "I was going to the first gay liberation meetings in London that year," he recalls, "and then going into the studio, where there were gay actors, but all in the closet. It was so strange. I was out of the closet outside the studio, but in the closet inside. I wasn't going to create havoc for Ken by coming to work as a radical fairy or something."

Jarman's first feature, *Sebastiane* (1976), was certainly nothing short of radical. It was spoken entirely in Latin, shot in Sardinia with money sup-plied by a sympathetic industrialist, and shown in gay porn houses in the United States due to all the naked and seminaked boys in his decidedly S&M interpretation of the iconic saint's life. His next film, *Jubilee* (1978), didn't fare much better commercially, but it marked the real start of his cult following. The signal success of *Caravaggio* (1986) should have opened the doors to an ironclad art film career for Jarman. It didn't, and Jarman contends the reason was overt homophobia:

> The censorship was incredible. Ian Charleson, the actor who starred in *Chariots of Fire*, was told when he was hired to say that he'd never worked with me. He was told that *Chariots of Fire* was to be listed as his first film. The film establishment, and [producer] David Putnam in particular, ac-tively worked against me. He was the one who personally told Charleson that he had to take Derek Jarman's *Jubilee* off his resume. Because of Mrs. Thatcher and Mr. Putnam, I couldn't work for five years.

Jarman found a pragmatic solution to his funding woes: making beauti-fully crafted, jewel-like films and videos, assembled on next to or no money, contemptuous of narrative constraints, and created with a dedicated cadre of talented associates, including the young Tilda Swinton. His decidedly avant-garde films—*The Angelic Conversation* (1987), *The Garden* (1990), and *The Last of England* (1988)—found their way to international film festivals, while his work in music videos with groups like the Pet Shop Boys won him a new audience among the younger generation. Finally, funding came through for a new feature, and *Edward II* came into being. It was a double victory, since Jarman recovered from tuberculosis and temporary blindness, the worst of his AIDS ailments, to direct it.

Ironically, *Edward II* has attracted some criticisms for the alleged misogyny of the Queen Isabella role, played by Swinton. Jarman protests, "They don't seem to understand that I'm saddled with a four-hundred-year-old unreconstructed collaborator [Marlowe]." He also emphasizes his collaboration with Swinton herself, who comes close to being Jarman's official muse. Already being discovered as a major actress in her own right, Swinton "made all the decisions on how she was going to play the character."

Jarman finds it sad that the ideological excesses of the "gay community" have frequently claimed films as victims, pointing to his friend Ron Peck's film *Night Hawks* (1978), about the tormented life of a gay schoolteacher, as an example. "It transgressed the era's rigid sexual politics, the ideas that people had about putting up positive images, and so got left out of the gay film histories." He sees today's openness of debate and disagreement as a positive sign. With typically devil-may-care heresy, Jarman speaks his mind:

> Half of the gay community could be sunk at the bottom of the ocean, if you know what I mean. I was under no illusion that I was joining a particularly enlightened group of people by coming out. I'm glad to say that this sort of illusion is being dispelled more, at this moment. We can all quarrel again. And we don't have to pretend that we like each other. It's really important. It's a sign of maturity and growing up.

At the same time, Jarman has welcomed, with gratitude, the new feeling of gay community that exists among filmmakers, mentioning his meetings with Gus Van Sant, Todd Haynes, Isaac Julien, and Tom Kalin, and the "real feeling that we're in this together." In addition to his films, Jarman has been contributing to the sense of collective endeavor by publishing a series of books on his life and work: *At Your Own Risk: A Saint's Testament*, an account of his experiences as a media-styled "AIDS victim."[2]

Jarman worries most about being treated as a saint, fretting that a note of worship has replaced the old indifference. He doesn't seem to realize that he's just made his best film yet and that, for once, the public, and maybe even the press, know enough to respond accordingly.

Notes

This chapter originally appeared as "King of Queer," *SF Weekly*, April 1, 1992.

1. This and all other Jarman quotations are from personal communication via telephone, 1992.

2. Jarman published a sequence of books, journals, and diaries that chronicle his life in the United Kingdom in cinema, under Thatcher, and with HIV/AIDS. See *Dancing Ledge, At Your Own Risk, Modern Nature,* and, published after his death, *Smiling in Slow Motion* and *Derek Jarman's Garden.*

TRUE STORIES OF FORBIDDEN LOVE

6 *Forbidden Love* (1992) is the film to see—for every lesbian wannabe out for a quick fix, every heterosexual queer curious about the past, every out-of-it straight who's read *Newsweek* and wants to know where lesbian chic came from. It's the movie of choice for dykes who suffered through *Claire of the Moon* (1992), tore their hair out after *Fried Green Tomatoes* (1991), who wondered when—when, oh lord, when—someone would get around to telling the truth about *the life*. Take heart. Lynne Fernie and Aerlyn Weissman have made the film you've been yearning to see (figs. 6.1–6.3).

Okay, so you didn't think it would be a documentary. Okay, maybe you didn't expect it to come from that bastion of sobriety, the National Film Board (NFB) of Canada. Okay, so you weren't thinking "historical." But I swear this is not just one critic's desperate attempt to find a lesbian feature worth championing. After all, can 1,500 dykes be wrong? (Don't answer that.) That's how many packed San Francisco's Castro Theatre for the opening night of the national June ritual, the lesbian and gay film festival—getting hoarse, screaming and hollering, sighing and lusting, over the venerable dykes of history up there on the great big screen. History, herstory. This is one for the archives, an item as rare as the attractions on a carnival midway—the truth about the lesbian past, gutsy and glorious stories of life after dark in days gone by.

By the way, that's *lesbian*. Not *lesbianandgay*, ladies first in the name but never primary in the game. Years after *Word Is Out* (1977), *Before Stonewall*

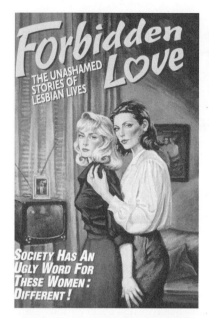

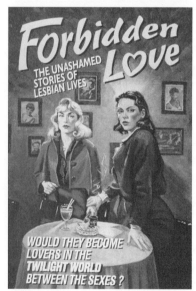

6.1–6.3 Pulp-paperback-style posters, created as fictitious replicas for *Forbidden Love* (1992). Courtesy of the National Film Board of Canada and Lynne Fernie.

(1984), and a host of other classics of the shared homosexual past, finally there is the beginning of a sweeping history of lesbians only. And surprise, it looks different. Nine women (culled from forty interviewed) tell their tales in *Forbidden Love*, as photo albums get juxtaposed with archival footage, mixing the personal and the political in the characteristic format of historical documentaries. Fernie and Weissman hunted through archives for a year, a pair of girl detectives out to solve the mystery of lesbian disappearance. As their reward, they found images that animate their stories in fresh ways, like the liquor control board's files with photographs of bars in the 1950s, and detailed inspectors' reports of deviant behavior, itemized to force the closing of said establishments. Searching through piles of 35mm negatives labeled merely "police," they found scraps of stock footage of bar raids on lesbian bars and fights between butches.

"This is our history!" crows Weissman, while sadly noting that new copyright laws make it nearly impossible for independent filmmakers and scholars to get future access to such materials.

Weissman, Fernie, and I talked for hours in Toronto, North Beach, and on the phone. Their fond hope is that this movie forces straights to look at their family albums and hometown memories differently—all those shots of mom with her "best friend," all those aunts who claimed they never married because "he" died in the war, mainstream history forever transformed.

Fernie and Weissman didn't go in for so-called political correctness, nor did the lesbian survivors who share their tales. One of the most powerful lines in the film is the warning delivered by a bar mate to Ruth Christine, as she sat in a lesbian bar stunned by the breakup of her marriage to her (male) husband: "Honey, if you think this is bad, just wait till you get your heart broke by a woman." Stephanie recalls pragmatically switching from femme to butch after an abusive relationship, showing off her new look to an approving bar crowd. Nairobi admits she had to disband her musical group when the male musicians got too jealous of her getting all the girls after every show. Amanda remembers never feeling comfortable as a First Nations woman in the always-white lesbian bars, coming out in a black bar instead. Lois, assessing the sorry state of the world at present, insists, "I think post-menopausal women should rule the world."

The filmmakers freely acknowledge their debt to the pioneering oral histories of Joan Nestle, Liz Kennedy, Madeleine Davis, and others. "It's really the S&M controversy that made this film possible," argues Fernie. "It threw a hand grenade into the lesbian discourse and made other kinds of stories possible. Now we have a new kind of lesbian feminism, not the old essentialist feminism of the 1970s that agreed: women good, men bad."

Were *Forbidden Love* merely a document of history, it would be valuable enough. But its true genius lies in the filmmakers' decision to explore the play of fantasy as well.[1] Tracking lesbian life in the 1950s (actually 1949–67), Fernie and Weissman learned a lot about the dreams that fueled those lives. They tracked down Ruth Dworin, a collector of more than four hundred lesbian pulp novels from the period, and questioned their dyke witnesses about the effect of those books on their lives, how they'd read and interpreted them, even got the famed pulp author Ann Bannon to reflect on the times. Then, putting together everything learned and imagined, they made up their minds to give something back—to design a fictional element for the movie, a sort of B-movie trailer: "We wanted to give these women the film they never got to see back then." They give the audience a visceral flashback to the film that might have been if, say, Douglas Sirk had optioned a script from a Beebo Brinker novel.

How does a film like *Forbidden Love* come to pass? The answers say a lot about why there are so few lesbian features. All that Fernie and Weissman needed was an executive producer with guts, major institutional support, a decent budget, and the license to do a full year of research. They found them all at Studio D, the "women's studio" at the NFB—once better known in the United States for producing the antiporn manifesto, *Not a Love Story* (1981)—in the Rina Fraticelli era. After Fraticelli, their producer-turned-studio-mogul Ginny Stikeman ran Studio D. Fernie and Weissman scanned the NFB's big Silver Anniversary catalogue and discovered there wasn't even a lesbian, gay, or homosexual *listing* in the book. Simultaneously Fraticelli realized that Studio D had never commissioned a lesbian film.

"You have to realize," say the filmmakers forgivingly, "how hard it was to start up a women's unit at the NFB in the 1970s. They didn't want to be dismissed as a bunch of dykes." But by then it was 1988. Weissman was well known as a sound recordist (*Pumping Iron II*, 1985) and was becoming a filmmaker (*A Winter Tan*, 1987). Fernie meanwhile had a long history as an interdisciplinary artist, curator (*Sight Specific*), even an arts journal editor (*Parallelogramme*). Fraticelli invited them to submit a proposal for a lesbian documentary.

The two knew perfectly well that they were embarking on the project in a backlash period: "We kept everything about the film quiet. Our working title was *B-Movie: A Women's History*. We didn't want any Tory backbencher to get hold of some internal NFB document and stop our project to make a point about tax dollars." Their strategy was to keep quiet long enough to get the film shot: "Once it was in the can, we knew we had something to defend." And they give kudos to the NFB for standing behind their controversial production, even devising strategies to head off any possible attack. (PBS, take note.)

Finally, though, it's these filmmakers who deserve kudos. They've resurrected a crucial chapter of lesbian history in living color, neither recasting the 1950s in our terms nor glossing over its realities. They wish they had the money to deposit the outtakes ("Our favorite cut was the four-hour version") in places like New York's Lesbian Herstory Archives. With the critic Becki Ross already working on a book, *The House That Jill Built: A Lesbian Nation in Formation*, based in part on the film, Fernie and Weissman felt they could move on to do a documentary on Jane Rule. But for all of the revisionist historians out there, they make a final passionate point:

> There's this attitude that lesbian feminists are to blame for coming along and wiping out the bar culture. Untrue. They were completely separate generations, parallel universes. Most of the Lesbian Nation came from university backgrounds, civil rights, et cetera. More middle class than working class. They would have been scared to go to those skid-row bars. Once in a while, some young lesbian feminist would come down to try to recruit. And the bar dykes told us, "Look, we thought they were so crazy we didn't even bother beating them up."

Ah, the lessons of history.

Notes

This chapter originally appeared as "Making Love," *Village Voice*, March 24, 1992.

1. For a detailed and inspired account of *Forbidden Love* and the larger world of pulp novels in the 1950s, see Villarejo, "Forbidden Love." See also Villarejo's extended study, *Lesbian Rule*.

GOINGS AND COMINGS,

THE *GO FISH* WAY

7 This is a fish story about, not the one that got away, but the one that got caught and won the trophy. Caught big-time, in other words. But it's also a cautionary tale, one about marketing, identity, and innocence. *Go Fish* (1994)—the movie, the trailer, the legend—wasn't always such. It once was just like its title, derived presumably from the corny classic sign ("Gone fishin'") once hung on office doors throughout America when spring fever, that most uncapitalistic and antientrepreneurial syndrome, struck. It's probably fitting, then, that a little, low-budget, black-and-white independent film with a title signifying play at its most elemental, least hip, almost provincial best should evolve so immediately into a festival hit and legendary deal.

This kind of success, of course, is the other kind of American fantasy, the one that's not exactly about play at all. In the process, though, care has to be taken that the fragile innocence and labor-of-love sincerity of the original doesn't evaporate on its way to the bank. If this article has a hidden agenda, it's the attempt to head backlash off at the pass and argue that this film is far more than any mainstream distributor's fishing expedition.

Go Fish started life as a little film called *Max and Ely*. It was written in Chicago in 1991 by Rose Troche and Guinevere Turner, a couple of twenty-somethings smitten with each other and their project. It was a lesbian film, by, about, and for lesbians, inspired less by what its creators were seeing in the clubs than what they weren't. It was a lark. As Turner says, it was "the little film that could."[1]

For a while, though, it couldn't. In 1992 they ran out of cash. Their all-volunteer crew began losing faith. Everybody had been suckered into working for free because they shared the dream of bringing a lesbian cinema into being. Troche says, "If you don't think that you can walk up to any lesbian and say, 'Hey, do you want to make a film because look at the shit that's out there,' and they're, like, 'I'm with ya,'" well, the consequences go without saying. So that's how it was. When they found themselves with little money, fewer friends, and a film only partly made, they sent a letter to Christine Vachon in New York. As bad as things were, there was now actually a lesbian producer in the United States helping independent films like *Poison* (1991) and *Swoon* (1992) get made. And they knew that her production partner, Tom Kalin, was a Chicago boy. They still believed in fairy tales, and fairy godmothers. Vachon read the letter, saw their twenty minutes of film, read their script, and signed on. The girls were back in business.

By 1992 John Pierson's Islet Films came up with enough money that shooting could be completed. By 1993 the ex-lovers Turner and Troche were working and playing in New York. Troche was editing the hell out of the footage, Turner was fine-tuning the voiceovers, and the Sundance Film Festival would soon decide to show it.[2] I was enchanted and started composing the catalogue copy in my head: "*Go Fish* begins just about where coming-out films used to end." I wasn't particularly restrained in my choice of adjectives: wistful, lyrical, seriocomic, fanciful, and "an assured cinematic ability to confer grace."

Go Fish came to Park City, Utah, in 1994 with high hopes and lots of fears. By opening day, Rose Troche, the director and co-screenwriter, and Guinevere Turner, the actor and co-screenwriter, had arrived; a box of nail clippers to be distributed as promo hadn't. Troche and Turner wondered if anyone would like their film up there in what is, after all, boytown. But at its first screening the crowd went nuts. "God, are they hot," said the straight women about the lesbians on screen. "Give her money to make another one quick," said the straight man about the lesbian director on stage. Troche called her cast and told them to get there quick. Tom Kalin, a Sundance veteran, guided them around town protectively. Sundance's first-ever lesbian dinner was held, and Goldwyn made festival history by signing them to a distribution contract on opening weekend.

Then came the marketing: unprecedented ads matched two women kissing (except that when it's printed too dark, one looks like a man, intentionally or not) to quirky handwritten copy. Trailers were in the theaters by May, playing backup to other big-time quality product. Then the press kicked in:

Turner had a whole page in *Interview* with her hair arranged in front of her face like a beaded curtain, touting her as a writer to watch; Rose got a pitch in *Rolling Stone* as the hot director for 1994, all pierced and intense-looking; and the two together got the number 2 slot in the *New Yorker* "Talk of the Town" section, which would be a major status symbol even if the writer (anonymous back then, as was customary for Talk contributors, even though Jacqueline Kennedy once wrote an item) hadn't gone on and on about what a good flirt Turner was and how much all the adulation was pleasing Troche and, well, how charmingly full of themselves and hand-rolled cigarettes and beautiful women and Café Tabac these two were.[3] It was unprecedented respect for a lesbian movie. And keep in mind, all that time *Go Fish* hadn't even opened yet.

Go Fish offers up a lovely little fable: the little film that gets saved from extinction, hits the bull's eye, and gets swept into the marketplace, leaving its hard-core fans to worry that the hype might start a backlash, that the innocence and fervor that are the film's finest qualities will be mistaken for mere artifice once the context changes. Fears, then, that could best be encapsulated in a joke like *Will Madonna buy the remake rights?*

If *Go Fish* is to get the respect it deserves, and get it on its own terms, undistorted by the context of reception, it's important to understand the birthright of the film. Consider these ten origin myths then, a start.

Origin 1: A Comedy in Six Unnatural Acts

In 1975 Jan Oxenberg made *A Comedy in Six Unnatural Acts*, the first (and nearly last) lesbian comedy. As a send-up of both political correctness and homophobic stereotypes, it was ahead of its time. Technically raw and politically sophisticated, it was shot on a shoestring budget and went on to play for years at women's film festivals and cultural womyn's evenings. For me, *Go Fish* is the daughter of *Comedy*, the living, breathing proof that lesbian camp does exist and even has a lineage. Except that Troche and Turner have never seen it.

Origin 2: Puerto Rican Rhythm

Rose Troche's parents are Puerto Rican, from the island. She says that they couldn't understand why moving to the United States didn't make them automatically able to pump out blue-eyed, blonde-haired babies instead of the kids they got. They moved all over the country, thereby obliging her to change schools midyear; she learned to fight and make people laugh. With no vocabulary for racism, Troche could never understand why their house was egged in the white suburban neighborhoods they favored or why her mother's accent on the telephone was cause for social ostracism.

During a conversation in a Park City boîte, she looks around the room, pointing out how differently she'd be treated at Sundance if she had a heavy-duty accent instead of assimilation speech. Moving around and switching communities became a theme: she went to a public university where students commuted and never really knew each other. She had time to study lots of things in the nine years she spent at the University of Illinois, Chicago: industrial design, for instance, which was her major for several years. "Can you imagine anything more shallow than designing the *outside* of things?" jokes Troche, in wonderment at her younger self, a woman who has clearly moved on to designing the guts instead.

Origin 3: Commune Crisis

Guinevere Turner doesn't like to talk about her past or her childhood, though she finally admits she was a commune kid. "That's the book I want to write: the children of the flower children." I ask if she was the radiantly happy type or a damaged commune kid, and she indicates the latter. Her college experience at Sarah Lawrence continued the commune theme—in other words, an isolated and mutually dependent group, sure of themselves, with cultish tendencies. Probably great boot camp for the lesbian nation. She moved to Chicago to get away from scrutiny and try to write. She was afraid her long-haired, straight-girl look would make it hard to find dykes, so she went to an ACT UP meeting, where she met Troche. The rest is history.

Origin 4: The Bars, Negative

Turner and Troche did what any young self-respecting dyke couple in love would do: they went out clubbing. And what did they see? "Oh no, not the rain scene from *Desert Hearts* again. Not *Personal Best*! Oh, *The Hunger* again." Video clips are the entertainment staples of lesbian bars all over the United States. The dilemma is that there's so little to clip. The pair didn't have anything against most of these films. In fact Turner saw *Desert Hearts* at eighteen and was totally fixated, as much by the lesbian couple in front of her as by the film. No, it was the paucity that got to them.

Then, in 1991, that hideous Blake Edwards vehicle came out: *Switch*. That's what did it. Troche remembers, "We thought, well, if they can do it, we can do it." Vows were taken. They stopped making T-shirts, staging ACT UP benefit performances, making lesbian safe-sex erotic photographs, and got themselves a new concept. They'd make a film instead. "We loved having a project. It wasn't even a labor of love. It wasn't labor."

Origin 5: The Bars, Positive

They loved what they found in the bars: the energy and camaraderie, the fierce commitment to a life choice. And, I venture to add, the video. Not the video clips of mainstream movies featuring historical or farcical lesbians, but the alternative videotapes that were being produced, starting in the late 1980s and early 1990s, in and for the community. Just as disco music fueled gay male culture in the 1970s, I'd argue, so did the bar video explosion fuel lesbian identity.

Turner and Troche see their allegiances to this sector very clearly. Troche says, "I really hope the connection between our work and the work of people like Cheryl Dunye [in Philadelphia] and Sadie Benning [in Milwaukee and Chicago] is clearly recognized. It would be terrible if *Go Fish* were to be put up on a pedestal just because it's a feature." The language that's being elaborated in the videotapes and then spoken in dialogue back and forth across the film-video boundaries goes on display every spring in the lesbian and gay film festivals, which are some of the only film festivals to include video in their mix as full equals. They're the future. Film critics, though, tend to live in the East and outside this subculture; to them, *Go Fish* must look like it dropped, uniquely, out of the sky instead of out of a community with a shared aesthetic voice.

Origin 6: Happy Writers Write Happy Characters

"No, we were miserable." Turner and Troche insist they fought like cats and dogs when they were together and that *Go Fish* was a very deliberate attempt to imagine lesbian happiness. They wanted to make a feel-good movie in spite of themselves. "Yes, yes, this is so excellent" was their mantra for being a lesbian.

"We needed a jolt in our lives to remember: Girl, don't hold your head down." Pride, you might say, was on their minds. Once there was a car accident in their script, a suicide, and a confrontation with some violently homophobic men. But they got over it. Charming everyone who crosses their path, they insist that their characters are much nicer than they are. Turner, for instance, insists that she's not obnoxious like Max, whereas Troche claims she's exactly that character, just wearing a different hat off-screen.

Origin 7: Chicago

Rose Troche is a product of the Chicago avant-garde tradition and is proud to say that she wants her audience to know that what they're seeing is a fiction. Thus the eloquent bridges between scenes that link emotion and gesture in a series of tops, games, hands. She studied at the University of Illinois with Hans Schall, her hero. "I owe it all to Hans," she insists, in tribute to the man who taught her that, given three minutes of footage and an optical printer, you could make a feature. "I like to see film grain." She prides herself on doing all her own opticals and freely admits her avant-garde training. "My negative cutter hated me because there are so many cuts in the film."

Troche remembers struggling to find a film analogy for the scratch in hip-hop music when she was cutting to "Feel That Love" at the end. She thinks it's a question of rhythm, wanting to get the groove. She jokes that, being Puerto Rican, she ought to have rhythm. "But I'm so white-washed, it's like, *Excuse me, could I have some of my culture back now?*" Of course, the University of Illinois wasn't all a piece of cake. Wayne Boyer, the resident authoritarian, would never let her near the "good" optical printer.

Origin 8: Literary and Filmic Formation

They, uh, vary. For Turner, studying fiction writing at Sarah Lawrence, the major influence was Jeanette Winterson's writing. She's still her hero. Turner writes short—very, very short—pieces of fiction and great one-liners. That's why *Go Fish* has such a coherent sense of vignette. Since the pair virtually finish each other's sentences, Troche immediately launched into a polemic about her desire to find a way to put the passion, the intensity of a novelistic love story like Winterson's *Written on the Body* into a film that could taste and smell and breathe like books do.

For Troche, some of the influence was counter. She bemoans the way that Lizzie Borden and Chantal Akerman switched from their core lesbian audience to a mainstream where heterosexuality has to rule on screen, but stops short of dissing the sisters. "Go girl" is more her style. She loved *I've Heard the Mermaids Singing* (1987). Patricia Rozema is another hero. Unmet so far, like the rest.

Origin 9: The Lesbian Community

When Troche and Turner rounded up their lesbian gang for the years-long *Go Fish* shoot, they still had a euphoric view of lesbianism and lesbians. In the beginning, the crew was all women, and Roche can still recall the energy field produced by that gathering. "Some days you'd see fifteen women laying down the track for the camera." It was evidently a fantastic experience. "There's just so much strength in this community," says Troche, bemoaning how little it's mobilized. When the tide turned and the gang got haircuts, got attitude, took off, well, that's the lesbian community too. "They won't believe this is happening." Troche and Turner have a philosophical view of their film now: "Even if lesbians who see it say, 'Damn that *Go Fish*,' that's a success." If they swear they can top it, and they make their own, great, let it spur successors and oppositions and debate, so long as it generates more films.

In this sense, their film becomes poised as a sort of Molotov cocktail tossed, like a bridal bouquet, to the throng.

Origin 10: Genre Traditions

The original press kit for *Go Fish* has a fascinating statement from its director. She tries to talk in one and the same breath about the need to carry on and build a tradition of lesbian filmmaking and her desire to be recognized as a filmmaker, period. She bemoans the fact that reaction thus far is so fixated on content, that comments on the film's complex structure and associative image cutting go unexpressed. She argues that the genre need is so great that *Go Fish* is moved into the new slot "regardless of its merit" and earns its place "purely because of lesbian content."

Troche talks wisely about how a starved market is asked to prove its loyalty over and over. She finally ends her press kit statement as follows, reconciled: "I believe I should deal with a subject I have a relationship with, and be able to make my art without taking a political vacation, and hope that with the fulfillment of these beliefs I will gain the momentum to see me through the tasks ahead."[4]

Ah, you go, girls.

Notes

This chapter originally appeared as "Goings and Comings: *Go Fish*," *Sight and Sound* 4.7 (1994), 14–16.

1. This and all other quotations from Troche and Turner are from personal communications in person and via telephone.

2. Actually, I had a role in that decision. Producer Christine Vachon, worried that the festival hadn't made up its mind yet, shipped a double-system work-print for me to view. This meant tracking down an editing table where I could watch the spliced film in progress: before all editing was digital, that's what you did. I loved it and lobbied the festival on its behalf.

3. See Elizabeth Royte, "A Couple of Lesbians, Sitting around Talking (Mostly about Their Film)," *New Yorker*, May 9, 1994, 40. "Talk of the Town" authors are now identified in the online archive of formerly anonymous columns.

4. For an excellent in-depth study of the film, see Henderson, "Simple Pleasures."

HISTORICAL FICTIONS, MODERN DESIRES

The Watermelon Woman

8 Forget about Philadelphia, city of brotherly love. Welcome, in its place, Philadelphia, city of sisterly lust. Just as *Rocky* redefined the city in the image of white ethnic testosterone, so has the filmmaker Cheryl Dunye now spun her hometown around all over again with her feature film debut, *The Watermelon Woman* (1996). In it, Dunye plays the character of Cheryl, a cheeky and tongue-in-cheek version of herself, as she did in the series of videotapes that carved out a territory somewhere between sitcom and stand-up comedy, and evidently prepared her for prime-time moviedom. This time, in her most ambitious work yet, Dunye takes us on a wonderfully inventive journey through the annals of film history, African American culture, dyke attitudes, race relations, and the elusive mysteries of lesbian attraction. Did I mention that this too is a comedy?

Cheryl, you see, is a video store clerk. Think of *Clerks* (1994). Think of Quentin Tarantino, for that matter, since Cheryl plays a wannabe filmmaker who ravenously devours rental videos while she gears up for the big time by videotaping people's weddings, parties, and nightclub engagements.[1] Her loyal but increasingly fed-up pal and partner in crime is Tamara (the thoroughly captivating Valarie Walker), who's as adept at playing Cheryl's foil as she is at puncturing her self-importance when she needs to be cut down to size. They work side-by-side in the video store, and they tape side-by-side on weekends. Tamara is happily hitched to Stacy (NYC downtown denizen Jocelyn Taylor). Between gigs, Tamara and Stacy try to fix Cheryl up, resulting in one of the funniest and grimmest blind-date sequences ever seen on celluloid when Cheryl's tipsy but tuneless date decides to cover Minnie Ripperton's "Loving You" at the karaoke mike. Dunye is hilarious at sending up a full spectrum of Afrocentric habits alongside the bittersweet tropes of dyke philandering.

Then the film heats up. Cheryl becomes obsessed with uncovering the history of a mysterious "mammy" actress who went by the name of "the Watermelon Woman" and starred in such silent and early sound films as *Plantation Memories*. Anyone who's ever seen *Birth of a Nation, Imitation of Life,* or *Gone with the Wind* can easily fill in the blanks. The actress turns out to be a woman by the name of Fae Richards (played by Lisa Marie Bronson). Seemingly an unknown synthesis of Butterfly McQueen and Hattie McDaniel, she's eventually discovered to have been a sister in all senses. A forgotten African American actress of race-film fame who was also a dyke, and who in fact had an affair with a Dorothy Arzner–style white director? Too good to be true! Richards becomes the "Rosebud" riddle that Cheryl just has to solve.

While Cheryl is assiduously tracking down clues, unreeling fabulous old black-and-white footage of Fae in her early roles, and interviewing those who knew her back when, she takes a detour. Why? Because who should sashay into her video store but Diana (the sultry Guinevere Turner of *Go Fish* fame), a skillful safari hunter who immediately casts her net for the willing Cheryl. Given how savvy Cheryl and Tamara seem to be about independent production and lesbian culture, however, I confess I was puzzled. I fully expected them to yell, "Hey, it's Guin from *Go Fish*!" But, no, everyone stays in character, and this hip, screwball comedy in the key of queer is off and running.

Cheryl remains the rock-solid center of the film as subplots begin to compete for attention. A riot grrrl–style punker starts working at the video store, inflaming Tamara even further. A trip to the library comes up against racist arrogance and gay-boy attitude. Cheryl gets increasingly testy toward Diana and, soon enough, toward most of the white bitches that seem to populate this little world. But hope beckons from such kindred spirits as a black film historian and a stone butch of the old school. The film has a loopy structure that effectively pulls together the sketches, monologues, and set pieces that make up its narrative.

As Dunye has begun to appear at festivals with her film, she's garnered some unwelcome attention: attacks from the usual forces of the anticulture Right (an article in the notoriously right-wing *Washington Times*, a House of Representatives floor fight, the rote accusations of using National Endowment for the Arts funds to advocate homosexuality).[2] More positively, she has been compared to Spike Lee, and her *Watermelon Woman* to his *She's Gotta Have It* (1986) for their obvious affinities for wit, sex, and directorial on-screen presence, despite the obvious differences on all counts. Others have invoked Yvonne Rainer for Dunye's use of avant-garde disjunctions and to-the-camera address, or Isaac Julien for her film's irreverence toward cultural icons and its black-on-white sexual action.

I'd like to offer a different set of comparisons and sketch another kind of lineage—a lesbian one. If *The Watermelon Woman* has antecedents, and I'd argue that it does, then they can be found much earlier than *Go Fish*. Check out Jan Oxenberg's dyke satire, *A Comedy in Six Unnatural Acts* (1975), which was such a hit on the old lesbian-feminist circuit that she spun off a stand-up act for a few years in the 1970s; or Lizzie Borden's battle cry, *Born in Flames* (1983), which mixed sexy black-on-white shower scenes with all-girl revolutionary action; or Sally Potter's long-overlooked feature from the early 1980s, *The Gold Diggers* (1983), which cast Julie Christie opposite the black actress Colette Lafonte, who crashes a cruise ship's ballroom on a white horse to carry Christie's character away; or, for that matter, Sheila McLaughlin's passion play, *She Must Be Seeing Things* (1987), which was similarly obsessed with a forgotten historical figure and a filmmaker protagonist intent on resurrecting her.

These films are all monuments to particular moments in lesbian culture. They represent serious attempts to think through the complicated political and aesthetic debates of their day. They all wanted to reconcile ideological work with entertainment. I'd also point out the shared collaborative nature of their production, not just because of some vague notion of democratic recognition but rather because the community-based process was key to what these films represented—and how they come today to embody a sort of zeitgeist of their moment.

That's what *The Watermelon Woman* does as well. Dunye has packed so many issues into her film—from the fights over cross-race attraction to the need for cultural heroes and the racism of history making—that it's a testimony to her talent (and the talents of her collaborators, the director of photography Michelle Crenshaw, the photographer Zoe Leonard, the professor and actress in a cameo, Alex Juhasz) that the movie remains so sprightly and engaging throughout.

The movie is not flawless. Ambition has its limits: if only Cheryl the editor had cut some of the scenes that Cheryl the director includes of Cheryl the actress delivering Cheryl the screenwriter's recurring monologues. Even Spike Lee threw his actors more bones. Walker and Turner deserve more screen time

8.1 Zoe Leonard created a Fae Richards faux-still purportedly
from the fictitious *Plantation Memories* for Cheryl Dunye's
film *The Watermelon Woman* (1996). The Fae Richards Photo
Archive, 1993–96. Courtesy of the artist.

than they get and would keep Cheryl from wearing out her welcome. And
while Dunye's parodies ring true, they can also be mean: Sarah Schulman's
cameo as a staffer at the all-volunteer Center for Lesbian Information and
Technology (CLIT for short), which is obviously a stand-in for the actual, real-
world Lesbian Herstory Archives, comes off as more vicious than playful, but
that could be an effect of Schulman's performance as much as Dunye's script.

Even so, Dunye balances any shortcomings with a buoyantly inclusive approach to casting. She manages to shoehorn in cameos by Brian Freeman
of the former performance group Pomo Afro Homos (1990–95), the singer-
songwriter Toshi Reagon, the poet Cheryl Clarke, and even the infamous
Philadelphian Camille Paglia, whose hilarious explication of watermelon's
cultural significance leaves the viewer baffled as to whether it's self-parody
or a full-court display of Paglian earnestness.[3] Only the fellow Philadelphian
Louis Massiah, a filmmaker and recent MacArthur fellow, is missing. *The
Watermelon Woman* works its sources well and turns its limitations to strik-

8.2 Zoe Leonard created a fictitious Fae Richards publicity shot for Cheryl Dunye's film *The Watermelon Woman* (1996). The Fae Richards Photo Archive, 1993–96. Courtesy the artist.

ing advantage. The resulting film is a fresh, bracing, rough-and-ready work that repays our attention with bursts of delight.

Lest anyone think that Dunye's concoction of her African American film history is far-fetched, here's an anecdote: last year, when the British critic Richard Dyer came to town to speak at the San Francisco Museum of Modern Art, I had the pleasure of being on stage with him to chat about queers and queens, stars, race, and representation. There he dropped the bombshell: he'd uncovered anecdotal evidence that Tallulah Bankhead had once had an affair with Butterfly McQueen. Just a few months earlier, Judith Mayne published her magnificent study, *Directed by Dorothy Arzner*, which detailed for the first time Arzner's lifelong, live-in relationship with the choreographer Marion Morgan. In Zoe Leonard's faux stills, a 1930s-era director whose clothing style is reminiscent of Arzner's signature look is played by none other than Alexandra Juhasz, this film's producer and Dunye's off-screen partner (at home and on the set) at the time (figs. 8.1, 8.2).[4]

Sometimes truth is stranger than fiction and fiction just as intriguing as the facts that inspire its inventions. *The Watermelon Woman* shows us how, and then it shows us why. Finally, this is a movie that begs to be seen *à deux,* a welcome addition to the slim pickings of lesbian date movies. And for the singletons, it needs to be seen with a crowd, so nobody should be tempted to wait to see it alone at home with a VCR and a bowl of popcorn.[5]

Notes

This chapter originally appeared as "She's Gotta Film It," *San Francisco Bay Guardian,* July 23, 1997.

1. With video store clerk and convenience store clerk already the basic biographical currency of young white guys out to break into the indie film business, Dunye's casting of herself in this role was deeply transgressive and was a conspicuous bid to claim this territory for her and her kind, then and now.

2. On June 14, 1996, Julia Duin published a scurrilous article in the *Washington Times,* using as its excuse a (positive) review of the film by Jeannine DeLombard in Philadelphia's *City Paper* (March 3, 1996). Deliberately pinpointing the film's funding from the National Endowment for the Arts, she set off a political firestorm, just one in a long list of congressional attacks on the agency's funding.

3. Full disclosure: I was invited to perform the Paglia role of deluded academic but was unable to oblige due to a family medical crisis. Ah, cruel fate.

4. Dunye went on to direct *Stranger Inside* (2001) for HBO, *My Baby's Daddy* (2004) for Miramax, *The Owls* (2010) and *Mommy Is Coming* (2012).

5. Of course, by now, the VCR has been displaced: with Netflix streaming or the DVD option,Wolfe Video or HBO, the stay-at-home options have grown and diversified.

CHANNELING DOMESTIC VIOLENCE

In the Den with Todd Haynes

and Christine Vachon

9 In one corner of a pristine gallery, a crummy sofa and tattered armchair flank a cocktail table piled with magazines, while an old color television set plays the same roster of odd videotapes over and over. A plaque of mock needlepoint identifies the scene for the visitor as *Domestic Violence*, a museum installation by Todd Haynes and Christine Vachon.

The gallery is located at the Wexner Center for the Arts in Columbus, Ohio, where the traveling show *Hall of Mirrors: Art and Film Since 1945*, a big-ticket survey of obviously monumental ambitions, was on exhibition.[1] The irony is that this tiny, quirky installation—the only collaboration ever between Haynes and Vachon in which both have been equal artistic partners (and far outside the movie theater milieu that always dictates hierarchies of roles)—was handily stealing the thunder from the giant show that should have dwarfed it. Wexner's curator Bill Horrigan had commissioned this adjunct piece on a lark, intrigued by the idea that Vachon and Haynes dreamed up and the particular problem (public hysteria over the immorality of cinematic violence) that they wanted to "solve."

In fact *Domestic Violence* was a provocative video intervention that simultaneously tackled the assumptions of both the art world and popular culture. Approaching the television set from behind, as viewers were required to do, one encountered an inexplicable barrage of soundtracks that slowly clarified into excerpts from a canon of famously violent movies: *A Clockwork Orange, Deliverance, Dirty Harry, Reservoir Dogs, Natural Born Killers*. Once on the sofa, however, visitors were ambushed by the discovery of a television screen filled, not with the familiar actors in their signature roles but with a substitute cast of performing cats, dogs, and babies.

Vachon and Haynes restaged ultraviolent classics using their original soundtracks and casts composed of the most beloved (and anthropomorphized) of family tropes: domestic pets and toddlers. All scenes were shot and edited in exact imitation of the originals while decisively altering their essential nature.[2] *Domestic Violence* ambushed its audiences at the intersection of sentimentality and outrage, splicing discourses of violence and innocence onto a screen the two were never meant to occupy simultaneously. If some viewers' systems of identification had trouble surviving this crazy blend of sacred images and demonized soundtracks, other gallery visitors had equal trouble withstanding the assault of popular culture, represented by the trashy objects and plebeian sounds of this artistic Trojan horse.

The television's juxtaposition of a level of violence that has been frequently denounced and condemned with the signposts of unquestioned innocence demanded that viewers decipher a system of conflicting codes initially resistant to coherent readings. Puppies and kittens inflicting humiliation upon each other? Toddlers with guns reciting lines they couldn't understand? Very queer indeed.

Some context was provided by the setting: a shabby sort of den with wagon-wheel couches, cheap furniture, and the kinds of magazines more readily found in a dentist's office or supermarket check-out line than a museum. This was meant to be a house of zero sophistication, really an urbanite's imagining of "trailer trash" interior decorating and taste.

Haynes and Vachon archly posed a question with their needlework and their set: Does violence really come from outside, or from within? And further, is evil always in the form of a threatening outsider, or in the far more palatable form of a trusted member of the household? With an extraordinary economy of means, the two threw down a gauntlet to the forces of family values and entertainment censorship: *Look in the mirror*. While their provocation might have relied on class triggers that were not necessarily accurate or reliable, so did the movie clips they chose to restage.

Their question was not one of provenance but of evidence. Was morality in the eye of the beholder or the images on screen? Posed in the midst of the Culture Wars that beset the United States in the 1980s and 1990s, their domestic mission was a crucial one. And while this wasn't the usual brief for such post-NQC principals as Haynes and Vachon, it did carry forward the mission of queering popular culture, even if this time around that extended to excoriating obliquely the questionable standards of the moral majorities.

It's not incidental that the installation was commissioned for the Wexner's presentation of *Hall of Mirrors*. The Wexner is an unusual presence in the U.S. arts scene: built in 1989 under the old-fashioned aegis of a single patron, it has nevertheless been such a visionary enterprise that it included, from the beginning, in-house video postproduction facilities and a commitment to a program of bringing artists in to use them. Horrigan, the Wexner's media arts curator, has long overseen an art and technology division where editing rooms and online suites welcomed twenty or thirty artists a year, in the era before Final Cut and other software introduced new options and budget accommodations. In fact when I visited to see *Domestic Violence*, I found the Mexican video artist Ximena Cuevas hard at work, finishing the edit of Jesusa Rodriguez's satiric version of *Cosi fan tutte* (1996).

While there were no immediate plans to send *Domestic Violence* on tour, its makers were hardly sitting still. *Velvet Goldmine*, the follow-up to *Poison* (1991) and *Safe* (1995), was starting production in London in January 1997. Set in a fictionalized world peopled by the likes of David Bowie, Iggy Pop, Lou Reed, and the glam-rock scene of the 1970s, *Velvet Goldmine* had Jonathan Rhys-Myers and Ewan MacGregor as its stars. Haynes admitted to a long fascination with glam rock, which he listened to in college, and professed himself eager to turn his vision to the era of androgyny that preceded today's rugged version of homosexuality. "Glam rock was so Wildean in its notions of artificiality and completely constructed identity. And it had such a spirit of curiosity about multiple selves and sexual orientations."[3]

Velvet Goldmine would be their biggest-budgeted project to date. But there in the faux den of the Wexner, in that stunningly simple set, it was possible to see their ideas turned inside-out, its very simplicity masking the complexity of the sources and missions. Even the term *domestic violence* comes rife with possibilities. Haynes has set many of his films in the domestic sphere: *Dotty Gets Spanked* (1993) seems particularly apt here, as it targets precisely the kind of violence, both spiritual and (sometimes) physical, visited upon queer youth trapped in conventional families. Of course, leave it to Haynes to avoid anything resembling a didactic or realist piece: his little boy expresses his fantasies via cheesy 1950s-style television shows. And for Julianne Moore in *Safe* (1995), of course, even the sofa was dangerous, as even the rugs and the furniture wrought violence upon her.

The exhibition seemed to me to be an invitation into the brains of two of the most successful figures of the NQC: the depth of thinking about popular culture, the deeply felt repulsion at the dark side of American populism, the honest repudiation of easy answers. These were the thoughts on their mind, anyway, in 1996: four years after the start of the NQC and in the very epicenter of the Republican-fabricated Clinton sex scandal that would castrate his administration for the balance of his second term. Maybe some day Vachon and Haynes will make a film about *that* and figure out how to queer the story.

Until then, the installation will have to do. Its message to those who stumbled into the ad hoc living room there in the Wexner Center was damn serious. Visitors would have caught the grim pun of "domestic violence," and hopefully the far more subtle punt: an exercise in giving up preconceptions about violence in the movies and learning, for a moment, to separate cause and effect.

Notes

A shorter version of this chapter originally appeared as "Violence to Glam Rock," *Sight and Sound* 6.12 (1996), 5.

1. Special thanks to Bill Horrigan for staging this exhibition and inviting me to see it.
2. This predated Gus Van Sant's remake of *Psycho* (1998).
3. Todd Haynes, personal communication, by telephone.

THE *I.K.U.* EXPERIENCE

The Shu-Lea Cheang Phenomenon

10 Step right up, ladies and gentlemen, the carnival is about to begin. Come inside, surf the Net, play the video game, dive into the screen, cruise the future, come get fucked, just come, come, come. Bodies are packages made to be opened, minds are penetrable, sensations communicable, orgasms collectable.

Shu-Lea Cheang's *I.K.U.* (subtitled *This is not LOVE. This is SEX.*) invents a future cybersexual universe where trained replicants roam the empty spaces of unseen metropolises, hunting willing prey for orgasmic sexual marathons conducted in the service of science. The irresistible replicants are equipped with unicorn-like arms which—presto—turn into dildo machines specifically calibrated to collect and transmit the specifications of orgasms into the centralized, corporatized databases of the future. Meanwhile the species of the future are wildly indeterminate, gender-blurred or homosex, oversexed, or just, well, willing. Shorn of emotion, stripped of procreation and provocation, sex isn't just work. Data have their pleasures.

And the audience? Like it or not, we're implicated in it all, swept up by the throbbing techno soundtrack, plugged directly into the action by the animation tunnels that materialize at the onset of arousal. Remember the origin moments of hypertext and interactive video? Every technological invention of the twentieth century has been designed in the service of either pornography or the military. Those early demonstrations of camcorders and interactive video games always featured some version of cyber blow-up dolls gauged to fulfill every fantasy of the male users. Well, *I.K.U.* democratizes all that: *I.K.U.*

frees the body from gender restrictions, empowers the object of fantasy, and merges the user and the used, the carrier and the carried, into a cyber satyricon of impulses, stimulants, and gratifications.

I.K.U. is a phenomenon that wants to refuse definition and, to a certain extent, succeeds in that effort, even as it crosses all categories—geographic, physical, conceptual—with a demented flourish. As much transgenre as it is transgender, *I.K.U.* also wants to merge video and film into a fresh digital universe large-scale enough to overwhelm the viewer. Narrative, nationality, and production medium are all certainties easily thrown into question. The actors are drawn from the Japanese porn world. They speak broken English. They mutate into shape-shifting manga characters. It's a whole new world, but one that's deliberately low-budget and manageable, shot with digital cameras, edited on Premiere using home computers, then blown up to 35mm, exaggerated like Godzilla, to conquer its audience. Sure, sometimes it's flat or hokey, one-dimensional or predictable, but more often it surprises and triumphs, the love child of the writing of Samuel Delaney and *Flaming Ears* (1991).[1]

Cheang is the mastermind behind *I.K.U.* The Taiwanese runaway and former scion of the New York City art and video scene has now self-reinvented as a "digital drifter." She roams from commission to commission, from Osaka to Amsterdam, London to Tokyo, relaying her transmissions to the Internet banks of the present. Until the legendary Japanese producer and distributor Asai Takashi (known for promoting such cutting-edge work as Derek Jarman's last films to Japanese audiences) proposed this sci-fi porn movie for her to direct, Cheang had been deploying her visions straight into cyberspace through her websites, *Brandon* (a commemoration commissioned by the Guggenheim Museum in 1998, predating *Boys Don't Cry*) and *Bowling Alley* (commissioned by the Walker Art Center).

It's hard to believe that Cheang started out as one of the Paper Tiger gang, producing low-budget community video with DeeDee Halleck's activist acolytes and flying back to Asia to champion those who died at Tiananmen Square with a five-part camcorder tribute memorial, *Will Be Televised* (1990). She simultaneously began her move into the art-video world with *Color Schemes* (1990), an installation that indicated her future interests: it focused on the body, in the form of performance artists, and on playing with viewers' relationship to the work—in this case, scrambling video into Laundromat machines and, double trouble, locating those machines in the sacrosanct space of the Whitney Museum. The next project revealed the shape of her future: it was a collaborative installation of sex secrets and video loops, installed in a gallery space transformed into an old-time porn emporium. Machines were central to her vision, whether washing or watching.

Then she was off. Leaving the gallery space, in 1994 Cheang made her first feature film, *Fresh Kill*, written by Jessica Hagedorn (*Dogeaters*) and set in a sci-fi New York City where fish are radioactive and the cast multicultural. With the combination of their talents, the film was able to unite conspiracies of world contamination with the investigations of a lesbian couple under threat. It was made in 35mm, a true change of gears for the low-budget artiste, yet it embraced the worlds of hacking and ecoconspiracy so totally that it had a hard time finding traditional distribution even in the heyday of the NQC.[2] Not one to be typecast, Cheang also tossed off a pair of lesbian porn tapes, *Sex Fish* (1993) and *Sex Bowl* (1994), in this period that showed what a flair she had for sex work in the idiom of cutting-edge video.

Then she was off again, this time into cyberspace. She gave up her New York City digs and became a global wanderer, a "floating digital agent," jacking into power supplies around the world and reachable only through websites and email. Did she really exist? Happily, yes. When spied in 2000 at Sundance and at Pitzer College, where we shared a residency, Cheang looked like one of her characters: her head shaved except for a sprig of hair that Jessica Hagedorn's daughter had dubbed an "island," swaddled in a wraparound butcher's apron made of a material that managed to suggest a cross between black leather and latex. Perched on platform shoes that upped her stature, fusing fashion and fetish, Cheang easily fulfilled her self-appointed role as avatar. Never mind that, characteristically contrarian, she preferred to ignore all this synthetic construction and talk about the future as she saw it: organic farming, her new passion.

Cheang defines *I.K.U.* precisely: it's a porn film that takes up where *Blade Runner* (1982) left off. The elevator door that closed now reopens. A new corporation has taken over. The *I.K.U.* characters have names, identities, and missions, but I don't think the story is the point, however carefully calibrated it may be. Narrative, which once was the weak spot in Cheang's work, has become its strength. Or, rather, it is the very absence of narrative that has now supercharged her work, suffusing its every choice. Cheang's mix of sensation and suggestion is perfectly suited to the post-hypertext world of postverbal storytelling. What's most intriguing about *I.K.U.* is its daring disposal of older forms and its unabashed effort to pioneer a visual text in which pornography and science fiction, film, video and computer, matinee and late night, gallery and porn arcade, all merge into a single movie experience.

As collaborative as ever, Cheang involved a range of Tokyo figures from the worlds of club culture, night life, and adult movies. Production designer Sasaki Takashi and VJ E-Male usually work the club scene, creating visual effects. The character of replicant Reiko is played by Tokitoh Ayumu, an erotic actress from the world of satellite television. Another character, Dizzy, is played by Zachery Nataf, who's identified in the production notes as an F2M transsexual (transman, in newer parlance) and founder of the Transgender Film Festival in London. Other parts are played by humans drawn from the ranks of magazine models, strippers, porn stars, even a "rope artist."

I suspect that none of this is remotely fringe for Cheang. Rather these are the personae of a future that's just now coming into view; she has simply given them a context. In the process, she's given her audience a challenge. A whirlpool (cesspool?) of ideas, *I.K.U.* has usefully provoked meditations on the nature of sex, narrative, and representation that we'd be well advised to put to further use, here and now, on the cusp of the alleged media future.

Having leapfrogged over narrative, updated porn, and utterly transcended the seemingly binary universe of the New Queer Cinema, Cheang has become a genre, if not a gender, unto herself. Whether her work can be considered postporn, postgender, or postqueer, it pushes audiences to think hard about the most basic assumptions. If joining a theater audience means entering into a relationship of complicity with the representational productions that appear on the screen, then *I.K.U.* presents audiences with an explosive futuristic imaginarium in which all acts are recalibrated to lie outside any possible set of experiences or code of taboos. Identification? Unlikely. Participation? Impossible.

Naturally, not everyone has been ready for what Cheang had to offer, even in the Y2K era in Park City, Utah. At its world premiere at Sundance, despite the word *porn* in its catalogue description that ought to have reset audience expectations appropriately, *I.K.U.* managed to scandalize a midnight crowd that's usually self-congratulatory and proud of withstanding, if not embracing, anything thrown at it by the most fiendish of minds. But clearly that brand of hipness has its limits.

In place of self-satisfaction, the *I.K.U.* experience sent folks scurrying for the exits whenever the action got explicit (40 percent fled, according to Cheang). Shu-Lea Cheang was taken aback, troubled: she thought Sundance was more sophisticated. I, on the other hand, was delighted: in the post-NQC days of posed tolerance, how reassuring it was to see that people still could be shocked by something.[3]

Notes

Originally published as "The I.K.U. EXXXperience: The Shu Lea Cheang Phenomenon," *Cinevue*, Asian Cine Vision Film Festival, July 2000.

1. Cheang is good friends with Hans Scheirl, one of the codirectors of *Flaming Ears*.

2. For an in-depth discussion of *Fresh Kill*, see Chua, "Interview with Shu Lea Cheang."

3. When last glimpsed in 2010 in Paris, Cheang had slowed down enough to live there for a while; as of this writing, she's still there. She's making films, challenging norms, touring, and, yes, growing organic vegetables in upstate New York with a gang of collaborators and cyberspace controls. For information on the Sprouts Society, see http://www.watershedpost.com/tags/shu-lea-cheang.

JONATHAN CAOUETTE

What in *Tarnation*?

 In 2003 buzz was circulating on the streets of Park City, the kind of buzz to which people pay attention because it emanates from audiences, not just a paid publicist (as if there isn't always a hidden push from that maligned profession). Word was that a newcomer, Jonathan Caouette, had made a powerful debut film about his painful life and his mother's near-destruction in the Texas mental health system, produced for no money flat, to spectacular effect.[1]

Tarnation is an adrenaline-fueled mix of documentary and performance relating a tragic autobiography through home movies, purloined television footage, and a mix-master full of sampled tunes. Even the most ignorant press and industry folks safely pronounced the film genius, given that the names of Gus Van Sant and John Cameron Mitchell appeared on the screen as end-stage executive producers. Caouette, who had quit his day job as a jewelry shop doorman to finish in time for Sundance, had grabbed the golden ring.

Where, though, could *Tarnation* go next? That was the follow-up buzz. After Sundance, what? Its emotional bravery and stylistic audacity made an intoxicating mix, but as one distributor pal confided, "It would take two million dollars just to clear the music rights!" As it happened, it reportedly cost less than a quarter of that. By then, *Tarnation* had nabbed a distributor, gone to Cannes, won a prize at the Los Angeles Film Festival, and penetrated that shrine of cinephilia, the New York Film Festival. Not bad for a little digital movie edited on iMovie from scraps Caouette had recorded since early adolescence.

According to the apocryphal yet true saga, Caouette had burned the midnight oil on his boyfriend David Sanin Paz's consumer iMac, with nothing but its built-in software to edit the melancholia out of his system and onto the screen, like some sort of latter-day digital Goethe. Editing to music, a private VJ without a club or show, Caouette channeled his way into a format and style true to the subject matter. The total cost—just over $200—has proven just as fascinating to the press pack as the autobiography. "Yes, now I have a William Morris agent," admitted the sheepish but transformed Caouette when he passed through San Francisco recently to promote the film.[2]

The focus on budget isn't fair. What's important about *Tarnation* has very little to do, ultimately, with either its iMovie genesis or its lunch-money budget. What marks *Tarnation* as so important is its originality and emotional courage, its formal approach to depicting mental states as POV on screen, its wrenchingly unanticipated stories that unfold before the viewer's startled gaze, and its matter-of-fact queerness. Finally, it's the creative synchronicity of subject and style that makes *Tarnation* worthy of the public's attention now that the party's over and the judgment of folks who actually pay for their tickets begins to kick in.

Testifying to Trouble

Hit the rewind button. Back up twenty years or more. On screen there's a young boy, already battered and bruised, but clearly a survivor. The boy's got enough spunk to busy himself with dropping bread crumbs that will one day show him the way out of his Jewish white-trash Houston existence, out of a netherworld of foster homes and drug overdoses and mental hospitals, into the magical world of movies and clubs and . . . New York City.

Tarnation is first and foremost an autobiography. Texts pop up on screen early on like a graphic tattoo, detailing the life and history of one Jonathan Caouette, his mother, Renee, and his grandparents Adolph and Rosemary. Like a fable, the on-screen titles tell of terrible things that befell our heroes, rendering them damaged in the world. The opening words? "Once upon a time in a small Texas town in the early 1950s a good woman met a good man. Rosemary and Adolph got married. They had a beautiful daughter, Renee. Everything in their lives was bright, happy and promising." Ah, we viewers know to brace ourselves when a narrative starts out like that, especially when the film has already opened with a flash-forward to the present, revealing Renee felled by a lithium overdose and Jonathan, her son and chronicler, ill with worry and guilt.

Hordes of voyeuristic documentaries have been made over the years about the powerless or victimized, from early cinéma vérité classics like Richard Leacock and Joyce Chopra's *Happy Mother's Day* (1963) to Nick Broomfield's pair of Aileen Wuornos docs. Unlike them, *Tarnation* is suffused with a compassion and tenderness virtually without precedent. Its spotlight of empathic love bathes its sinners in forgiveness and redemption. That's true even for the one who's the filmmaker himself. Indeed Caouette is on screen nearly nonstop, emoting, performing, and finally even mugging for the camera, saving himself in life by preserving himself on film. He records "testimonies" repeatedly and, like a video cheerleader, gets his kin to do the same, delivering star turns aimed at salvaging their lives and making sense of it all, just this once. Tell it to the camera!

At his San Francisco screening and interview sessions, Caouette proved to be a seasoned pro already, yet with a touching enthusiasm not yet sucked out of him. Rumpled, short on sleep, he sucked on cigarettes and blinked into the sun poolside at San Francisco's late beloved Phoenix Hotel. He still couldn't quite believe how far *Tarnation* had taken him, but there's no doubt he sees film as his life's calling:

> I was always a diehard packrat. I always just held on to everything. I accumulated 160 hours of stuff. I always wanted to be a filmmaker, since I was four years old. I always wanted to tell a story about my life, by way of a narrative, utilizing actors. I never realized I was inadvertently making this movie for twenty years. That is one reason I wanted to use text, to invoke personality disorder. It sufficed as a kind of frame because the movie is going off in so many weird places anyway.

Electroshocking a Narrative

Caouette began *Tarnation* at the age of eleven. No, that's not quite right. He began consciously performing for the camera at that age. No longer a mere participant in home movies, he stands alone in front of the camera speaking in a first-person address. But he's not exactly himself, as if we know what that was. Instead, in drag and distraught, the young Jonathan offers up an impersonation, presenting "a testimony" about Caroline and her husband who drinks and does dope and beats her, fidgeting with "her" hair, weeping. Who is this? Whether his mother, or a neighbor, or a fantasy of a movie star, she's a show-stopper.

So are the texts that interpolate and structure the narrative, an intelligent device for conveying the unrepresentable. For example, continuing the fable: "In 1965–99, Renee was treated in over one hundred psychiatric hospitals. Records now indicate there was nothing initially wrong with her." She was originally sent to a hospital for help by Adolph and Rosemary, after a fall from a roof left her paralyzed. Today she'd get therapy and antidepressants; back then, she was given electroshock therapy twice a week for two years. And then more.

If much of *Tarnation*'s exposition is delivered in an electroshock blast straight from the screen with graphic intensity, the texture of the lives it explores is nothing less. His mother and grandmother vamp for the camera, he delivers confessions alone in the night, and peril lurks between the reels. Caouette's brilliant grasp of the visual clearly goes way back: at moments, *Tarnation* plays like a catalogue of consumer video effects of the past twenty years, some cheesy, some poignant, some both. The screen splits along with Jonathan's and Renee's mental anguish and institutionalizations, images mutate and multiply, the wholeness of the screen becomes fractured, and subjective states swamp all objective stability.

His mother is central to *Tarnation* and to Caouette's life, to the point that we witness his driving back to Texas to rescue her and bring her home to live with him and boyfriend David in Brooklyn. Renee is what Divine was to John Waters, what the Factory stars were to Warhol: a larger-than-life presence who eats up the camera and rewards all attention with unique performances. In Renee's case, she claims links to Elizabeth Taylor and tells her own tales of tragedy. And indeed life has been cruel to her; the difference is that she's Jonathan's mom, and he never stops loving her or paying attention to her. It's his intoxication that the audience picks up, a passion made manifest by the subjective eye through which we are thrust into this story of mother and son.

Some pundits have forged links for *Tarnation* through scandal, claiming it's what Andrew Jarecki's *Capturing the Friedmans* (2003) would have been if directed by the sons themselves, not first-timer Jarecki and editor Richard Hankin. For others of us, an entirely different documentary comes to mind: the Maysles brothers' *Grey Gardens* (1975), an indelible portrait attacked by critics of its time as exploitative but vociferously and publicly defended by its subjects, Big Edie and Little Edie, who came across then as just as nutty as Caouette's grandmother, grandfather, and mother do today—and just as thrilled to be documented.

Except when they're not. To his credit, Caouette includes several scenes in which his mother or grandparents tell him to turn off the camera; notably, all occur toward the latter part of the film, when he clearly knew he was on to something and had begun working on "my movie." (In one scene, Grandpa Adolph even tries to call the police to stop his grandson's filming him.) If those moments disturb the loving harmony that otherwise prevails, they're a necessary reminder of the power relations that lurk behind the surface of most documentaries and, however disguised, contribute to their shape and direction. The difference is that, here, Jonathan is son, grandson, director, cinematographer, and coeditor (helped by Stephen Winter, producer, and the director of the MIX festival in New York, where a three-hour *Tarnation* first premiered).

By now Caouette has seen *Grey Gardens* and, of course, loved it. But he doesn't consider his own film a documentary: "I prefer to call it a DIY," he confesses. Asked to name film influences, he bypasses any reference to documentaries in favor of an excited litany: "David Lynch, *Mulholland Drive*, Derek Jarman, Alejandro Jodorowsky, *El Topo*, Sidney Lumet." Months later he expands the list: "There's so many, it's so hard to choose. I was as inspired by acid-trip animated madness like *Dirty Duck* as by *My Beautiful Launderette, Love Streams, Do the Right Thing* or *Rashomon*. I'm very equal-opportunity when it comes to movies and there's still so much I haven't seen that I can't wait to get a chance to!"[3]

As a Texas kid, Caouette had joined a Big Brothers program that paired fatherless boys with role models; he was matched with Jeff Millar, a film critic for a Houston paper, who took him to screenings and obviously changed his life. The clips from childhood and adolescence that cycle through *Tarnation* favor horror and splatter genres; they alternate with the hyperreal encounters with his family and his poignant narrative of his own travails, from childhood trauma to his-and-her drug overdoses and mental health interventions. Throughout he maintains his particular brand of creativity. One of the rare scenes videotaped outside the home is a record of his high school play, cowritten with an old boyfriend; it's a musical, based on David Lynch's *Blue Velvet* with songs by Marianne Faithfull.

Queering Documentary Style

In cinematic terms, *Tarnation* is poised at a complex intersection of trends and lineages. In spirit, it harkens back to the euphoric days of the New Queer Cinema, suggesting nothing so much as that earlier wunderkind, Sadie Benning, and her Pixelvision masterpieces. Like her, Caouette is a master of the late-at-night-in-my-room-with-cheap-technology ode, a bard of queer adolescence coming into being on videotape, but with Texan sensibility and a touch of Tennessee Williams decay shifting the balance. Long after the marketplace has taken over the NQC label and filmmakers have opted for deals over discoveries, Caouette brings it all full circle with his raw and absolutely new style perfectly matched to the pains and passions of his life.

His queerness marked him from an early age and informs *Tarnation* throughout, even as he has gone in other directions within this one piece. His club-kid immersion in a counterculture mythos inflects the work as well, so it was no surprise to find that his years in Houston and New York were indeed club-centered. He was a natural at thirteen, smuggling himself into Houston clubs as a "petite Goth girl." At one point, he tried to support himself as an actor and ended up doing stints in *Hair* and a European tour of *Rocky Horror Picture Show*.[4] Throughout he "always was a film bug, but the cut-throat part, the finance, was all so daunting." Props to the gay and lesbian film circuit: it was the introduction to MIX through a friend that led Caouette to the film world, recognition, and the important assistance of MIX's Stephen Winter.

Tarnation isn't being released into the world of the early 1990s when the NQC was the rage of the moment. Instead its documentary credentials ensure that it flies in the face of two dominant trends of the moment: on the one hand, the move in the United States toward big theatrical-release documentaries in the wake of box-office successes like *Capturing the Friedmans* and Michael Moore's *Fahrenheit 9/11* (2004); on the other, the cultural obsession with reality television shows, as even the Osbornes lurk in semiparallel in the background. Caouette may well be pointing the way to a new approach to both documentary and autobiography precisely by refusing categories and insisting instead on a hybrid approach that accurately encapsulates the tone of his life. Purity isn't his game. But he's generous and inclusive, posing a casual model of what life looks like today in America for a damn talented queer boy who has just turned thirty-two, for whom the contents of his life and the stuff of film have merged:

> It's weird for me to think back on it because although I never, ever, in my wildest dreams, thought the stuff I was shooting would ever get into Cannes or even be shown outside my bedroom, I always did kind of know that all the craziness that I was going through and all the footage I was shooting would come in handy somehow, somewhere. I would even

sometimes invent weird scenarios, like: I'd die alone in my apartment and my footage would be discovered by someone, Blair-Witch style and then *they* would build something out of it, which then made me mad, which is funny. I was like, *I'm not waiting till I'm dead for this film to get made!*[5]

Not a chance, Jonathan Caouette. *Tarnation* is out, and there's a wonderfully mad idea in the wings: a new story stitched together from a series of cult films from the 1970s, all starring the same actress, redeployed into a completely different and original Caouette narrative.[6] "I like always to be doing ten things at the same time," admitted Caouette. "It's just how I'm hard-wired."[7]

Notes

This chapter originally appeared as "Tell It to the Camera," *Sight and Sound* 15.4 (2005), 32–34.

1. Thanks to Alexis Fish for insisting that I see *Tarnation* and arranging for me to do so.

2. This quotation and all others, unless indicated otherwise, are taken from an interview conducted in person with Caouette in San Francisco in 2004, when he was on a press tour for *Tarnation*'s impending theatrical release.

3. Quotation emailed to me after the interview by his producer Stephen Winter, "as dictated by" Caouette.

4. He returned to acting again in *Short Bus*; see below.

5. Also via Winter's email.

6. Caouette had a cameo as an actor in John Cameron Mitchell's *Short Bus* (2006), playing the "Blondie-Grabber." He has since made a short film, *All Flowers in Time*, starring the sublime Chloë Sevigny, and a follow-up documentary on his mother, *Walk Away Renée*, in 2011.

7. Also via Winter's email.

APICHATPONG WEERASETHAKUL'S

TROPICAL MALADIES

12 The young Thai director Apichatpong Weerasethakul blames his film career for his lack of a boyfriend. Talking in San Francisco recently on the occasion of a U.S. retrospective in his honor, he explains, "I think guys are afraid of me. Because to be with me now would mean being so public, and in Thailand, people prefer not to attract attention. Me, too! But it's too late for that now. It's my karma."[1] With such a plea, I promised Apichatpong (or Joe, as he's known in the West) to include this detail for any readers who may be interested: yes, he's gay and he's available.

Considering that he's based in Bangkok, a virtual destination for the gay imagination as well as a mecca for gay tourism, his loneliness seems an anomaly. But Apichatpong is quick to turn the tables, pointing out all the ads in my local paper: "No, it looks to me as though San Francisco is the sex capital of the world."

Apichatpong's films are a revelation. Set in villages and forests, they look beneath the surface of Thai life, exposing his characters to an unblinking scrutiny that probes their yearning, desire, and heartbreak with eyes wide open. At the age of only thirty-four, this enfant terrible, with an MFA from the School of the Art Institute of Chicago and a growing reputation in Europe, already boasts a signature style. His newest film, *Tropical Malady* (2004), was opening in the United States after making history as the first Thai film ever to screen in competition at Cannes.

Tropical Malady is a wildly erotic film that traces a romance between a

12.1 A village boy and a soldier enjoy each other's company in *Tropical Malady* (2004).

handsome soldier and a village youth, then suddenly shape-shifts into a fable about a forest ranger (who just might be the same soldier) and his romance with a tiger (who just might be a ghost; fig. 12.1). This is a film to see in the movie theater, if at all possible, for the spell it casts over the audience. Mixing pop culture and village wisdom, Apichatpong focuses our attention on male bodies and female stories. There's an emotional resonance seldom found in hipster urban dramas and a sexiness that could knock you right out of your seat. "I think my film has been taken up in Thailand by university students and more mature, open audiences," he says. "And if smart gays think it's their movie too, that's fine with me."

The mix of elements comes naturally to "Joe," who grew up in Khon Kaen, a small village in northeastern Thailand. His parents were doctors who practiced there but also took the family traveling internationally. Despite his cosmopolitanism and urban base today, Joe is still most at home in the villages of his youth. But what about growing up gay in one? "I knew I was gay as a child, and I knew I felt uncomfortable, but it was not a big issue for me. It's quite natural." The real problem, he explains, is that he wasn't a transvestite. "That's the only idea that most Thai people have of homosexuality. You have to be flamboyant if you're gay. There's just one word that means both transvestite and gay in the Thai language."

That stereotype explains why Joe's excursion into popular movie-making, *The Adventures of Iron Pussy* (2003), codirected with its star, Michael Shaowanasai, was a bigger hit than any of his art films. Who could resist the sight of Shaowanasai morphing from subservient shop-boy into a transvestite super-hero, modeled on legendary avenger Diana Rigg? Yet Apichatpong refused to be pigeonholed into comedies. "You know, in Buddhist culture, being gay is the result of bad karma." He sighs. "I know this is against the whole gay movement's beliefs." Despite his international perspective, he confesses that he's become more Buddhist since his father's recent death.

Apichatpong's films—full of warm communities and hot men, cool heads and warm desires—are apt reflections of the contradictions he's working out. A central scene in *Tropical Malady* shows the village youth and the soldier out on a date. At a local cabaret, an older woman dedicates a love song to the soldier and invites the young man up on stage to sing with her. Can you imagine it? A beautiful youth takes the stage to belt out a karaoke love song to a hunk in uniform clearly smitten with him, in a popular community space, his action legitimated by the older woman who is beaming—approvingly? knowingly?—at his side. The scene, like *Tropical Malady* itself, is simultane-ously sexy as hell and mind-bogglingly astounding. The same goes for the love scene with the tiger (supposedly censored on release back home).

Apichatpong has a film company in Bangkok with three compatriots, where he turns out lots of short videos, serious ones, but with titles like *Boys at Noon* (2000) and *Secret Love Affair* (2001). He's also active in music video production and has staged a giant pop concert with multimedia screens in an arena-like space, while also carrying out museum installations.[2] Nothing seems to faze or intimidate him. He works across media, recently adapting a comic book into an episodic production with the names of his friends as characters.

For good reason, he likes to think of himself in the mold of the old Holly-wood directors, who were always working and churning out product, but with an experimental approach that he discovered in art school back in Chicago. His next project? A film set in a hospital, a space that's obviously charged with childhood memories, and one that will most likely contain a love story or a tale of heartbreak if it's going to be a true Apichatpong Weerasethakul film.[3]

Acknowledging the follies of the heart, he defends the near-inevitability of love gone wrong. "It's universal," he explains patiently to this American interviewer. "When you're attached, you suffer. It's Buddhism 101. It doesn't matter if you're gay or straight."

Notes

1. Personal interview, Piccino restaurant, San Francisco, May 2005. Thanks to Marcus Hu for arranging the conversation.

2. His four-channel video installation *Unknown Forces* was presented at REDCAT in L.A. in 2007. For a comprehensive guide to his activities and his large number of installations shown throughout Europe and Asia, see the website of his production company Kick the Machine: http://www.kickthemachine.com/works/index.html.

3. This film would become *Syndromes and a Century* (2006). He canceled its commercial release in Thailand after the Thai government's Censorship Board demanded that a number of scenes be cut, and he has since become more outspoken about political conditions in Thailand, especially as they affect artists: "I, as a filmmaker, treat my works as I do my own sons or daughters. I don't care if people are fond of them or despise them, as long as I created them with my best intentions and efforts. If these offspring of mine cannot live in their own country for whatever reason, let them be free. There is no reason to mutilate them in fear of the system. Otherwise there is no reason for one to continue making art." In response to its censorship, he launched the Free Thai Cinema movement with other cultural figures. For the complete text of the petition from which these sentences are extracted, see the Petition Online website, http://www.petitiononline.com/nocut/petition.html. His next film, *Uncle Boonmee Who Can Recall His Past Lives*, won the grand prize, the celebrated Palme d'Or, at the Cannes Film Festival in 2010 and opened in the United States in 2011. As of this writing, Apichatpong Weerasethakul continues to distribute all his films through Strand Releasing.

BEYOND DOOM

Gregg Araki's *Mysterious* Film

13 Anyone who has ever been a fan of a Gregg Araki film can give thanks to the gods of culture that he can't carry a tune or play an instrument. "My biggest regret is that I was never in a band," he admits, as we talk in his press tour hotel room in downtown San Francisco. Ah, I can't help but think: the films, dear Gregg, are a fine compensation.

Chatting with him in this unlikely setting, the day after his Frameline Award and a week before the local release of *Mysterious Skin* (2004), I got a lesson in the Araki concept of life as a soundtrack. "I think I was born at the perfect time," says Araki, who has taken his birthday (December 17, 1959, if you must know) as a signifier of his musical generation: "We got to experience all the great music events at the actual time they happened. I was sixteen when the Sex Pistols were hitting in America and punk-rock culture took over: the whole DIY status of it, anticorporate, march to your own drummer, who cares what people think of you, that was such a powerful influence on me. Punk rock, new wave music, and the whole world of alternative music was creatively so exciting." Araki insists his films are explicitly linked to that alt music catalogue. *The Doom Generation* (1995), he says, is his Nine Inch Nails film, and "a lot of them are the Jesus and Mary Chain, in the sense that there's a kind of naïve romanticism at their heart, surrounded by chaos."

Araki was the bad boy of the New Queer Cinema, the one willing to send his characters in *The Living End* (1992), my favorite of his early films, on

guerrilla godard

13.1 Gregg Araki's affinities with the French New Wave were obvious from the start, as the *LA Weekly* recognized when *The Living End* premiered in 1992. Courtesy of Craig Gilmore.

an HIV-positive spree across the American badlands, with the black-leather-jacket guy from the corner offering the geek a taunt in place of an invitation (fig. 13.1).

One year at Sundance, though, everyone was whispering about his new behavior. I remember John Waters's version the best: "It's so boring now that everyone is coming out. How great that Gregg is going back in." Araki laughs, "Yeah, that was the year I tried dating girls." He's matter-of-fact about it now. How exactly does he define his sexuality these days? "I'm a person," he says calmly. "I have a boyfriend, but I'm a person." That very boyfriend is now web-surfing in the corner of the hotel room and calls out, "Ed Koch"—former mayor of New York City—"just gave your film a positive review!"

Araki claims an affinity with today's younger generation and says that his actors, Brady Corbet and Joseph Gordon-Levitt, "have this whole 'who cares' attitude about their sexuality." He adds, "I think that's so modern and healthy. It's not like being in the closet or hiding, or being on the 'down low,' it's just that it doesn't matter. There's such an open-mindedness among kids their age."

It's becoming awfully hard to connect this well-mannered, reasonable guy to the wild-man films he's created. Araki recognizes my dilemma: "People always think, because of my movies, I come from some family of drug addicts. . . . But I have this unnaturally normal childhood, this perfect suburban life. It's shocking how normal it is." He didn't even grow up in Los Angeles, where his films until *Mysterious Skin* were always set, but rather in Santa Barbara, where he remained to go to college at the University of California, Santa Barbara—even living with his family! He laughs. "You have to have a super-normal background to be able to take the plunge." So while Araki may give his damaged characters in *Mysterious Skin* his favorite childhood cereal boxes and have them eat SpaghettiOs like he did, the story of parental indifference and serious emotional harm is, yes, fiction.

Araki knows about cinematic fiction, what with a degree in film studies from UCSB, schooled by auteurists. "I'm super old school," he says, reeling off the names Sarris and Kael, Ford and Lang, Renoir and Truffaut. Then came a whole semester of Jean-Luc Godard, thanks to a new professor, Michael Renov, today an associate dean at the University of Southern California. "I was so Godard-damaged!" Araki recalls. If the influence is still apparent, imagine his crash landing at USC film school, where he was supposed to learn industry standards and three-act structures but instead proved himself "a pretentious dickhead" who kept bringing up Godard. He got out with an MFA and a unique cinematic view produced by melding his disparate influences.

I've always thought that Araki's films, filled with hip music and TV-star actors, offer an index to American pop culture, that, if lined up from 1987 to now, would synthesize the tastes of the coolest teenagers. So it makes perfect sense that Araki, relaxing at the Hotel Niko in his jeans and T-shirt, scuffed black shoes and single pierced ear, would be a rocker at heart. And one that's still defiantly "old school." Despite his TV-actor casting, he claims not to follow TV. As for the Internet, it bores him. And downloading music? Nope. "I love CDs. I have thousands of them. I like to be able to hold the music in my hand and see the art."

The rocker is clearly different now, shorn of the old wink, removed from the po-mo style and satiric delivery of yore. Departing from the original stories that have always been his signature, Araki adapted Scott Heim's novel into a wondrous, beautiful, and disturbing fable about adolescence, extraterrestrial abduction, pedophilia, trauma, and sexuality. *Mysterious Skin* conjures a universe in which a baseball coach has a radical impact on two boys, one who grows up testifying to his abduction by aliens, the other who evolves into life as a hustler. It resonates deeply, transporting viewers into the dark universe of a troubled childhood, precisely because Araki sets irony aside. Also left behind are the songs that made his films so top-pop playable. Instead he commissioned his first original score from his idols, Harold Budd, ambient-music legend, and Robin Guthrie of Cocteau Twins fame. The first film score for both, its release was timed to the film's opening.

Araki credits the musical score for the film's success in transporting the audience back to a childhood time of dreams and violations. "It's called 'shoe-gazer' music because of the way that the bands would come out on stage and just look at their shoes instead of the audience. It's hypnotic but not in the way that trance music is. It has a dreaminess, a melancholy, with lush washes of guitar that take you away." Hmm, maybe that's it. But I suspect something bigger, as if a sort of harmonic convergence has taken hold: Araki's chops as a director, his genius with actors, his years of fearlessness with subject matter have conspired to transform the biggest risk of his career, miraculously, into a modern masterpiece.

Note

This chapter originally appeared as "Araki Rock (Greg Araki)," *San Francisco Bay Guardian*, May 25, 2005.

A WALK IN THE CLOUDS

Julián Hernández

14 *A Thousand Clouds of Peace* (2003), the debut feature of the young Mexican writer-director Julián Hernández, is a sublime meditation on love, heartbreak, sex, and loneliness.[1] Hernández is too smart and too sensitive to join his compatriots in their race to match Hollywood's action output.[2] Instead *A Thousand Clouds* offers up romantic pleasures that would not be found in a quickie and delivers its love bites with the smooth, deliberate tempo of a bolero. It's a film for anyone who ever went to bed forlorn, comforted only by Frank Sinatra or Billie Holiday—or Sara Montiel—on the stereo.

The star of *A Thousand Clouds,* on screen at every moment, is a sexual flâneur named Gerardo who wanders Mexico City, traversing and transgressing its physical boundaries in search of love and affection but finding only sex for hire. No hustler could be more different from the model of Warhol's narcissistic stud. Gerardo is an avatar of heartbreak, a lonely soul seeking connection.

He works in a pool hall and services some of the men who frequent the place. He lives in an anonymous room, with little to call his own apart from the intensity of feeling, physicality, and sexuality that marks his existence. Not content to let the camera dwell happily on first-time actor Juan Carlos Ortuño's face and body ad infinitum, Hernández breaks up the shots, jump-cuts his transitions, disrupts time and place with voice-overs and nonsynchronous sound, and even ends scenes with an abruptness that can make us lose equilibrium as surely as Gerardo loses his own. It's clear Hernández wants us totally immersed.

Hustling may be a life, but love isn't a hustle. When Gerardo finally falls for a guy, an offer of money breaks his heart—and a Dear John letter from the beloved john fractures it even more. Gerardo wanders the streets in search of his lost love, finding consolation, not in the anonymous sex he performs with the mechanical urgency of a heroin addict copping a fix, but instead, surprisingly, from the many high-spirited women he encounters. One pair of women is conducting a sidewalk sale, where Gerardo searches for a long-lost song he remembers from a movie. They recognize the tune and laugh uproariously at his rendition, even as they boost his spirits and find Sara Montiel's old LP record, *El Último Cuplé*, for him.

This memory and purchase aren't scripted randomly: Montiel was the preeminent femme fatale, actress, and singer of the 1950s–60s in Latin America and Europe. She captured hearts and sympathies on screen and off, including an infamous romance with the director Anthony Mann that ended in a disastrously short-lived marriage. Montiel's songs form a soundtrack for heartbreak, as cherished by her lovelorn fans as by lovesick Gerardo. Her songs bind us to the movie, turning the audience into a virtual shoulder Gerardo could cry on, if only he knew we were there.

Mexico City is a bifurcated, gendered universe in this film. Apart from a school friend who offers desultory advice and a melancholic queen whose attention he half disdains, it's the women Gerardo encounters who understand the damage wrought by men. A sympathetic waitress offers him advice and free food; she turns out to be pregnant, alone, dreaming against the odds of a better life ahead. He meets another woman on a bridge; she seems dangerously close to the edge, emotionally and geographically, yet she pauses to sympathize and share a utopian dream of the return of her own lost love. In this strange city emptied of masses and peopled only by the compass points of Gerardo's subjectivity, women dream and men act. Badly.

In one episode, Gerardo encounters a visitor from the dark side, an icon of macho masculinity straight out of somebody else's movie. Needless to say, Gerardo's erotic encounter with this stranger in an abandoned industrial landscape (which he enters on one of his quests to find his true love) goes so wrong he's left bleeding. It's bad enough to send him running back to Mama, but alas, there's no comfort to be had from the astonishingly young and hostile woman to whom he cannot even talk.

Hernández doesn't mention Fassbinder when he reels off his influences to me during a phone conversation from the midst of the Guadalajara Film Festival, where in 2003 he won the award for best director. But Fassbinder's dystopic universes have something in common with the one Hernández brings alive for us here. The difference is heart: Hernández loves his characters, he loves his city, and he's not afraid to let his story veer toward the sentimental as well as the sexually graphic. Nor is he afraid to let his vision unspin in a visually original fashion. Shot by the talented Diego Arizmendi in luminous 35mm black and white, the graphic splendor of the images rescues the film from ever toppling over into the full-color sordidness of an Arturo Ripstein film or those of the many younger Mexican directors who've followed his lead into the lower depths of ever more predictable squalor.

Think of *A Thousand Clouds,* then, as the anti–*Amores Perros.* Its use of black and white is a tribute, Hernández says, to the black-and-white television sets on which he and so many other Mexicans (and so many of us too) once watched the movies that fixed their fantasies—like photographs developing in a darkroom—with a monochromatic signature. But I suspect it's also a gesture toward cinephilia itself, a proclamation of connection to a cinematic past that was so much more colorful than color.

Recent Mexican films, from María Novaro's *Without a Trace* (*Sin dejar huella*, 2000) to Carlos Reygadas's *Japón* (2002), have been busy trying to reconfigure the harsh gender conventions of their national cinema. Hernández is doing that and more. In a decisive break with New Latin American Cinema's disavowal of pop confections in favor of a gritty realism, Hernández names as two of his biggest influences the men responsible for everything the New Latin American Cinema movement sought to overturn. First, he cites Mexico's Emilio "El Indio" Fernández, king of the golden age of popular movies and cinematic godfather to the wondrous María Félix and Dolores del Río; Hernández points in particular to El Indio's cinematic elevation of women and their suffering. But he might also have had El Indio's problematic race politics in mind, since Gerardo's dark skin has a clear relationship to his marked, tragic life in which, incidentally, his runaway love and bitter mother are both lighter by far. Interestingly, Hernández also mentions the relatively overlooked Argentine director Leonardo Favio, whose movies fused politics and pop culture into some of the highest-grossing Argentine films ever, citing his formalism as a strong influence.

It's important to note, though, that Hernández has also been nurtured and shaped by an international world of queer cinema. He and his collaborators first met while students in the Centro Universitario de Estudios Cinematográfico and showed their early shorts in the MIX festival of gay and lesbian films, a forum for experimental work that started in New York City two decades earlier and became an important presence in Brazil and Mexico in the 1990s, where the MIX festivals have continued.

Imagine if Wong Kar-Wai's *Happy Together* (1997) had been directed by Antonioni in his *L'Avventura* (1960) period, since Hernández worships the master. Imagine the kind of urban adventure Derek Jarman might have brought to life, complete with deadpan acting and nonnarrative edits, had he been born Mexican instead of English, since Hernández professes adoration for Jarman too. Or follow the lead of the third point on the holy trinity of influences that Hernández recited to me: Pier Paolo Pasolini. I like to imagine *Teorema* (1968) turned inside out, with the stranger now the one disrupted, alone, and unloved.

There goes Gerardo, wandering Mexico City—often running, inexplicably, with total desperation but no real destination. *Run, Gerardo, Run*? No, he's not Lola, emblem of a new German cinema out for kicks. There's no heist, no boyfriend, no gun, no father. Just a lack, a wound, a heartbreak, out of which Hernández's assured direction and Ortuño's astonishing performance have created a moving, romantic surplus.[3]

Notes

This chapter originally appeared as "A Walk in the Clouds (A Thousand Clouds of Peace)," *San Francisco Bay Guardian*, March 31, 2004.

1. Its original title is *Mil nubes de paz cercan el cielo, amor, jamás acabarás de ser amor* (*A Thousand Clouds of Peace Fence the Sky, Love; Your Being Love Will Never End*).

2. This is a reference to the contemporaneous defection of the "Three Caballeros" (Guillermo del Toro, Alfonso Cuarón, and Alejandro González Iñárritu) from Mexico to Hollywood movie-making and L.A. residency.

3. Since this debut, Hernández has gone on to make two further features: *El cielo dividido* (*Broken Sky*, 2006) and *Rabioso sol, rabioso cielo* (*Raging Sun, Raging Sky*, 2009) and more than a dozen shorts.

PART III

GENRE MEETS GENDER

LETHAL LESBIANS

The Cinematic Inscription

of Murderous Desire

15 In the late 1980s and early 1990s, just as the New Queer Cinema was picking up steam, a parallel cinematic phenomenon was also surfacing. In 1984–93 instrumental factors fed its development: the prominence of an ascendant queer culture, empowered female sexuality, a new "lesbian chic," heightened U.S. militarism, infamous serial killings, and a couple of hit movies in the multiplex denounced by pundits for glamorizing the murder of men by women. With a perfect storm of pop culture, celebrity fashion, and violence, these elements would coalesce (ca. 1991–95) into a new cinematic vogue for murderous women, killers who turned the table on the formula that had long insisted lesbians had to die by the end of the movie. It is this lethal lesbian category which invites analysis in the context of the NQC.[1]

When cultural attention coalesces so acutely on a combination of crime and sex, something bigger than the individual parts is driving it. My inquiry here looks, not at intentions or conspiracies, but rather into the forces shaping these narratives, the use to which audiences were putting them, the ways in which they answered an inchoate need. The United States was increasingly in the hands of resurgent neocon forces that demonized anyone outside their narrow zones of tolerance. Republicans were still in office, AIDS still going strong, culture wars still raging in the halls of Congress. It's not hard to imagine why lesbians, queers, uppity women, and kindred outsiders were in need of fantasies for sustenance and courage. The arrival of a spate of films in which women teamed up with each other to commit murder was welcomed—at a fantasy level. Off-screen, men in uniform were murdered in the name of the U.S. government, but no filming was allowed.

In New York City, though, popular culture took a surprising turn. In the late 1980s and early 1990s, a radical remodeling of the dyke into a new figure of desire was under way. The lesbian, the age-old creature from the black lagoon, was abruptly transformed from scorned humorless outsider into glamorous insider.[2] It may have been Madonna's fault.

In 1984 Madonna had released "Like a Virgin," the song that made her a star and inspired girls everywhere to take charge, claim their sexuality, and defy society's rules; in 1985 she appeared in Susan Seidelman's *Desperately Seeking Susan* as the impossibly hip, sexy mystery woman who inspired a New Jersey housewife to leave her marriage to search for her.[3] In 1988 Madonna and then-pal Sandra Bernhard appeared together on *Late Night with David Letterman* for what would be its most notorious show of the era.[4] They rushed the stage for a full-body embrace, flirted, danced, bantered, and shouted "Cubby . . . Hole," the name of a popular Greenwich Village lesbian bar, when Letterman asked how they spent a typical night out on the town. Dressed in matching outfits, they tried to shock their host and studio audience: "I slept with Sean!" giggled Sandra. "And you were much better!"[5] Shredding talk television's heterosexual rule book, delightedly watching Letterman squirm, they did as much for lesbian status as any demonstration. When rumors circulated that Madonna "stole" Ingrid Casares away from Sandra, lesbian and maybe-lesbian credibility hit the stratosphere.[6]

The new lesbian became ubiquitous. Everybody wanted one! It was as though lesbians had been appointed the new gay men, filling in while the guys dealt with AIDS. Nobody said so, but you had to wonder. This newly stylish lesbian didn't have to wear flannel shirts anymore or announce ideological positions; she could just buy clothes and go to dinner parties. The fad culminated five years after the *Letterman* show with the media invention of Lesbian Chic, which appeared in 1993 in cover stories in three magazines, nearly simultaneously.[7] First kd lang was on the cover of *New York* magazine; then she was on the cover of *Vanity Fair*, her face covered with shaving cream, being shaved by Cindy Crawford; then the "Lesbian Chic" cover story appeared in *Newsweek*. No fame comes unencumbered. Lesbian visibility was attained at long last, freed from the stale stereotype of asexual spoilsport, but the terms of visibility were set by the media and would eventually prove problematic.

In between *Letterman* and Lesbian Chic, two films were released that magnetized public attention around these issues of gender and power: Ridley Scott and Callie Khouri's *Thelma and Louise* (1991) and Paul Verhoeven and Joe Ezterhaus's *Basic Instinct* (1992).[8] Two different takes on the nexus of women, glamour, and violence, they were received differently.

Thelma and Louise became an instant cause célèbre: women went with friends to see it over and over, while male pundits wrung their hands and wrote editorial pages that denounced the film as immoral for glamorizing murder.[9] A deadly gender war was trumpeted by the media in response. Reaction to *Basic Instinct* was different: men loved it, so did a lot of women, but gay and lesbian community leaders, papers, and the GLAAD media-watch organization denounced the film as homophobic for reviving the image of the crazed pathological lesbian. There were demonstrations with pickets that snitched "Catherine did it!" and calls for boycotts.[10] I crossed the picket line on opening night. I loved the movie and wondered why, with half a dozen films in the multiplex showing men murdering women, I was expected to boycott the only film in which a woman killed men instead.

The two films signaled a shift in feelings around women's acceptable place in society just when U.S. society was in the midst of being remasculinized and heterosexualized. These films were a counterweight, a pop culture imaginary that was desperately needed by women engaged in vital political struggles as well as glamorous cocktail parties. Both films echoed the NQC's contention that "negative images" could be reclaimed within a new, postmodern queer moment: the cultural attitudes evolving at breakneck speed into "queer" required the redemption, even transfiguration, of the negative into the positive. Just as Tom Kalin's *Swoon* redeemed villains of the past, many lesbians were happy to trash the compass coordinates of good and evil that had mapped morality in older, more tremulous times. The deck had been shuffled and the roles changed up: the villainess could be a new heroine.

The plot of *Thelma and Louise* is well known: best friends Thelma (Geena Davis) and Louise (Susan Sarandon) take a weekend getaway from the men in their life (one good, one bad), but on the way, Thelma's rape by a good ole boy outside a country-western roadhouse is prevented only by Louise taking out a gun to stop it and then to kill the arrogant bastard. The twin acts of violence (a rape interrupted, a homicide) may have set off an initial reaction of hysteria and dysfunction for the two protagonists, but the shedding of blood transforms them into a team buoyed by the euphoria of the open road. They defy former limitations as their new selves carve paths through the world with a gun and a car. By the time the film reaches its famous shot of the two women driving off the mesa into the Grand Canyon, their hands clasped as they kiss and a Polaroid photograph of the two joined together soars into view, they no longer seem to need the asphalt to get to where they're going.

So Thelma and Louise are heroines, best friends, partners in crime, but can they be called lesbians? Consider the argument made by the late Lynda Hart in her landmark study, *Fatal Women: Lesbian Sexuality and the Mark of Aggression*. Hart's analysis of the powerful effect of structured absence is helpful for understanding this film and those that follow:

> Summoned through negation in both the film's action and the critical responses is a history of identification between the female criminal and the lesbian. Given this history, the expectation for lesbianism between women who violate the law is so strong that the film works overtime to disavow it. If the lesbian has been constructed as the manifest figure of women's latent criminality, we can expect that representations of violent women will be haunted by her absent presence. . . . The female protagonists of these films make "shameless liaisons" which expose the dominant culture's underwriting of lesbianism when the violence of women enters representation. . . . It is not too surprising . . . that when women enter representation ineluctably together, they do so as criminals.[11]

The story of two women fighting and killing for the chance to be together, yet doomed inevitably to fail, is the narrative that will animate the lethal lesbian genre. Men may indeed appear along Thelma and Louise's journey (notably, the young Brad Pitt), but Hart's theories of expectation and disavowal suggest that the very presence of the men becomes proof that there is something so intense going on between the women that it must be masked. Once Thelma and Louise improve their driving, challenge men on an almost routine basis, and become inordinately fond of their new life and each other, naturally they must die. Criminals "ineluctably together," they stay that way for all eternity, or at least the movie version: the freeze-frame.

What does Hart's theory, then, imply about *Basic Instinct*? It's a sexual thriller in which a detective (Michael Douglas) tries to solve a murder in which Catherine (Sharon Stone) is the target of suspicion. Displaced by the arrival of Catherine's lesbian lover, the angry detective ends up killing her. A complex series of events lead to another murder and another woman; meanwhile the detective discovers that Catherine is surrounded by a circle of friends who have all served time for killing their husbands or male lovers. Ignoring the evidence, he decides Catherine's not guilty and ends the film in bed with her—as she reaches, in the last shot, for an ice pick, the weapon in two of the film's murders. Attention to the film focused on Sharon Stone as the central figure and central killer, but in truth the film makes clear her allegiances to the other "fatal" women who share her distaste for men.

The taboo of reversing roles runs deep, though: normatively both killer and victim hold deeply gendered positions. Messing with them away from the glamour and klieg lights can carry a high price. Enter Aileen Wuornos, a real-life example who received treatment very different from that enjoyed by the Hollywood stars.[12]

Ah, societies are packed full of contradictions. In January 1989 George H. W. Bush (the first one) was sworn in as president; in August 1990 Iraq invaded and occupied Kuwait. U.S. troop deployment built throughout 1990 as bases emptied and soldiers shipped out. In January 1991 Operation Desert Storm began: the United States attacked Iraq and Kuwait. A very different deployment, meanwhile, was under way in Florida as police hunted for the "angels of death" believed responsible for killing a series of men along the state's highways. In January 1991 Aileen Wuornos was arrested in a biker bar in Daytona Beach and dubbed "the first woman serial killer" by the media. One of the reasons she'd had to resort to the dangerous work of turning tricks on the highway, she explained, was that the military buildup had depleted her usual supply of customers on the military base. One of the reasons she had to kill, she disclosed, was that men were attacking her.

Thelma and Louise would premiere at the Cannes Film Festival in May 1991. *Basic Instinct* would open in theaters on March 20, 1992. By then Aileen Wuornos had been sentenced to death. The murder of men by unglamorous, off-screen lesbians did not carry the allure of the movie versions. Instead it caused anxiety. As Miriam Basilio pointed out, "The use of Wuornos to redefine the category of criminal deviance known as the serial killer to include women occurs at a time when women's greater social mobility is causing anxiety in conservative sectors of American society."[13] The timing is not incidental: Wuornos's case is tied to the basic changes under way in the American sociopolitical landscape of the time. That's the reason the criminal justice system made an example of her.

None of the tragedies of her life were allowed to affect the tabloid fantasy construction of an inexplicably predatory killer. Hysteria seized Florida. Evidence that the first murdered man, Richard Mallory, had a record of violent rape and battery for which he'd served time was never introduced to support Wuornos's spurned plea that she'd acted in self-defense. The idea of prostitutes turning on customers who abuse them, of women grabbing power over men who think they hold the monopoly on predatory action, had to be extinguished. A male desire for revenge combined with class prejudice and Wuornos's own unpredictable and unrepentant courtroom appearances to seal her fate with an unsympathetic Florida jury.

Aileen Wuornos entered the popular imagination along with the fictitious heroines of *Basic Instinct* and *Thelma and Louise* at an intense level that goes to the heart of the disturbances set off by the so-called Reagan Revolution. Clearly it meant something different to audiences and critics when women instead of men picked up the guns or the ice picks or flexed their bare hands. But for women, these women of fact and fiction were meaningful to an extraordinary degree: they entered into the culture for good. At a tremendous demonstration for gay and lesbian rights in 1992 in Washington, D.C., banners announced the Aileen Wuornos Defense Committee and a brigade of women collected money for her trial. At a huge march on Washington for abortion rights the same year, I saw contingents of women with buttons that proclaimed, "Thelma and Louise Live!" On the tenth anniversary of the film, Sarandon happened to be vacationing at the Grand Canyon, where she encountered fans on a pilgrimage to the site.[14] When mainstream films and real-life events give rise to a community response so powerful that it resonates in the culture at large over a period of years, even decades, lodged in the collective imagination, then something larger than just a movie or a trial is at stake. The symbolic violation and reclamation of women's agency was a lesson that cut to the bone for women. Alas, only one was fantasy. Perhaps in the magazine culture of the metropolis, it was safe to imagine a cosmopolitan lesbian killer, but that fantasy could be sustained only by disassociating the real-life criminal from the beautiful actress cast in the role.

As the image of the lesbian killer coalesced, other films followed, launching careers and capturing attention. The lethal lesbian genre is grounded in this moment of fascination, one that would continue to multiply and build on itself through the mid-1990s, following and then rewriting the celluloid tales of women who kill. It was in 1994 that a trio of art house films premiered: Rafal Zielinski's *Fun*, Peter Jackson's *Heavenly Creatures*, and Nancy Meckler's *Sister, My Sister*. All three featured women or adolescent girls who team up to kill. Within just two more years, their numbers multiplied as the lethal lesbian cinema evolved, expanded, and finally wore out its welcome. Nearly all the killer lesbian films were directed by men, responding to ideas in the air that were as threatening as they were exciting.

If the set of films and real-life events in 1991–92 effected a merger of lesbian glamour and criminality, it was left to the independent fiction films that followed to lead the genre forward into an updated vision of pathology with a twist. They revised the old movie formulas, which prescribed that a lesbian character either had to kill herself in a scripted act of narrative closure or else murder her girlfriend in order to effect a similar closure. Those were the only lesbian roles on offer: destroy oneself or destroy each other. The lethal lesbian genre adds a new option. It converts the depression and self-hatred of the old-school movie lesbian into something more positive, more self-assertive, healthier: it converts introjected rage into outer-directed action. Specifically, murder.

No central network dictated codes for the new screenplays. To the extent that *Thelma and Louise* and *Basic Instinct* set in motion an enjoyment of women who kill with a soupçon of desire for one another, they tapped into a zeitgeist. No lineage of intention, then, but certainly a direct line of reception can be discerned due to the ways the audience of the 1990s shifted and reconstituted itself under the aegis of an emergent queer community—on the prowl for relevant cultural objects, unrestrained by the nervousness of previous generations, and willing to embrace all kinds of representations and narratives.

In all three independent films—*Fun, Heavenly Creatures*, and *Sister, My Sister*—lesbianism was moved off its old hell-and-brimstone version of deviance as despised, pathological evil. Instead, taken by the potential of the new lesbian killer, the lethal lesbian phenomenon offers a new species of sympathetic villains to animate its narratives and win our hearts. Unreliable women, fatal attractions, and twisted plots have always been the stuff of noir. It was no surprise, after the fall of the Berlin Wall (1989), the end of the Soviet Union, and U.S. war(s) in the Middle East, that noir, which once matched threatened postwar American masculinity with unsettling cold war politics, should now be revived in a new form.

What's different now is an element of lesbianism that turns the old noir protagonist plural: not a single lonely killer, but a pair, a couple acting on desires transmuted into bloodshed. *Fun, Heavenly Creatures*, and *Sister, My Sister* share a focus on anger, love, and adolescence that is compellingly cathartic for audiences hungry for the shape that social fantasies can assume on screen. In all three, narrative distance is abandoned: the audience enters into the "friendship" and eventually recognizes their crime as a frenzy of fulfillment, a commitment ceremony taken to an extreme.

Heavenly Creatures is the best known of the three, but all share a core of necessary elements. First, the young women in these films typically have families in which they are abused, ignored, or misunderstood. In *Fun*, Hillary (Renée Humphrey) tells Bonnie (Alicia Witt) that her dad calls her a slut, then abruptly changes the subject when her new friend reacts to the father's inappropriate sexual innuendo and tries to question her further.

There are generally no glamorous sexy babes ensnaring men but out-of-control adolescents or young women, lashing out against female authority figures in *Fun, Heavenly Creatures, Sister, My Sister, La Cérémonie*, and *Freeway*, among others. The young women are reminiscent of characters in the cold war cycle of juvenile delinquency films. At the same time, their cusp-of-adulthood age emphasizes the liminal space in which the stories unfold, emphasizing the loose boundaries that lead to mayhem.

The two women inevitably have a special connection to one another: in *Sister, My Sister*, it's a literal sibling connection that goes wrong; in *Heavenly Creatures*, a bond formed by shared physical illness; and in *Fun*, it's a friendship or crush culled from loneliness and identical music tastes. Later in the film, when they've been jailed for murder, Hillary tells a prison psychiatrist, "When we met, it was like a door opening. First I was alone, then Bonnie came in."

There can be special behavior too, such as a marked emphasis on running. In *Heavenly Creatures*, Juliet (Kate Winslet) and Pauline (Melanie Lynskey) run to the movies, fall for the music of Mario Lanza ("the world's greatest tenor"), and run straight into a pseudo-coital moment. Most insistently, all the protagonists kill with and for each other, either to seal their bond or to avoid being separated, or both. Murder is a joint activity—whether planned (*Heavenly Creatures*), spontaneous (*Fun*), or some combination (*La Cérémonie, Freeway*)—in which both join.

The murders themselves are generally an exercise in manual labor. With no guns involved, they're brutal, a form of overkill with lots of blood, guts, and destruction. The emphasis on bloody mayhem becomes a central feature. These are artisanal killings, handmade, and atavistic.

In the early films, the protagonists are always caught because they never run away (in *Sister, My Sister*, they are found in bed together) or because they can't be bothered to lie. They end up in prison in the initial three. As the genre moves away from its true-crime origins, their destinies shift until finally the genre will end with a happy-ending getaway in 1996.

There are more than a few scenes worth pointing out for the precision with which they pinpoint the identifications that will lead the pairs of women to perform unspeakable acts. It is these scenes of bonding between the protagonists that are most interesting, not the scenes of violent murder that are mostly overdetermined.

In *Fun*, the key scene is the first encounter between Hillary and Bonnie at a bus stop after school. Instant best friends, they take off on one of those seemingly endless peregrinations that teenagers favor, spinning a euphoric present into an imaginary future by simply prolonging it. They run, of course. They talk and talk. They discuss *Frankenstein*, which is most significant for Hillary's misremembering that the little girl is "too stupid" to be afraid of the monster; in fact, in both the novel and the movie, she is actually blind. Turning a blind eye? The characters are communicating something important through this exchange, captured by the script with uncanny accuracy: the pattern of adolescent speech, the sing-song lift at the end of sentences, the interchangeability of expressions. The monster's deadly tossing of a girl into the water becomes, in their telling, an act of brutal havoc, not a tragic mistake. Thus the tale of a girl's kindness and a monster's misapplied tenderness is converted into a tale of mayhem, as *Fun* too will be.

In *Sister, My Sister*, the twist of class that haunted the Wuornos case gets a classic treatment through an upstairs/downstairs tale of employers done in by their servants, a ruling-class nightmare played out on screen. However, in keeping with this genre, there's a parallel denouement of desire: two sisters, who murder their mistresses, also share a bed and an obsessive attachment. (At least, one does; these films and the Wuornos details play out a distressing formula by which the "real" lesbian is the one deemed responsible.)

Nancy Meckler based her television film not on Jean Genet's famous play *The Maids* (*Les Bonnes*), written in 1947, but on the true-crime story that had inspired it. The crime was that of the Papin sisters, who in Le Mans, France, in 1933, brutally murdered their mistress and her daughter. They inspired passionate commentary: besides Genet's play, Jean-Paul Sartre and Simone de Beauvoir attended the trial, and Jacques Lacan coined the term *folie à deux* to explain their brutal act.

In *Sister, My Sister*, a crescendo of passion precedes the murder, crosscutting between a mother-daughter card game in the parlor and sister-on-sister sex in the attic. Not unlike the arias of action in *Fun* or *Heavenly Creatures*, the run-up to the crime is used to establish a mood of euphoria that binds murder and desire together. Again, it's the female figures of authority who are killed to preserve, prolong, or enable a mutually felt or enacted desire, an object choice that suggests multiple avenues of inquiry into the role of oedipal attachment in lesbian desire, or destruction.

Heavenly Creatures pushes the themes and consequences even further. As with Wuornos, the original crime and trial were extraordinarily sensational. In 1997, while I was at New York University, the New Zealand author Alison J. Laurie came for a visit and talked about the case in depth. I was able to interview her at length about the Parker–Hulme case, which she had researched after gaining access to sealed trial records.[15] Her revelations were extraordinary, and she shed light on the wave of moral panic set off by the case in Christchurch in the 1950s, where the link between lesbianism and murder was graphically forged in tabloid coverage.

In 1954 Pauline Parker and Juliet Hulme, eroticized best friends with an extreme co-identification, murdered Pauline's mother in a park by hitting her with a brick. The New Zealand media pinned the girls to a nexus of evil, lesbianism, and murder that made for a brilliant morality tonic: every mother would prevent her daughter's lesbian leanings or overwrought friendships, lest she meet the same dreaded fate. *Heavenly Creatures* makes the girls' unnatural attachment to one another the center of attention, and the act of murder is clearly marked as an attempt to avoid separation.[16]

Following Lacan, the girls' defense attorneys pleaded *folie à deux* and got the girls a light sentence. The court ensured that they'd be separated in prison, based on the psychoanalytic theory that only together did they constitute a menace. Today *folie à deux* sounds suspiciously like lesbianism; then, it was a convincing enough diagnosis to merit five-year prison sentences instead of life in an insane asylum.

In a period of only four years, the affiliation of murder with lesbian attraction would be reproduced in a range of films that fit the lethal lesbian category either directly or tangentially. The ties that bind and character constructions are mostly shared, though the narrative arcs widely vary: Jon Avnet's *Fried Green Tomatoes* (1991), early but oblique; Clarence Fok Yiu-leung's *Naked Killer* (*Chik loh go yeung*, 1992), where killing takes precedence over eroticism; Michael Winterbottom's *Butterfly Kiss* (1995), though Amanda Plummer's avenging wrath was reserved for girls who were not Judith; Herbert Ross's *Boys on the Side* (1995), with a script by Don Roos, also oblique; and Shimako Sato's *Wizard of Darkness* (*Eko eko azaraku*, 1995), with satanic schoolgirls and supernatural battles. Then the focus begins to move back toward male targets: Claude Chabrol's *La Cérémonie* (1995), with its revival of the class struggle of *The Maids* in a contemporary bourgeois family; Andrew Fleming's *The Craft* (1996), with more supernatural intervention; Annette Haywood-Carter's *Foxfire* (1996), in which gendered but nonfatal vengeance was led by Angelina Jolie; Jim McKay's *Girls Town* (1996), another nonfatal case of high school vengeance led by Lili Taylor; F. Gary Gray's *Set It Off* (1996), with Queen Latifah in action; Jeremiah S. Chechik's *Diabolique* (1996), with another Don Roos script, which took advantage of the moment to revive the twisted sapphic homicide of Henri-Georges Clouzot's *Diabolique* (1955).

The genre definitively changes with Matthew Bright's *Freeway* (1996), which overlays Little Red Riding Hood with a serial-killer plot: two young women (Reese Witherspoon and Alanna Ubach) flirt in juvie, then kill their prison matron to escape; eventually Reese solos and kills the serial killer too.

Just as it was all becoming too much to bear, one film delivered an unambiguously happy, sexy ending. In Lana and Andy Wachowski's *Bound* (1996), Corky (Gina Gershon) and Violet (Jennifer Tilly) make the link between lesbian desire and crime utterly explicit, restore the male as sole target of violence, escape punishment, and get to drive off into the sunset, not just the Grand Canyon, after committing the perfect crime: they get away with murder, and money, a gun, and, most of all, each other. It took five years to get there, a half decade of eroticized vengeance.

The explosive expansion of the genre at a time of ever-increasing queer presence on the political and cultural front suggests a complex set of meanings attached to the production and reception of images of lesbian killers, at the real-life and fantasy levels. Two other figures should be mentioned here as parallel influences seasoning the broader culture. One was a television show, *Xena: Warrior Princess* (1995–2001), in which Xena (Lucy Lawless) and her constant companion and lover, Gabrielle, roam the world fighting for justice and redemption. With a huge following and an always visible lesbian subtext, *Xena* did a lot to bolster women's sense of agency in perilous off-screen times.

The other inspirational warrior was less ancient, more historic: Tura Satana, star of *Faster, Pussycat! Kill! Kill!* (Russ Meyer, 1965), hit the screens again in a thirtieth-anniversary rerelease by Strand, the distribution company for much of the NQC.[17] Leading her squad of bad-ass women into the desert in sports cars, killing with her bare hands and deadly Aikido moves the man who dares challenge her, sneering at heteronormative American society at every turn, Satana's Varla matched Lawless as a role model and was a hit all over again, albeit with a different audience than the all-male one to which *Pussycat* was originally marketed.

The interaction between these films and their queer (and lesbian, at a time when the category was in danger of vanishing into the queer moniker) publics at this mid-decade moment is what interests me here. If my experiences at multiple screenings are any indication, these films were thoroughly consumed, claimed, and reclaimed by a queer audience. But why? I followed a hunch into the past.

In the groundbreaking lesbian-feminist scholarship of the early 1970s, there was a foundational fight to rethink the long-unacknowledged affective, romantic, and sexual relationships of key writers and social actors. Such scholars as Blanche Wiesen Cook, Nancy Cott, Ellen Carol DeBois, Lillian Faderman, Estelle Freedman, Rayna Rapp, Carroll Smith Rosenberg, Nancy Sahli, Catherine R. Stimpson, and many others were key to this scholarship of reclamation. A founding document was Rosenberg's "The Female World of Love and Ritual: Relations between Women in Nineteenth Century America," published in 1971 in the inaugural issue of *Signs*, volume 1, number 1, page 1. Thereafter every new *Signs* and *Feminist Studies* carried revelations that would reorder the past and reorient a sense of lesbian history written on the blank pages of erasure and indifference.

One aspect of that early historical research and literary interpretation was the reclaiming of key spinster couples as lesbians, arguing that these platonic companions had in fact been lovers, sanitized by history and the men who wrote it. One reexamination focused on what had been called the "Boston marriage," a nineteenth-century term for women's romantic friendships that bound couples together in joint households, sometimes for a lifetime. In the new scholarship, close readings of literary texts and archival documents proved the existence of relationships where none had been discerned. At the time, the strategy was controversial: male traditionalists argued there was no "proof" of genital sex, nor could it be asserted retroactively. Nonetheless revisionist scholarship prevailed in repositioning these women within updated notions of relationship structures which today are seen as transparent.

To be sure, these women were not committing murders. Using the same approach, however, I make a different but similarly inspired claim: that in the lethal lesbian films, the proof that the women on screen are lesbians is precisely that they commit murder together. On the screens of the mid-1990s, in other words, killing replaced sex as consummation. Nor is the timing incidental. The first half of the 1990s is a time dominated by anxieties prompted by the AIDS crisis. The death toll of the 1980s had burdened sex with fear; it's entirely possible, then, that sex could no longer provide a catharsis on screen for audiences in the early 1990s. Violence took its place, conveniently filling a vacuum of narrative need.

Violence has a particular history when it comes to lesbianism, one that complicates the genre modification. History, once again, has a lesson to teach, as Lisa Duggan revealed in her essay "The Trials of Alice Mitchell," first published in *Signs* in the summer of 1993, when so many of these films were beginning production. Duggan was investigating a period one hundred years prior to the Parker and Hulme, Papin, and Wuornos slayings, tracing the emergence of lesbianism in the popular press at the end of the nineteenth and early twentieth centuries. Guess what she found there? Murder, she wrote:

> This focus on violence was partly an artifact of the moralizing sensationalism of the press. The late nineteenth century newspaper narratives of lesbian love featured violence as a boundary marker; murders or suicides served to abort the forward progress of the tale, signaling that such erotic love between women was not only tragic but ultimately hopeless. The selective nature of the reports made the exceptional cases of violent conflict among women seem characteristic of female sexual passion. The stories were thus structured to emphasize, ultimately, that no real love story was possible.[18]

The circulation of any story of a woman who killed her lover, or who killed herself over a lover, made for a good early-warning system to prevent such indulgences if women wanted to live. Just as the Parker and Hulme case was a terrific motivator in getting mothers to police their daughters' sexualities, so was the Alice Mitchell case a great device for convincing women to reject any other woman's advances (she might kill you) or attractions (you might kill yourself).

The lethal lesbian genre has something a bit different going on. These films can't be warning women off lesbian desire for their own good, because it's someone else that's getting killed; these women in love are teaming up to kill a third party, not each other, not themselves. Murder, in this sense, may be the Boston marriage of the 1990s, the spinsters sprung from the attic with a knife—or a hunting rifle, like the ones held by the murderous pair of maid (Romaine Bohringer) and postmistress (Isabelle Huppert) in *La Cérémonie* who interrupt a bourgeois family's night at the opera in order to kill them all: blood spills while an aria fills the room.

It may be that lesbianism is literally "in the blood," at least as imagined in this genre of films. In April 1982, at a notorious conference at Barnard College, "Towards a Politics of Sexuality," antipornography forces denounced its speakers, funding was withdrawn, and "pro-sex" women became scapegoats.[19] One of the flash points of the attack was an off-campus panel organized by local women in sympathy with the conference's subject. They wryly dubbed themselves "the lesbian sex mafia" and sought to discuss unacceptable and untraditional sexual practices. One of the panelists was my friend Jewelle Gomez, who spoke about the erotic attraction of blood; she'd go on to publish *The Gilda Stories*, exploring the consciousness of lesbian vampires of African descent from the era of slavery into the future. Gomez thus linked the actual blood of menstruating women to her mythical heroines.

Ah yes, the vampire. That, of course, is the other film genre in which there has long been an appreciation of lesbian murder, from Stephanie Rothman's groundbreaking *Velvet Vampire* (1971) and Harry Kumel's cult hit *Daughters of Darkness* (*Les levres rouges*, 1971), with the late Delphine Seyrig, to Tony Scott's *The Hunger* (1983), with Catherine Deneuve and Susan Sarandon, a lesbian bar staple for decades.[20] These films provided audiences with a glimmer of fatally erotic fascination years before Buffy or *Twilight*.

Nor has the lesbian vampire remained the province of cinematic fictions. Consider the Australian scholar Deb Verhoeven's analysis of a true-crime vampire story in "Biting the Hand That Breeds." The case occurred in 1991, though it was little reported outside of Australia. Verhoeven tells of an alleged "lesbian vampire" and the four women who killed under her spell. "Vampire killer Tracey Wigginton was obsessed with a sickening desire to perform oral sex on her lesbian lovers while they were menstruating," read one tabloid, typical of the general media response to the "sickening" murder.[21]

I do not intend to finish with the age-old figure of the vampire. I want to recall, not the agent, but the essence. Blood itself was central to early lesbian culture in the 1970s and early 1980s. Blood was celebrated in feminist and lesbian art and poetry—until the arrival of AIDS caused everything to change. Then blood became instead a symbol of contagion, a sign of mortality, a carrier of death, a fatal flaw. The new plague took precedence, and old meanings disappeared under the tidal wave of death. These films of the 1990s announced on screen, presumably without meaning to, that blood was back with a new set of meanings: bloodshed became the new form of lesbian courtship, murder the new foreplay.

In 1977 the Greek American poet Olga Broumas published her collection of poems *Beginning with O* in the Yale Younger Poets series to instant acclaim and notoriety. Broumas celebrated blood in her poems, as in this one, celebrating lesbian passion in the public streets of the metropolis:

where red is a warning, and men
threaten each other with final violence: *I will drink
your blood.* Your kiss

is for them
a sign of betrayal, your red
lips suspect[22]

It was menstrual blood that Broumas was celebrating, and it's startling today to realize how very brief the fluid's revival as a cultural totem actually was; the attention was limited to feminism of the 1970s, when films and songs and articles sought to redeem menstruation as a female cycle to be claimed, not shamed.[23] With the advent of AIDS, blood ceased to be recognized as a female essence.

In the cycle of lethal lesbian films in the 1990s, it was not menstrual blood, nor a lover's blood, nor that of an enemy on the battlefield that was being spilled; rather the blood inevitably belonged to a female enforcer of repression, a mother substitute, or anyone who threatened a couple with separation. If they interfere, they pay with their blood. It's a horror movie of sorts, a *Carrie* for dykes. These new blood sisters did what Broumas wrote then that only men did: they vowed, "I will drink your blood." Killing together made them into blood sisters forever; even Corky and Violet, in their happy ending, drove off in a 4×4 that's blood red.

In the cycle of lethal lesbian films that I've examined here, the haunting figure of the pathological lesbian killer has been rescued from historical neglect and social isolation, given a partner and even a celebration. But, again, why? Given the timing of the genre, fixed between complex coordinates—shifts in global alignments, independent film developments in neo-noir and neoviolence, the influence of true-crime stories, and the pop culture spin on lesbian chic—there are multiple signs in play. Perhaps the films constitute a sign that lesbians have become dangerous enough to take seriously. Perhaps they are cautionary tales warning what lesbians might do if they stopped processing long enough to get in touch with their anger.

Or else, in the age of queer-positive, out-of-the-closet lesbianism, it may be that something from the past is beckoning, unrepressed, rising once again to the surface to claim attention: a desire to act out, against respectability, against the social tolerance of the cleaned-up, well-mannered lesbian. It's the desire to be an outlaw again that these films detect and celebrate. In that sense, they restore to lesbian viewers a sense of the once omnipresent risk and criminality, lost in the shift to the acceptable, well-regulated lesbian life. As if *The L Word* girls took up reading *Hothead Paisan* to refresh their palate.

The teams of lesbian killers in these films were built to satisfy a range of fantasies, seductive in their mixture of desire and disaster but ambiguous in their ultimate message. For all the celebration and pleasure taken in their bravura actions, there are certainly dangers too in the redeployment of such figures in the notoriously uncontrollable world of popular culture. Lesbians, like gay men and transgendered persons, are overwhelmingly the targets of violence, not the perpetrators. The films in the lethal lesbian genre reverse the actual power dynamics by which lesbians are more likely, outside the movie theater, to be murdered than be murderous. In that sense, the films invert actual power relations at the risk of camouflaging them.

The explosion of the genre in a scant half decade is a testimony to the extreme pressures set loose in society by the open proclamations and demonstrations of lesbian identities and eroticisms, freeing both progressive and deeply regressive responses into the public sphere. Insofar as the uncanny is set loose in these films, it would be provident to recall the pleasures and dangers of the uncanny, in literature as well as in religion and society.[24] And its limits.

Aileen Wuornos continued to haunt public culture and lesbian imagination long after the other movies had passed into the half-life of DVD.[25] Then glamour returned in force. Patty Jenkins's *Monster* dramatized the life of Aileen Wuornos, with Charlize Theron cast as Aileen. Nothing remotely like the orange-suited woman of fury seen ranting in the courtroom in the Broomfield–Churchill documentary, Theron was widely praised for her performance and for her embodiment of the tragic woman. The film failed to take Aileen's side entirely, transferring audience sympathy from her to an about-to-be-murdered man in one scene and in other ways. Still, it conveyed the pathos of her life: she really was turned in to the police by her lover Selby Wall, replaying the betrayals of her youth, and it illuminated the class aspects of her story.

Monster opened in 2003. By then Aileen Wuornos was dead, executed by the state of Florida on October 9, 2002. The timing of her execution led to her being exploited yet again: her death became a successful prop for tough-on-crime Governor Jeb Bush's reelection campaign. And it certainly helped *Monster*'s Academy Award campaign. Aileen Wuornos, the off-screen original, was punished with death, made into an example, a deterrent, a scapegoat. She had to be literally extinguished so that dubious men might safely travel the Florida highways again, so that powerful men could sleep at night, so that other women didn't go getting any ideas. The governor won his second term. And Charlize Theron won her Oscar.

Notes

This text derives from original lectures delivered between 1994 and 1999. Elements of this chapter appeared as "Lethal Lesbians," *Village Voice*, April 25, 1995; "Introduction to U.S. Edition," *Parker and Hulme: A Lesbian View*, ed. Julie Glamuzina and Alison J. Laurie (Ithaca: Firebrand Books, 1995), i–xi; and in German, "Lethal Lesbians," *girls-gangsguns: Zwischen Exploitation-Kino und Underground*, ed. Carla Despineux and Verena Mund (Marburg, Germany: Schüren Verlag, 2000), 127–50.

1. In 1994 the Pacific Film Archive in Berkeley invited me to participate in its "Scary Women" summer series. The double bill I chose of Paul Verhoeven's *Basic Instinct* (1992) and Russ Meyer's *Faster, Pussycat! Kill! Kill!* (1965) set off the ideas that evolved into this chapter. Thanks to Edith Kramer and Kathy Geritz for the invitation.

2. While I used the term in my original lectures, I must offer a tip of the hat here to Amy Villarejo for her fine redeployment of the phrase in "The Creature from the Black Lagoon."

3. Jackie Stacey was the first film scholar to call out the subtext in "Desperately Seeking Difference." See her *Star-Gazing* for her early theories of film and spectatorship.

4. This show was widely considered the most notorious television of its era, a time when cable was in its infancy, gay and lesbian characters weren't part of the TV landscape, and coming out on national television was certain career suicide.

5. See YouTube, http://www.youtube.com/watch?v=wtC4hhd4ZoI, and part 2 at www.youtube.com/watch?v=CT3R55posvU. Watch out for 1980s hair.

6. Casares would later be linked to the singer kd lang before becoming a celebrity in her own right as a club owner in newly glam South Beach. For details on the rumors, see Jonathan Van Meter's profile, "Who's That Girl?," *New York*, July 27, 1998. In "The Bitch Is Back," *New York*, October 19, 1998, he followed up with Sandra Bernhard: "In Bernhard's 1993 book of essays and short stories, *Love, Love and Love* . . . there is a nakedly honest, moving piece very obviously about Madonna. 'She never loved me,' it begins. 'I swear to you nothing ever happened.'" Both are archived on the nymag.com website. Casares was widely compared to an earlier Cuban lesbian, Mercedes de Acosta. For more on her, see Gever, *Entertaining Lesbians*, chapter 5, "In Retrospect: Legends of Mercedes de Acosta and Company"; White, "Black and White."

7. There were many such articles in those early days, including Lindsy Van Gelder, "Lipstick Lesbians," *Los Angeles Times Magazine*, March 15, 1992.

8. I deliberately credit the screenwriters on these films, as the screenplays are in both instances key to the films' success and notoriety.

9. For an excellent perspective on the film and its reception, with the hindsight of a ten-year delay, see Dawn Taylor's review of its commemorative DVD release on DVD Journal, www.dvdjournal.com/reviews/t/thelmaandlouise.shtml. Geena Davis acknowledged reading Susan Faludi's *Backlash: The Undeclared War against American Women* to understand the extreme reactions from columnists, given that only one murder took place in the film, compared to the many murders (by male characters, of course) in the rest of that season's theatrical releases. She also disclosed that they tried to require any mainstream press interviewers to read *Backlash* before they'd agree to do the interview. Geena Davis, personal communication, 1992.

10. The San Francisco press reported on disruptions and protests throughout. See, for example, Joan Smith, "Film Forges Ahead Despite Gay Protest: 30 Arrested; Producers Balk at Script Changes," *San Francisco Examiner*, April 30, 1991; Rob Morse, "Catherine Did It, but You Won't Care," *San Francisco Examiner*, March 17, 1992 (four days before the film's opening).

11. Hart, "Chloe Liked Olivia." (Also see chapters 7–8.) Her astute analysis of narrative strategies identifies, for example, why Brad Pitt appears in *Thelma and Louise*: he is disavowing lesbianism.

12. For documentaries that explore the chilling details of the Aileen Wuornos case, see Nick Broomfield, *Aileen Wuornos: The Selling of a Serial Killer* (1992); Nick Broomfield and Joan Churchill, *Aileen: Life and Death of a Serial Killer* (2003). For a fine analysis and comparison with Jenkins's movie *Monster*, see Horeck, "From Documentary to Drama."

13. Basilio, "Corporal Evidence."

14. DVD commentary track.

15. See Glamuzina and Laurie, *Parker and Hulme*. A comprehensive historical investigation of the original Christchurch crime and court case of 1954, the book was originally published in New Zealand in 1991 by the New Women's Press. The authors had unprecedented access to the sealed court records, but they also conducted original research on the period through interviews with lesbians who had come of age in the shadow of the trial. According to Laurie, the authors and publisher were in negotiation with Jane Campion's producer, Jan Chapman, for the film rights when Peter Jackson and his wife, Frances Walsh, secured funding for a screenplay based on the very same story, while denying any debt to Glamuzina and Laurie's research. Note that Jackson was then known primarily for another matricide film, *Dead Alive* (*Braindead*, 1992), a splatter film in which a son kills his zombified mother in order to be with his girlfriend. He's a hero, not a criminal, and there's no outcry, but of course it's fantasy horror.

16. Ironically, they killed "the wrong mother," as some newspaper accounts re-

ported. While they murdered Pauline's mother, it was Juliet's mother who was causing their separation on account of her affair, pending divorce, and return to England.

17. Satana prided herself on breaking through the racial barriers of the time: part Apache and part Japanese, she stood 5'9" without boots or stilettos. She was discovered at the Pink Pussycat strip club, but she had a Go-Q belt in Aikido and did all her own stunts. After her death, newspapers revealed that she'd been imprisoned in the Manzanar camp with her family during World War II. See my interview with Satana, "What's Up, 'Pussycat'?"

18. Duggan, *Sapphic Slashers*.

19. See the landmark anthology edited by Carol Vance, *Pleasure and Danger*, for full details of this conference and its period, and my own essay, "Feminism and Sexuality in the Eighties."

20. In interviews at the time of the release of *Go Fish*, Rose Troche and Guinevere Turner spoke of making the film because they were sick of lesbians being shown so often as vampires instead of flesh-and-blood women. For more on reclaiming the lesbian vampire, see Weiss, *Vampires and Violets*.

21. I presented my *Lethal Lesbians* show at the film festival in Brisbane, the very town in which Tracey Wigginton had lived and murdered. I couldn't help but notice a bit of audience discomfort. Afterward, though, the festival director, Anne Demy-Geroe, took me on a detour to dinner, driving down a dark lane, through a park, finally stopping with a flourish: Look, here is the very boathouse where Tracey Wigginton took her victim and killed him! Hometown pride, then, places Brisbane in the unlikely pantheon (with Christchurch, New Zealand; Daytona Beach, Florida; and Le Mans, France) of lesbian murder sites. For more on this case, see the incisive, well-informed essay by Deb Verhoeven, "Biting the Hand That Breeds."

22. Broumas, "Sleeping Beauty," 62.

23. Blood was explored widely in the 1970s despite its disappearance so soon after. In 1974, for instance, the filmmaker Linda Feferman made *Linda's Film on Menstruation*, a short, sharp satire that doubled as an educational film. In the same period of 1973–74, using blood and tempura paint and natural elements like rooster feathers, the late artist Ana Mendieta made a series of drawings, photographs, and Super-8mm performance pieces that are now identified as "Untitled," with subtitles like "Sweating Blood," "Blood Tracks," and "Self-Portrait with Blood." These are not isolated cases: blood was widely reclaimed in feminist work of this era.

24. While the uncanny is beyond the scope of this essay, see Castle, *The Female Thermometer*, as well as essays in "The Return of the Uncanny," special issue of *Paradoxa: Studies in World Literary Genres* 3.3–4 (1997), ed. Michael A. Arnzen, in particular Lesley Stern's "I Think, Sebastian, Therefore I . . . Somersault."

25. Artists across mediums have paid tribute to Wuornos: Deb Margolin, Lois Weaver, and Peggy Shaw, Split Britches Co., *Lesbians Who Kill* (1992), and in 1994–95 Millie Wilson's installation *Not a Serial Killer* and Tammy Rae Carland's *Lady Out-*

laws and Faggot Wannabes. Lynda Hart dedicated her *Fatal Women* book to Aileen Wuornos and "all the women who have been vilified, pathologized, and murdered for defending themselves by any means necessary." Music tributes include Diamanda Galás's version of "Iron Lady" (1998); Carla Lucero's opera *Wuornos*, a "tragic love story of operatic proportions" (2001); Bitch's "Aileen Wuornos" (2006). Galás claims Wuornos as "a huge hero" and has recognized Tura Satana as one also.

16

When Monte Bramer and Lesli Klainberg's moving documentary, *Paul Monette: The Brink of Summer's End*, played on the cable channel Cinemax in the summer of 1997, it established a record of sorts. Frolicking around a European hotel room, the eulogized author can be seen (if only for a few seconds) playfully wagging his cock for the benefit of his boyfriend's camcorder. It is a significant moment not for reasons of censorship, though that was usually the sinister presence attending projects like this in the 1990s, but for its departure from the usual sober tone of contemporary documentaries on gay or lesbian figures.

Paul Monette: The Brink of Summer's End does a very good job of balancing sainthood against mere-mortal status. Perhaps its job was made easier by Monette's own personality or the checkered quality of his career. Even though the director Monte Bramer and the producer Lesli Klainberg clearly want to celebrate both Monette's life and his work, they resist any urge to gloss over his failings. We learn that his early books were popular but trashy reads suitable for a day at Fire Island, that he betrayed the trust of his first lover by involving himself in a serious "extramarital" affair, and that he chose to spend years of his life writing never-produced scripts for the money he required to fulfill his class-envy ambitions, a holdover from his youth as a prep school scholarship student. None of this is exactly the stuff of nobility.

Where *Paul Monette* does enact the genre to which it clearly belongs is in its elegiac pacing, its constant sense of hindsight vision, its respectable and laudatory witnesses who fuse our approval of them into a second-hand worship of their late friend and brother, and in the obvious postmortem intentions that drive the footage being shot before our (and his) very eyes while Monette was still alive.

As a result of cancer and AIDS, a virtual genre has sprung up around the celebration of dearly departeds of sufficient fame to attract production financing. There's a larger genre too, of biographical films in general that target gay or lesbian figures of note, even if still alive or long-lived. And while the category doesn't yet have the status of longer-term subjects, such as Holocaust documentaries, the gay biography does already exhibit some shared elements: reverence, injustice, martyrdom.

Does that sound too cynical? Never fear. I believe in the worth of these films and their value in setting history straight (or better yet, queer) while attending to the necessary restitution of faith and dignity in their protagonists and bereaved communities. But the fact that there's now a mini-genre makes this an apt moment to stand back and take stock. As the San Francisco Lesbian and Gay Film Festival reminded us recently with a tribute, this year signals the twentieth anniversary of three landmark documentaries: *Word Is Out, Gay USA,* and *In the Best Interests of the Children.* While none was a biography of a single individual, and while all of their protagonists were still alive and seemingly well at the time of the films (such health being in itself a sign of an earlier and more innocent era), the films collectively signaled a coming of age of gay and lesbian cinema and a coming together of community.

The 1970s was the era of positive images: make "us" look good for "them." This trio of films was aimed at both gay and lesbian audiences and the mainstream. After all, a lot was at stake. Stop taking children away from lesbian mothers, pleaded *In the Best Interests of the Children.* Homosexuals deserve the same respect as anyone else, argued *Word Is Out.* We're gay and we're proud and there are millions of us, celebrated *Gay USA.* This was the era of "affirmation" films, to use the term of the British critic Richard Dyer. They carried a heavy burden: to affirm our identity to ourselves and at the same time to carry a message of strength and tolerance to the wider society.

Of course, this burden has yet to be unshouldered. It may be that the collective "queer ego" is unlikely ever to gather the strength—in the modern climate of alternating liberal tolerance and homophobic backlash—to move beyond the reinforcement that gazing upon venerated iconic figures in public can supply. Indeed, as Rob Epstein remarked, "How wonderful that we're now at the point that Cinemax wants to be involved with a Paul Monette biography."[1] For critics like this one, however, with a wary eye always fixed on the dangers of uncritical acceptance and the manufacture of heroes and heroines, 1997 is also a time to take stock and examine the cinematic history of the laudatory biography and the pros and cons of its flourishing.

The contemporary elegiac biography can be said to have arrived with an event of far-reaching consequences on the morning of November 27, 1978, in San Francisco, when city supervisor Dan White climbed through a City Hall window and assassinated Mayor George Moscone and the openly gay supervisor, Harvey Milk. *The Times of Harvey Milk* (1984), one of the landmark films of the gay documentary movement by anybody's standards, was made by Rob Epstein and Richard Schmiechen. Rob had been the youngest member of the Mariposa Film Group that made *Word Is Out*. Interestingly, he recalls, "The film didn't start out to be a strictly biographical film. *Word Is Out* was all about the personal aspects of being gay and working through coming out and through internalized oppression and about embracing one's own gay identity. But meanwhile, right around the corner, the reaction to all that was building: the backlash." Epstein had actually started work on a film about the Briggs Initiative while Milk was alive. In fact it was his role in defeating that historic homophobic legislation (the do-you-want-a-homo-teaching-your-kid? campaign) that brought him to Epstein's attention. "I guess in my ignorance I didn't understand his significance as a politician." After Epstein hooked up with the producer Richard Schmiechen and after Harvey Milk was assassinated, the film started to take shape as a documentary focusing on Milk as "a man of his times."

Made collaboratively with money raised in part from work-in-progress screenings for gay and lesbian communities coast to coast, *The Times of Harvey Milk* may paradoxically have succeeded so well precisely because of the richness of its mixed genesis. More than any other biographical documentary, it opens up the examination of its central character to include the signal events of his era: the gay rights movement, the struggle for civil rights, the backlash, and the start of "family values" and Christian coalition–style political movements. Its great power comes from the skill with which it involves the viewer in a sophisticated historical analysis along with a heart-rending elegy for a demonstrably extraordinary human being. Two factors, of course, helped this mission along: first, unlike many other subjects, Milk was a public person who was constantly shaping his own image and projecting himself onto the public stage; second, Milk was assassinated both for being gay and for being part of a larger progressive agenda that left behind a wide range of witnesses.

Isaac Julien was just starting his own filmmaking career when *Harvey Milk* was released, but he remembers being incredibly moved by it: "I adored that film," he recalls.[2] Still, when he began his own examination of Langston Hughes soon after, he took a very different approach, resulting in *Looking for Langston* (1989), its very title marking it as a provisional alternative to the definitive genre. In part, he recalls, this was possible because Hughes was so well known in the United States as a poet, yet paradoxically so unknown as a gay man due to the efforts of the Hughes estate to "protect" his good name. "Because there was such a controversy and such secrecy over his sexual identity, and it was such a touchy subject for his estate, the selling point for the film became not to embark on a teleological approach to his life and origins, but rather to start from the point of the imaginary."

When Julien and the producer Mark Nash went on to do a biography of the legendary revolutionary Frantz Fanon in 1996, however, they found they couldn't do the same thing; not enough people knew who Fanon was, so they had to resort to traditional documentary devices like interviewing the family. Julien observed, "I've always tried not to have a hagiographic approach to portraits or biographies, but I think the audience sometimes actually wants that approach, and that's where one gets into trouble over how to satisfy both the audience's desires and your own. Because the last thing I want is to end up with a completely celebratory approach to icons. Who needs another black male hero? I don't think so."

Or do we? Today, in the midst of what Richard Dyer has termed "post-affirmation" films, it's interesting to see what time has done to our concepts of biography and how different filmmakers have coped with new sets of challenges and opportunities. Several recent biographical documentaries seek to inscribe the lives of Audre Lorde, Marlon Riggs, and Martina Navratilova into history. *A Litany for Survival: The Life and Work of Audre Lorde* (1995), directed by Michelle Parkerson and Ada Gay Griffin, was begun when Lorde was still alive but diagnosed with terminal cancer. With Lorde's cooperation and that of her partner, Parkerson and Griffin began a sort of emergency salvage operation to videotape as many interviews as possible with Lorde reflecting on her life and work.[3] Years in the making, the result is a magnificent tribute to this extraordinary figure, who was one of the major poets and essayists of our time, and a key figure both for the lesbian-feminist movement and for those pre-Stonewall lesbians who felt sidelined by feminism. Lorde was an oracular figure, a mode that the interviews handily capture. But the film derives much of its power from its historical material, featuring archival footage of Lorde in younger days, expounding with her signature boldness on poetry, writing, race issues, sexuality, illness, and the other themes she sounded throughout her life.

The documentary has a harder time, ironically, filling in the facts of her life that are the mainstay of other such biographies. Because her partner at the time of her death was not the woman with whom she'd spent much of her life, the film has peculiar lacunae. One can only assume that the filmmakers had to honor Lorde's surviving partner by leaving her predecessor out of the film—an understandable strategy, but one that damages their documentary's narrative drive and may leave the uninformed viewer confused about the sequence of Lorde's life.

Karen Everett's approach to the life of her former teacher, the documentarian Marlon Riggs, takes the opposite approach to a different partnership controversy. When Riggs made the video that earned him his fame, *Tongues Untied* (1989), he closed the piece with the following motto: "Black men loving black men is the revolutionary act." The epigram turned out to be just as controversial as the film. Some thought he was being essentialist, treating race as an all-determining category; others thought he was being too individualistic, annexing the statement without crediting its actual author, Joe Beam; still others began to sniff around Riggs's personal life enough to criticize him for hypocrisy, since he turned out to have a long-term relationship with his white lover, Jack Vincent.

One of the great contributions of *I Shall Not Be Removed: The Life of Marlon Riggs* (1996), which Everett and the producer Evelyn C. White made with incredibly scant resources, is the restoration of Vincent to his rightful place as the official domestic partner of Marlon Riggs. No longer an abstract figure manipulated by strangers' debates, he emerges as a heroically unassuming partner and a central presence in Riggs's life, along with Riggs's mother and grandmother. The documentary covers the high points of Riggs's video career, including both clips from his work and clips from the television coverage of the right-wing attacks on him that accompanied the National Endowment for the Arts debates. Everett brought the work relentlessly up to date too, with hard-to-take footage of Riggs in the hospital and at home on his deathbed. His death shapes his life's narrative, not only because it always does in such biographies of those felled while still in their prime, but also because Riggs acquired a public dimension to his life only in his last years. Even then, like Paul Monette, he's essentially a private artist thrust by the AIDS epidemic into the public eye—not, like Lorde or Milk, charismatic leaders whose mortality instead removed them from the public's embrace.

Martina: Farewell to a Champion, which premiered in the United States at the 1997 New Festival in New York City, distinguishes itself by its focus on a subject who is still, happily, very much alive and healthy. The producer Clare Beavan landed what must have been many a lesbian producer's dream assignment when she apparently convinced Martina Navratilova to participate in a biopic for the BBC. Handsomely produced in a mainstream television format, this biography is clearly made with the most mainstream audience in mind, but it still manages to pay equal attention to Navratilova's tennis and her lesbian identity. There's something charming about other tennis stars (Chris Evert, Billie Jean King) talking about the hard time she's had. And something chilling about seeing a clip from the infamous Judy Nelson palimony court case, the event that upset the careful balance Navratilova had always maintained for her image as a serious tennis player who happened to be a lesbian. Navratilova herself comes across as an extremely sympathetic figure, not only comfortable in her identity but open to what the rest of her life, postretirement, will be like.

With so many film biographies in release and in production, it may seem that there's no problem at all about how they turn out and how they view their subjects. Not quite. Allow me for a moment to revisit *The Times of Harvey Milk* a decade later. It's still moving. But at a recent screening of the film for a group of twenty-somethings educated by years of gay activism and "queer theory," it was ruled deficient. Where was Harvey Milk's sexuality? Did he have to be cleaned up to earn hetero-respect? Why wasn't his lover in the film? Was it true, as one article argued, that he used to go to the Castro's legendary sex clubs until he decided to run for supervisor? Was this a whitewash? What was Harvey Milk really like, then, if the protective veils could be stripped away and we were allowed to see him in all his public and private guises? And why weren't we allowed to?

There's another film about Audre Lorde that would seem the perfect answer to these new generational questions. *The Body of the Poet* (1995), by the British filmmaker Sonali Fernando, follows in Julien's footsteps by imagining and dramatizing Lorde's life and era—but Fernando also inserts quasi-vérité scenes of women debating the wisdom of making a film about Lorde at all, of valorizing any one woman to such an extent. What's the big deal about Audre Lorde, asks one fiery lesbian unwilling to be pulled into any scenario of veneration.

In the end, I suppose, we are left with the perennial debate over how we want our heroes or heroines: writ large, perfect in all ways, fit for monuments and idol worship, or flawed, human, mortal, imperfect enough to inspire us to think we can follow their example. I'm a postmodernist at heart: I want my heroes and heroines to be shown in all their extravagant and exposed details, even if that includes feet of clay; I'm happy to have them in fragments, in sketches of half-remembered memory and fantasy, because that's how I read my own life. But, at minimum, I want to have them. And if that means that there's a genre of films that write them into history without the cracks, without the secrets, well, I'll make do with that until something else comes along. After all, heterosexual icons still get shown that way most of the time.[4]

Notes

This chapter originally appeared as "When the Saints Come Marching In," OUT 6.2 (1997), 65–67.

1. All Rob Epstein's quotations are from personal communications, 1997.

2. All Isaac Julien's quotations are from personal communications, 1997.

3. Two recent documentaries add to the record: *Audre Lorde—The Berlin Years 1984 to 1992* and *The Edge of Each Other's Battles: The Vision of Audre Lorde.*

4. Of course, queer biographical documentaries have gone right on their merry way deifying their subjects in fairly traditional fashion ever since. So much for critical intervention.

A QUEER AND PRESENT DANGER

The Death of New Queer Cinema?

17 *Boys Don't Cry, Being John Malkovich*, and *The Talented Mr. Ripley*: all U.S. hits in 1999, all solidly released as mainstream art house fare, all lavishly praised, rewarded, and awarded for their originality, nerve, and flair. Could they possibly owe a debt to the pioneering spirit of the New Queer Cinema nearly a decade earlier?

Back then, the big news was the arrival of NQC; by 2000, the film that would seem most fit to qualify for category inclusion, *Boys Don't Cry*, directed by Kimberly Peirce and produced by Christine Vachon, had become one of the most acclaimed films of the year. Based on the best true-crime story since *In Cold Blood* made Capote famous, *Boys Don't Cry* told the tale of a small-town boy from the land of country-western music who transgressed the rules of gender and finance and paid with his life. The fact that he turned out to have been a biological female who changed clothing, haircut, name, and town to pass as male was central to the case and, by now, the legend; the fact that he had forged checks, less so. Passing checks, passing as male: a natural connection of aspiration at work. Not only had Brandon Teena started life as Teena Brandon, but he'd won girls over with his special brand of romantic charm, sorely lacking in the male of the species in the backwaters of America.

Critical raves poured in, from the Fédération Internationale de la Presse Cinématographique Award at the London Film Festival in 1999 to the breathlessly awaited Oscar nominations of 2000, the moment when *Boys Don't Cry* made history of a sort by winning an Oscar for its luminous star, Hilary Swank. Independent Spirit Award nominations similarly lauded the film, recognizing its first-time director, Kimberly Peirce, as well as Swank and costar Chlöe Sevigny. Critics' associations throughout the United States bestowed honors on director and cast. Peirce even picked up a Five Continents Award at the European Film Awards. And no less an authority than PopcornQ, the pioneering and immensely popular queer film website, polled its visitors and named *Boys Don't Cry* one of the top queer films of 1999.[1]

Insofar as Peirce's true-life saga of Brandon Teena (a would-be transman who died as a biological woman, murdered for passing as a man by the men who had befriended Brandon but despised Teena) can be counted as the timely flowering of NQC's early shoots, then the movement may really have arrived, hitting the big time at last. But not so fast: the story is more complicated than that, its conclusions less clear-cut, the movement itself in question, if not in total collapse.

From the beginning, *New Queer Cinema* was a term more successful for a moment than a movement. It was meant to catch the beat of a new kind of film- and video-making that was fresh, edgy, low-budget, inventive, unapologetic, sexy, and stylistically daring. Creation is ultimately never explicable. Elements can be identified, yes, but not how they came together, or why, or when. And even when we see something happen, there's rarely an explanation that satisfies. Why me? Why now? Even those caught up in the maelstrom are unlikely to know the answer. Similarly, when it's all over, there's never an adequate reason for why it had to end so soon. So it was with NQC and its short sweet climb from radical impulse to niche market.

In the 1980s Hollywood was too busy manufacturing blockbusters to take much notice of the independent world. That changed famously in 1989, when Steven Soderbergh's *Sex, Lies, and Videotape* won the audience award at Sundance and proceeded to fill the bank accounts of an upstart distribution company by the name of Miramax. The queer moment for independent film was different. It owes its genesis not to money but to repression, namely the savage attacks by U.S. right-wing politicians on government funding for such films as Marlon Riggs's *Tongues Untied* (1989) and Todd Haynes's *Poison* (1991). The bad politics made for great reviews, respectable box office (not yet called "grosses"), and an impassioned following.

More features followed, laying claim to the same category: *Young Soul Rebels* (1991), *Swoon* (1992), *Go Fish* (1994), *All over Me* (1997), *Lilies* (1996), *The Delta* (1996), *The Watermelon Woman* (1996), and dozens more. These works spawned a whole sector of queer filmdom—not just genres but viewers, distributors, and venues. By the late 1990s there were well over a hundred film festivals billed as LGBT or queer: thus, in contrast to the integration of the most successful work into theatrical sectors, the explosion of queer film-making and video was screening largely in an enclave circuit without other options for distribution—unless Strand Releasing or Wolfe Video picked something up for theatrical or home release.

There were downsides too, and they came along fast. First, the sheer volume diluted the quality. For critics, the consequences could be dispiriting, as queer audiences flocked to films every bit as mediocre as those pulling in heterosexual dollars at multiplexes down the road. Soon enough, the draw of the queer dollar and the aura of a queer fashion began to attract heterosexual directors eager to make their mark and skilled enough to do it well, very well, especially when returning to that age-old trope: male director, lesbian subject, that tired formula.

Queerer than thou? Identity politics doesn't meld well with market considerations, so the new films dumped the politics overboard. Love stories, coming-out stories, and star-crossed romance tales sweetly proliferated, all executed in a normative dramatic style and deeply soothing to audiences long deprived of any such thing. Soon enough, distributors were blaming the glut of product for the receding public: lesbian and gay ticket-buyers were no longer reliable and could no longer be counted on to rush to the box office in support of queer work. By 1999 the problem had become so acute that the PopcornQ site started a first-weekend club to try to fill seats for queer films.[2]

But what's a queer film? The films and their receptions in the late 1990s have rearranged all such definitions. Bill Condon's *Gods and Monsters* (1998), for instance, was such a crossover hit with both queer audiences and straight crowds that it propelled its star, Sir Ian McKellen, into an Oscar nomination and won writer-director Condon a best adapted screenplay Oscar and a thriving future career.[3] The film, which emotionally excavated the life of James Whale (creator of the *Frankenstein* movies), crossed over in part because of its Hollywood history theme. I suspect it was also helped by the homophobia of the Brendan Fraser character, the gardener, who provided an identificatory figure for audience members suffering from the same ailment. And, of course, by the participation of such a class act as McKellen. Finally, though, I'd wager that *Gods and Monsters*, a film I dearly loved, could achieve success beyond the previous run of queer films not only for these reasons but also because it was set in a particular corner of the modern edition of *Brideshead*-land, a place in the imaginary not-so-distant past where British accents of the proper

rank and vintage can still be heard and money is still required for entry—
except, à la Sirk, for the gardener.

The same American affection for upstairs-downstairs dramas helped John
Maybury's exquisite *Love Is the Devil: Study for a Portrait of Francis Bacon*
(1998); the box-office triad of high art, rough trade, and a tragic death rarely
fails, however queer the particular application. It's enough to turn me cynical,
yet I wouldn't give up Tilda Swinton's fabulous turn as Muriel Belcher, the
barmaid-proprietor of Bacon's favorite club, The Colony Room, nor the film's
many other visual and narrative pleasures, just because it appealed to some
viewers for the wrong, retro reasons.

Richard Kwietniowski's *Love and Death on Long Island* (1997) took the
category into a different direction. Based on the Gilbert Adair novel, it cast
John Hurt as an aged British writer who becomes inexplicably besotted with
an American B-movie star, played by Jason Priestley. When Hurt flies to Long
Island and begins to stalk the object of his affection, the film has fun tracing the intersecting arcs of class and desire onto the myopic, unsuspecting
landscape of suburban America. Its core of defeated desire never quite lives
up to the *Gods and Monsters* pathos, despite an inventive plot that taps into
celebrity worship while playing for mainstream laughs. Yet it was certainly
something fresh on the screen that year.

The three films combined to open up an Anglo beachhead in the NQC, all
well crafted, supremely literate, and adept at translating upper-crust tales of
rough-trade attraction into a fanciful twist of narrative collusion. In retrospect,
two other films, neither Anglicized but both contemporaneous, gilded the lily
and therefore also sounded the death knell of NQC: one was Wong Kar-Wai's
Happy Together (1997), the other, Lisa Cholodenko's *High Art* (1998). Both could
tear your heart out with one hand tied behind their respective backs.

Indeed tragedy seems paradoxically to have been the favored tone of much
of NQC.[4] Wong's *Happy Together* illustrated how brilliantly a heterosexual director could capture the essence and nuance of queer romance, lust, jealousy,
and rage. Cholodenko's *High Art* defied all prior taboos of contemporary lesbian cinema by showing the dark side of lesbian society and having the nerve
to go for an unhappy ending. But it also did something else: like *Boys Don't
Cry*, it made stars of its actresses instead of the other way around. Ally Sheedy
launched a much deserved comeback after winning awards and praise for
her daring role, while Radha Mitchell showed she could play American, and
Patricia Clarkson, who played German so well, expanded a cult following into
a nonstop star career.

Such films could have signaled a moment of triumphant consolidation for the NQC, yet the opposite would seem to suggest itself: the NQC has become so successful that it has dispersed itself in any number of elsewheres. Lacking the concentrated creative presence and focused community responsiveness of its origin moment, NQC has become just another product line pitched at one particular type of discerning consumer. At a time when casting has become essential to getting independent films financed and produced, it's clear why actors have to be involved. On the other hand, it's the runaway success of the NQC films that has turned them into such welcome vehicles for actors, reversing the trend that in the past saw actors turn away from films that in any way pushed sexual identity into a zone of ambiguity—a move, in other words, from career poison to career honeypot.

And so back again to *Boys Don't Cry*, made at a time when suddenly queer directors could get actors. "We actually got to cast this film," said Christine Vachon, in reference to *Boys Don't Cry*.[5] And cast it they did. Hilary Swank made the audience hold its collective breath at the magnificent, fine-tuned cockiness of her performance. And it was Swank who made the awards juries and audiences hold their breath once more: the boyish Brandon transmuted into sexy babe as Swank showed up in form-hugging dresses, batting her eyelashes and thanking her (then) husband. The good news? That was all acting. The bad news? The same.

In 1998 the Australian director Ana Kokkinos benefited from the trend when she was able to cast an Australian television idol, Alex Dimitriades, as the star of her passionate coming-of-age tale, the gut-wrenching, Greek immigrant family drama *Head On*. One of the first and only films to address the dilemma of queers struggling inside immigrant or ethnic families, *Head On* brilliantly excavated the pain of running straight into undeniable desires that automatically ensure ejection from the family of origin. Sexuality was the taboo, gender an assumption rather than a problematic.

In the old days of NQC, films and videos tended to be filled with friends or lovers of the director or the occasional sympathetic actor who wanted to help put the picture over. Now it's turned out that starring in an LGBT film can be good for one's career!

Boys Don't Cry has another problem fitting into the contemporary NQC canon: it's not about a lesbian. When the real Brandon Teena murder took place, a slew of stories followed in the gay press. One, by the U.S. journalist Donna Minkowitz, took a lot of heat for presenting Brandon as a butch lesbian, an identity roundly rejected by the trans community that turned out en masse for the murder trial. As an earlier documentary, *The Brandon Teena Story* (1998) by Susan Muska and Gréta Olafsdóttir, made clear, Brandon saw himself as a transgendered person (without surgery or T), not as a lesbian and certainly not as a woman. Gender confusion haunts the reviews of the film and even showed up at its big premiere bash at the Toronto International Film Festival, where Lindsay Law, then head of its distributor, Fox Searchlight, rose to offer a toast to Brandon and "her bravery," only to be followed by director Peirce toasting Brandon for letting them film "his story." The same gender confusion reigned when I appeared on television with Roger Ebert to give the film a thumbs-up. Even Ebert, a long-time champion of LGBT films and adventurous cinema in general, was momentarily stymied by the trans pronoun challenge.[6]

It's the murder at the center of *Boys Don't Cry* that links it, perhaps perversely, with *The Talented Mr. Ripley* (1999), another lethal cocktail of covert queerness and killing. Back to back, the two make a new sort of sense. Step out of the cosmopolitan world of big cities at the turn of the millennium, switch time zones into the lockstep past or redneck present, switch identity so that attraction to the same sex comes without the baggage of modern queer sexuality, wander into the land where the U.S. military policy under the Clinton administration (don't ask, don't tell) becomes instead a social habit, and presto, there's a perfect setup for a new cinematic code of conduct: either kill or be killed. Ripley kills; Brandon is killed. Both of them were invented: one by a writer, one by the subject himself. Both based their lives on a driving need to be something they were not (wealthy in the first instance, male in the second). And both characters depended on not being found out, lest the price be death, spilling either one's own blood or someone else's. Ripley becomes, in this scenario, the mirror image of Brandon.

Is either one a New Queer Cinema product? I think not.[7] But I can think of another film entirely that I'd have to nominate for the honor: Spike Jonze's *Being John Malkovich* (1999). Now there's a movie that's all about gender confusion, gender trading, and the kind of identity destabilization brought about by celebrity worship. Its characters are deeply implicated in the project of gender repositioning, a crisis precipitated by the now-familiar device of discovering a portal leading into John Malkovich's brain. As a result Lotte (Cameron Diaz) is bowled over by her unexpected attraction to another woman and immediately assumes she's going to need gender-reassignment surgery, as though lesbianism or becoming butch were beyond the pale, a less sexy alternative. *Malkovich* is just the sort of cheeky and original film that first made

NQC possible. And it's got something neither of these other films can offer, apart from its box-office numbers: it offers a lesbian happy ending, though I never saw a single newspaper review that mentioned it. Hey, I noticed.

Being John Malkovich is a mainstream movie made possible by the advances of NQC. I would have loved to hear the kind of television voice-overs that accompany the awards ceremony in which it might figure say *that*. I can just about imagine the stentorian tone, acknowledging the debt as rewards are bestowed, as though movies followed the traditions of science, rock music, or pharmaceuticals. For truly, madly, deeply, without all that groundbreaking and heart-stopping work of the early days, it's impossible to imagine the existence of the more mainstream films coming along now to play with the same concepts, cast bigger stars, and shuffle the deck for fresh strategies. Don't get me wrong: I'm happy to have them. I'm happy to be part of a new market, really I am. And, yes, I'm working on my ability to synthesize current fashion with my memories of the good old days, a sort of personal millennial strategy to get ready for whatever might be next.

Notes

This chapter originally appeared as "A Queer and Present Danger," *Sight and Sound* 10.3 (2000), 22–25.

1. This article was written within months of the film's being released. By now a veritable publishing industry surrounds Brandon Teena's life and death. See in particular the special section "The *Boys Don't Cry* Debate," with contributions by Michele Aaron, Julianne Pidduck, Patricia White, Judith Halberstam, Lisa Henderson, and Jennifer Devere Brody, published in *Screen* and reprinted in Stacey and Street, *Queer Screen*. Also see Halberstam, *Female Masculinity*.

2. With an increasing glut of films, the opening weekend box office has become the decisive factor in any film's lasting more than a week. Thus it was crucial to get the audience in there immediately if word of mouth were to have any chance to build.

3. Condon would go on to direct *Chicago, Kinsey,* and *Dreamgirls*, as well as to produce the Academy Awards ceremony in 2009.

4. For a detailed rumination on this subject and its intersection with race, see Muñoz, "Dead White." Muñoz would go on to explore questions of racial identities in greater depth in his much-cited *Dis-Identifications*.

5. Christine Vachon, personal communication, 1998.

6. Since this article was published, the body of scholarship on *Boys Don't Cry* has been considerable. At the time of writing, I knew very little apart from what *Boys Don't Cry* relayed in its narrative; by now the historical record has been corrected

to include the others who were murdered: Lisa Lambert and Philip DeVine, who is oddly not in the film at all, probably because his being African American would complicate the three-act story.

7. I've been roundly and rightly criticized for this statement; in my defense, I spend much of the article arguing that virtually *all* the films I discuss were beyond the boundaries of the original NQC. In terms of trans qualifying as queer or postqueer, obviously that's the case. See the conclusion for more recent thoughts on trans cinema.

PART IV

QUEERING A NEW LATIN AMERICAN CINEMA

PREFACE TO A HISTORY

18 We can never tell which subjects will call to us, which regions will draw our attention, which zones of meaning preoccupy our lives. Latin America has had a grip on my imagination since my college years, when I caught limestone fever in Yucatán and briefly thought I'd become a Mesoamerican archaeologist. By the time I returned nearly a decade later to spend months in Ecuador, Bolivia, and Peru, I was already involved in film and meeting filmmakers and curators along the way. Later I'd journey to film festivals in Guadalajara, Havana, and Rio; I'd be invited to speak about film at a Catholic University in Puerto Rico; and I'd get to report for *Variety* from a film festival in Fortaleza, Brazil. I'd return to Havana over and over, for juries and panels, conferences and parties.

If the fit was never easy for a critic making no secret of her lesbianism in the heterosexual, masculinist structures and values of most Latin American film festivals and institutions, life wasn't necessarily any easier in the LGBT circles back home in the United States, where misguided notions of Latin America prevailed. All sorts of Anglo gays and lesbians confidently pronounced judgment on Latin America's LGBT mores, speaking out in reviews, at panels, or in the LGBT press, yet rarely traveling to test their stereotypes against the flesh-and-blood realities. They were more comfortable staying home and pitying those far-off homophobic societies, assuming total repression in the places where I was discovering instead a rich underground of house parties, cafés, ice-cream parlors, and opera circles. Over the years, an insistence on a single standard for the acceptable queer life, as expressed by

LGBT folks in the United States, obscured the actualities of LGBT and queer lives as lived on a daily level rather than in official versions in many parts of Latin America (and the rest of the world).

In the last decade of the twentieth century and the first decade of the twenty-first, that began to change: a New Queer Cinema emerged within the resurgence of energy (and outside interest) in Latin American cinemas, and in fact has provided a crucial counterweight to the drift toward global movie industry norms in national cinemas which once had been the site of innovative, groundbreaking experiments in political and aesthetic oppositionality.

The New Latin America Cinema movement (Latin America's *el nuevo cine latinoamericano*, Brazil's *cinema novo*) had developed in accord with national liberation movements in postwar Latin America, inspired by the example of Italian neorealism in the years following World War II as well as by the French New Wave (*la nouvelle vague*) that shaped the postwar era into an alternative cinema for an alienated populace.[1] Exile was a condition of this period, as filmmakers were denounced, deported, or murdered or escaped. Between 1964 and 1990 Latin America was characterized by coups, kidnappings, and assassinations.[2] The dire situations threatened—and inspired—filmmakers who, in hiding or exile, sustained by underground political groups and by their cultural wing, the *cine clubs*, revolutionized the modes of representations and the very purpose of cinema. It was a thrilling time, but with few exceptions, the films of this time were overwhelmingly heteromasculinist, leaving gender as much as sexuality out of their cinema-style call to arms, very typical of its time in this respect.

The neorealist influence and New Wave aesthetic radicalism shaped a New Latin American Cinema that unified the continent with oppositional energies until democracy finally began to return in the 1980s, when new conditions of production propelled a shift to the popular and commercial. It was then that the issues omitted from earlier cinema—notably gender and sexuality—came into their own, as a return to democracy began to shape alternative political trajectories.

The antecedents for a native New Queer Cinema can be located in earlier Latin American cinemas, both commercial and independent, in which the most interesting narratives and characters were often gay and lesbian. They were often embedded in concerns that predated modern queer concerns or were helmed by an older generation of established, usually heterosexual directors. These early depictions of gay and lesbian characters are often problematic for contemporary viewers, yet they were vitally important in creating a presence on screen where none had been seen previously. Even in the 1970s and 1980s Latin American films often used LGBT characters symbolically, only rarely as figures of interest in their own right. Still, they were present. Gay, lesbian, and transgender characters and narratives, all there, indelibly visible on screen.

These early directors (Mexico's Arturo Ripstein, for example) drew on their own cinephiliac sensibilities and used LGBT characters or narratives symbolically. They were making films to play in international film festivals and art houses and for their national intelligentsia, not usually mainstream or subcultural audiences. Yet they were important to LGBT viewers and communities; in fact, as some of the only screen representations of their times, they were crucial. They may have been supplanted by a queered New Latin American Cinema emergent in the 1990s, but these early films are nonetheless integral to investigations within and across national boundaries.

Traditions and developments vary widely from country to country in Latin America, each with a distinct cinematic history of its own. The early manifestations of an LGBT cinema tended to be exceptions, not movements, and the strongest proponents of a queer sensibility were usually curators or writers, not the filmmakers who had to struggle with financing, equipment access, and professional aspirations tied to industry standards.

Eventually, against formidable odds, a new generation of Latin American filmmakers would come into its own, creating films to be discovered at home as well as on the festival circuit; their emigration was not into exile this time but rather a move to gain access to international resources by virtue of residence, however provisional or nomadic.

Notes

1. Influential Latin Americans traveled to Rome to study at the famed Centro Sperimentale di Cinematografia, established under Mussolini but ironically a laboratory for antifascist filmmaking after the war. These pilgrims adapted the "new realism" to their own countries: Tomás Gutiérrez Alea, Julio García Espinosa, Fernando Birri. Early influences were Alberto Cavalcanti, a Brazilian of Italian origin who learned filmmaking in Europe and carried neorealism back to Latin America, and Luis Buñuel, the famed Spaniard who settled permanently in Mexico City and influenced the Mexican strain of realism. Later Joris Ivens and Chris Marker were strong influences, in solidarity, through their work and material assistance. Many have written about these histories. For my own views, see "An/Other View of New Latin American Cinema." Equally influential aesthetically were the early works of

the French *nouvelle vague,* or New Wave, which offered a way to use cinema to alter perception and perspective, creating a counterculture of the screen well suited to Latin American needs.

2. Few countries were spared. Dictatorships and military juntas dominated their epochs with repression, terror, censorship, torture, and disappearances, most notably, Argentina, 1976–83; Brazil, 1964–85; Chile, 1973–90; Paraguay, 1976–83; and Uruguay, 1973–85.

REFASHIONING MEXICAN SCREEN SEXUALITY

Ripstein, Hermosillo, Leduc

19 In Mexico, the best-known figures to emerge parallel to and following the militant New Latin American Cinema era were the filmmakers Arturo Ripstein and Jaime Humberto Hermosillo, who directed two of the earliest films with serious gay characters: *El lugar sin límites* (*The Place without Limits*, 1977) and *Doña Herlinda y su hijo* (*Doña Herlinda and Her Son*, 1985), respectively. Together with Paul Leduc, whose *Frida: Naturaleza Viva* (*Frida*, 1983) extended their dominion into a partial queering of sacred history, they retrospectively can be seen to have laid the foundation for a New Mexican Queer Cinema.

Ripstein and Hermosillo constitute a complementary oppositionality, their perspectives forged in diametrically divergent positions of sexuality, aesthetics, and location. Arturo Ripstein, born in 1943, was the heterosexual son of a successful commercial movie producer and was himself a protégé of Luis Buñuel. He was born into and raised within Mexico City's artistic and financial elite, and his cinematic obsessions led him to return again and again to the lower depths of its marginalized citizens. Jaime Humberto Hermosillo, on the other hand, was born in 1942 in Aguascalientes, lived in Mexico City's middle-class environment, and for decades has lived as an openly gay man in Guadalajara. His tastes, sexuality, and observations led him to become a chronicler of the Mexican bourgeoisie in all its habits, hypocrisies, and sexual behaviors. Influenced by their sexuality and social strata, the two became very different sorts of directors, choosing narrative themes of abjection or empowerment and drawn to opposing tropes of comedy or tragedy. Yet both filmmakers won international recognition with signature films centered on gay material, and both created distinctive cinemas that continued to encompass gay characters and dilemmas.

Ripstein's *El lugar sin límites* represents an ingenious study in the intrinsic connection between overstated masculinity and the homosexual desire that underlies it. Set in a small town with a claustrophobic moral code, the film focuses on the characters of Manuela, a drag queen and brothel owner, and Pancho, a hot-tempered drifter with an attraction/repulsion thing for Manuela. The overpowering pressure of the macho social order to which Pancho feels obliged to prove his allegiance will become fatal for Manuela by the end of the film, but until then it's a breathtaking ride through gender allegiances. Though its narrative drive and tragic resolution would seem to place *El lugar sin límites* squarely in an older category of films that stigmatize homosexuality, it differs in its solicitation of the audience's sympathy for Manuela and in convincingly denigrating the *machismo* that warps what could have been a love story. Indeed the film scholar Sergio de la Mora has argued that it is "the first Mexican film to take homosexuality seriously."[1]

The film is an exposé of the fragility of Mexican masculinity as it ricochets between the *travesti* and the *macho* in its revolving brothel door of sexual desires. Ripstein manages to set up intriguingly subversive scenes that call *macho* identity into question by exposing the desire it is meant to conceal or by showing its failed usefulness to its own social order—yet the predictably tragic ending undermines those gains.

El lugar sin límites would not figure into any operative code of a New Queer Cinema work. But given its provenance of 1977—contemporaneous with Sidney Lumet's *Dog Day Afternoon* (1975), Edouard Molinaro's *La cage aux folles* (1979), and William Friedkin's *Cruising* (1980)—it is hardly out of step with its time, whether viewed through a U.S. or a Mexican lens. Ripstein pathologizes gay characters no more, and possibly much less, than was common at the time. It's also important to point out that he always pathologizes his characters, even the *machos* that find themselves trapped in the brutal demimonde of his cinematic oeuvre. By placing the infernal dynamic of the *macho* and the *reina* at the center of the film, Ripstein created a space for the discussion of queer life in Mexico's underclass and for its future revised depictions.

Hermosillo's *Doña Herlinda y su hijo* offers the polar opposite of this dark tragedy: a sunny view of reconciliation. No doubt the optimism was made possible by a shift in setting, from patriarchal regime to the benevolent rule of the mother, Doña Herlinda, a marriage broker of gay and heterosexual unions.[2] As director, Hermosillo offers an idealized and utopian image of mutual tolerance in his tale of a mother whose desire to bring about both her son's happiness and her own contentment leads her to welcome his male lover into her house while simultaneously arranging for a wife and grandson in residence.[3] *Doña Herlinda* offers a spin on domestic melodrama, removing conflict by imagining an extended family able to integrate individual wishes without rupture; thus the ideal of the family can continue so long as all members can be united under its singular roof, from which no one can be evicted for their sexual or reproductive desires. In essence, the ideologies of family and of motherhood are refashioned in favor of an expansion that enables the survival of both, despite an apparent violation of society's normative prescriptions. Notably missing from *Doña Herlinda* is any Ripsteinian patriarch to disrupt the harmony; instead, under the benevolent law of a matriarch, peace and happiness prevail.[4]

As an openly gay director, Hermosillo has made a career of creating thematically sophisticated yet stylistically accessible films that question Mexico's social hypocrisy. They serve the additional purpose of creating a cinematic space within which his own gay sensibility can flourish uncastigated, successfully and productively deployed. His films attract international attention and support, while he continues to spend time in Guadalajara, wellspring of his cinematic universe. For years he was isolated and lacking in cinematic comrades in the ranks of Mexican directors, left alone to fend for himself. He's been increasingly accompanied by the many gay and lesbian filmmakers and festival curators in the international world of cinema—both within Latin America and beyond—whose ranks he joined as a fully accepted member.

Indeed Hermosillo has been a crucial elder for the queer cinema that has followed in his wake. He pointed the way out of tragedy as obligatory formula and found international favor and the possibility of realizing a queer sensibility on screen. Later he took up digital technologies as a way of encoding conflicts of identity and frustrations of desire in increasingly plastic and baroque explorations, most notably in his supernatural experiment, *eXXXorcismos* (2002). This digital film chronicles the tale of a new night guard at a mall that is haunted by the ghost of a young gay man who committed suicide over a failed love affair. The lover who jilted him? This same guard, come back to make amends—in fact to make what turn out to be very explicit and X-rated amends to the naked body of the rematerialized spirit-lover. Hermosillo was free to limn such radical fantasies of regret and fulfillment precisely because he'd removed himself from the financial constraints and censorship of market and government, beyond even the independent cinema. He was set free to explore new technologies and visualizations of queer desire, moving beyond taboo into explorations of a universe barely imaginable in earlier decades.

Nearly queer subject matter and sensibility could be seen in the same period in an unusual film by Paul Leduc. Leduc was one of the best-known filmmakers of Mexico's post-'68 era.[5] In *Frida: Naturaleza viva*, his prophetically revisionist portrait of the artist Frida Kahlo, Leduc rejected straightforward narrative entirely to make visible, through a dream-like spectacle and operatic structure, the texture of Kahlo's life and art. Along with the expected elements of Mexican folk culture, indigenous religion, and political life that inspired Kahlo's work and her later veneration, Leduc incorporated her range of sexual expression: her flirtations and affairs with both male and female suitors figure into the film's cinematic tableaux. Indeed *Frida* stands out for being ahead of its time in matching a life of broken rules and undaunted sexuality with a fittingly nonnormative cinematic style.

Further, Leduc's matter-of-fact inclusion of lesbian lust as an unpunished and unrepressed aspect of life's pleasures was something entirely new for Mexican cinema. Lesbianism was suddenly freed from the mandate to be metaphoric, tragic, or instructive. In *Frida*, lesbian sexuality was presented as an intrinsic aspect of the artist's nature: Leduc simply showed, in detail, that Kahlo embraced aspects of life ignored or stigmatized by bourgeois Mexican society, in the process transforming denigration into celebration. The film's international success created a viable example for subsequent expressions of lesbian and gay identity on Mexican screens and another heritage for the future Queer New Latin American Cinema to claim.

In 1994 Ripstein returned to his earlier terrain of Mexico's demimonde with another film, *La reina de la noche* (*The Queen of the Night*), an "imaginary biography" of the legendary singer and actress Lucha Reyes (portrayed by Patricia Reyes Spíndola). Reyes was adored on both sides of the border, in Los Angeles, Mexico City, and Guadalajara, for her *ranchera* singing and the enormous popularity of her movies. Given the deep fascination of Ripstein and his screenwriter and wife, Paz Alicia Garciadiego, with cinematically representing the tragic workings of greed, injustice, family traumas, and love gone bad, any lesbian or gay attachments in their films are unlikely to prove any exception.

For Ripstein, as ever, it is the sordid that captures his (camera) eye. While Reyes appears never to have had a moment of happiness or romance in her life, she comes closest in her moments of affection and longing for La Jaira, her lifelong friend, a kept woman who seems to reciprocate Reyes's passion emotionally but rejects her own desires physically. In the film, Reyes makes a bad marriage, visits brothels to find girls, even buys a daughter, all based in fact. Yet in the Ripstein oeuvre, any lesbian impulse serves as a sign of danger and degradation. (True, heterosexuality fares no better in the Ripstein universe, where everything is tainted and any human interaction is bound to end badly.) Patricia Rayes Spíndola as Reyes and Blanca Guerra as La Jaira are terrific together, generating heat whenever they have a scene—but the camera is always positioned too far away for intimacy, leaving the audience stranded in the voyeuristic purgatory that Ripstein prefers.

Lucha Reyes was notorious for the combination of qualities that made up her performing persona and captivated her public. If her husky voice and ribald performances weren't enough to defy her gender position, then surely her breaking taboo to lead a *mariachi* band, a previously all-male activity, and her deep connection to other women—to La Jaira, above all—gave her a sexual ambiguity that has retroactively marked her as queer. She was done in by alcohol and grief, a nightmarish mother and equally wretched husband, and perhaps the toll of defying the border for a career both in Los Angeles and in Mexico. Her life was bedeviled by multiple factors beyond her sexuality that could have been responsible for her death by suicide or overdose at the unspeakably young age of thirty-eight. Her story continues to haunt Mexico, especially its bohemian and queer enclaves.

Lucha Reyes followed the tragic path of those brave women on the cusp of modernity who broke with a patriarchal society's expectations in order to pursue a personal agency, both sexual and artistic; all too often, they paid with their lives. She was an actress in films of the 1930s and 1940s. Sergio de la Mora has observed, "Most often recognized for the sexual agency and unique lyrical interpretation encompassed in her rendition of *rancheras*, Reyes embodied modes of desire, pain, and tragedy that transcended heteronormative sexual economies of the time."[6] Something queer, maybe.

Notes

1. See de la Mora, "Fascinating Machismo." Also see de la Mora, *Cinemachismo*. For a different articulation, see Subero, "Fear of the Trannies."

2. It is tempting to see the NQC happy-ending classic, *Big Eden*, as its descendent, and to see Ang Lee's *The Wedding Banquet* as an homage.

3. For an incisive analysis of Hermosillo's work as well as many of the other films mentioned in this chapter, see Foster, *Queer Issues in Contemporary Latin American Cinema*.

4. Well, the happiness may not be total: Sergio de la Mora notes that Ramon/Moncho is clearly not happy sharing his guy with a wife (email communication, 2011).

5. Leduc was a prominent member of the film generation that emerged from the cultural upheaval of the late 1960s and the Tlatelolco massacre of students in 1968 to form the New Mexican Cinema movement, in opposition to the established style and subject of Mexico's official cinema.

6. De la Mora, "*Por un amor.*" See too de la Mora's *Cinemachismo* for his analysis of Mexican cinematic masculinity in depth. For other perspectives, see Nájera-Ramírez, "Unruly Passions"; Mitchell, *Intoxicated Identities*, 163–64.

GAY AND LESBIAN TRACES

20 In the 1970s, when the New Latin American Cinema flourished, there was a unity of purpose and style due to shared radical agendas, but by the mid-1980s, values were more diverse, in keeping with evolving societies and governing systems; it was more productive to scan for traces of shared concerns than unities. In the case of LGBT cinemas, national differences are particularly acute: ubiquity has yielded not coherence but rather individual works of inquiry and promises of discovery yet ahead.

In Brazil two films, both eponymous, became prominent for their central gay and lesbian characters: *Pixote: A lei do mais fraco* (*Pixote: The Law of the Weakest*, 1981) and *Vera* (1986). Both films updated older notions of sexuality with new accommodations.

Héctor Babenco had his breakthrough success with *Pixote*. Incorporated into its unvarnished depiction of the lives of young outcasts on the streets of São Paulo is a pair of boys who form a symbiotic sexual union. The international attention lavished on *Pixote* was closely linked to its shock value, in which homosexuality played a part. *Pixote* can't be held up as an example of how gay desire can be depicted, given its sensationalistic and sordid treatment of gay sex as accommodation, substitution, and punishment, but again, its very registering of the subject matter was unusual for its time and arguably helped to open future spaces for gay desire on Brazilian screens.

On a smaller scale, Sérgio Toledo's *Vera* centered on a working-class protagonist whose experience of abjection as a lesbian butch in prison leads her to seek fulfillment on the outside as a man.[1] *Vera* detailed its theme of sexual identity and desire with a clear expression of sympathy and subtlety. Its protagonist was derived from the life of Anderson Bigode Herzer (born Sandra Mara Herzer in 1962); Herzer was similarly imprisoned, identified eventually as transgender, and published a book of poems, *A queda para o alto* (*Descending Upwards*), which Toledo admitted basing his film on, in part.[2] Even though Ana Beatriz Nogueira, the actress who played Bauer/Vera, won the best actress award at the Berlin Film Festival in 1987, *Vera* never attained much international fame, possibly due to its twofold lack of shock techniques and Hollywood stars; evidently empathy and identification do not sell as well. *Vera* was perhaps ahead of its time, forced to wait in the NQC lobby until the rise of a trans cinema within which it could finally find a home.

The construction of gay or lesbian characters by Latin American female directors in the 1980s took an entirely new and different turn. Instead of embodying tragic tales of identity conflict, the LGBT characters in their films now represented zones of tolerance, agents of protection, signifiers of a better way of living.

In Argentina, María Luisa Bemberg directed *Señora de nadie* (*Nobody's Wife*, 1982), the first in her series of films examining repression, stigma, and individual courage. The film follows a conventional middle-class woman who, betrayed by her husband, finds a new life under the encouraging wing of a gay man in her support group; his open homosexuality suggests a larger scope of freedom and liberation from social constraints.

Three films later, Bemberg made *Yo, la peor de todas* (*I, the Worst of All*, 1990), a portrayal of the legendary seventeenth-century Mexican writer, theologian, and nun, Sor Juana Inéz de la Cruz, played by Assumpta Serna. Privileging the imagined eroticism of the convent, Bemberg focuses on Sor Juana's intense friendship with her protector, a sexy vicereine played by Dominique Sanda.[3] The *virreina* is able to use her station to protect the embattled nun, allowing us the pleasure of witnessing the two meeting and exchanging deeply erotic looks and heartfelt words. Alas, Sor Juana is left to her mortal destiny (punishment for heresy) when the *virreina* and viceroy are ordered to return to Europe, possibly on account of her indiscretions.

Sor Juana is a legendary figure in Mexican history, even appearing on its currency, yet she also belongs to another tradition: a global lesbian fantasy of lust and passion in the convents of yore. By eroticizing the story, *Yo, la peor de todas* appealed to audiences for reasons that exceeded its historical interest. Bemberg, a legendary figure in her own time as Argentina's leading director, managed to overcome the film's unexpected controversy, less for its sexualization of the revered nun than for the more modern heresy of an Argentine appropriating one of Mexico's most revered figures.

One year later, María Novaro, a Mexican filmmaker based in Mexico City, won international distribution and acclaim for *Danzón* (1991). The film follows Julia, a meek switchboard operator and dance-loving mother, played by the beloved María Rojo, as she journeys from Mexico City to Veracruz in search of Carmelo, her mysterious dance hall partner. Lost and adrift, she is befriended by a drag queen and attendant coterie, all of whom accept, educate, and encourage her. Energized by her newfound identity as honorary drag queen (she even has a daring fling with a young hunk), Julia is able to see herself differently. She returns home a changed woman: confident, self-realized, courageous. In this simple fable, the drag queen has become an agent of transformation, enlightenment, and tolerance—quite a change from the fatality of drag in Ripstein.

The success of *Danzón* demonstrated that such a character could now be redeemed and retrofitted into a form of melodrama that no longer mandated death or punishment. Julia herself avoids any tragic end, instead acquiring a level of agency and a sense of power as a single mother, a previously unimaginable fate in the genre. Finally, the film's international distribution suggested that, far from hurting a film's chance of acceptance, the inclusion of such a modern trope as the drag queen as mentor might actually enhance its prospects in international distribution circuits.

In virtually all these films, the prescient interest in LGBT subjects was a byproduct of a particularly enlightened cinephilia that recognized and embraced otherness as a route into the complex narratives and subjectivities that make for a richer cinema. Not a unified movement, these films were often singular works within oeuvres that otherwise left queer characters unexplored.

Consider, for a moment, the legacy of Manuel Puig, arguably the central figure in the evolution of a gay Latin American cinema and sensibility. Puig, a cosmopolitan and exile who left his native Argentina to live in Italy, Brazil, London, New York, and finally Mexico, is today the definitive writer to read—for his sexuality, sensibility, metropolitan wanderings, and radical refashioning of literary conventions.[4] He created a literature that merged his sexuality with his *latinidad* and begat a powerful new kind of postmodern writing.[5]

The cultural critic Ilan Stavans, writing on Puig, pinpoints the deep contradiction that would distinguish his experience in his time from that of the readers and viewers who came after him: "Like most gays in the Hispanic world, Puig was trapped between his sexual preference and the prejudices of the larger society. And yet, what is distinctive about him and the literary generation that came of age in the wake of the sixties is the desublimation of the phallus."[6]

This coming out into the open was indeed the fulcrum that pitched Puig into a more spacious, rapt, but contrary public. His novel *Kiss of the Spider Woman* (*El beso de la mujer araña*), published in Spanish in 1976 and in English in 1979, was made into a feature film, directed by the now gay-friendly and bankable Héctor Babenco in 1985. The screenplay, adapted from the novel by Puig, had the screenwriter Leonard Schrader, brother of Paul Schrader, as cowriter. Puig's book and screenplay managed to merge three themes not previously unified: the sensibility of the queen, the fetish of the cinephile, and the passion of the revolutionary. Desublimation times three.

Shot in Brazil and annexed to Hollywood through star performances by Raúl Juliá as the revolutionary and William Hurt as the movie-mad queen, plus Brazil's Sônia Braga as the femme fatale of its film-within-the-film, *Kiss of the Spider Woman* was unprecedented in its fusion of a radical politics of sex with a sexual politics of revolution. The phallus desublimated, indeed.

With a narrative structure less radical than Puig's novel, as dictated by the genre formulas it both obeyed and tried to escape, *Kiss of the Spider Woman* became a classic. As an opening salvo for the promise of a future queer New Latin American cinema it issued an unprecedented permission slip, allowing transgressions of Latin American cinema's status quo of gender and sexuality. Its depiction of an alliance between the queen and the revolutionary (up to and, yes, including sex), in which the pair for a moment shared and exchanged roles, constituted a radical representational act. Unsurprisingly, the story, director, and stars were transposed into U.S. production economies. Only in that hybrid laboratory—one, incidentally, with a large enough population to ensure ample U.S. niche markets to turn a profit—would a cinematic revolutionary understand a queen's desires well enough to offer up his body, and only there would a queen reciprocate by leaving prison as a revolutionary, sworn to make contact with a political cell. The film was released in 1985, the very year that Brazil's military junta stepped down and a constitutional government took over, auguring more changes to come. (Puig himself would die in 1990 at age fifty-five in Cuernavaca, supposedly of complications from gallbladder surgery.)[7]

Notes

1. See the longer analysis in de Lauretis, "Guerrilla in the Midst," as well as its analysis as a case in point in Halberstam, *Female Masculinity*, 216. My original article appeared at the time of its release: "Tough Girls Don't Dance."

2. Sérgio Toledo, personal communication, New York City, 1987.

3. In another example of symbolic casting, Dominique Sanda carries in her persona the history of her role as the sexy bisexual Anna Quadri in Bernardo Bertolucci's *Il conformista* (*The Conformist*, 1970).

4. Virgilio Piñera and José Lezama Lima should be well known too, but they faded behind the greater notoriety of their compatriot Reinaldo Arenas.

5. The Hong Kong director Wong Kar-Wai explained in interviews that his film *Happy Together* (*Chun gwong cha sit*, 1997), was set in Buenos Aires specifically because of Puig, whose work he cited as a major influence on his narrative style. The film's working title was the *Buenos Aires Affair*, after the Puig novel.

6. Stavans, "The Latin Phallus," 62.

7. In the same essay, Stavans casts doubt on the gallbladder explanation and raises the possibility of AIDS. However, Ronald Christ, who knew Puig, endorses the surgery explanation in "A Last Interview with Manuel Puig." Two uncanny observations: first, that Puig died in 1990, the same year as García Mesa; second, that Christ credits my late friend and colleague, Gregory Kolovakos, who arranged for him to interview Puig for the gay journal *Christopher Street*. Gregory, who died of AIDS soon after, deserves recognition for his passionate support of Spanish-to-English translation and the publication of Latin American writers, especially if they were gay. For an appreciation of Puig that encompasses the 1993 musical by Kander and Ebb, also titled *Kiss of the Spider Woman*, as well as the relationship between Latino and gay studies, see Román and Sandoval, "Caught in the Web."

MEXICO IN THE FORTIES

Reclaiming a Gender Pioneer

21 In 1990 I traveled to Tijuana for "*Cruzando Fronteras*, Crossing Borders," a landmark conference that brought together Latina, Chicana, and Mexicana filmmakers, video makers, and critics from both sides of the border. The event was hosted by the Colegio de la Frontera Norte (COLEF), the multicampus university that specializes in border studies.[1] In the masculinist context of so many Latin American conferences, its radical impulse lay in the simple fact of its focus on women as well as a cross-border configuration more commonly claimed by the men of Aztlán; indeed it was due to criticism of just such a lopsidedly male event that the Colegio sponsored a women's event. Amid a joyous recognition of shared sensibilities and goals, screenings of film and video, and vigorous bilingual debates, a historical reclamation transpired. We witnessed a belated fortieth-anniversary tribute to a woman filmmaker whose contribution to Mexican cinema had gone unrecognized for four decades: Matilde Landeta, pioneering elder, was there in person.[2]

If queerness resides as much in the eye of the beholder as in texts or intentions, then it's tempting to claim Landeta's scandalous landmark *La negra Angustias* (1949) as such. The film was based on the novel by Francisco Rojas Gonzáles, which in turn was based on an actual figure: an orphaned mulatta shepherd who rose to the rank of colonel in the revolutionary army. Landeta created her protagonist, Angustias, as an independent woman shaped by a total identification with her (deceased) father and the Mexican Revolution.

Angustias casts off the gender codes of her village to join the revolutionary battle, leading a cadre of loyal male followers on horseback. Later, as *colonela*, she orders the castration of a captured brigand who had (seemingly) raped her. She laughs triumphantly when she hears the screams that testify the deed has been done (off-screen). Though *La negra Angustias* is forced by the time's characteristic codes of narrative closure to lead its heroine into love with a lackluster man—and by its racial codes to feature an actress in blackface, despite her otherwise authentic sense of agency—the protagonist's force of personality survives: she triumphs and rejoins her troops by film's end.

As with other mainstream works, the lesbian viewer is free here too to turn away from the horrific lapse of minstrel impersonation and heterosexual romance and to invest instead in the spectacle of a strong, brave, mixed-race, male-defying Mexicana in the 1940s who literally wears the pants in the movie and lacks only a girlfriend to complete the fantasy—all this, five years ahead of the treasured Mercedes McCambridge–Joan Crawford showdowns in Nicholas Ray's *Johnny Guitar* (1954). Angustias's gender transgressions mark her as an early figure of queer aspiration in an epoch of social and cinematic norms.

Consider Matilde Landeta, then, a force in the problematizing of gender dynamics and their cinematic representations in the years prior to NQC. Landeta made her feature debut just a few years after the end of World War II, amid a Mexican film industry rife with corruption and bolstered by U.S. interests.[3] To assess her achievement in context, consider that the roots of the New Latin American Cinema are always traced back to Luis Buñuel's neorealist *Los olvidados* (*The Young and the Damned*), shot in Mexico City in 1950—a year *after* Landeta's achievement in gender defiance. Aesthetically, Buñuel is widely credited with pioneering neorealism in Mexican film, whereas Landeta practiced the traditional melodrama then dominant in Latin American cinema; it was Landeta, however, who introduced gender while Buñuel hewed to the unexamined masculinist dominance of the era.

Like him, Landeta is a cinematic pioneer, albeit far less credited. *La negra Angustias* is proof that gender disruption was there from the very beginning of a modern Mexican cinema, an inherent component of its birthright, long unrecognized, hiding in plain sight (just as queerness so often has).

Notes

1. The conference was organized by COLEF's Norma Iglesias with Lourdes Portillo. The catalogue and anthology of its proceedings, *Miradas de mujer: Encuentro de cineastas y videoastas Mexicanas y Chicanas*, was edited by Iglesias with Rosa Linda Fregoso and published by UC Davis and COLEF in 1998.

2. For in-depth perspectives and details on Landeta, see Huaco-Nuzum, "Matilde Landeta"; Burton-Carvajal, *Matilde Landeta, hija de la Revolución*; Rashkin, "An Other Cinema."

3. The United States was intent on punishing Argentina for its fascist sympathies (i.e., its "neutrality") by economically encouraging the ascendancy of Mexican film.

REVOLUTION, SEXUALITY, AND THE PARADOX

OF QUEER FILM IN CUBA

22 My professional trips as a critic and curator to Cuba in 1978–2003, to Mexico in 1970–2002, and throughout the intervening decades to Argentina, Brazil, and Puerto Rico alerted me to the ways in which cultures shape sexual mores as much as cinematic tastes. Havana was the place where I first began to make sense of sexuality in Latin America and where I first heard the dictum that has rung in my ears ever since: *Se hace todo, se dice nada* (Do everything, say nothing). I learned the differences between official and off-the-record discourses and market-rate and black-market sexual economies, along with the culturally determined consequences of being out in distinct Latin American societies. Gay life there seemed the opposite of the more easily visible U.S. lifestyle, but certainly no less rich for its earned availability.

In the early 1980s I became involved in hotly contested debates over the issue of Cuba and homosexuality. Together with my coauthor Lourdes Arguelles, I published a series of articles exploring the histories and lived realities of gay and lesbian life both on the island and in the Cuban enclaves of the United States. We dug deep into political and cultural attitudes, researching histories and traveling widely; as a result, we frequently had to defend ourselves from libel threats and editorial attacks.[1] We understood that we were intervening in a complex system of rights and pressures. American discussion of LGBT life in Cuba at that time wasn't obscure: it was positioned at the very center of foreign policy strategies and immigrant ideologies.[2] Ronald Reagan was president and had made Cuban Americans his "model minority," citing economic success and virulent anti-Communism as the ideal to which all immigrant communities should aspire. Even though the Cuban exile community had its fair share of poverty, and even though political views had diversified with the birth of a second generation, the cold war was still raging. Such propaganda was useful. When imagining options available to Latin American LGBT filmmakers living and working in their home countries, it's important to remember the extent to which sexuality is always linked to context and annexed to ideology. Cinemas, however individual or inventive, are inherently implicated in their specific moments. Nothing is simple.

In 1983 I became a member of a joint U.S.-Cuban committee that came together to organize the programming and presentation of a sidebar for the Latin American International Film Festival, which we titled *La otra cara*, or *The Other Face*. We had responded to a request by Cuba's national film institute, Instituto Cubano del Arte y la Industria Cinematográficos (ICAIC), to showcase "the other face" of American cinema. It was the birth of the American independent cinema movement: this new style of low-budget films, like Charles Burnett's *Killer of Sheep* (1981) and Victor Nuñez's *Gal Young 'Un* (1979), could engage with the world on new, more equitable terms far removed from the Hollywood empire that (at that time) independent filmmakers opposed. Regionally based, often working-class, this new filmmaking could claim a position of solidarity with the Cubans.

In December 1983 I traveled to Havana to present our showcase and participate in a special conference with its films and filmmakers. We'd selected a short version of the Mariposa Film Collective's landmark documentary on the history of gay and lesbian lives, *Word Is Out: Stories of Some of Our Lives* (1977), in defiance of Cuba's history of institutionalized homophobia, prevalent in the 1960s through brutal doctrines of incarceration, but once again a focus of concern in the United States in the 1980s. *Word Is Out* was included in our program, but we worried that we might encounter opposition on the island.

In the event, ICAIC's brass were too sophisticated to censor the film outright, knowing that such a move would draw U.S. and international attention. Instead they simply neglected to prepare the translations of subtitles that were read aloud during screenings—a conspicuous oversight, given that texts for all the other films were already completed. The ICAIC also failed to translate my essay for the *La Otra Cara* conference. In "The Aesthetics of Liberation," I presented my argument for gay aesthetics as an integral companion to cinematic strategies emerging from feminist, African American, and other liberatory movements in the United States. Everyone else's essay had already been

22.1 Héctor García Mesa shows off his T-shirt on Playa
Santa Maria outside Havana, 1983. Photo by B. Ruby Rich.

translated into Spanish, copied, and distributed to participants' mailboxes in
advance of the sessions. Not mine.

I was upset: I had trusted our group's collaboration (with Cuban co-
curators), only to fall victim to a strategic silencing of my text and of the dialogue in *Word Is Out*. Dejectedly slumped in a chair in the hotel lobby, I met
Héctor García Mesa, the founder and head of La Cinemateca de Cuba (technically a division of ICAIC but strikingly independent in its program choices),
who had been a collaborator on the selections, and not incidentally was a gay
man. His knowledge was extensive, his taste impeccable. He knew everything
about Latin American film and literature, especially when it involved anyone
"in the life." It was with him that I first discussed Manuel Puig; he introduced
me to the Cuban writers Virgilio Piñera and José Lezama Lima, still officially
off-limits for Cubans, all of whom he had known personally (fig. 22.1).

I didn't know if his skills would extend to cultural diplomacy, but I explained the situation in detail, certain as I was that there was no way he could
influence a decision that had already been made and implemented by those
over his head. But I was underestimating García Mesa; he paid close attention,
then vanished, even uncharacteristically absent from the nightly party in the
Hotel Nacional's legendary courtyard. The next morning, I was summoned

to the office of Pastor Vega, then director of ICAIC. "*No hay problema*," Pastor assured me. There's no problem. Pastor Vega had rewritten the scenario: at that very moment, subtitles were being translated, and so was my text, both of which would be in all the mailboxes by the end of the day. Most surprisingly, Vega offered an official apology, blaming unnamed people who were undermining ICAIC and making it look bad by misinterpreting official policy.

My head was spinning by the time I returned to the Hotel Nacional and encountered García Mesa. I asked him what on earth he had said to make the officials change direction so drastically. Smiling, he said he told them "it would be better for Cuba" to respect the curatorial and critical "sovereignty" of our program. Then he took my hand and bought me a drink. Using the rhetoric of the Revolution as a tool against its own policy, he displayed mastery of the codes of ideology and appearance and intervened in their outcomes.[3]

So that is how *Word Is Out* came to be shown in Cuba in 1983, with subtitles. And how I came to deliver my speech, with translation in hand, on the conference panel the next day—despite walkouts by the Cuban attendees. And how I came to consider García Mesa the best friend a girl could ever have.

Fast-forward to 1994. Sing the song "I Scream, You Scream, We All Scream."[4]

Tomás Gutiérrez Alea (Titón, to his friends) had finally completed a long-promised film about homosexuality on the island, *Fresa y chocolate* (*Strawberry and Chocolate*). One of the founding fathers of ICAIC, Gutiérrez Alea was identified with its most progressive forces. In the 1970s he'd supported Afro-Cuban struggles for visibility, and in the 1980s, feminist positions within the Cuban Revolution as well as an emergent gay and lesbian cultural politics. By the 1990s his ease with people and issues across a range of sexualities led some people outside Cuba to insist he was secretly gay, despite his two marriages, the second to the actress Mirta Ibarra. Across many encounters with him, I witnessed a remarkably enlightened man who empathized with marginality, outsiders, and freethinking, and was entirely comfortable in any setting, no matter his own identity or relationship to it.

By the 1990s, in the Special Period of extreme devastation following the loss of Soviet economic support, Gutiérrez Alea was able to use his considerable national and international stature to influence ICAIC to permit the production of a film dealing with homosexuality within the framework of the Cuban Revolution—and to allow it to circulate inside Cuba, where the subject was still taboo. Presumably his terminal lung cancer gave added weight to his request.

Fresa y chocolate was approved and completed; it was programmed in Havana's official film festival of December 1993 and won all of the festival's top honors. At the reception with Fidel Castro following the awards ceremony, a dessert of strawberry and chocolate ice cream was served.[5] The film opened commercially in Cuba immediately afterward and played for three months, drawing tremendous audiences. With distribution by Miramax Films, it went on to considerable attention in the United States, including a screening at Sundance which Gutiérrez Alea was well enough to attend, an Oscar nomination for best foreign-language film, and considerable European play.[6]

Cuba's first feature film with a gay central character, *Fresa y chocolate* was based on the play and novella by Senel Paz, who adapted the screenplay from his earlier piece, *El lobo, el bosque y el hombre nuevo* (*The Wolf, the Forest, and the New Man*), which had been provisionally titled *La catedral del helado* (*The Cathedral of Ice Cream*). *Fresa y chocolate* needed the imprimatur of the untouchable maestro to come into being—even though he was already so ill that he needed a codirector. Its production on the island was an unprecedented cinematic act for Cuba in the age of Fidel.[7]

That said, both novella and film hedged their bets regarding revolutionary fealty through a strategy of time travel. Instead of a contemporaneous setting, the director and screenwriter set their story in the far more benign days of 1979, an era of prosperity in Cuban society when the economy was stable, the island was beginning to open up to the world, Cuban exiles' grown-up children returned for the historic *Dialogo*, ICAIC held its first international festival of Latin American cinema in Havana, and neither the Mariel exodus nor AIDS was yet a factor. Thus 1979 was a setting less likely to register as a criticism of the policies of the 1990s.

Fresa y chocolate is structured in terms of a friendship between David, a young party-line heterosexual typical of the "new man" who came of age after 1959, and Diego, an older gay aesthete whose initial interest in the young functionary-in-training is one of seduction. Here the gay character humanizes the heterosexual: Diego brings David into a wider world of art and literature, while Diego's neighbor Nancy (played by Mirta Ibarra) supplies the young man with sex too. The eroticized friendship and eventual admiration that the young David brings to Diego, in turn, restores the older man's sense of self-worth. Restored, Diego is poised to relinquish both the Revolution and its men—and opt for the Cuban version of a happy ending: a new life abroad.

Here Gutiérrez Alea has opted for added value, returning to the earlier use of gays as metaphors: on screen, a heterosexual-homosexual drama transpires, but their debate over tolerance, political parameters, and the acceptance of "difference" within the ideology of Cuba's Revolution is pitched to a broader public and discourse. Who wins? Who loses? It is Diego, the sophisticate, who is marginalized and yet who could be of more use to an evolving society, while it is David, the party-liner, who knows only what he's been told, who is groomed to continue a system already set in stone.

I'd met Senel Paz in the 1980s at the Havana Film Festival when he was starting his career as a writer. It's a small island, where the literary, film, and art worlds overlapped: Senel, Héctor, and Titón knew each other. How much was the character of Diego portrayed by Jorge Perugorría inspired by Héctor García Mesa?[8] Had Senel or Titón borrowed his elegance and brio for the character of Diego? I remembered details: García Mesa's apartment, with its perfect arrangements and shrines; the time he took me to the Heladería Coppelia ice-cream parlor, where Diego takes David, and pointed out the distinctly gay clientele congregating separately around the outdoor tables. I can't remember if he ordered strawberry or chocolate, but I do remember his lamenting the narrow choice of flavors compared to its menu before 1959.

Fresa y chocolate was released into a decade already full of debates and attacks over homosexuality in Cuba, initiated by the documentary *Improper Conduct* (*Mauvaise conduite*, 1984). Made by the Cuban exiles Néstor Almendros and Orlando Jiménez Leal, it played theatrically in the United States to considerable acclaim. *Improper Conduct* gathered individual testimonies, including one by Susan Sontag, into a chorus of denunciations of Fidel Castro and the Cuban Revolution on the basis of the oppression of homosexuals. Most of the testimonies were incomplete, misleading, or out of date, yet *Improper Conduct* sparked considerable controversy; coinciding with Reagan's second term as president, it worked in concert with his administration's demonization of the island and aggressive foreign policy toward Cuba.[9]

At the time, Gutiérrez Alea was one of the few Cuban voices raised against the veracity of the film.[10] He later acknowledged that he had conceived *Fresa y chocolate* partly as an on-screen retort to it.[11] Almendros, alas, died before *Fresa y chocolate* began shooting. Such an intent makes the film especially notable for its inclusive politics of acceptance and its refusal to condemn either side or any border. Rather the film reads as an olive branch held out in all directions, a gesture that has led some to see this "Can't we all just get along?" posture as naïve or disingenuous or as outright capitulation.

To be sure, the film's attitudes are old-fashioned, better suited to 1979 than to 1994. Dated even for 1979, though, these attitudes and cinematic conventions belong more to the 1960s, the era of Cuba's grievous treatment of homosexuality and notorious forced labor camps, or UMAPS (Military Units to Aid Production). Gutiérrez Alea's memories of this traumatic era may well have shaped his film's style: one part *Tea and Sympathy* (1956), one part *Philadelphia* (1993). Further, the film's antiquated cinematic codes are hardly unique to *Fresa y chocolate*; Gutiérrez Alea's cinema always had a deeply sentimentalized side alongside its grittier, more modern one. The conventional side was more dominant in his oeuvre after the 1970s: a relaxed studio style, overly expressive acting, normative narrative structures, and an operatically comic or romantic tone. *Fresa y chocolate* fits that template.

In that sense, it could be argued that the film was fundamentally for Cuba and Cubans, not for international gay or lesbian publics—evidence of changed attitudes within Cuba rather than of any demonstrable reciprocity between Cuban cinema and the NQC moment. Nonetheless, through his creation of deeply sympathetic characters and a narrative structure that invites empathy and identification, Gutiérrez Alea was able in his last days to deliver a gay critique of the system to which he'd dedicated his entire life.

Notes

This essay is dedicated to the memory of Héctor García Mesa.

1. See my articles coauthored with Lourdes Arguelles: "Homosexuality, Homophobia and Revolution," parts 1 and 2. We were attacked publicly and privately for these and for a related article that appeared in a local gay paper *New York Native*, in the same period.

2. The rhetoric concerning women's rights that was mobilized by the Bush administration to justify intervention in Afghanistan is a contemporary example of the same strategy. In just such cynical fashion did the Reagan administration mobilize a gay rights discourse (which they opposed elsewhere) as a means to neutralize left support for its attacks on Cuba.

3. My essay, "Héctor García Mesa: Man of My Dreams," was commissioned for La Cinemateca de Cuba's monograph in his honor in 2009. García Mesa died in 1990 of a stroke while preparing to host a major international conference of film archivists.

4. Apologies here for title theft! See Chua, "I Scream, You Scream," a refreshingly nuanced view of the film and the director at the time of its release.

5. West, "Strawberry and Chocolate, Ice Cream and Tolerance."

6. For a consideration of *Fresa* in the context of Cuban cinema, see Davies, "Recent Cuban Fiction Films." Also see Smith, "The Language of Strawberry" and "*Fresa y chocolate* (*Strawberry and Chocolate*): Cinema as Guided Tour." For an in-depth

analysis of *Strawberry and Chocolate* as compared with Gutiérrez Alea's *Memories of Underdevelopment* (1968) see Shaw, *Contemporary Cinema of Latin America*, 9–35. See too Nero, "Diva Traffic and Male Bonding in Film."

7. Recently another film with a gay theme has been made by a Cuban filmmaker: *La casa vieja* (*The Old House*, 2010) by Lester Hamlet. It is an adaptation of Abelardo Estorino's play of the same name, written in 1964. In this case, unlike *Fresa y chocolate*, the story is updated to the present, right down to a neighborhood character who's always dressed in an Obama T-shirt.

8. For a completely opposite and antagonistic reading to my own, see Santí, "*Fresa y Chocolate*: The Rhetoric of Cuban Reconciliation." He argues that David and Diego are stand-ins for Gutiérrez Alea and Almendros, a claim I consider ludicrous.

9. I was embroiled in these debates. My article "Bay of Pix" was my last assignment for the American Film Institute's journal *American Film*: the AFI made space for Almendros and Jimenez-Léal to attack me. Vito Russo published an attack on me, too. To this day, I owe thanks to Michael Ratner and the Center for Constitutional Rights for defending me from libel threats that were a common right-wing tactic in those days, meant to control public discourse on Cuba.

10. In fact Gutiérrez Alea provided a rebuttal in the form of a published interview with the editors of the *Village Voice*, which I helped to arrange.

11. Tomás Gutiérrez Alea, personal communication, Park City, Utah, January 1995.

QUEERING THE SOCIAL LANDSCAPE

23 Queer visions, classed and racial interventions, and scandalous satires can all be found on the margins of the official national industries of Latin American image-making. When the film industry itself was hopelessly sclerotic, male-dominated, and heteronormative, the alternative sphere of performance spaces, cabarets, and alternative video were all the domain of outsiders. As such, they were fertile ground for the cultivation of oppositional voices, including matters of gender and sexuality.

As the energy of the performance sector began to bleed into the film world, video artists grew up to write feature scripts and digital technologies obliterated the old industrial film hierarchies. Economic crises that had obliterated screen potentials began to relax, making new fantasies possible, including, at long last, queer ones.

Latin American queer visions differed from country to country, and certainly from Anglophile versions. Instead of one unified rebellion against formal standards and formulaic tropes, there was a dispersed range of strategies that traversed normative boundaries of gender and sexuality. A cinema of nuance and feeling emerged, a moody landscape of longing and heartbreak, with figures who daydreamed and pursued desire wherever it might be found, who upset expectation and invaded pop culture. In this, the Queer New Latin American Cinema would resonate more with queer cinemas emerging in Europe and Southeast Asia than with the original Anglo versions of queerness on screen. And yet they are very much their own, belonging to their regions and peoples as much as any other cinemas that have emerged in a period of reinvigorated life and cultural expression in Latin America, where progressive political leaders have supplanted the old dictators yet economies have flourished, at least for a while.

Performing Mexico

Much of Latin America has a long tradition of cabaret, vaudeville, dance hall, carnival, and festivals—all popular cultural sectors that run parallel to, and at times intersect with, the film industry. In Cuba, for instance, in acknowledgment of their populist importance and artistic power, cabarets and circuses were included along with cinema under the Ministry of Culture (at least through the 1970s).

In Mexico City, decidedly nongovernmental players have transformed the cabaret genre into a particularly vibrant space of political satire and critique. Interestingly, the new cabaret has also nurtured strong women, with outstanding feminist and lesbian cabaret works in the 1980s–90s. As the scholar Roselyn Costantino has noted:

> Many Latin American performance practices . . . are homegrown, deeply rooted in cultural traditions and theatrical styles not recognized by elite culture but which nevertheless have existed for centuries as modes of expression for the peoples of the Americas. These include revue theatre, cabaret, street theatre, body art, religious rituals, popular celebrations . . . and oral and written literature with a critical, often humorous, edge.[1]

Lesbian and feminist energies, largely shut out of the Mexican film industry until the 1990s, were flourishing in the worlds of theater, cabaret, and alternative video, where originality and attitude could be rewarded. This world, in opposition to official culture, communicates an unapologetic energy that can be claimed as queer. Following Costantino's lead, the queer seeker set adrift in Mexico City in this time would have been well rewarded for visiting the live stages and bars in the neighborhoods of Mexico City; they were far more energetic than the fare on view in the city's movie palaces, themselves in danger of collapse with the onset of video technologies. In the cabarets, unlike in the Hollywood-dominated movie theaters, live entertainment was always entirely local in origin, subject, and performer. The unofficial status of the cabarets, the frequently oppositional tone of the lampooning, the carnivalesque upending of bourgeois society, all combined to make these spaces

queer-friendly if not precisely queer. That would be no surprise to Costantino, who points out that "performance in its multiple styles and manifestations constitutes a fundamental articulation of realities and memories of
communities not represented within official, constructed notions of nation."
Lest her point be lost, she reiterates, "Performance . . . traces these 'unimag-
ined communities.'"[2]

Performance, then, was a medium through which women, feminists, gay
and lesbian performers, and outsiders to class and privilege could "make a
spectacle" of themselves and refashion official society to their own liking.
Kitsch and camp were central elements, humor reigned, and the sacred could
swap places with the taboo without warning. Inherently heretical performances were prized at a time when political consolidation rendered official
routes compromised. Women performers in the cabarets, bars, restaurants,
performance spaces, and streets included Maris Bustamante with No Grupo;
Jesusa Rodríguez with Liliana Felipe at El Hábito; Astrid Hadad with Los
Tarzanes; Lorena Wolffer, Paquita la del Barrio, and numerous activists and
artists at El Closet de Sor Juana; and countless other locally renowned performers with fervent followings. Performances ranged from adaptations, such
as Rodríguez and Felipe's all-woman *Don Giovanni* to original parodic revues
like Hadad's send-up of Mexican officials or the appropriation of songs reversing power dynamics, as in Paquita la del Barrio's "Rata de dos patas" (Two-
legged Rat), a song insulting men. Cabarets, outside the mainstream, were
not restricted in their audience appeal; indeed Mexican politicians have been
known to drop into performances that ridiculed them. Up-to-the-minute in
their satires and pointed in their political wit, the cabaret acts of the D.F.
(Mexico City, Distrito Federal) were as fully a part of popular culture as any
Saturday Night Live episode might claim to be in the United States, albeit with
a smaller audience of cognoscenti.[3]

Jesusa Rodríguez and her partner, Liliana Felipe, were probably best
known in this era. They had created their own performance space, El Hábito,
purchasing and restoring a historic space (the former Teatro la Capilla) in
fashionable Coyoacán by redeploying a U.S. foundation grant into real estate. With El Hábito, they established their La Capilla theater company and
staged their fierce satires, taking on every aspect of Mexican life, culture, and
politics. Even their blatantly lesbian spectacles drew broad and appreciative
audiences, and they could always be counted on to launch fusillades inflected
and infected with gender, puncturing the foibles of political actors on the
Mexican national stage as well as celebrating insider figures. They opened

the space to others who shared their sensibilities. It was there that the adored lesbian troubadour Chavela Vargas was given a regular slot in El Hábito's weekly schedule in the 1990s, singing the songs that had originally made her famous in the 1950s and 1960s and would again when Pedro Almodóvar declared her to be his muse and cast her in *La flor de mis secretos* (*The Flower of My Secrets*, 1995).

Another cabaret featured the well-known Lebanese Mexican performer Astrid Hadad, whose shows in Mexico City in the early 1990s combined a fierce love of Mexican popular culture with savage critiques of its worst attitudes toward women.[4] A central player in the cabaret renaissance, Hadad took gender as both target and ammunition; she frequently donned traditional folkloric clothing like that which Frida Kahlo had revived with reverence, now draping it in irony. Strapping giant papier-mâché cacti to her back or sporting impossibly huge sombreros, Hadad sang of women's pain with a vibrato of protest that Lucha Reyes and all the tragic women of Mexico's past would surely have applauded. Making Mexican women's suffering into a spectacle, she effortlessly deconstructed the ideology of sacrifice. In her guise as nightclub singer, she carried out a heretical assault on Mexico's sacred *marianismo* (the worship of the Virgin Mary) for her audience's amusement.

A young Mexico City video artist was also part of the cabaret circle around these women. I first met Ximena Cuevas in 1992, when she was already working with Hadad and Rodríguez/Felipe, shooting video of their performances and creating new and original works of her own design in collaboration with them. Her wildly inventive music video, *Corazón sangrante*, based on one of Hadad's performances, led to her being recognized on the U.S. side of the border (fig. 23.1).[5] *Corazón sangrante*, arriving from Mexico City in sync with the New Queer Cinema's reign at Park City, showed at Sundance in 1993 and alerted U.S. audiences to the queer energies south of the border. In *Corazón*, Hadad cut up the screen in a madcap succession of official and populist religious iconography through parodic enactments for which Cuevas provided video pyrotechnics.

Not a narrative, not explicitly lesbian, her video *retablo* is such a joyous celebration of unrepentant, fed-up, and disobedient womanhood that it provided a useful corrective to the cinematic indignity, denial, and death that usually accompanied any female representation in Mexican cinema. The bleeding heart, of course, references both the most sacred of Catholic images and rites and the embodiment of women's punishment and life's work. It was Hadad's genius to identify such multilateral points of contradiction and social

23.1 Ximena Cuevas, crossing the globe, suitcase in hand.
Courtesy of the filmmaker.

vulnerability, with Cuevas orchestrating a frenetic succession of cartoon-like images that lacquered additional coats of irony and critique onto the performance of gender, Mexican-style.

Cuevas was not the only video artist seeking to redefine Mexican popular culture. Others began to inject a queer presence into the official iconography of Mexican stars, the true saints of the secular church. Out in the provinces, Agustín Calderón took up the male flesh-and-blood counterparts to the Virgin of Guadalupe: Pedro Infante and Jorge Negrete, celebrated romantic stars of Mexican cinema in its classical golden era (*Época de Oro*), a parallel state religion all on his own. In 1995 Calderón made a short, *Así se quiere en Jalisco*, which echoed *Corazón sangrante* in parodying the sacred, in this case, the popular *Dos tipos de cuidado*. Calderón reframes the traditional suitor, seen in classic fashion, petitioning his loved one from beneath her window with Mariachi band in tow. But the hero encounters an entirely different brand of heartbreak when a couple, in dishabille, in a clear state of coitus interruptus, emerge onto the balcony. It's immediately clear from the reaction shot that it wasn't the woman whom he was serenading. The punch line rewrites the plot line, and in one deft move casts doubt on all the hypermasculine romantic leads of Mexican film history—and thrills the queer viewers who respond with raucous appreciation.

As digital video spread and oppositional cultures gained and lost traction amid Mexico's shifting political regimes, Ximena Cuevas matured from young video sorceress into a video and performance artiste with a distinct sensibility, blending Mexican popular culture with her autobiography, adoration of women, and love of Mexico City itself.[6] Her intervention into Mexican television's heart of darkness, the tabloid talk show, is a perfect prototype for an emergent Queer New Latin American Cinema.

La tómbola (*The Raffle*, 2001) follows Cuevas as she agrees to appear on a scandalous talk show of the same name that's just as determined to capitalize on her father's celebrity as she is to resist any such vulgar appropriation.[7] Cuevas appears on *La tómbola*'s television screen in unusual garb. In marked contrast to its cast of characters—the exaggeratedly lascivious dress of one female guest, the proper-matron wardrobe of the wronged mother seated next to her, the personality-in-charge suit of the host—Cuevas shows up in a uniform of denim overalls and straw hat with feather, carrying a battered old-fashioned suitcase. Though known for her signature hats in her private life, Cuevas here calls to mind a beloved historical figure: Cantinflas.

Cantinflas (Fortino Mario Alfonso Moreno Reyes) was the star of innumerable Mexican popular movies and theater productions throughout the 1930s–1950s, an everyman and champion of the downtrodden. On screen he assumed a simple worker's outfit, sometimes with a suitcase, in a refusal of the macho-businessman-politician attire, for he steadfastly aligned himself with the simple folk (and labor sector) who formed the audience for his endless procession of movies.[8] I like to think that Cuevas is dressed in a genderswapped Cantinflas uniform as she breaks with the gender expectations of commercial television as well as the normative standards of the entertainment industry itself. How? She deflects the host's innuendos about her father's having a mistress by exuding an utter lack of interest in the whole question. Next, in the most scandalously transgressive action possible on a tabloid show, she declares, "I am incredibly bored." Cuevas wields boredom as a defense against the salacious assaults of mass-market television. To be bored is, by implication, to be outside the net(work) of entrapment, to be protected from an unwilling incorporation into its workings.

She is not content to rescue only herself, as it turns out. Cuevas goes considerably further than mere refusal. Opening her suitcase with low-key suspense, she retrieves a small consumer video camera and begins to operate it as she approaches the studio's giant counterpart. "Why are you watching this?" she asks, as she moves her lens closer and closer to the giant studio equipment that can deliver her into the home audience's vision. She challenges this imagined audience, those who want to watch the horrific pantomime of fame and fortune on offer.

"The only thing I hope," Cuevas explains to the host and studio guests, "is that there is at least one person out there who has a life of their own . . . who is interested in their own life." Like Diogenes roaming Athens with his lantern in search of one honest man, Cuevas roams the airwaves with her video camera in search of one lone soul outside the grasp of the entertainment-industrial complex, one perhaps marginalized by its dictates but still capable of generating self-representations outside its deadening regime. Her camcorder ruptures the laws of television: gender, yes, but also sheer passivity and acceptance. Perhaps she is searching for a new Mexican queer cinema, nascent in a room somewhere . . . out . . . there.

Just as Cantinflas was much more than a clown, so Cuevas too is far more than a court jester. She's up to something else, something that penetrates further into the sphere of an unsuspecting Mexican society to rupture its complacency. For an article in the tabloid magazine TV Notas published on January 9, 2001, Cuevas allowed a photographer and a journalist to chronicle her daily life at home with her woman lover, making a public announcement of her sexuality. The tabloid trumpeted its scoop on the cover with a photo of the two women kissing. But the joke was on them: while Cuevas had indeed decided to reveal her sexuality, she did it satirically. The woman pictured was not, in fact, her lover. Kathy High, a good friend and U.S. video artist, agreed to be the stand-in for Cuevas's actual lover, who could thus remain undetected and unidentified, outside the maw of the Mexican media. Just as La tómbola was a mock-acquiescence to the rules of tabloid television, so too was her appearance in TV Notas a fraudulent capitulation to tabloid abjection. In both cases, Cuevas used the tabloids for her own purposes, injecting their discourses with her own ongoing performances.

A comparison to Cantinflas is useful in another way too. The populism that shaped his performances matches the *rascuache* tradition of Mexican art and culture once described by Tomás Ybarra-Frausto: "Propriety and keeping up appearances—*el que diran*—are the codes shattered by the attitude of *rascuachismo*. This outsider viewpoint stems from a funky, irreverent stance that debunks convention and spoofs protocol. To be *rascuache* is . . . to seek to subvert and turn ruling paradigms upside down. It is a witty, irreverent, and impertinent posture that recodes and moves outside established boundaries."[9] Ilan Stavans applied Ybarra-Frausto's *rascuache* manifesto to Cantinflas himself and posits him as a foundational figure for Chicano culture and cultural studies. Stavans laments the passing of Cantinflas, who came of age in a utopian past when Mexico was a model that others looked to, whether for art, cinema, or literature, when everything seemed possible.[10] But Stavans is too quick to grieve: the *rascuache* habit of recycling scraps into new fashions, of building new genres out of discarded ones, might well apply to its emergent queer cinema rising out of the shards of the old movie industry.

The recoding that Cuevas enacts in her ventures into journalism and television is parodic, yes, but it's fundamentally queer as well. She cross-dresses in a parodic drag that subverts gender and sexual identity, violating cosmopolitan expectations of sexual allure. Outfitted in clothing that would mark her as an outsider to her class position and urban identity, she finesses seeming contradictions with attitude and technology. She defiantly contests the popular culture framework that would seek to account for, and discount, her presence. She could well be enacting not only a refusal of Mexican celebrity worship but also a phrase more commonly heard north of the border: "We're here, we're queer, get used to it."

Queering the Past in Brazil

The Algerian Brazilian filmmaker Karim Aïnouz has forged new queer cinematic possibilities, in his case, by tracing queer desire back to the early twentieth century. In 1991 Aïnouz was living in New York City and codirecting the MIX film festival. In 1993 MIX Brasil was founded, soon joined by MIX Mexico. A key figure in queer Latin American diasporic culture, Aïnouz eventually returned to his native Brazil to make his debut feature. He carried with him not only a script but also the widely shared NQC impulse to look to the past to unearth new heroes. He turned to the past and to the mythic figure who awaited him there: Madame Satã.[11]

Madame Satã (2002) is an extravagantly stylized and theatrical reimagining of the transgressive life of the legendary João Francisco dos Santos, who defined queerness long before any culture was there to claim or shape him/her.[12] Notorious for his life and escapades as a bandit, convict, boxer, transvestite, cook, father, and drag performer, Madame Satã was the boss, anchor, and protector of the community of outcasts in Lapa, Rio's notorious bohemian slum. With this story and film, we are instantly in the world of the *malandro* and the *malandragem*, a genre unto itself in Brazilian cinema.[13] The *malandro* can be roughly characterized as a street tough, a Mack the Knife–type who lives by his wits, outside the law, shifty and seductive, turning society's codes upside down and enjoying life. Born to former slaves in 1900, João fought to claim a place for himself in a society that would deny him even his personhood. In his chosen community, a *malandragem* of outlaws and criminals who violated multiple categories and boundaries of law, Madame Satã was a self-invention begging for a big screen.

Aïnouz succeeds in queering the *malandero* genre that predates the film and is attached to its "true story" origins. His revivification of João's life and milieu launches a fascinating story of gender defiance in a reclassed society. As Lorraine Leu explains in her study of Brazilian music, Madame Satã was "the most notorious *malandro* of all." Leu defines the moral code that governed this universe as "courage, elegance and the *jeitinho* (or ability to find a way around laws, rules and regulations), which were important in the alternative order that the *malandro* created from his position at the margins of society."[14] Aïnouz sees João/Satã through contemporary queer eyes and refuses the disavowal that had previously made such a figure invisible.

Madame Satã is a historical saga that crucially invests its meaning in the visual. Collaborating with the great cinematographer Walter Carvalho, Aïnouz creates a magical world that is utterly captivating and persuasive.[15] The story of Madame Satã becomes a color-saturated funhouse of sensuality and brutality, so lush that nearly every shot could be productively reproduced as a still or a painting. That visual approach is well suited to the film's queer homage, setting the compass points of the era's delirium with an unerring eye for detail. Couture and interior design, costume and performance take the place of narrative to transmit through symbols and codes the subjective scope of João's self-invention, split between the tough macho João and the captivating Madame Satã, a high-wire act of gender acrobatics.

Madame Satã convincingly revives an era in Brazil when questions of identity were anything but fixed. In a society where slavery was legal until

1888, where the mere color of João's jet-black skin would have marked him as chattel, what did it mean for him to redefine himself in a new universe, outside the laws of society at every level? These are questions that are not commonly operative in what has become, over time, a much more normative queer cinema, but they are essential to the reinvention of the category by a new generation in Brazil—and, like issues of class, should be essential for any truly relevant New Queer Cinema.

Race and class are often too incidental to queer narratives. In this tale of Brazil's unlikely hero/heroine, such omissions were impossible, for they are the core of Madame Satā's life and narrative. In *Madame Satā*, João's twists and turns of gender reveal a filmmaker's commitment to inhabiting all the spaces of marginalization to which he, and the viewer, have access.

By rewriting the rules and inhabiting the roles of both tough *malandro* and femme fatale, João/Satā defies easy stereotyping and confounds the codes of gender. It's as though breaking through the barriers separating slave from free person and black from white or mulatto has exposed the categories of gender and sexual identity as equally arbitrary. Not for João the fatal binarism of *reina* or *macho* (but never both) that doomed La Manuela in Ripstein's *El lugar sin límites*. Thanks to Aïnouz, João/Satā can claim dignity as well as heartbreak, robust masculinity as well as seductive femininity. Convincingly, neither one can be seen as the real João or the real Satā, for that figure is defined precisely by the contradiction, inhabiting the sphere of demons as well as the nourishing bonds of a chosen family and a despised but generative community. The streets of Lapa coexist with the stage of the Blue Danube.[16] Aïnouz makes *Madame Satā* into a time capsule of what was as well as what might have been, a queer view of a time and place that gives the viewer a glimpse, however brief, of new categories of personhood suggested by the trail-blazing, powerful, and tragic figure of João Francisco dos Santos.[17]

Queering a Continent

Alfonso Cuarón's *Y tu mamá también* (*And Your Mother Too*, 2001) broke the ice for same-sex desire in contemporary Mexican cinema. His crossover success, after years in Hollywood, was reportedly aimed at his son's generation. About-to-be stars Gael García Bernal and Diego Luna play best friends passing the time while their girlfriends are away by hitting the road with sexy Luisa (Maribel Verdú), whom they've met at a wedding celebration. Searching for a mystical beach that may or may not exist, the three end up drunk in a hotel room. Our protagonists Julio and Tenoch lose control: they have sex with Luisa, yes, but also with each other. Oops. That broken taboo marks the end of the trip and the friendship; with Luisa left to die of cancer off-screen, the myth of heteronormative masculinity is restored.

But the viewer doesn't forget so easily. The gasps of horror and nervous laughter emitted by mainstream Mexican and American audiences during the boy-on-boy sex scene would have been fatal to the film's commercial prospects in an earlier era. Now $33 million in ticket sales and a raft of Oscar nominations signaled that homosexuality was no longer off-limits—and no longer a source of box-office poison or social ostracism for Latin American cinema. Perhaps the shock waves that spread for most of a decade had an emboldening effect on a new generation.

The new queer filmmakers in Latin America were creating work suffused with sexuality and life's quotidian rhythms, pushing further into new territory, blinking at sexual disorientations no more than at ruptured narratives or nonnormative styles. Instead each opened up a previously unanticipated space for queer lives and desire.

In Argentina, Lucrecia Martel, a filmmaker close to the generation of Cuarón's son, took out her own camera to explore the underbelly of family dynamics, including a lovelorn daughter besotted with another woman, all observed with a whipsaw vertiginous style that alerted viewers to just how nonnormative her debut feature, *La ciénaga* (*The Swamp*, 2001), would prove to be. Another young Argentine, Diego Lerman, released a quirky lesbian-themed comedy, *Tan de repente* (*Suddenly*, 2002). Back in Mexico, Julián Hernández made an experimental narrative, *Mil nubes de paz cercan el cielo, amor, jamás acabarás de ser amor* (*A Thousand Clouds of Peace Fence the Sky, Love; Your Being Love Will Never End*, 2003), about a gay hustler with a broken heart. All three films renegotiated de facto compacts with their own national cinemas.

Lerman's debut, *Tan de repente*, based on the novel *La prueba* by César Aira, starts out as a classically neorealist depiction: its chubby protagonist, Marcia, is an unhappy working-class girl who seems to be the sole employee of a lingerie store. But Marcia's lonely life gets turned upside down when she is accosted in the street by a pair of lesbian thugs with knives and the dubious street names of Mao and Lenin. The monikers suggest ideological intentions, but the two declare their motive as purely sexual: they think she's hot, and one wants to have sex with her. Paradoxically, they also want to gain Marcia's acquiescence by trading her something she wants: to see the ocean for the first time.

One stolen car later, they're on the road. The trip is complicated by a detour to visit Lenin's aged auntie, where emotions deepen, unexpected switches occur, and true love wins out in the end. It's a black-and-white film that charms as thoroughly as anything from the era of the original black-and-white classics, utterly lovely in its transcendent innocence and sense of the world being remade for the better. Unlike any Argentine film before it and any Lerman film after it, *Tan de repente* is a cinematic vision, called into being perhaps by a queer moment suffusing the atmosphere.

In Mexico, Julián Hernández's work was also examining the nature of queer desire in previously unexplored landscapes. In his debut, *A Thousand Clouds*, Hernández also settled on a black-and-white palette and urban setting. The film follows a gay hustler as he tracks his lost love through the streets of Mexico City. An experimental, off-kilter narrative, its long and defiantly opaque title announces an insistence on playing outside industry norms. This languorous tale of a hustler's heartbreak has traveled the queer festival world, piercing the hearts of sympathetic viewers along the way. *A Thousand Clouds* maps a geography of love and desire, paid sex and unpaid romance, puncturing its sadness with surprises: a delightful encounter with two women selling records on the sidewalk, a brutal one with rough trade by a railroad track. Unapologetically shorn of both heterosexual signposts and narrative conventions, *A Thousand Clouds* creates itself as it goes, its gay working-class melancholia scored to the soulful tunes of Sara Montiel, and "Nena" in particular.

Hernández does more than spin a story. A veteran of MIX Mexico, he is deeply committed to a vision of queer cinema. Too avant-garde in his formation to churn out commercial movies, he's taken experimental cinema into the mean, lovely, and addictive streets of Mexico City. The second film in his trilogy, *El cielo dividido* (*Broken Sky*, 2006), slowed the dreamy pace of his debut feature to a somnambulant stroll in its version of schoolboy love, betrayal, and possible reconciliation. He observes no limits, either, in the rules of duration: *Rabioso sol, rabioso cielo* (*Raging Sun, Raging Sky*, 2009) is over three hours long. (Even so, this finale of the trilogy won the Teddy Award at the 2009 Berlin Film Festival.) It's as though Hernández is testing us. He needs to be absolutely sure of his audience and certain of viewers' identification before giving away anything so sexy as filmic pleasure. Between features, he tosses off shorter and even less commercial, though no less sexy, projects.

23.2 The "headless woman" tries to ignore her niece, on her motorcycle out the window, who is trying to seduce her. Screen grab from Lucrecia Martel's *The Headless Woman*.

Deeply embedded in this work of unruly imagining, he's one part Antonioni, one part Jarman, adrift in the land of Buñuel, and he keeps testing the ground beneath his and our feet to verify that it is terra firma.

Lucrecia Martel represents a unique kind of auteur, with a style and a set of interests that have remained remarkably consistent while evolving since *La ciénaga*. First, there's her regionalism. Nearly every other Argentine director hails from Buenos Aires, but she's firmly grounded in the north of the country, where she grew up and where her family still resides; she has returned to Salta for all three of her features. Second, there's her style: formed neither by Argentina's original golden age of cinema nor by oppositional New Latin American Cinema, she's a child of video. Initially self-taught with the cameras that her father brought home, Martel stationed herself in the kitchen and let the camera roll; later she'd take a camcorder into the countryside to shoot her siblings and cousins on rat-killing expeditions. Storytelling in the kitchen, a jungle outside, and a still-primitive technology to record their essences: there were no rules. So finally, a very queer vision emerged: gazing wide-eyed and unapologetically at absolutely everything and listening without judgment to all that was said.[18]

When Pedro and Agustín Almodóvar saw *La ciénaga*, they must have recognized in Martel a kindred spirit, for they offered to produce her next film, *La niña santa* (*The Holy Girl*, 2004) and would produce her third one, *La mujer sin cabeza* (*The Headless Woman*, 2008; fig. 23.2), too. Some combination of her talent, queer vision, provincial upbringing, and scandalous titles clearly called out to them. There is an innocent perversity to her films that works in perfect synchrony with her and their Catholicism and a subversive humor that underlies brutal turns of plot. And just as Pedro Almodóvar has centered many of his films on divas, so too has Martel recruited some of Argentina's most dazzling divas to anchor her casts of unknowns and nonprofessionals.

Sexuality in the Martel universe is always illicit and frequently incestuous across generations and inside families: father and son share a woman while mother and daughter compete for another; in a hotel, a man has an assignation with his wife's best friend, who is also his cousin and married to his own good friend. These are not tragic love stories, really, but the sexual ties contribute to the mise-en-scène. And always, sooner or later, there is a girl pining for another girl, or for another woman. In *La ciénaga*, it is the neglected daughter who pines for the indigenous Bolivian maid; in *La niña santa*, it is the two girls who practice kissing with each other, in that ambiguous but common adolescent ritual that so often exceeds its alleged purpose; and in *La mujer sin cabeza*, it is a wild niece cruising on her motorbike, unencumbered by the men of the family as she boldly propositions her older aunt.

With sexuality as repressed or expressive as the life around it, the maybe-lesbian protagonists participate in erotic exchanges to uncertain and ultimately unsuccessful effect. Martel's films are concerned with lesbian desire in both vague and offhand ways, but her characters engage that desire within worlds that lie beyond the formal control or norms of society. There, in Martel's worlds of refuge and subterfuge, rules are obscured and actions improvised. Desire is felt as much in the subtext as on the surface; backstory or aftereffect, it's rarely her main focus. Lesbian desire is neither tragic nor scandalous in Martel's films, but it's always there. The desire of one woman for another is one element positioned within the clotted sexuality of an environment (hotels, school, or home) where desire turns back on itself. Basically the world of attraction is as small or as large as the cast.

Martel is a cinematic naturalist, observing and cataloguing the follies that she calls into being as manifestations of her memories and fantasies. It's a queer world all around, captivating and repellent in turn, a puzzle that challenges viewers to dare to play. She offers a wondrous example of how queer cinema, done right, is cause for a radical expansion of possibility. She parses queer questions, not queer answers.

Though working in entirely different nations and sensibilities, Martel and Hernández both posit queer desire as a matter of assumption: it already exists before each of their distinctive films begins and is never resolved by the final frame. It's a cinema that's queer, not a queer cinema; an assumptive cinema, not a declarative one.

Notes

1. Costantino, "Latin American Performance Studies," 461.

2. Ibid.

3. For an in-depth history and analysis of Mexico City's oppositional performance sector, see McCaughan, "Gender, Sexuality, and Nation in the Art of Mexican Social Movements."

4. Interestingly, Hadad had long nurtured a project on Lucha Reyes, performing the songs and even writing a script, but had to abandon it after Ripstein secured the rights. For more on Hadad and the tradition of political cabaret performance to which she belongs, see Taylor and Costantino, *Holy Terrors*, particularly the introduction, "Imagined Communities," and the chapter on Hadad herself. See too Gastón Alzate's study of the broader cabaret sector in Mexico City, *Teatro de cabaret*.

5. See Gutiérrez, "Reframing the Retablo"; de la Mora, "Mexican Experimental Cinema and Ximena Cuevas" and "Chili in Your Eyes."

6. For more on Ximena Cuevas, consult the website of her U.S. distributor, the Video Data Bank, http://www.vdb.org/smackn.acgi$artistdetail?CUEVASX.

7. She is the daughter of the well-known Mexican artist José Luis Cuevas.

8. For an analysis of Cantinflas in Mexican culture, see Stavans, "The Riddle of Cantinflas." Cuevas disavows the comparison, citing Tin Tan instead.

9. Ybarra-Frausto, "Rasquachismo," 155.

10. Stavans, "The Riddle of Cantinflas," 46.

11. For more on both Karim Aïnouz and Madame Satã, see Aïnouz, "Interview with Tania Cypriano," in which he explains, "Madame Satã was an emblematic character. In Rio he was legendary. A black guy, very exuberant, a gay man who throughout his life was very outspoken; he was accused of murder; he adopted seven kids, he spent 25 years of his life in jail for petty crimes and sometimes serious crimes. . . . What is fascinating about him was that in the circle that did know him, every person you asked would tell you a different story and describe a different character since he went through so many transformations throughout his life. He was almost a superhero. When I began to think about the movie, I wanted to see the superhero after he has taken his cape off." Accessed online at http://bombsite.com/issues/102 /articles/3046.

12. For a review in appreciation of the film and the figure, see Edward Guthmann, "A Fascinating Symbol of Resistance: Black Gay Man Fights for Respect in 'Madame Satã,'" *San Francisco Chronicle*, July 11, 2003. For an analysis of the film in the context of Latin American gay culture, see Subero, "Fear of the Trannies."

13. See Shaw, "Afro-Brazilian Identity." Also see the work of Robert Stam, especially his *Tropical Multiculturalism*, published prior to the release of this film but clearly applicable to its modes of representation.

14. Leu, *Brazilian Popular Music*, 32–33.

15. Carvalho worked with both Walter Salles and Héctor Babenco and remains vitally connected to the resurgence of Brazilian cinema.

16. It is satisfying too that the cabaret's name should invoke that other tale of cinematic despair, Josef von Sternberg's *The Blue Angel* (1930), in which gender is firmly bifurcated and its codes upended by Marlene Dietrich's sexual power.

17. Aïnouz's follow-up film, *O céu de suely* (*Love for Sale*, 2006), seeks to do the same for women, examining the roots of gender, race, and class through an investigation of the body and its material value.

18. For more on Martel's formation, see my article, "Making Argentina Matter Again." For a closer analysis of *La Ciénaga*, see my notes to the DVD (Home Vision Entertainment, 2005).

19. As this chapter was completed, remarkable changes were taking place in Latin America. First Mexico City legalized gay and lesbian marriage in the city, then the Argentine Senate defied the Catholic church and voted to legalize gay and lesbian marriage throughout the country. In Buenos Aires, Lucrecia Martel published a newspaper piece celebrating the occasion and included best wishes from Almodóvar. In "Soy: Una ayudita para Salta" in *Pagina/12,* Martel quotes a note from Almodovar: "*Creo que Argentina se sentirá más justa y más civilizada, después de haber aprobado esta ley. Enhorabuena.*" ("I think Argentina feels more just and civilized since passing this law. Congratulations."). Online at http://www.pagina12.com.ar/diario/suplementos /soy/1-1490-2010-07-16.html.

At the same time, new films began to emerge that extend the boundaries for a Queer Latin American cinema. For example, young Argentine filmmaker Lucía Puenzo released two daring films: *XXY* (2007) and *El niño pez* (*The Fish Child*, 2009). The first explores an intersex adolescent with well-meaning parents and an awakened libido, the second a rich daughter who becomes her father's rival for the affections of their maid. In the first, the intersex teenager wins the boy; in the second, the daughter wins the girl. Puenzo's invention of deeply transgressive happy endings marks a radical leap forward in narrative possibility.

Shifts in political and social sectors always have an influence on the kinds of films that can be made. Perhaps soon Arturo Ripstein's early title can be rewritten to fit an optimistically envisioned new moment for a Queer New Latin American Cinema: *un cine sin límites*, a cinema without limits.

PART V

EXPANSIONS AND REVERSALS

24 *I. Cowboy Queer: Perambulations around Brokeback Mountain*

Every once in a while, a film comes along that alters our perceptions so thoroughly that cinema history thereafter has to arrange itself around it.[1] Ang Lee's *Brokeback Mountain* is just such a film. Lee accepted the grand prize at Venice just as Heath Ledger and Jake Gyllenhaal were accepting wild ovations from crowds at the Toronto International Film Festival, and an alert listener might well have heard the crack of the Earth splitting open and the history books rewriting themselves. Even for audiences educated by a decade of the New Queer Cinema phenomenon, it's a shift in scope and tenor so profound as to signal a new era. For never before has there been a film by a brand-name director, packed with A-list actors at the top of their careers, with the scope and cinematography of an epic, that has taken an established genre by the horns and wrestled it into a tale of homosexual love with such a monumental scope. It's a film made to ensnare a general audience, and it likely will.

The vast majority of New Queer Cinema films in the United States and United Kingdom were gritty urban dramas, set in New York or Chicago, Portland or London. Firmly grounded in the realities of gay life, they sought a vocabulary for a new AIDS and post-AIDS experience.[2] From the early days of Gus Van Sant, Todd Haynes, Cheryl Dunye, and the other trailblazers of a transgressive cinema, they prioritized a new mode of storytelling geared to their unprecedented narratives. These were usually sidebar festival films, not galas—certainly not multiplex programming. It's as though there were two different universes: one composed of the big majestic mainstream movie, empowered to order off the menu of any genre it damn well pleased; the other tucked into the boutique café, where independent films and small-budget specialties thrived within their constraints. *Brokeback Mountain* has blown it all wide open, collapsing the borders and creating something entirely new in the process. With utter audacity, the renowned director Ang Lee, the legendary screenwriters Larry McMurtry and Diana Ossana, and the revered novelist Annie Proulx (on whose story the film is based) have taken the most sacred of all American genres, the western, and queered it.

The story is a simple one. Ennis Del Mar (Ledger) and Jack Twist (Gyllenhaal) are two drifters in search of work who show up one day at a shabby trailer in the summer of 1963. Hired on as a team to guard the sheep that their employer wants to fatten illegally over the summer on protected government land, the taciturn cowpoke, Ennis, and the chatty rodeo rider, Jack, bond—and more—in the majestic isolation of Brokeback Mountain. The cinematic vocabulary of those scenes on the mountainside progresses from rough-riding, ranch hand realism to romantic idyll as the summer days pass. Finally, the sheep are shipped out, and Jack and Ennis go their separate ways, back to a Wyoming town and off to a Texas rodeo circuit, holding secret the bone-deep truth of a sexual love that dare not speak its name. They both marry; their wives give birth. Five years later they meet again, and it starts up all over again. My warning to menfolk in the heartland: fishing trips will never be innocent larks again.

The depth of Ennis's and Jack's attachment to one another gives their lives meaning, while at the same time draining out all other meaning, leaving them both emotionally enriched and destitute. If the film never shies away from the sexual truth of that attachment, well, it doesn't settle for the merely explicit either.

Brokeback Mountain is a great love story, pure and simple. And the story of a great love that's broken and warped in the torture chamber of a society's intolerance and threats, an individual's fear and repression. It's a great romantic tragedy, in the end, with no possibility of a happy ending. Setting the film in 1963 places it squarely prior to the modern gay liberation movement and the politics of modern queer identities. Tuning into the pre-Stonewall gay experience in all its euphoric and foreboding chords, Lee has used the skills he honed in *Sense and Sensibility* (1995) for etching heartache and in *Crouching Tiger, Hidden Dragon* (2000) for conveying emotion through action.

The first wave of film critics to see *Brokeback Mountain* began to riff on the obvious, pointing out that the western was always gay, de facto, anyway; wantonly, they started to nominate cinephile favorites to reconsider. It's irresistible, I suppose. But Noah Cowan trumped them all: the man who programmed the film at Toronto, he wisely held up *Red River* (1948) as an apt point of comparison. Actually, ever since the dawn of feminist film criticism and theory in the 1970s, film scholars have been analyzing the homoerotic subtexts in the homosocial world of the classic western. *Brokeback* goes further: it turns the text and subtext inside out, reading back the history of the West through a queer lens. Not only does *Brokeback Mountain* out its own cowboys, but it outs the Wyoming landscape (actually Alberta, Canada) as a space of homosexual desire and fulfillment, a playground of sexuality freed of societal judgment, an Eden poised to restore prelapsarian innocence to a sexuality long sullied by social shame.

Brokeback Mountain certainly isn't devoid of precedents. One obvious choice is *Giant* (1956), the film starring James Dean in his final role, as the black sheep on a Texas cattle ranch. Given the rumors of Dean's bisexuality and his claims to having worked as a street hustler, the cowboy duds in *Giant* must have been the frosting on the cake. Cowboys had long been a gay fantasy, even as being labeled a girly-man was a frontier threat; the camp cook might be seen in films in an apron, but all the lampooning equally served to enforce standards of masculinity. There are gay cowboys back in the days of silent films, but it's hard to be certain that they're not being played for laughs.

Andy Warhol knew all about the appeal of hunky cowboys for the gay imagination—and the dangers they posed. He and Paul Morrissey shot *Lonesome Cowboys* in 1968 in Oracle, Arizona, where a movie-ready Main Street (dubbed "Old Tucson") had been constructed nearly thirty years earlier for use in western movies and TV shows.[3] Warhol found himself investigated by the FBI when locals and tourists complained of immoral goings-on. An online archive of Warhol films and superstars details what happened there in Oracle when the star, Eric Emerson, made the mistake of using a local hitching post as a ballet barre for his warm-up exercises. Reportedly, he and the Warhol crew were accosted by a pack of locals who snarled, "You perverted easterners, go back the hell where you came from."[4] The completed film was a hit with Warhol fans, and *Lonesome Cowboys* won the best film award at the San Francisco Film Festival at the end of the year. After all, it was 1968, the counterculture was rapidly taking over the mainstream, and morality seemed to be up for grabs. Warhol's hip version of aberrance was wildly appealing—even though, as the FBI investigation demonstrated, just as widely condemned by Nixon's Silent Majority.

The following year, Dustin Hoffman and Jon Voight would rocket to superstardom with *Midnight Cowboy* (1969), another trailblazing movie, which followed Warhol's lead in coding queerness into the cowboy's duds and physique. When Voight's character arrives in New York, he has no idea of his western costume's true appeal; by the end of the film, he knows quite well whose fantasies he's there to serve. Yet he's also glimpsed true love in the flinty lessons dispensed by his street-smart buddy. *Lonesome Cowboys* and *Midnight Cowboy* cemented the cowboy hustler motif in the popular imagination and lifted a subculture to the surface, writing the cowpoke into the book of gay desire for decades to come.

To be sure, Lee sets *Brokeback Mountain*'s opening scenes in a time prior to any such shift. As its protagonists grow older and their lives unfold, though, they age into an era of much greater tolerance—in the cities, anyway. Keep in mind that the film's source text, Proulx's story of the same name, had been published in the *New Yorker* in 1997; one year later Matthew Shepard, a student at the University of Wyoming, was brutally murdered for the crime of being gay. Bright and promising, Shepard was tortured and killed outside Laramie on October 12, 1998, just shy of his twenty-second birthday. Among his other interests, he loved to fish and hunt. The cruel fate of Matthew Shepard for the simple sin of homosexuality was a horrific reminder of exactly how provisional and geographically specific contemporary tolerance remains. (And remember, Shepard actually had the benefit of class denied to Proulx's hardscrabble sheep herders.) Shepard's widely publicized death has been commemorated by *The Laramie Project*, performed throughout the United States in regional theaters and high schools.

Nonetheless the fantasy of the cowboy continues to exercise a mighty fascination. The most benign view to date was the romantic comedy by Thomas Bezucha, *Big Eden* (2000), which conjures an idyllic Montana where the only challenge gay men pose to old cowboys and mountain ladies is how to fix them up with each other. Funny and surprisingly moving, *Big Eden*'s love story centers on a native son who returns from his New York art world life to care for his dad and becomes so besotted with his high school love object (a jock, of course, and still heterosexual) that it takes him the entire movie, and a lot of help, to notice the Native American hunk who has long loved him from afar. The two-step has never looked sexier than it does when danced by two men in love, celebrated by their whole Montana clan.

When the British filmmaker and artist Isaac Julien created his poetic tribute to cowboy lust, *Long Road to Mazatlan* (1999), the queerness of cowboys was almost overdetermined. He told me, "It was really striking to walk around in Texas and see people in this iconographic cowboy costume, and to recognize it as the same dress code of gay men on the streets of London."[5] As if anticipating *Brokeback Mountain*, Julien (working as always with the cinematographer Nina Kellgren) staged a cowboy-cruising scene at a San Antonio cattle auction hall, choreographing bodies, stances, and glances into a ballet of desire as effectively and efficiently as Lee and the cinematographer Rodrigo Prieto would do five years later on that Alberta mountaintop.

Julien explained the title of his three-screen installation with a reference to a message that Tennessee Williams once wrote on a postcard to a friend: "I'm going to Mazatlan, please don't bother to ring." The notion of taboo and borders, whether crossing from Wyoming to Texas or from Texas into Mexico, is never far from the homosexual narratives of days of yore, for danger and desire were inseparable. And, it must be stressed, race is implicated as well. After all, why is it that Mexico is projected as the place where cowboys can perform the unspeakable? Crossing the line, whether out of the country or out of heterosexuality, meant risking disapproval, dishonor, or even death. *Brokeback Mountain* shows that it knows that perfectly well. Even if its fealty to the period precluded any critique of the racism inherent in Jake's crossing of that symbolic and real border, it's there.

But Lee also knows something else from his years of making films that tread with exquisite delicacy on the suffering of the human heart, from *Sense and Sensibility* to *Crouching Tiger*. He knows that great love and great suffering often come packaged together. Further, he understands that self-denial is as finely tuned a punishment as the physical damage any posse could inflict. He knows that the death of the heart, to quote Elizabeth Bowen, knows no bounds of gender, nationality, or era.

It is fascinating indeed that after the misstep of *Hulk* (2003), Lee has returned to the gay subject matter of his earliest triumph, *The Wedding Banquet* (1993), released a decade earlier to considerable praise.[6] *The Wedding Banquet* was a far sunnier film, free of fatalism and fatalities, but it also addressed the toll of social disapprobation. Times have changed, both historically and contemporaneously, between the two films. *Brokeback* carries the burden of a societal threat so crushing that it will not be solved, not even by the forgiving parents of the earlier film that are so conspicuously missing from the stern households here.

With *Brokeback Mountain*, Lee has done nothing less than reimagine America as shaped by queer experience and memory. Alas, it cannot be a sunny picture, not in Wyoming, not in the early 1960s, not here or there, not yet. In Toronto even the notoriously hardened press corps emerged from the advance screening in tears. One friend of mine, a gay man from the South who's been known to wear the occasional pair of cowboy boots, swore to me that never had he seen a film that spoke to his experience so directly. Fixing me with a look of intensity bordering on worship, he swore, "This is our *Gone with the Wind*." Not *Doctor Zhivago*? I wanted to ask. But why quibble. *Brokeback Mountain*, by raising the stakes, merits endless comparisons.

II. Meanwhile, Back at the Ranch

The claims that I made for *Brokeback Mountain* in the *Guardian* were issued within three days of seeing the film for the first time and published months before its actual theatrical opening. One of the great pleasures of attending film festivals as a critic, when the stars align and things go your way, is the chance to help determine public reaction and critical debate by the simple act of being first into print. It's the supreme critical luxury, one that's increasingly rare in a world of blogs, Twitter, and the diminished authority of the corps of publicists who formerly set the rules regarding publication windows. ("Hold Review" lists were always a basic feature of press packets, a courtesy extended by the press to distributors and filmmakers in order to maximize media attention when it could do the most good—on opening weekend. A piece such as the one in the *Guardian* was a feature rather than a review, and as such was allowed, even encouraged, as a way to marshal attention for the release.)

As *Brokeback Mountain* debuted and as its commercial release widened and widened again, I was frequently asked to comment anew. My initial festival review had been reprinted in Australia and South Africa, thanks to the *Guardian*'s reach into the Commonwealth countries. Subsequently I was interviewed for newspaper articles, interviewed for a documentary on queer film, and even appeared in a cameo in the "extras" on the Collector's Edition DVD.[7]

Without a deadline breathing down my neck, I could think more deeply about the significance of the film. I decided that it wasn't trying to invent a new style exactly. It was trying to mobilize the most classic and accepted of styles in support of a grand love story, the scope of which we hadn't seen before with a homosexual theme.[8] In this reliance on familiar forms and mainstream affect, of course, *Brokeback* was virtually the opposite of the NQC that had come before it, and yet it was impossible to imagine Lee's film ever being made, or even imagined, without that precedent.

While so many others ably analyzed the film's relationship to nature, so queer as to sometimes seem a throwback to Walt Whitman, and to the representation of sexuality between men, a feature alternately idealized and ridiculed by critics, I began to focus instead on a central theme of the film that actually runs through all of Ang Lee's work: the determinant power of the father-son relationship.

Brokeback's most terrifying scene, for me, was the chilling visit that Ennis pays to Jack's parents on the ranch, where an encounter with the bitter patriarch fills in for Ennis every blank ever left in Jack's character. This visit concludes with his momentous discovery of the shirt from their Brokeback summer, still hanging in Jack's closet—a torn garment that Ennis brings home with him. It is arguably this act that finally puts the love story into context and allows Ennis, at last, to fully express his love for Jack and to live with him "happily" ever after. Yes, it's ironic that Ennis finds true love only in the closet, where Jack's shirt literally hangs, and posthumously to boot. Yet it is undeniably that sacred shroud that heals his own wounds and brings peace to this heartbreaking love story.

I reread Proulx's original volume, *Wyoming Stories*, which ends with the story from which the film's screenplay was adapted, even then titled "Brokeback Mountain." What I discovered is that it's a collection of horror stories about the fatal effects of masculinity run amok, as it so often tends to do. Interviewed by Neva Chonin in the midst of reading the book, I told her, "*Brokeback* disrupts gender codes. It's more than just a love story with a Western setting. . . . It's a film about two young men who have been absolutely brutalized by their fathers and by toxic masculinity—exaggerated masculinity, Marlboro-man masculinity. A masculinity that denies tenderness and defines itself in terms of doing harm."[9]

In every story in the collection, men do terrible things to other men, and sometimes to the women as well. Neighbor to neighbor, father to son, brother to brother—weakness is dangerous, strength pathological. In this regard, the specter of homosexuality was not solely about itself, for as we know, it was long used as a yardstick by which to measure and authenticate masculinity in general. Proulx (who lives in Wyoming) and Lee (the immigrant, the urbanite) show the tragic effects of such a masculinist rule.

I began to think more deeply about the film and to seek a context for its story. I know that whenever we go into the past, whenever anyone writes a historical novel or makes a period film, we're always, in a sense, engaging in an argument about the present. Therefore I knew it was essentially impossible to be off-base in laying any interpretation whatsoever on the *Brokeback* story, given the interplay of contemporary projection and historical fact and the influence of the film experience itself. On the other hand, it *was* a different time in the early 1960s in Wyoming.

As I did further research, I didn't have to look far: the files of the Mattachine Society, an early gay rights organization, have been a major resource for gay historians. Consider the tale of one man, "Tom Forman," a survivor of the *Brokeback* era, discovered by Martin Meeker in his article on the Mattachine Society and gay life in the punitive 1950s and 1960s. The file is dated 1963, the very year in which *Brokeback* is set. Here is what Meeker relates about the pseudonymous Tom Forman, who wrote to the Mattachine folks for guidance, just as he was writing elsewhere to find a job and relocate to the city to live freely:

> Forman was but one voice of many crying out from the nation's hinterland, alerted to the Mattachine Society by word of mouth. . . . While it is not clear whether Forman ever made it to San Francisco, he did send . . . at least one more letter that indicates he marshaled his resources to make such a move. On 24 March 1963, he wrote that his contact at the placement agency in San Francisco "stated he could place me anytime . . . [so] I think I'll be able to make it by Summer." He imagined that upon his arrival in San Francisco, "it sure will be wonderful to be able to . . . be among friends. I have nothing here [in Kentucky]. No friends, no one to talk to." . . . The Mattachine Society . . . regularly heard stories of how bad things were in other parts of the country.[10]

The Mattachine Society was contacted by gay men suffering ostracism and imprisonment (Forman reported a six-month jail term for purchasing illicit publications) in isolated places throughout the country. The organization was a beacon of hope for those who knew about it. Both "homophile" organizations, the Daughters of Bilitis (for women) with its publication *The Ladder* and the Mattachine Society with its *Mattachine Review* (for men), were very aware of *Brokeback*'s type of tragic story: that was exactly the status of gay and lesbian life they were working to change.

A year after my piece in the *Guardian*, *Film Quarterly* invited me to contribute to a special section of critical responses to *Brokeback Mountain* after its theatrical run had ended. Having had my say early, I decided to examine not the film itself but rather the reactions it had elicited, to trace the film's remarkable journey through societies and popular cultures more fully.

III. Brokering Brokeback:
Jokes, Backlashes, and Other Anxieties

Word on *Brokeback Mountain* had been building long before its release. Distributors, publicists, and other industry representatives speak of the initial impact of Annie Proulx's story.[11] Passed around in tattered Xeroxes in a decade when Internet links were not yet ubiquitous, the story deeply moved many people. Among them was Diana Ossana, who immediately made her writing partner, Larry McMurtry, read it too. The pair contacted Proulx and, once she agreed to their plan to turn it into a screenplay, used their own money to option the rights.

They didn't expect it to take seven years to be made, but it did. Eventually Ang Lee's longtime screenwriter and producer, James Schamus, assumed a leadership position at Focus Features, putting him in a position to exercise an option on the screenplay and finance the project. Schamus and Lee announced the project in 2002. The casting of Heath Ledger and Jake Gyllenhaal was announced in 2003. *Brokeback Mountain* became real to the press, launching the tag "the gay cowboy movie" into the American vernacular.

While the signing of up-and-coming actors with major sex appeal was thrilling to some and titillating to others, the gay press was preoccupied with rumors: Lee and Schamus were going to downplay the homosexuality and make the story more heterosexual, the actors had no chemistry, and so on. The distrust was somewhat peculiar, given that the team had started their partnership on *The Wedding Banquet*, an early gay comedy; Schamus had been an executive producer on such early New Queer Cinema films as *Poison* (1991) and *Swoon* (1992); and Good Machine, the precursor to Focus Features, had produced *The Laramie Project* for HBO in 2002.

Brokeback Mountain had its world premiere at the Venice Film Festival on September 2, 2005, its U.S. premiere at the Telluride Film Festival the next day, and its Canadian premiere at the Toronto International Film Festival on September 10, almost simultaneously with its winning the Golden Lion at Venice. In the six months between these premieres and the Academy Awards ceremony, *Brokeback Mountain* became a cultural phenomenon, the rare film that could jump out of the film section entirely to become hard news and editorial-page fodder, a subject of parody, a controversy, a matter of pride. The uses that were made of the film transformed it from a marketplace product into a signifier of personal worth, political position, and cultural values, accelerating the process by which, more commonly, classic films organically acquire meanings and communities years after their initial release.

In the fall of 2005 Focus Features carried out a canny marketing strategy.[12] Its platform release first rolled the film out to the prestige festivals, opened selectively in major markets, and only then moved to more theaters in ever-wider sectors of the United States, expanding from 483 to 1,200 screens by late January and finally far more in the lead-up to and after the Oscars. Interestingly, during this process, the anxiety that had characterized the gay (or, to use current nomenclature, the LGBT) community's response prior to the film's completion now shifted to the mainstream.

Instead of fretting over whether the film would be heterosexualized, the mainstream press focused on how the film would perform: Would it make much money? Would anyone who wasn't gay pay to see it? Would anyone outside major cities go to see it? Would it break any box-office records? In other words, the anxiety had moved from whether the film was gay enough to whether it was too gay. The breathless coverage seemed to increase with every benchmark that was passed. Watching the reports and opinion pieces mount up, I became convinced that the unprecedented coverage, in terms of both column inches and speculation, represented a form of heterosexual panic. The language of economics and market forces masked hysteria and homophobia. While many on the Conservative Right tried to ignore the phenomenon, there was considerable attention from its electronic bully pulpit, as the watchdog reports posted on the gay website AfterElton.com make clear:

> David Kupelian of WorldNetDaily.com wrote an article titled "The Rape of the Marlboro Man" and then appeared on Fox to share his opinion. Charles Kincaid, of Accuracy in Media, has managed to be even more homophobic. Even Larry King invited anti-gay pundits on his show to debate and criticize a movie they couldn't be bothered to see. Fox commentator Bill O'Reilly can scarcely imagine himself catching the movie, but if he did, he imagines that when the romantic scene in the pup tent occurs he will find himself wondering what would happen if the cowboys from *The Good, the Bad, and the Ugly* were to stumble upon Jack and Ennis. Says O'Reilly, "Gunfire would be involved I imagine." MSNBC's Chris Matthew and radio personality Don Imus referred to *Brokeback* as

"Fudgepack Mountain" among other derogatory comments they offered on-air.[13]

The relentlessness of the satires, parodies, and jokes indicated a transparent use of humor to alleviate anxiety and provide symbolic protection. Mainstream media settled on a dominant response of ambivalent snickering. The cartoon *Boondocks* developed a running storyline concerning its homophobic grandfather's desire to see this "manly" western, while jokes about *Brokeback* proliferated on talk shows. On *Late Night with David Letterman*, for example, Nathan Lane issued a correction when his host spoke of "that gay cowboy movie," retorting, "Oh, it's so much more than that." But it was a set-up: the stage was transformed into a *Brokeback* musical, Lane belted out double entendres, and dancing cowboys made a wink-wink mockery of the very idea of the film.[14]

Jokes showed up repeatedly in op-ed pieces and newspaper columns. Larry David, in a New Year's Day opinion piece, wrote that he was afraid to see *Brokeback* because he might hear a little voice in his head saying, "Go ahead, admit it, they're cute. You can't fool me. . . . Go ahead, stop fighting it! You're gay!"[15] This parodic stance in relation to the film reached its zenith in Jon Stewart's Academy Awards show montage of gay western moments, still found on websites.[16] In print, the montage was manifested as an endless series of articles that sought to alert readers that the western had really always been gay—and, by extension, that this was therefore nothing new.[17]

Jokes most often took the form of a heterosexual man's reluctance to expose himself (so to speak) to on-screen homosexuality, a new-fangled revival of the old-fashioned contagion theory. One MSNBC contributor, Dave White, kept his tongue firmly in cheek with an advice column entitled "The Straight Dude's Guide to *Brokeback*." Posing as a queer-eye-for-the-straight-guy movie critic and acknowledging the discomfort that heterosexual male readers might be experiencing at the prospect of seeing the film—a prospect that he assigned to coercion by their wives or girlfriends—White offered reassurance. It's a western, he advised, plus you get to see Anne Hathaway topless, there's only one minute of kissing, and so on. White even appealed to a sense of fair play: "It's your turn. Really, it is, and you know it. Imagine how many thousands of hetero love stories gay people sit through in their lives. So you kind of owe us. Now get out there and watch those cowboys make out."[18]

Another tactic in the cultural mud wrestling was the "chick flick" accusation, made with apparently no awareness of how sloppily it conflated homophobia with misogyny.[19] This tactic offered an exit strategy to heterosexual men trying to avoid going to the film on dates: they could simply say they never went to "chick flicks." Focus Features acknowledged that their strategy involved targeting a female audience with, for example, a poster that resembled the one used for *Titanic*.[20] Still, it's arguable that the label allowed pundits to dismiss the film without charges of homophobia. John Powers, writing in the *L.A. Weekly*, identified the tenor of the commentary:

> The most fascinating thing about Ang Lee's wrenching "gay cowboy" picture (as it's lazily known) may well be the unlikely responses it's provoked. . . . The media have been filled with pieces . . . either saying "I don't want to see *Brokeback Mountain*" or asking whether the refusal to go makes you homophobic. I don't know about you, but I can't remember . . . anyone asking if skipping *Memoirs of a Geisha* means you're a racist. Gee, do you think gayness may still make some people uncomfortable?[21]

Later, gay bloggers would rebuke the LGBT community's leaders for not responding forcefully to the parodies, if not as hate speech then at least as a calculated campaign to "trivialize" the film. A major LGBT response was issued, though, to someone not identified with conservative positions at all but rather with film appreciation. The television movie critic Gene Shalit reviewed the film on the *Today* show and made reference to the way Jack, "who strikes me as a sexual predator, tracks Ennis down and coaxes him into sporadic trysts."[22]

Shalit's casual use of the term *sexual predator*, historically leveled to demonize gay men, quickly brought down upon him the wrath of the Gay and Lesbian Alliance against Defamation (GLAAD), a media watchdog group. A press release urged its readers to write to NBC to complain. This campaign, in turn, led to a rejoinder by Gene's son, Peter Shalit, whose statement was published in the national gay magazine, the *Advocate*. "I am a gay man, a physician, serving a mostly gay patient population in Seattle," he wrote. "I am hurt by your mischaracterization of my father, a man who does not have a molecule of hate in his being." In particular, he criticized GLAAD for attacking his dad when so many real enemies lurked. "Incidentally, I loved the movie," he added.[23]

Surveying the mainstream press, responses can be grouped according to the political position occupied by each columnist, television commentator, or organization, with their responses to *Brokeback Mountain* slotted into the relevant categories of tolerance, antagonism, or ridicule. As the film began to move in larger and larger circles, there was an effort to conscript more voices into the debate. For a while, no celebrity, actor, or political figure was safe from the *Brokeback* roll call.

Catherine Deneuve was questioned by reporters at the Bangkok Film Festival, where she was receiving an award. She acknowledged her surprise at the film's success. "You wouldn't think that because of homophobia it could be popular," she said. Ever the diplomat with her public to consider, she quickly added, "But it's also one of the strengths of the American people that they are surprising."[24] President George W. Bush was asked his opinion during a question-and-answer session at Kansas State University and answered grimly that he hadn't seen the film.[25] The fan who'd asked the question recommended he check it out. Soon enough, in a striking display of the film's viral mutations, Bush was cast opposite Cheney in a cartoon parody of *Brokeback* on the cover of the *New Yorker*, following the notorious Cheney shooting incident.[26]

While *Brokeback*'s cycle of mainstream attention ended after analysis of the Oscar results, the LGBT community's connection to the film has continued. During the film's initial run, writers had been overwhelmingly celebratory of the film. Marcus Hu, co-president of Strand Releasing, was one of the first gay voices in the industry to express unequivocal support, calling it "a gay *Romeo and Juliet*" in a column for the trade website indiewire.com, written just prior to its release.[27]

Just as mainstream critics were overwhelmingly positive, so were the LGBT press and blogosphere largely euphoric. Focus Features set up a "Share Your Story" feature on its website that brilliantly fused marketing and community service, shepherding gay autobiography and history under the *Brokeback* brand. There thousands of anonymous writers told their stories. Among them are tales as heartbreaking as anything in the film: stories of isolation and abuse in rural America, suicide and loss, marriage and denial, and finally escape (for it was mainly the ones who got away who wrote in).

AfterElton.com started a *Brokeback Mountain* forum, compiled links to articles on the film, and provided a link to Dave Cullen's Ultimate Brokeback Guide, a dedicated website with multiple discussion threads on the film.[28] Its articles and discussion sites are a convenient representative index of gay responses to the film: "Culture: How America and the World Is Reacting to *Brokeback*," "The Backlash against the *Brokeback Mountain* Backlash," "Has America Passed the *Brokeback* Test?," "More Actors Willing to Play Gay for Pay," and so on. A year after the film's debut, "The Impact on Society and Ourselves" thread alone had 26,545 postings; a post written in mid-September 2006 was from a man announcing he had come out to his family with the help of the film and this online community. As the film escaped its status as a commodity to become a compass by which people fixed their own coordinates, it also escaped the expiration date common to films released into a generally unforgiving marketplace, achieving a shelf life of indeterminate longevity.

A joke for some, a banner for others. And for still others, a target of criticism. Gay male viewers and reviewers, in particular, had bones to pick. Some criticized the emphasis on emotion over sex, or contended it wasn't relevant to gay experience (shades of chick flicks again, this time meant to evoke the feminization of rugged homosexuality). Some, like Gary Indiana, questioned the legitimacy of the characters' attraction, arguing that while the isolationism of small-town life was credible, what "seems less real, despite the months that separate each of Jack and Ennis's reunions, is the unfailing high voltage of their sexual connection. It's . . . rare for people to stay sexually interested in someone they love for much longer than two years."[29]

Other gay writers circled back to the original charge that Focus Features was going to defang the film and turn it heterosexual. In a notorious piece in the *New York Review of Books*, Daniel Mendelsohn argued exactly that. Even the press kit, he charged, had sought to conceal its central theme and to further the agenda of the advertising campaign tagline "Love is a force of nature."[30] His central argument concerned the sense of a betrayal of queerness caused by a marketing of product based on a hypothetical universalism. In his answer, Schamus interestingly noted, "Mendelsohn is rightly nervous about what happens when a gay text is so widely and enthusiastically embraced by mainstream hetero-dominated culture; and it is true that many reviewers contextualize their investment in the gay aspects of the romance by claiming that the characters' homosexuality is incidental to the film's achievements."[31] Nervousness again, this time making an appearance due to visibility, not invisibility.

But visibility on what terms? Here, finally, is the heart of the *Brokeback Mountain* dilemma: on the one hand, a friend reports visiting his eighty-four-year-old mother in a Republican stronghold on Long Island and is thrilled to discover a *Brokeback* DVD in her den; on the other hand, sophisticated gay men in urban enclaves complain of conservatism and retrogression, a soppy package wrapped around an out-of-date stereotype. Is *Brokeback* merely the kind of gay-themed film that the marketplace can support? And is it, then, important to make or support such a product? The gay fans of the film who placed a full-page ad in *Variety* after it failed to win the Academy Award for Best Picture thought so.[32] Such an act was unprecedented in the trade journal's history and attested to the powerful loyalties the film had inspired by bringing its story out into the open of mainstream release.

Brokeback Mountain was an event movie, one that sought with old-fashioned ambition to straddle marketplaces and move beyond self-identified audiences. That strategy is unlikely to appeal to all members of the LGBT community prepared to cast judgment on any such gesture. Universalism, for good reason, is suspect by now. But what takes its place, then? Limited releases? Mutually exclusive niches in our increasingly niche-fueled society? No-budget digital stories distributed by download? *Brokeback Mountain* was a mainstream release inspired by a widely read story by an established author, written by highly regarded screenwriters, directed by a name-brand hetero-sexual director.[33] A post–identity politics epic. And a hit. Whether that's a good or a bad development will have to be decided, as usual, in hindsight.

Notes

Part I was originally published in a shorter version as "Hello Cowboy," *The Guardian*, September 23, 2005, and reprinted as "Queer Eye for the Cowboy," *Sydney Morning Herald*, October 22, 2005, and "How the Western Was Won," *Mail & Guardian*, South Africa, January 24, 2006. Part II is new material. Part III was originally published as "Brokering Brokeback: Jokes, Backlashes, and Other Anxieties," *Film Quarterly* 60. 3 (winter 2007): 44–48.

1. Thanks to Andrew Pulver, *Guardian* editor, for commissioning my feature article, "Hello Cowboy," which ran in the *Guardian* on September 23, 2005, filed from the midst of the Toronto International Film Festival, where I'd just seen the film. And thanks to Linda Williams and editor in chief Rob White for inviting me to contribute an article, "Brokering Brokeback," on the online uses of the film for a special section of *Film Quarterly*. This chapter incorporates elements of both, and then some.

2. This is shorthand: it was a response to the AIDS epidemic *before* the invention of the drug cocktails that kept people from dying and then *after*, when AIDS was no longer fatal, at least for people with access to the drugs.

3. Note that the official history of "Old Tucson" omits *Lonesome Cowboys* from its roster of movies shot there and makes no mention of Warhol, his superstars, or the FBI.

4. My sources included numerous accounts and online records of the FBI investigation as well as direct quotes from Gary Comenas. *Brokeback* has spawned a small publishing industry since I wrote this chapter. See Needham, *Brokeback Mountain*, 70.

5. For a much longer and more informative discussion of *Long Road to Mazatlan*, see Rich, "The Long Road."

6. *The Wedding Banquet,* a small art house film typical of the era, was a gentle romantic comedy of errors in which a young Taiwanese gay man, living happily in lower Manhattan with his Caucasian boyfriend, is so panicked by his parents' sudden visit that he recruits a Chinese woman to portray his fiancée; problems, pranks, and a happy ending ensue.

7. Neva Chonin, "Midnight Cowboys," *San Francisco Chronicle,* December 18, 2005; Cole Akers, "Giant Queer Movies!," OC *Weekly,* December 21, 2005; *Brokeback Mountain Collector's Edition,* DVD release by Universal, 2005. I also talked about the film, immediately after seeing it, for the IFC documentary *Fabulous! New Queer Cinema* (2006), directed by Lisa Ades and Lesli Klainberg.

8. Chonin, "Midnight Cowboys."

9. Ibid.

10. Meeker, "Behind the Mask of Respectability," cited in Akers, "Giant Queer Movies!"

11. For speaking with me, thanks to James Schamus and Harlan Gulko, Marcus Hu, John Murphy, Andrew Pulver, Stephen Raphael, Charles Wilmoth, and many others.

12. The marketing strategy was elaborated in a *Hollywood Reporter* story that is no longer available online to nonsubscribers (#1001956880).

13. See http://www.afterelton.com/archive/elton/movies/brokeback.html.

14. Originally broadcast on December 21, 2005. For another take on the episode and the use of humor to deflect gay dangers as well as powers, see Creekmur, "Brokeback: The Parody."

15. Larry David, "Cowboys Are My Weakness," *New York Times,* January 1, 2006.

16. See "78th Academy Awards: Homoerotic Westerns," http://www.milkandcookies .com/link/42908/detail and YouTube postings.

17. See David Thomson, "Who Are You Calling Butch?," *Independent* (U.K.), September 13, 2005, and a later piece on the decline of the Western by Alex Cox, "A Bullet in the Back," *Guardian,* May 5, 2006.

18. White, "The Straight Dude's Guide to 'Brokeback.'"

19. See, for instance, *Newsweek*'s Susanna Schrobsdorff, "Chick Flick Cowboys." While young women have long been recognized as the primary audience for gay male films in Japan, the argument that American women would be the audience for a gay male film is new. It's tempting to read this as a gendered corollary to the notorious male audience for lesbian-themed sex movies, only substituting romance for the former's porn focus.

20. Sean Smith, "Forbidden Territory," *Newsweek,* November 21, 2005.

21. John Powers, "Hollywood's Newest Age of Liberal Cinema," *L.A. Weekly,* January 13, 2006. See also the astute Manohla Dargis article, "Masculinity and Its Discontents in Marlboro Country," *New York Times,* December 18, 2005.

22. Shalit delivered the review as part of his "Critic's Corner," *Today,* NBC, January 5, 2006.

23. Http://www.advocate.com/news/2006/01/07/gene-shalit-trashes-brokeback
-mountain-antigay-review, posted January 10, 2006.

24. Agence-France Press, February 20, 2006, Bangkok, web link now defunct.

25. See Peter Wallsten, "Bush on Brokeback, Didn't See, Can't Tell," *Los Angeles Times*, January 23, 2006.

26. *New Yorker* cover art by Mark Ulriksen, February 27, 2006. It was titled "Watch Your Back Mountain" and was occasioned by Vice President Dick Cheney's hunting accident, when he shot and injured Harry Whittington.

27. See http://www.indiewire.com/article/first_person_marcus_hu_on_broke back_mountain. Similar comparisons to classic films appeared in Anthony Kaufman, "Range Rovers: Subversive Western Poses Special Challenge for Ang Lee and Focus," *Variety*, October 26, 2005, among other articles.

28. "The Ultimate Brokeback Guide," http://www.davecullen.com/brokeback /guide/.

29. Gary Indiana, "West of Eden," *Village Voice*, November 29, 2005. In a posting a year later to The Evening Class (http://theeveningclass.blogspot.com/2006/06/2006 -frameline-xxxb-ruby-rich-on-q.html), Indiana objected to my use of his quotation. His clarification: that sex between *any* two people "gets stale" after two years (posted on January 1, 2007). My thanks to Michael Guillen for his terrific website.

30. Mendelsohn, "An Affair to Remember," and the exchange of letters between Mendelsohn, Schamus, and Joel Connaroe in *New York Review of Books*, April 6, 2006.

31. See Schamus's letter on the *Filmmaker Magazine* blog, "Focus(ed) Debated," March 24, 2006, http://www.filmmakermagazine.com/blog/2006/03/focused-debated .php.

32. The ad appeared in *Variety* on March 10, 2006. See Jim Emerson's defense on Roger Ebert's website: http://rogerebert.suntimes.com/apps/pbcs.dll/article?AID =/20060309/SCANNERS/60309006. Emerson champions the Ultimate Brokeback Forum fans' ad as an act of love, not anger. The site and its forums are archived at http://www.davecullen.com/brokeback/guide.

33. Yes, married to a scientist wife and proud father of two children, Ang Lee is a professed heterosexual (as is the similarly married James Schamus). But after Lee's gay trilogy of *The Wedding Banquet*, *Brokeback Mountain*, and *Taking Woodstock*, tongues are wagging again, though nobody accused him of being a swinger after *The Ice Storm* or an assassin after *Crouching Tiger, Hidden Dragon*. Notions of gay contagion die hard.

ITTY BITTY TITTY COMMITTEE

Free Radicals and the Feminist Carnivalesque

25 A persistent problem of New Queer Cinema, which I've addressed repeatedly, has been its lack of gender balance. Even including the low-budget productions where more lesbians have tended to work, the imbalance has only worsened. Hopefully there's a new generation ready to jump into action, but I fear they are more likely to show up on YouTube than on film festival circuits, more likely to surface on blogs than in the newspapers I still read. I fear for their visibility. The NQC has been dominated by gay male directors who build oeuvres; lesbians pass through like comets, lighting up the screen before disappearing into *The L Word* credits and an otherwise unknown universe. Status differentials trump the category of queer.

From the start of NQC, there were only a handful of women, many already invoked in these pages: Alex Sichel, Shu-Lea Cheang, Rose Troche, Maria Maggenti, Cheryl Dunye, Hilary Brougher. For argument's sake, include those who came just before: Patricia Rozema, Donna Deitch, Léa Poole, Sheila McLaughlin, Yvonne Rainer, Monika Treut.[1] The ranks are woefully thin, the prospects dim.

Luckily, in 2007 one project snuck through: Jamie Babbit (*But I'm a Cheerleader*, 1999) found assistance in one of the few bright spots in lesbian production and financing: POWER UP, a nonprofit founded by Stacy Codikow to produce work by lesbian writers and directors.[2] Babbit had already established a reputation with her earlier features, shorts, and stint as a television director (including, yes, *The L Word*). She was a good bet and she had a great idea: *The Itty Bitty Titty Committee*, a film that went back to the source for new inspirations.[3] The source, in her case, was Lizzie Borden's legendary pre-NQC classic *Born in Flames* (1983), her inspiration the idea of reviving those gritty, exciting days of early lesbian-feminist feature filmmaking.

"She says I'm the inspiration, but I don't see it," Borden wrote me.[4] Babbit certainly does: she always introduces *Itty Bitty Titty Committee* (IBTC) as an homage to *Born in Flames* and credits the earlier film for her film's style, tone, and kick-ass spirit. If Babbit was looking for a route out of lifestyle narratives and back into the pent-up rage and political energies of lesbians in the 1970s and early 1980s, she found the right model. Borden was working in New York City at a moment in between the women's liberation movement and a full-scale AIDS epidemic, in between feminism's consciousness-raising groups and lesbian power-brokering, in between Reagan and . . . Reagan. Babbit, filming in L.A. in 2006, updated *Born in Flames*'s downtown punk-dyke attitude to reflect the lives of young lesbians today—if they live in a world of postpunk, pansexual, anarchist, communalist, anticonsumer-ist acting-out. Thanks to IBTC, there was a rerelease and reconsideration of *Born in Flames* unmatched since it first appeared in 1983, when audiences packed theaters to see it and a generation of theorists wrote about it.[5]

Babbit appears to have taken to heart the lessons of *Born in Flames*. She echoed its production commitment to an all-woman crew, or nearly so.[6] She respected and updated the driving musical soundtrack that had made early *Born in Flames* fans want to dance all the way to the revolution. She shot scenes in Super-8mm and 16mm, emulating the production formats used by Borden and other indie filmmakers of that time. Babbit's long-time partner, the producer Andrea Sperling, personally masterminded the production, using the low-budget pickup style of the early storied NQC.[7] And of course, there's the title, impossible to hide behind, brandished like a fiery sword in front of the film itself, warning all and sundry what to expect.

In addition to her tip of the hat to Borden, Babbit invokes an entire roster of names with this film, a blast from the past, as though she'd synthesized a mixtape of lesbian and feminist Greatest Hits into the shapes, politics, and subtexts of her screenplay in a bid to make once-powerful ideas live and breathe again. Decoding her film becomes both a great game for the viewer and a process of enlightenment—that is, a subcultural lesbian-feminist Enlightenment, not necessarily the rationalist kind.

Itty Bitty Titty Committee opens with Anna (Melonie Diaz) a young Latina, facing a life crisis: she's been dumped by her girlfriend and rejected by the only college to which she applied, she's living at home with her parents, and her sister expects her to dress up as a bridesmaid for her upcoming traditional wedding. Her dead-end job has her manning the receptionist desk at a local plastic surgeon's office, where a steady stream of women show up for boob jobs. She steels herself for a grim summer.

And then, just like Alice in the looking glass, one fateful encounter changes her life. Leaving work late, Anna discovers Sadie (Nicole Vicius) spray-painting graffiti on the clinic walls: incendiary slogans exhort women to love their bodies and abandon surgical "improvements." Sadie invites Anna to her group's next meeting, flirting madly while she describes it: Clits in Action, or C(I)A, a sort of underground cell carrying out mysterious actions. The film then morphs into a coming-of-age tale in which Anna is inducted, not into lesbianism (she already is one), but into politics, consciousness-raising, the duplicities of love, and the passion of activism. (Incidentally, it also appears to be her induction into a race and class to which she doesn't belong: a majority-white group with a style and lifestyle outside the realm of her simple Latino family.) The courtship of Sadie and Anna then plays out against the forward motion of C(I)A brainstorming and actions (fig. 25.1). The cell's members tag slogans, crash store windows, disrupt press conferences, infiltrate a television show, and pull off a major, spectacular action in the nation's capital as a

25.1 The leader of the C(I)A feminist guerrilla group, Shulamith Firestone (the nom de guerre for Carly Pope), lectures eager newcomer Anna (played by Melonie Diaz) on the fine points of ideology in *Itty Bitty Titty Committee*.

grand finale. In between, though, they play the age-old games of lesbian bed-swapping and heart-breaking.

That's the plot, but *IBTC* is more than its style or story, and its homages are not there just for fun. It's a history lesson and a call to arms, a guerrilla action keyed to audiences fed up with a status quo that seems to have left them behind long ago. And its strategies reach beyond the mise-en-scène.

Consider its hall-of-mirrors casting. Melanie Mayron is Courtney Cadmar, a second-wave feminist leader with a backstory: as a visiting lecturer at Smith, she'd swept away young Sadie. Mayron starred in of one of the earliest feminist independent feature films, Claudia Weill's *Girlfriends* (1978), and was in the cast of television's iconic show of the 1980s, *thirtysomething*. She's a perfect choice to embody this earlier era.

Cadmar appears on a television talk show hosted by the archconservative Marcy Maloney, played by Guinevere Turner of *Go Fish* and *Watermelon Woman* fame, a casting choice that links *IBTC* explicitly to the early NQC. The déjà vu continues. Another C(I)A member is Laurel, played by Jenny Shimizu, who was the It girl of the 1980s known for her modeling, rumored love affairs, and brief squiring of Madonna; she now describes herself as a "sober Samurai." When the C(I)A girls pick up sexy hitchhiker Calvin on the side of the road, s/he turns out to be Daniela Sea, who played transman Mac on *The L Word*.

In this use of casting as a way to "write" a film's meaning beyond its screenplay, Babbit is following Borden too. Flo Kennedy appears in *Born in Flames* as a strategy advisor, but she was defense attorney to Valerie Solanas in "real" life. The editor of a journal collaborating with men in power was a young Kathryn Bigelow, and the woman on the World Trade Center roof was Sheila McLaughlin.

In Babbit's case, the casting strategy encourages her publics to recognize their lineages on the screen and invest accordingly, while her considered choices of names and actions deepen the film's grasp of history and links it firmly to the *Born in Flames* era and influences. Carly Pope, boss-lady of the C(I)A, adopts Shulamith Firestone as her nom de guerre, invoking the uncompromising theorist whose book *The Dialectic of Sex: A Case for Feminist Revolution* was published when she was only twenty-five.[8] Firestone was a revolutionary futurist convinced that the fundamental key to women's liberation was to separate procreation from women's physical bodies; she's a visionary who used Marx, Engels, Freud, and Beauvoir to critique the structures of gender power, called on women to rise up against the oppression of their own biology, and helped found the first women's liberation organizations. This is no casual moniker that Pope's character has chosen. Naming, like casting, has power.

In keeping with the examples of both Firestone and *Born in Flames*, the C(I)A's politics are a brew of earlier clarion cries updated for the present. Its agenda too calls for women to repudiate patriarchal norms and stop playing by the rules, since politics-as-usual gets us nowhere. Purposefully interventionist, the C(I)A disrupts events both public and private, at one point even crashing a meeting at the home of the Cadmar character where fiery young Sadie hangs her secretly bourgeois hat. For the C(I)A, only direct action personally instigated can be trusted to turn the tide.

For years, women seeking their rights in the United States did the opposite: they played by the rules, to little effect. In a serendipitous intersection of history and imagination, *Itty Bitty Titty Committee* had its premiere in Austin at the South by Southwest Film Festival in 2007. The same year, a new campaign was launched to build support for reviving and passing the Equal Rights Amendment. The last campaign had ground to a halt twenty-five years earlier: it ran out of time, three states shy of the vote required, after incessant attacks by the right-wing orator Phyllis Schlafly, who declared, "ERA means abortion funding, means homosexual privileges, means whatever else."[9] She twisted arguments and whipped up hatred, dooming the amendment in the final months of 1982—the very year that *Born in Flames* opened in lower Manhattan, with its posters all over the wooden barriers that dominated New York City streets at the time.[10] The legislation was defeated at the very moment that Borden's film arrived on screen to rally women to rise up and fight. In a replay of that timing, just as *Itty Bitty Titty Committee* debuted in 2007, Sen. Ted Kennedy, Rep. Carolyn Maloney, and the National Council of Women's Organizations pushed for the amendment to be put back into play once again.[11]

If this back-and-forth of dates and campaigns is whiplash-inducing, keep in mind that the vital question of strategies and their limits motivates the women of *IBTC* throughout. Consider that the Nineteenth Amendment, the one that gave women the vote, was first announced as a goal in 1848 at Seneca Falls, where women seasoned by their successful work as abolitionists came together to petition for an equal right to suffrage for women, among other goals. They would encounter such insurmountable obstacles that Susan B. Anthony, Sojourner Truth, and Elizabeth Cady Stanton would all die before the right to vote was won. Over seventy years later, in 1920, the amendment finally passed by one vote—cast, ironically, by one Harry Burns, a young man from Tennessee who'd been urged to vote for its passage by his mother.

Similar hardships faced the ERA, which merely sought to ensure equal rights in the workplace for women. The ERA was first proposed at the seventy-fifth anniversary of the original Seneca Falls convention in 1923, three years after women won the right to vote. Submitted by Alice Paul as the Lucretia Mott Amendment and rewritten in 1943 as the Alice Paul Amendment, it has yet to pass.[12] Keep this history in mind: for more than seventy-five years, an alliance of well-connected and well-behaved women with considerable assets and connections has been unable to pass an amendment to guarantee equal treatment before the law in the workplace, regardless of gender. No wonder a girl might get fed up with the usual channels, let alone a gang of girls bent on revolution. In the 1960s oppositional positions were manifested to an extraordinary degree, in keeping with the cultural and political ferment engulfing the United States and the world at large.[13] The postwar age of change and rebellion, full of dreams of transforming societies, inevitably encountered the nightmare forces of repression aligned to prevent any such change. Amid such turbulence, second-wave feminism was bound to contain contradictory forces too from its very beginning.

In this corner, in 1963, Betty Friedan shakes up American society with *The Feminine Mystique*, which posits the unhappy state of women in the United States as "the problem that has no name," a depression resulting from social exclusion and devaluation. In 1966, after three years of traveling door to door to organize women, she founds the National Organization for Women (NOW). Among its first calls: the legalization of abortion and passage of the ERA.[14]

In the other corner, two years later, 1968, Valerie Solanas writes the legendary *S.C.U.M. (Society for Cutting Up Men) Manifesto* and declares, "Life in this society being, at best, an utter bore and no aspect of society being at all relevant to women, there remains to civic-minded, responsible, thrill-seeking females only to overthrow the government, eliminate the money system, institute complete automation, and destroy the male sex." Famously, she later went to The Factory and shot Andy Warhol, then surrendered to a traffic cop in Times Square.[15] In the same year, the women's liberation movement arrived and waved a bad-girl banner at NOW: the Redstockings held a whistle-in on Wall Street, the New York Radical Feminists gave testimony in support of prostitutes, and masses of radical feminists had attitude to spare.[16]

Even journals faced off: *Off Our Backs* on the one hand, *Ms.* on the other.

Don't be fooled by the history books: the relentless calls to action had an effect. They created virtually all the institutions taken for granted by women today, from Title IX to the Guerrilla Girls, academic fields of study, and laws on domestic violence. It was an enormous sea-change, followed by more battles, exhaustion, and conservative pushback.

Lizzie Borden knew this history well and built her film from its blueprints. Babbit and her writing partners multiply their pasts, stitching together Borden's and their own.[17] Choices of casting, naming, scoring, and narrative make the audience flagrantly aware of the C(I)A's connections to more recent and therefore better-known bad-girl histories. Cue the music. Enter the Riot Grrrls. As the *Bikini Kill* zine once declared, "BECAUSE I believe with my wholeheartmindbody that girls constitute a revolutionary soul force that can, and will, change the world for real."[18]

The Riot Grrrls were America's very own return of the repressed, the rewriters of history come to earth to rescue feminism from the "F-word." Bastard daughters of punk and bastard sisters of grunge, the Riot Grrrls were brought together by shared experiences of marginalization and a determination to kick open a place for girls in the rock 'n' roll scene of the times. Riot Grrrls wasn't just the name of a music genre or band; it was a whole culture of zines, clothing style, self-respect, and women in the mosh pit. With Kathleen Hanna and other musicians and writers in the media spotlight, the phrase announced a new generation. In their search for ideas and models, many of them even credited their feminist studies classes: "The whole point of riot grrrl was that we were able to re-write feminism for the 21st century. Feminism was a concept that our mothers and that generation had, but for teenagers there wasn't any kind of real access to feminism. It was written in a language that was academic, that was inaccessible to young women. And we took those ideas and re-wrote them in our own vernacular."[19]

Band members, writers, and fans saw themselves as reclaiming the ethos of feminism past—just like *Itty Bitty Titty Committee* one decade later, its soundtrack packed with songs for its revolution by Sleater-Kinney, Heavens to Betsy, and Bikini Kill. Riot Grrrl started in 1992, parallel with the New Queer Cinema. It bubbled up out of twelve years of Reagan–Bush and popped into visibility full-grown, surfacing in the area around Evergreen State College in Olympia, Washington, and the University of Oregon in Eugene (and Washington, D.C., where the name and idea reportedly originated).[20] Determined to rescue a new generation of girls, the singer-musician and Riot Grrrl leader, Kathleen Hanna, teamed up with Tobi Vail to write the first *Bikini Kill* zine and form a band with the same name. They helped spark a movement.

With the C(I)A posse as Riot Grrrls redux (too much so for some young audiences who fault its 1980s ambience), *Itty Bitty Titty Committee* mixes the bad-boy energy of early New Queer Cinema—helped by Sperling's formative link to Araki—with lesbian-feminist anger, boisterous boasts, and furious ambition, all aiming to shake things up. The *IBTC* has the born-again urgency of a new generation's desires, its pure and undiluted energy, and its fury over the injustices of life, love, and death.

Such connections are not speculative, just a reminder of a time when worlds collided. In 1995, when HBO decided to commission a series of short music videos for girls, the NQC wunderkind Sadie Benning teamed up with Kathleen Hanna to make *Judy Spots*. The five shorts feature Hanna as the voice of Judy, an animated cut-out girl who survives dead-end jobs, incest, and girl-on-girl jealousy, only to find happiness with—of course, an all-girl band. Hanna and Benning then teamed up to form an actual band together.[21] Le Tigre was a huge success. Its lyrics spoke directly to girls and women disheartened and craving just such inspiration.

> Ten short years of progressive change,
> Fifty fuckin years of calling us names . . .
> Yeah we got all the power getting stabbed in the shower
> And we got equal rights on ladies nite.
> Feminists we're calling you.
> Please report to the front desk.[22]

Violence against women, the ERA, Alfred Hitchcock, and a call to arms are all assembled into a feminist frame with lyrics reportedly inspired by Shulamith Firestone's ideas. Not such a stretch: in 2003, when Firestone's *The Dialectic of Sex: The Case for Feminist Revolution* is back in print, Hanna's words of praise will be printed on the back. It's no accident that the leader of the C(I)A pack is named Shuli. These aren't coincidences, for Babbit surely knew these histories, overlaps, and referents when she was putting *IBTC* together, naming its characters, picking its music, and creating the C(I)A posters in Guerrilla Girls style.[23]

I'd suggest that, in addition to Babbit's nods to a feminist history of politics, music, and zines, there's another politics here: the antics of the carnivalesque, a mode of sociopolitical intervention not unlike the C(I)A's seemingly chaotic working process. The carnival as model is the legacy of Mikhail Bakhtin, whose posthumous publications initiated an excited academic exploration into the carnivalesque as a mode of political interference.[24] Bakhtin's idea of the carnival as an instrument of power available to the powerless inspired feminist discourses in the 1970s for its suggestion that actions aligned with the grotesque, the disobedient, and the parodic could indeed be powerful enough to break through the laws of the state and effect change.[25]

In *Itty Bitty Titty Committee*, the guerrilla actions undertaken by the C(I)A are just as carnivalesque as any of the dump-your-bra-in-the-trashcan demos of the late 1960s, ACT UP "kiss-in" actions of the 1980s, or apolitical flash-mob actions of the twenty-first century. If they transpire in *IBTC* in the alternative universe of a movie script, that ought not preclude the power of cinematic fictions. Culture does not follow the linear track of political action: it works on perception, subterranean and subtle, and lodges in dreams. To act, in life as in film, we must first imagine acting.

A carnivalesque action frees the imagination to envision a different world, a sort of voluntary amnesia in which obstacles and disciplines can be "forgotten" long enough to be flouted, with the fond hope that they won't necessarily be "remembered." Shuli and Sadie and their crew stage symbolic actions to catch the world's attention: papier-mâché mannequins to redefine women's bodies or an elaborately silly action turning the Washington Monument phallic to make a point about male political power.

The off-kilter irrationality of many of the C(I)A actions in the film can render them illegible, as I've heard from friends who considered the monument an infantile gesture. And yet such actions are perfectly consistent with the language of groups shut out of systems of power. Just as terrorism is sometimes described as the last resort for groups deprived of any other political speech or avenue, left only with violence as a means of seizing attention, so does the carnival offer a peacetime alternative to those whose demands are otherwise rendered mute and illegitimate, even in a porous, so-called democracy. By this logic, since the C(I)A radicals don't have drones to deploy, they try tricks instead. The same charge of absurdity was leveled at Borden for the World Trade Center ending to *Born in Flames*. After 9/11, though, Carla Freccero incisively linked this guerrilla action in Borden's film to a sense of terrorism as violation, spotting "the semiotic logic of the cartoon" that rendered the action more symbolic than silly.[26]

Itty Bitty Titty Committee exercises a related brand of cartoon logic, but in a sly last act, Babbit goes out of her way to answer the prosaic criticism usually leveled at those who launch such all-consuming actions: How do you earn a living? Babbit takes care of her characters' futures with end credits—her film's final fantasy—that provide employment for Anna and the others in their imaginary, post-*IBTC* futures.

Babbit dares return to the funky, low-budget world of early NQC in order to engineer a revival of the spunky days of lesbian feminism and to situate it in a world as imaginary in its own way as Borden envisioned. Her film is a place where the professor runs away with the talk-show host, where terrorism of the televisual kind can launch careers, where an ideologue and a vet can live happily ever after, and where even Anna's mommy turns out to have a past. Babbit made *IBTC* in an era far removed from both feminism of the 1970s and early NQC. But that didn't stop her.

As lesbians continue to struggle to find legible zones of representation on screen in a post-NQC universe, in a film industry simultaneously locked down (to outsiders) and threatened (by technological change), yet as inhospitable to women and lesbians as ever, *IBTC* offers another way: not simply DIY, but rather DWO, "Do it with others."[27] Group action is her retort to lockstep, DWO her retort to hipster DIY, the current brand of individualism. No, we can make our own. (Michel Gondry must have listened: he cast Anna's actress, Melonie Diaz, in *Be Kind Rewind* [2008] playing Alma, a character who prevails over abjection to save the day.)

Itty Bitty Titty Committee has an infectious effect on viewers willing to exercise their suspension of disbelief. Its metafilmic incorporation of popular culture and lesbian history is slyly empowering. Babbit tills new ground here, modeling inspirations and aspirations very different from other post-NQC as well as her own earlier work. This is a film that solicits queer identification in the interest of agency, for both its characters and its audience. But it also has a clear mission to reclaim the specifically lesbian history that can be muffled by the category of queer.

I think of *Itty Bitty Titty Committee* as a banner rather than a product. It's out there in the world now, to be taken up by the guerrilla cinebrigades of the future, wielding whatever technomachines are waiting in the wings, turning those new gadgets loose on new sets of obstacles, blazing a trail into the next iteration of representations, fighting the good fight, ready for the next generation of lesbian heroines. You go, girl!

Notes

This chapter was developed from a lecture delivered in April 2009. Special thanks to Prof. Leslie Dunlap, whose invitation to speak at Willamette University in April 2009 initiated my reexamination of this film and led to productive discussions with her Willamette colleagues and undergraduate students on the history of feminist and queer filmmaking. Thanks to Rob Nelson for facilitating the arrangement.

1. I list directors of dramatic features only; the shorts list is much longer, of course. I also omit documentaries and avant-garde and personal works, where there are so many lesbian filmmakers: Jennie Livingston, Barbara Hammer, Su Friedrich, and more.

2. In 2009 POWER UP switched from "gay women" to "co-ed." No comment.

3. Many Blockbuster video stores, the main source at the time, censored the title to *Itty Bitty Committee* on the DVD boxes. I was shown just such a box at my lecture. Reduced to a download and streaming service, Blockbuster has restored the full title. The full title appears on the Netflix site.

4. Lizzie Borden, email, September 29, 2008.

5. De Lauretis, "Aesthetic and Feminist Theory." Annette Kuhn and others wrote on the film in the 1980s. See also Rob Nelson's essay, "Lizzie Borden Took a Bolex," http://blogs.walkerart.org/filmvideo/2008/06/26/lizzie-borden-bolex; Mackenzie, "*Baisemoi*, Feminist Cinemas and the Censorship Controversy."

6. Borden wasn't alone: Sally Potter did the same for her production of *The Gold Diggers* (1983), starring Julie Christie and shot in Iceland with an all-woman crew.

7. Sperling was behind the low-budget solutions to many of the original NQC films and was Gregg Araki's original producer.

8. For a view of Firestone when she was an art student, see Elizabeth Subrin's "restaged documentary," *Shulie* (1997).

9. It's a widely referenced quote that sounds eerily familiar. See http://www.great-quotes.com/quote/960770.

10. In the 1970s and early 1980s, NYC was in desperate straits economically, just out of receivership. Its landlords busied themselves with constructing wooden scaffolding over sidewalks to avoid lawsuits by pedestrians hit by chunks of stone. Ironically, the barriers were turned into large-scale community bulletin boards, where posters announcing movies, concerts, and record releases could count on being seen.

11. See Juliet Eilperin, "New Drive Afoot to Pass Equal Rights Amendment," *Washington Post*, March 28, 2007.

12. For all things ERA, see http://www.equalrightsamendment.org. Today it would be the twenty-eighth amendment. Alice Paul too died without seeing it pass.

13. Events and organizations key to understanding the 1960s–1970s include everything from the Kennedy assassination to the Black Panther and Young Lord movements (crushed by the FBI), the war in Vietnam, SDS, through to Nixon's election, Watergate, the Weathermen, and anticolonial struggles in Africa, the Cuban Revolution, May '68 in Paris, the Algerian War, Mao's Cultural Revolution, the Berlin Wall,

Red Brigade, Baader-Meinhoff Gang, Pinochet's coup in Chile, the Montoneros in Argentina, and more.

14. Everything wasn't rosy: lesbians were purged from NOW in the early years, labeled "the lavender menace." See D'Emilio and Freedman, *Intimate Matters*, 316–18.

15. See Mary Harron's *I Shot Andy Warhol* (1996) and pay special attention to the misogyny of the Warhol crowd. My rediscovery of Solanas predated the film; see my "Manifesto Destiny."

16. For detailed first-person histories of the period, see Shulman, "Sex and Power"; Willis, *No More Nice Girls*.

17. Two young writers, Tina Mabry and Abigail Shafran, are credited for the script, while the story is credited to Babbit and Sperling.

18. Bikini Kill declaration, date unknown, cited in Rosenberg and Garofalo, "Riot Grrrl."

19. Jesse Colin Young, Sleater-Kinney, and Heavens to Betsy. Source unknown; widely quoted and referenced in blogs, websites, and journalism.

20. See Laura Barton, "Grrrl Power: The Riot Grrrl Scene Brought Feminism to Alternative Rock in the 90s," *Guardian*, March 4, 2009; Monem, *Riot Grrrl*; the Bikini Kill entry in Mitchell and Reid-Walsh, *Girl Culture, an Encyclopedia*.

21. The band carried on without Benning when she quit in 2001. Johanna Fateman and Hanna remained in the band, JD Samson replaced Benning as drummer.

22. "FYR," from Le Tigre album *Feminist Sweepstakes* (2001), released by Mr. Lady.

23. See Guerrilla Girls, *The Guerrilla Girls' Bedside Companion to the History of Western Art* and *Bitches, Bimbos, and Ballbreakers*. For details on IBTC's influences and processes, see Karman Kregloe, "An 'Itty Bitty' Feminist Romp," AfterEllen.com, April 2, 2007, http://www.afterellen.com/movies/2007/4/ittybitty.

24. I first read Bakhtin in the 1980s: *The Dialogic Imagination* and *Rabelais and His World*. There's a huge volume of literature on Bakhtin. See Stam, *Subversive Pleasures*; Freccero, "Feminism, Rabelais, and the Hill/Thomas Hearings."

25. See Isaak, *Feminism and Contemporary Art*; Russo, *The Female Grotesque*; and artists Sue Coe, Nicole Eisenman, Marlene McCarthy, and the late great Nancy Spero.

26. Freccero, "They Are All Sodomites!," 454.

27. Thanks to Patricia Zimmerman for coining and circulating this term in 2011.

QUEER *NOUVEAU*

From Morality Tales to Mortality Tales

in Ozon, Téchiné, Collard

There's a saying by the French philosopher Montaigne: You have to think about death every day in order to tame it. Maybe that's what I'm doing.
—François Ozon

The inclusion of French cinema in any category of New Queer Cinema is neither automatic nor obvious. Indeed the suggestion that the work of François Ozon has a place in such a volume has been met with skepticism.[1]

In early histories of gay and lesbian cinema, of course, France played a prominent role. Any such summary would have to include the monumental influence of (Belgian-born) Chantal Akerman as well as Jean Cocteau and Jean Genet, three essential figures whose work of 1930–94, from *Le sang d'un poète* (*The Blood of a Poet*) to *Portrait d'une jeune fille de la fin des années 60 à Bruxelles* (*Portrait of a Young Girl at the End of the 1960s in Brussels*) defined a pre–queer cinema as well as a new way of making cinema, of any kind, for decades. There was also so much in the art cinema heyday of French film to provide pleasure for gay and lesbian audiences of yore that these films became shorthand for an international fascination for sex and romance *à la français*, all twisted bisexuals and glamorous more-than-friends included.

By the time of New Queer Cinema's arrival in the early 1990s, however, France was better known in LGBT circles for actress idolatry (Catherine Deneuve, Delphine Seyrig) and theory and philosophy (Monique Wittig, Michel Foucault) than cinema. The increasingly transglobal LGBT cinema has owed less to France than to North America, the United Kingdom, Australia, Spain, and Germany. In Europe the primary figures of interest in the 1970s–90s were Pedro Almodóvar, Rainer Werner Fassbinder, Derek Jarman, Ulrike Ottinger, Monika Treut, and, until his murder in 1975, Pier Paolo Pasolini. None of the major modern influences were French. Since then, however, French films have indeed appeared and excited interest and speculation about their directors or actors and actresses.[2] Many have found success in the U.S. market, either in theatrical release or on the LGBT festival circuit, but they share no common project and in many cases lack even a queer director.

There is one particular lineage, though, that makes France not only eligible but essential to considerations of the New Queer Cinema in the post-1990s era. For just as French cinema has sometimes been seen by Anglo-American audiences as "inadequately queer"—especially given its penchant for including heterosexual sex as a plot element in any queer story—so today does it offer routes to conceptualizing sexuality within and beyond moments of crisis or celebration. Its insistence on a sexually inclusive cinema seems a better match for a more fluid queer world of postmillennial, postidentificatory sexual styles. As with French culture in general, however, any such assumption requires an understanding of the exceptionalism that undergirds all considerations of French identity and "lifestyle" choices. Context is essential to discerning the nature of a "*nouveau* queer cinema" and its queer spin on the latest French generation of auteurs.

François Ozon is the one French director consistently tracked by LGBT festivals and audiences, written about as an openly gay director, and celebrated with awards and loyal audiences for his presumed sui generis status as a queer French filmmaker. Yet his films often fit uneasily into those programs in terms of tone, theme, and intention, nor does Ozon exist entirely on his own, without precedent or company. His well-remarked cinephilia connects him to queer directors from other countries and eras, by inference (Almodóvar, Cukor, Pasolini, Visconti, John Waters) and affiliation, as in his recycling of a Fassbinder play into the script of *Gouttes d'eau sur pierres brûlantes* (*Water Drops on Burning Rocks*, 2000). I'd like to argue that Ozon is also inextricably linked to two other French queer directors whose films, at least those I discuss here, both pre- and postdate his own: André Téchiné and the late Cyril Collard.[3]

They are different generations, these three. Ozon is the youngest and arguably the most commercially successful, at least at this stage of his career. By examining their artistic links and the French political contexts shaping their work, the particularly French version of cinematic queerness will become more comprehensible. The unifying elements for all three include death, rage, grief, and the tortured fluidity of a sexuality in which eros and thanatos eternally change places. Never has rage been so subtly embedded, so obliquely written, so elegantly lived, as in the work of these three. Never has death been met with such clear-eyed negotiations of acceptance and disavowal, nor sexuality been made so damnably complicated, as in their queer tales. I'd argue that these three filmmakers and their key films that I examine—Collard's *Les nuits fauves* (*Savage Nights,* 1992), Ozon's *Le temps qui reste* (*Time to Leave,* 2005), and Téchiné's *Les Témoins* (*The Witnesses,* 2007)—are linked not only by the filmmakers' sexual identities but by a set of histories, concerns, and dissensions every bit as significant as those which, in the United States, have marked New Queer Cinema as distinct.

In the French context, these films rewrite the themes and, in some cases, the styles of the classic moral tales, or *contes moraux,* that long carried aloft the Éric Rohmer brand as a guarantor of quality. These new films instead serve as a disrupting influence on genres and themes, creating in their place a new set of mortality tales or *contes mortels,* deathly fables for the French Republic in its post-Vichy, post-Algeria, post-'68 era.

They describe a battle that mobilizes another resistance entirely, in all meanings of the word from the political to the biological. All are set in the mid- and post-AIDS moment of France between today and twenty years ago. In this new home-front war, the hallowed term *resistance* acquired a new meaning: it became the resistance of the immune system against a virus rather than an ideological enemy. (Though certainly there were plenty of those too—and were the battle lines finally so very different?) This war involved another kind of cell entirely: those hidden deep in the body. And while these cells weren't located in the countryside or urban safe houses, they were just as clandestine. In these skirmishes, of course, there was no enlistment: conscription was involuntary, recruitment continuous.

At a time when the New Queer Cinema movement in the United States may be over and careers are once again defined by the industry and marketplace, perhaps these "mortal tales" from across the Atlantic can also offer lessons in an integration that seeks to bind queer issues to larger social concerns and to engage without fear of contamination or assimilation with mainstream societies and genres. For in their complex sexualities and avoidance of politically correct solutions, the French are forever on the edge of abandoning the radical positions that the early New Queer Cinema represented. At the same time, that very flexibility of identity position carries a knife that cuts close to the bone, and in so doing shows, if not the "lesbian continuum" that Adrienne Rich once posed in more utopian times, then at least a dystopian continuum that cuts below the surface of assumed gender positions to reveal the swamps of desire lurking there, shaped by family dynamics that underlie the mores of polite society.[4]

Ground Rules: The French Context

François Ozon was born in November 1967, six months prior to the land-mark moment of French political and cultural history, May 1968. He is thus a member of the generation that came *after*: after the upheavals of May '68, after the end of the Algerian War, after Vichy and the Occupation, after the foundational moments of so much that shaped modern French politics and culture. As a gay man, however, he just as explicitly came of age *during*—during the AIDS epidemic of the 1980s, which hit France hard with the high-est rate of infection of any Western European country.[5] He also came of age during a first generation of French AIDS activism, marked by the founding of the organization Aides by Foucault's long-time partner, Daniel Defert, in 1984 and by the founding of ACT UP Paris in 1989.

Ozon was born into a newly open and liberatory gay culture in Paris, one in which the Marais became a gay neighborhood and homosexuality was no longer illegitimate, secret, or free of capitalist complicity. He would have been just turning eighteen in July 1985, when France's landmark antidiscrimination bill was enacted, in no small part due to the Socialist Party's election victory at the time (the old politics of state power never, in the end, very far away). The first Ozon film to attract international attention, *Une robe d'été* (*A Summer Dress*), debuted in 1996, the very year that the effectiveness of Highly Active Antiretroviral Therapy (HAART), or the "AIDS cocktail," was first celebrated at the International AIDS Conference in Vancouver.

In France the politics of AIDS were played out against the philosophical and material structures that contravene any such "single issue" debate against the overarching idea of the Republic, which imposes a unified wholeness on the nation and cares for its citizens under that mandate. In the 1980s the kinds of questions originally raised in the wake of May '68 and the end of the Algerian War also began to be asked in terms of the rights of immigrants, *sans-papiers*, women, and gays and lesbians. For a moment, even notions of multiculturalism as a praxis could be entertained, if not implemented. Out of that period there emerged an exciting new French cinema, the *cinéma de banlieue* or *cinéma beur* (roughly, a ghetto cinema or North African diasporic cinema). These films broke open the molds of the existing French cinematic formulas to make room for others: the brown- and black-skinned sons and daughters of the Republic, born and raised on French soil, sometimes for two or three generations, whose bodies and streets had been so long exiled from the nation's screens.[6] If the *cinéma de banlieue* would seem to represent an example of how cinema could play to the metropole from an "other" position, it is also a reminder that antiracism organizing at the time was often in alliance with antihomophobia organizing, a connection sadly missing from much of U.S. queer politics in the same moment. During the 1980s, however, particular rights were seen as inherently in opposition to the imaginary universal upheld as an ideal—however flawed—of French governance, complicating the discourse of such alliances. What has played out since that time is an ongoing, if unresolved tension between the group and the nation, between the specific individual or collective demand and the unified demands of the state. Known as the *républicanisme-communitairianisme* debate, it reproduces a version of nationalism that some contend can be traced all the way back to the French Revolution. Demands for gay rights or targeted AIDS awareness campaigns, though, are consigned to a subset of the nonnational or tribal, virtually undifferentiated from Muslim headscarves or polygamy; in fact early gay pride marches were explicitly linked to Islamic fundamentalism by right-wing critics. All such debates are shadowed by the rise of Jean-Marie Le Pen's ultraright National Front party and an acceleration of anti-immigrant xenophobia, preying on the nationalist anxieties triggered by France's European Union membership. In summary, France today is like much of the rest of Europe and many Western democracies: a place where, as Andrew Asibong puts it, "coherent social identities are clung to within respectable public discourses more possessively than ever."[7]

In this left–right war of fearmongering and fear-allaying, republicanism becomes the bedrock upon which radically opposite interests stake their claims; indeed Carl F. Stychin asserts that republicanism, "the dominant ideology" in France, "privileges the nation state and its direct relationship to individual citizens . . . leaving little space within the public sphere for groups within civil society to become politicized entities."[8] The earlier slogan, *droit á la différence* (the right to difference), which sought "a means to fight racism through recognition of social diversity," gave way in the following decade to the more cosmopolitanesque idea of the *droit á l'indifférence* (the right to indifference), meant to signal "the reconciliation of cultural diversity with universal rights and equality."[9] Elaborating the foundational differentiations, Stychin is clear:

> Republicanism thus provides the ideological basis for resistance to any claims to difference, which are constructed as contrary to the Republic itself, and as exemplifying communitarianism. . . . These arguments are closely linked to a dissociation of French political practice from an Anglo-Saxon model of multiculturalism, in which group identities are said to have become politicized. Throughout the debates . . . there is much discussion of an Anglo-Saxon politics of multiculturalism, difference and "political correctness"; all of which is encapsulated by the term communitarianism.[10]

From such a perspective, communitarianism is not only a potentially disruptive move toward fracturing the organic unity posited as constituting France as a national entity, but also a foreign move, derived from American and British examples in its multicultural dimension and from Islamic examples in its repositioning of the secular, and in both cases, therefore, allegedly non-French.[11]

The opening in October 2007 in Paris of the Cité Nationale de l'Histoire de l'Immigration Museum at the Palais de la Porte Dorée, its long-awaited and disputed national museum on the history of immigration, offered another case study in the writing of that history—beginning with the boycott of its opening by the newly elected president, Nicolas Sarkozy.[12] Such a response to a museum of this kind brings to mind Armando Salvatore's warning, in the context of a misleading interpretation of the headscarf, that attention must be paid to such reactions, as it "should not be dismissed as a simple epistemic distortion, an ingrained ethnocentrism, a will to domination or a politics of fear, though it probably includes all of these at once."[13]

The requirement in France to define issues in accordance with a birthright of universalism mandates that grand rhetorical flourishes are necessarily employed in order to stake out claims that otherwise would be seen as communitarian and thus rejected.[14] Thus was France's nascent antidiscrimination law reframed away from gay rights to include such cases as that of a young man denied employment on account of his long hair: it parses lifestyle issues, not questions of identity. The ranks that had originally sought a law prohibiting antigay discrimination expanded to make common cause with others: feminists, the antiracism organizing group *sos Racisme*, and, crucially, the Socialist Party. It was a uniquely successful coalition.[15] And its timing was perfect: on April 4, 1981, the first Paris Gay Pride Parade took place, attracting ten thousand demonstrators. The next month, François Mitterrand, the Socialist Party's candidate, won the presidential election—and decriminalized homosexual acts.[16]

The conditions were then set for the passage of the antidiscrimination bill, as the argument for universalism could now be made, specifying that the law would redress a loophole in universal rights, not impose new specific rights on specialized groups. The bill's passage was evidence of such a strategy's success in the French context, where difference has often been stigmatized, demonized, and manipulated for political gain. No doubt, feminist organizing around the concept of *parité*—not special rights but the elimination of a difference in rights—also played a part in opening a space in the public discourse. At the same time, there was one very real and unique feature to this particular campaign that apparently fueled support for the legislation, according to Jean-Pierre Michel, the deputy who sponsored it: "AIDS may have been responsible not only for its getting heard but also for gaining the sympathies of many lawmakers."[17] With new research and writing on the phenomenon of AIDS in the French context of the 1980s by David Caron and others, a better sense of the period is beginning to emerge.[18]

The bill was passed in 1985, during Mitterrand's first term, as part of a sweeping slate of social reforms promulgated by his government. In the following year, Jean Genet died, as if he could not bear to live in a culture in which he, with his lifelong commitment to crime, transgression, and outsider status, was now legitimate. Keep the moment in mind: the mid-1980s are the setting for both the Collard and Téchiné films, set in 1986 and 1984, respectively, though Ozon has typically stuck with a contemporary frame.

For Collard and Téchiné, those brutal years of the mid-1980s were heavily symbolic terrains, the ground on which their identities were formed, their friends died, their worlds spun on their axes. It's no surprise that their touchstone films were set in the intensity of those years. Collard would die before making another film, while Téchiné would make many more. For Ozon, it was a different story. As the time of his emergence into postliberation gay life, it suggests a different kind of trauma, one that may have pushed him into an eternal present, a state of denial as well as remembrance.

A decade later, and in many ways a generation later, Jean-Pierre Michel, the sponsor of the antidiscrimination bill, shepherded another extraordinarily decisive and divisive bill. The *Pacte civil de solidarité* (Civil Pact of Solidarity or PACS) was a new legal process that legitimated unions between unmarried couples regardless of gender (or, it must be said, of sexuality, as the civil contract excises sexual relationship as a condition of entering into such union).[19] Debate was prolonged and acrimonious, predictably dividing the Left and the Right, those who argued that the PACS was a means to legitimate everyone within the Republic as equal (in other words, as a guarantor of modernity) and those who saw it as an attack upon the sacred centrality of the French family (in other words, as a threat to tradition). Recent work has indicated that the PACS actually continues or revives an older French tradition of nontraditional families and same-sex couples, but that does not appear to have been part of the debate.[20] Stychin offers an interesting view of the PACS as "a source of nationalist pride because it demonstrates that France is at the forefront of progressive legislative change within Europe. . . . The PACS becomes a new element in the national self-image, and part of the corporate identity of France on the world stage."[21]

Through a combination of coalition building, significant intellectual capital, and Socialist leverage within the government, the PACS was enacted in 1999.[22] Given the constellation of meanings and values that it crystallized—ranging from the very nature of family to the implications for immigration—there's no doubt that analysis of the passage of the PACS and the attendant rhetorical alignments will be ongoing for many years.[23] Indeed at stake in the arguments was the very nature of France as a republic, now and in the future, with notions of filiation and *parité* equally implicated.[24]

Among its wide range of meanings for modern France, the passage of the law announced the power of the gay and lesbian vote in French politics and the voting bloc of those in the capital, in particular. With *Le Monde* reporting that the gay and lesbian vote was "at the heart of the municipal electoral campaign in Paris," it's no wonder that new presences appeared at the next Gay Pride March, to the consternation of veterans:

At the Gay Pride March in Paris, in June, Pierre Bergé, the fiery CEO of Yves Saint Laurent Haute Couture, gay philanthropist, and former Paris Opera honcho, reportedly threw a fit when he saw Romero and other Séguinist elected officials marching (though their mentor had skipped the march). "Right-wing and homosexuality? That's impossible!" Bergé snarled, then yelled: "*Vous nos enmerdez, foutez le camp!*"—roughly, "You're fucking bothering us! Get da fuck outta here!" Bergé may have to bring a posse of Saint Laurent runway models to next year's Pride March to help him evict the gaggle of vote-hungry conservative politicians that might, just might, show up.[25]

In March 2001 Bertrand Delanoë was elected mayor of Paris as the candidate of a left coalition, running as an openly gay man who nonetheless disavowed any tie to a single set of interests; he presented himself as a man of the Republic prepared to serve all Parisians.

Can I be the only one who detected, in the initiatives of his term—the *Paris Plage* that brings the beach to the Seine's city shore every summer, the *Nuit Blanche* that mandates an annual open-all-night event in municipal spaces and museums, the *Paris Cinema* that shows films in every *arrondissement* and sets up a giant screen in front of the Hôtel de Ville city hall, the *Velo Libre* program of free bikes that extends his bike policy beyond street closings and bike lanes—an unmistakable sign of old-school gayness: the mayor in the guise of cruise director, staging parties, directing fun, and freshening up the old city? One might think so, were it not for their inclusion in his campaign promise to "change the era, change the air," that is, a promise to make Paris more livable, more lively, with less air pollution and more attention to the vitality of life for both residents and tourists.

Delanoë built a political career without any disclosure of his homosexuality. His coming out publicly in 1998 and his election as mayor, though, made him a target: he was stabbed in the Hôtel de Ville on October 5, 2002, at 2:30 A.M., during his first *Nuit Blanche*, by a deranged, right-wing would-be assassin, who claimed to follow the Koran and hate homosexuality.[26] Seriously wounded, Delanoë was hospitalized, recovered, and won a second term as mayor in 2008, the same year that the election of Sarkozy shocked the country. There had been hope that gay marriage would become legal with a Socialist Party victory—until it lost. In 2011 there was much back-and-forth about legalizing gay marriage, but France's Constitutional Court ruled against it, pronouncing its ban constitutional. Press reports speculated on how Sarkozy would respond in the lead-up to new elections, with one poll showing 58 percent of France in support of legalization.

Interesting times, for cinema no less. With massive shifts in French and Parisian society, and with film occupying a central position for the interpretation of mores, it was perhaps inevitable that even France's most sacred genres and auteurs were due for reconsideration and refashioning. And what better place to start than the most sacred auteur of all and a genre unto himself, Eric Rohmer, whose moral tales of heterosexual love, lust, and fidelity were finally being queered.

Retrospective Mortality:
In the Shadows of Collard and Téchiné

Jean-François Marmontel, one of the eighteenth-century originators of the French "moral tale" tradition, is largely forgotten these days, but his legacy of the *comtes moraux* is not. A trio of films—Ozon's *Le temps qui reste*, Collard's *Les nuits fauves*, and Téchiné's *Les Témoins*—can be seen to constitute a re-titled revision: the *comtes mortels*, a set of stories of mortal combat in less than moral times. Taken together, they constitute a contemporary French queer cinema open to flexible gender and genre choices, with latitude to confront or displace the centrality of AIDS as a marker of the time.

The films share a number of features. Each has at its center the figure of a doomed young man. Each studies a protagonist consumed by rage: a young man for Collard and Ozon, an older doctor for Téchiné. None is a coming-out story: each young man is already gay, or at least already having sex with men, when the film begins. Significantly, each protagonist is an active agent not only of sexual presentation but of representation as well. One is equipped with a still camera (*Le temps qui reste*), one wields a video camera (*Les nuits fauves*), and one uses a tape recorder (*Les Témoins*). If these men are not *representative*, in the sense of providing types or symbols, they are nonetheless *representing*: they are agents, not victims, of the short lives they lead and are determined to interpret those lives to their own satisfaction.

In all three, the protagonist is dying. In the Collard and Téchiné films, he is dying of AIDS; in the Ozon, though the protagonist assumes it must be AIDS, the script assigns him a different malady. The Collard and Téchiné films were made fifteen years apart, yet both set their stories in the same era, 1986 and 1984, at the height of the AIDS disaster in Paris. Ozon, who eschews period dramas, sets his instead in an indeterminate present. Interestingly, as a result, it is Ozon who must shift the protagonist's illness from contemporary cocktail-maintained AIDS to a fatal brain tumor, thus supplying the plot with the element of imminent death that AIDS provided twenty years earlier.

All three directors are publicly identified as gay men—in the case of Collard, also bisexual. Apart from the public acknowledgment of their sexuality, neither Ozon nor Téchiné appears to live a life that seeks to be in sync with their films' gay themes or public receptions; sexuality is a fact in their on- and off-screen material and personae, but in the end incidental. Collard was a different matter entirely. He based *Les nuits fauves* on his autobiographical novel, published in 1989, which brought him notoriety for the explicit sex life he detailed; he adapted the screenplay from his book, composed the music, and directed the film. He even starred in it, playing the central role of Jean after numerous actors allegedly turned him down, afraid of being stigmatized as a result of becoming identified with the role. Collard died of AIDS complications a few days before his film swept the César Awards in 1993.[27]

The film was an immediate success and became even more of a hit after the publicity surrounding his death and César Awards, with nearly three million tickets sold. Already notorious for the innumerable S&M encounters down by the Seine with anonymous men recounted in his writings, and soon to be even more notorious for having had sex with a young woman in love with him (yes, as in the film), this sinner was so immediately rehabilitated and retrofitted posthumously into the esteemed ranks of the Republic that a letter to his parents from Mitterrand himself, read at the funeral, praised him as an example for French youth.[28] The extreme swings of social condemnation and deification that attended Collard's work and life represent more than a cautionary tale; they expose starkly the values of French society within which, not so changed today, Ozon and Téchiné continue to produce their films.

In all three films the protagonists are in a state of despair and disrepair. All three end up having a surprising relationship to heterosexuality: Manu, in *Les Témoins*, by having sex and falling in love with a French Algerian policeman who has a wife and newborn child; Jean, in *Les nuits fauves*, by having sex with a woman in addition to his multitude of anonymous male lovers and North African boyfriend; and Romain, in *Le temps qui reste*, by agreeing to procreative sex with a heterosexual married couple. Interesting how the figure of the North African appears and reappears in French gay stories, as a partner, an erotic figure, a fetishized fantasy; the queering of race in these cases remains underexamined, if hardly mysterious.

In all three films too gay people are beset by heterosexuals who want something from them. Romain encounters a married couple who want his sperm; his family of origin wants his labor (as a photographer) to reproduce their heteronormativity through baby pictures of his sister's children. Jean gets involved with a young woman who wants to reproduce with him, not through a baby, but through a virus: to have unprotected sex in the hope of contracting the HIV virus and thus bonding through a shared illness and mortality.[29] And when Manu's solitude is broken by the intrusion of Mehdi, the cop whom he loved, it falls to Adrien, the doctor turned AIDS activist, to be the person who stays and cares for him. The two are united by the totality of lives which, in opposite ways, are given over wholly to the disease. Thus

Adrien in *Les Témoins* fulfills the role that Laura desires in *Les nuits fauves*: a bond with the loved one through AIDS, here based on medicine, not sex. And what Adrien the doctor—who may be an alter ego for Téchiné or a reference to Daniel Defert, or perhaps a synthesis of the two—gives to Manu is not romance and sex but true friendship: a gift of pills with which to kill himself.

Each film is a sort of fable. Manu is a sunny twenty-year-old who comes to Paris from the provinces: it's the 1980s, and he comes for work and sex, heading immediately to the park to cruise for men. He follows the sun, and a man, back out of the city, where darkness descends in the literal form of Kaposi's sarcoma on his body—the body that steals his love and life. In *Les nuits fauves*, Jean is already a creature of the night, storming around Paris in his sports car, fucking men down by the river, lashing out all around. Ozon's Romain is the hipster, flying high, brought down to earth by a tumor, the one who will reconcile only on his own terms, nobody else's, and refuses intimate, friendly, and familial connections until radically accepting another kind altogether.

These are mortal tales intent on telling stories we have not yet been told. For Téchiné, it's a furious return to the scene of the crime, a delayed eulogy to all those beautiful young men who died as the Republic carried on with life as though none of it were happening. Significantly, Téchiné, veteran of an older generation, is also the only one who consciously inserts race into these questions, into the erotics as well as social complications. The heterosexuals of his film get away with it all: the husband doesn't get infected, despite an explicit scene of anal sex; his wife, indifferent to infidelity with either gender, gets a book deal based on the tapes that Manu has left behind. For Collard, the film itself was his last will and testament, his bid for immortality, and it worked.

And for Ozon? His irony seems to have deserted him for this film. The candy colors and pop mood are gone. What does he want to tell us? (Note that, of all the NQC directors, the one whom Ozon most resembles is Todd Haynes, who has the same penchant for cinephilia, love of genre, and consummate taste in women actors, and who has achieved comparable success with his postqueer films such as *I'm Not There*, *Safe*, and *Far from Heaven*.) In the closing scene of *Le temps qui reste*, Romain goes to the beach. The seaside is the site of greatest pleasure in the Ozon universe, though also a place of danger, adventure, and threat. It's the not-city, a landscape where fact and fable mingle in a sun-drenched effort to shed inhibitions and recapture a mythical essence dubbed "the natural." Melvil Poupaud, who plays Romain, embodies terminal illness to an unnerving extent: in production, Ozon forced

26.1 Romain (Melvil Poupaud) lies down on the sand to die, in François Ozon's ironic appropriation of the classic family holiday at the shore. Screen grab from *Le temps qui reste*.

him to stop eating, and he lost twenty-six pounds in two months. His skin shines white against the bronzed bodies around him. His tongue licking an ice-cream cone seems to have absorbed all the color that his body has lost, shining too pink, like a trace of childhood poking through a near-corpse. Here too hides a reference in need of deciphering.

In Ozon's early *Une robe d'été*, the gay protagonist goes to the beach, frustrated by his vacation day with his flamboyant boyfriend, and meets a woman with whom he has sex; his return to the vacation cottage wearing her dress arouses his guy's interest, matches his flamboyance, and raises it one. Perhaps this is Ozon's cheeky rewriting of Éric Rohmer, with the beach expanded to include more options than a Rohmer film: he frames heterosexual sex as a stimulant to gay sex (instead of the more common reversal).

Romain's beach, alas, is no such place of pleasure and sexual invitation. Surrounded by other families, by children with whom he has now made his peace, kept company by his own boyish incarnation, Romain is finally at rest (fig. 26.1). His wrist doesn't go limp, but we know that he's gone, just as surely as Manu is gone, and just as surely as Collard himself is gone. The beach is gay, in the old sense, a happy place for all its heterosexual beachgoers—not gay in any sexual sense, for the gay man there on the sand is beached. It's not D-Day, not the beaches of Normandy, but the scene is deadly, the body count real, and any notion of an armistice merely provisional.

Acting Out, Not Coming Out

Ozon's early films were discussed in terms of shock, his later ones, of capitulation (to box-office success). Throughout, however, he has been or should be recognized for his casting. Usually ignored in discussions of cinema, casting is the great unrecognized talent, and casting directors the scorned auteurs who are treated as little more than craftsmen.

Consider Ozon's selection of Melvil Poupaud to star in his meditation on death, *Le temps qui reste*, the second (after *Sous le Sable* or *Under the Sand*, 2000) in an intended trilogy on mortality. As an actor, Poupaud is associated with the films of Éric Rohmer, sainted guardian of France's post–New Wave, heteronormative, quality art cinema.[30] Poupaud, in fact, had starred in *Conte d'Été* (*A Summer's Tale*, 1996), the third in Rohmer's Four Seasons quartet, a romantic comedy set in a summer resort in which he played a womanizer with a surplus of women. With characteristic irony, Ozon casts him as Romain, a fatally ill gay man, a lothario turned wraith, cut down in his youth.

Ozon is a writer of fables, and even here in one of his most normative works, the rules of the fable are at play. He waves his wand, and a dark curse straight out of a storybook descends on a thirty-year-old fashion photographer's sunniest days—filled with an adorable and exotic young boyfriend at home, a fabulous loft, the choicest photo assignments, a pending trip to Japan to cover the shows, and plenty of cocaine. And then it's all taken away: illness arrives, jobs vanish, the boyfriend leaves or more accurately, is left. Removal by fate (rather, by script) continues apace until he ends up like this, in the midst of a high-season resort beach, alone.

Romain is a photographer, as is the young gay man in Ozon's early *La petite mort* (*Little Death*, 1995), a short film that pivoted on the death not of the son but of the father from whom he was estranged. Both films, like so many of Ozon's other works, involve family and death, father and son, rage, transgression, troubled relationships—and, of course, thwarted, warped, or wild desire.[31]

If the male melodrama is one of Ozon's territories, these are not normative melodramas in which an all-suffering figure finds redemption by the end of the tale, allowing the audience to leave the theater instructed, hearts filled with tragedy, poignancy, identification, and forgiveness. Nor are they domestic dramas; in fact they are explicitly antidomestic, savage in their depictions of the violence—emotional, physical, even sexual—wrought by the family, in particular by the patriarch.

In *La petite mort*, the son is portrayed as utterly undone by a family legend: his father, absent at his birth, complained that the photo he was sent showed a baby too ugly to be his son. The damage is finally undone, posthumously, through the action of a suitably Ozonian deus ex machina: a box of photographs bequeathed to the son by his late father, handed over by the sister. (As usual in Ozon's cinema, she's a character detested by the protagonist.) In the box, in a special envelope, there's a never-before-seen photo of the father delightedly holding his infant son in an unambiguous gesture of love. The heretofore pessimistic film offers a last shot of the son's face as a gesture toward hope, his stilted loveless features softening almost imperceptibly into peace.

In *Gouttes d'eau sur pierres brûlantes*, the father takes the form of a twisted, sadistic lover who sends the son/lover to his death. In *Sitcom* (1998), the father is literally a monster. He brings home a pet rat from his lab that then "infects" the entire family with unacceptable desires (same-gender, cross-race, incestuous, etc.), until the father himself, transformed into a rat, can be murdered, thereby allowing the rest of the family to live happily ever after. As a partial remake of Pasolini's *Teorema*, it nonetheless bears the Ozon signature of the demonic father. In Ozon's most commercially successful movie, *8 Femmes* (*8 Women*, 2002), the drama is set in motion by the announcement that the father has been murdered. This announcement turns out to be a ruse for the hidden daddy to observe how his family behaves without him, a spectacle that finally drives him to suicide and thus the fulfillment of the original announcement. These are savage Oedipal dramas in which the son's rage is matched only by the father's power.

Ozon may be rewriting the family drama as a horror movie, one in which the soul is killed if not the body and there is no escape. When the murderous couple flees to the countryside in *Les amants criminels* (*Criminal Lovers*, 1999), it is only to meet and be imprisoned by a father figure even more feral than the rat daddy in *Sitcom*: an ogre who imprisons the woman and sodomizes the man. A comment on the dangers posed by the European Union and cohabitation with its untamed Eastern members? The suggestion is no more or less apt than other, more directly apprehended connotations in Ozon's films: the family, nuclear or national, is always a place of danger and death.

And yet . . . *La petite mort* makes explicit the double meaning of such a death, the "little death" that denotes orgasm. In Ozon's darkly wry universe, the estranged son makes a career of photographing men's faces just at the moment of orgasm. His final rapprochement with his father can occur only when he photographs the older man's naked body in the hospital room, eyes closed, power rendered moot. (A twist occurs in the darkroom, when the son is forced to rewrite what has transpired.) If eros and thanatos are explicitly conjoined in Ozon, so are comedy and tragedy, with a touch of horror thrown in for good measure. His bright colors, jukebox soundtracks, and glamorous actors all combine to seduce the audience into an ironic nightmare from which we cannot escape.

The families that Ozon creates for his characters are damnably complex. The maternal figures are often all-good or all-bad maternal figures. His *Gouttes d'eau sur pierres brûlantes* transpires in a fraught apartment where a sadistic older man, Leopold, has seduced a youth away from his fiancée only to change partners again and resist the entreaties of an interloper who's come back for more. The young man Franz describes his great love for his mother, who is cold and absent. When he calls her on the telephone to tell her he has taken poison and is going to die, and hopefully go to heaven, he reports her response laconically: "She says, 'Bon voyage.'"

The cold mother's place is taken by the interloper, Vera. She is a trans-woman and ex-boyfriend of Leopold's who has shown up at the apartment after changing gender in a vain attempt to reclaim her sadistic lover.[32] Inspired by Franz, she tries to interest the youth in a new liaison. With his death imminent, she stays by his side, comforting and grieving, a pastiched Pietà for a new age. We know when he's dead, as does she: his wrist goes limp. More surplus meaning? The film has no shortage of them. Since Ozon is frequently compared to Hitchcock, his final image of Vera pinned to the window seems like a reference to *Rear Window*, a deathly drama staged for a disabled witness recast as a savage musical. Ozon borrows from Brecht as much as Fassbinder, composing shots to privilege iconic sexual moments, laying bare the codes of power in the form of a faux-happy musical number.

Le temps qui reste shifts gears from this early excavation of destructive familial dynamics but still shows the pain of Romain's relationship with his family. The father, for once, isn't a monster; instead the sister is the object of her brother's hatred, along with her children, whom he refuses to photograph (though in a pivotal scene, we see him do just that, secretly). There's an alternative, though, embodied by Romain's grandmother Laura, played by Jeanne Moreau. When she asks why Romain is telling the secret of his terminal illness only to her, he answers, Because you're like me, because you're old, because you're going to die soon. Laura begs to differ. She displays rows of bottles, evidently borrowed from Moreau's own medicine cabinet: enzymes, vitamins, nutrients. "I will die in the best of health" is her answer, speaking in character, but perhaps also of herself and the French cinema she symbolizes.

Notably, Romain's visit to Laura transpires in a singular world cut off from the spaces that dominate most of the film: the city and the beach. Perhaps her home functions as his repository of childhood, for he goes there to reminisce about life when he was a boy. Subjective shots reveal a life-like boyhood spirit that shadows him more and more as the life force leaves him. Like Vera in *Gouttes d'eau*, Laura is the one who comforts him through a shared fate. When he departs, she gives him roses. But she gives him something else as well: it is en route to her house that he stops at a roadside café in a scene that becomes pivotal. Using the washroom, Romain eyes the guy at the next urinal checking him out. He is, but not for the kind of sexual encounter that Romain expects.

In another bit of fable plotting Ozon-style, the man has a different proposition in mind: for Romain to have sex with his wife, the café's waitress, in order to give them the child that his own sterility prevents. Romain's coming to terms with this request and its consequences may well be the most shocking part of the film. In essence, he creates a new ideal family for himself, in which he gets to have sex with Mommy and Daddy and reproduce himself as a child. Such is the shape of a happy ending in an Ozon universe in which happy endings and biofamilies can never coincide.

Witnessing: Queer Casting in Téchiné and Collard

Téchiné's title *Les Témoins* suggests another way to gauge the three films: through a comparison of "the witnesses" that the three directors construct. For his witness, the mysterious Noria, who advises Jean that AIDS can teach him to love, Collard chose none other than Maria Schneider.[33] Schneider was a veteran actress as well as a kindred figure of notoriety: she blazed to attention as the star of Bertolucci's *Last Tango in Paris* (1972), playing Marlon Brando's mysterious sex partner, then reappeared opposite Jack Nicholson in Antonioni's *The Passenger* (1975), before causing a tabloid storm over rumors of her lesbianism and drug use.[34] Schneider performs a character who is essentially a deus ex machina and key to my notion of Collard's revision of the moral tale. It is the message that Noria delivers to Jean (and which is taken up by Jean's mother later) that offers an option of transformation through suffering.

Téchiné also reaches outside the customary vernacular of his casting choices to make a particularly apt one: the character of the editor and secret lover of Mehdi's wife, Sarah (Emmanuelle Béart), is played by Xavier Beauvois, an actor and director.[35] Relevant here is his feature N'oublie pas que tu vas mourir (Don't Forget You're Going to Die, 1995), an early film on AIDS that won the prestigious Jean Vigo Award for its importance to a French public that was slow to recognize the impact and danger of the AIDS epidemic. It's impossible that Téchiné would have overlooked the import of this symbolic reference.

In keeping with its retrospective eye on the period in which Collard was immersed, Les Témoins also has two other witnesses who deliver a more ambiguous message to the audience. One is Julie, Manu's sister, who seems determined to live life fully for the two of them after his death, through art. She's an opera singer who, in a final scene on stage, channels her grief into performances so enriched by suffering as to suggest future stardom. The other witness is Sarah, the writer poised for her own career breakthrough thanks to the book based on Manu's taped memoirs. Are heterosexual women the ones who will carry forward Manu's passion for life and keep his spirit alive? Or are they, in a darker sense, profiting from his death, like latter-day vampires? The film gives no answers: it's an elegy that refuses easy lessons.

For Ozon, the privileged witness is the character of the grandmother, Laura. She is the one to whom Romain chooses to expose the truth of his condition, and she is the one who accepts what he has to say without judgment or shock. As Laura, Moreau serves to model the behavior that the French film industry can emulate when the film and its director are received with newly open arms, box-office success, and awards. She is yet another Ozon love letter to the grandes dames of French cinema and a comment too, through Romain's privileging of her, on the younger generation's attitude toward that history, those veterans.

But there's another witness as well, or rather, a pair of witnesses: the couple for and with whom Romain agrees to make a child. They see a different side of the protagonist that is fundamentally in contradiction to his other interpersonal relationships, and they bear witness to it in irreversibly concrete terms: a legal document filed with a notaire and an actual child, the product and proof of their intimate witnessing.

Ozon constructs out of his actors an imaginary cinematic family of gods and goddesses. The gods, of course, have feet of clay, the goddesses bear gifts, and all of them bear witness through the audience's apprehension of their identities to this queer story. Their presence attests to the status of this queer tale—directed by a filmmaker who happens to be gay, about a gay protagonist who happens to be dying—as an integral part of French cinema, an accepted member of the family, deserving of our full attention.

Ozon may not reckon directly with AIDS in his films, yet it can hardly be disregarded as the code beneath the surface, driving the engagement with death that makes an appearance in virtually every one of his films. Desire is linked to it, at once understandably and inexplicably, as if AIDS had been displaced from the text to the subtext, from the plot to the mise-en-scène. Any markers of queer desire not bound up with mortality can be tracked back to the father, who must be fought to a draw if not to death, and back to a mother figure who advises, consoles, and lays roses on the grave. If François Ozon was considered a bad fit for the early days of New Queer Cinema, how telling that he has arrived at this point as a seemingly perfect fit for its aftermath, mapping a trail between the republican and the communitarian that just might suit the queer—or postqueer—cinema of today, in the United States as well as in France, a perfectly exportable French fashion designed to fit without undue alterations.

Notes

1. Happily, the Camargo Foundation did not share this reaction. I am indebted to it for the residency fellowship in Cassis, France, in 2007, that enabled me to write this chapter. Thanks in particular to the directors Jean-Pierre and Mary Dautricourt for their support of this project, and to the fellows in residence during the fall and winter of 2007 for invaluable feedback and generously shared information. The epigram that appears at the start of this chapter originates in a published interview by the British film critic Sheila Johnston. See her Ozon profile, "Death Every Day," 13.

2. See, among others, Josiane Balasko's *Gazon maudit* (*French Twist*, 1995); Alain Berliner's *Ma vie en rose* (*My Life in Pink*, 1997); Anne Fontaine's *Nettoyage á Sec* (*Dry Cleaning*, 1997); Cédric Klapisch's *L'Auberge español* (*Pot Luck*, 2002) and *Chacun cherche son chat* (*When the Cat's Away*, 1996); Patrice Chéreau's *Ceux qui m'aiment prendront le train* (*Those Who Love Me Can Take the Train*, 1998); Claire Denis's *Beau travail* (*Beautiful Work*, 1999) and *J'ai pas sommeil* (*I Can't Sleep*, 1994); Virginie Despentes and Coralie Trinh Thi's *Baise-moi* (*Fuck Me*, 2000); Sébastien Lifshitz's *Presque Rien* (*Come Undone*, 2000), *Wild Side* (2004), and *Going South* (2009); Olivier Ducastel and Jacques Martineau's *Drôle de Félix* (*Adventures of Felix*, 2000) and *Ma vraie vie à Rouen* (*My Life on Ice*, 2002).

3. In addition to Téchiné's *Les Témoins*, obvious key works are *Les Roseaux Sauvages* (*Wild Reeds*, 1994), *Les Innocents* (*The Innocents*, 1987), and *Les Voleurs* (*Thieves*, 1996), all with central gay and lesbian relationships which complicate sexuality with race and class.

4. Adrienne Rich's wonderful essay "Compulsory Heterosexuality and the Lesbian Continuum" was first published in 1980 and sparked considerable controversy, and still does, by wildly different camps united only by their objections to her notion of fluidity in matters of sexual desire. It has been reprinted many times since it first appeared in *Signs: Journal of Women in Culture and Society* and is included in Rich's collection, *Blood, Bread, and Poetry: Selected Prose, 1979–1985* (New York: Norton, 1994).

5. See Moatti, Dab, Quenel, Beltzer, and Pollak, "Social Perception of AIDS in French General Public," as cited in Grémy and Beltzer, "HIV Risk and Condom Use in the Adult Heterosexual Population in France Between 1992 and 2001."

For an expansive view of AIDS and the politics of sexuality in French culture, see Caron, *AIDS in French Culture*. Among the many explanations of AIDS in France in this period, the case of the *sang contaminé* deserves mention, as this scandal of the knowing dispersal of HIV-contaminated blood in the mid-1980s riveted public attention upon its exposure in 1991 and the subsequent trials in 1992–99. These implicated a range of politicians and cabinet officers and no doubt laid the groundwork for some of the later legislation discussed in this chapter. See Feldman, "Blood Justice."

6. For an astute early essay on *banlieue* cinema, see Reynaud, "Le 'hood." For an extensive study of the topic, consult Tarr, *Reframing Difference* and Ginette Vincendeau's single-film study, *La Haine (French Film Guide)*. Arguably, *La Haine* has an unacknowledged gay subtext in the scene of one friend's inexplicable entrée to a wealthy gay man's apartment, where he's recognized and initially welcomed. The film was released in the United States with the support of Jodie Foster and her Egg Productions company.

7. Asibong, "Meat, Murder, Metamorphosis," 205.

8. See Stychin, "Civil Solidarity or Fragmented Identities?," 351. I follow him too in citing Brubaker, *Citizenship and Nationhood in France and Germany*.

9. Ibid., 353.

10. Ibid., 354, 363.

11. There is a rich and increasingly urgent literature on the subject. See, for example, Salvatore, "Authority in Question."

12. See Michael Kimmelman, "Ready or Not, France Opens Museum on Immigration," *New York Times*, October 17, 2007. Noting that Sarkozy may have been reacting to the museum's status as a pet project of his rival Chirac, the article managed to suggest that the French public was snubbing it too. See Angelique Chrisafis, "France's First Immigration Museum Opens," *Guardian*, October 10, 2007.

13. Salvatore, "Authority in Question," 136.

14. See Scott, *Parité*, and Scott's comments on Perry Anderson's articles "Dégringolade" and "Union Sucrée" in the *London Review of Books*, September 2004, cited in a speech delivered at the New York University Institute of French Studies symposium on April 22, 2005. For further thoughts, see Schor, "The Crisis of French Universalism."

15. Gunther, "Building a More Stately Closet," 340.

16. For a view of the French sex club scene then undergoing further revival, see Guy Trebay, "Le Relapse: Libertinism Makes a Comeback in French Clubs," *New York Times*, April 28, 2002, which references the moment of decriminalization for its purported role in stimulating a new libertinism.

17. Gunther, "Building a More Stately Closet," 344.

18. See, notably, Caron, AIDS *in French Culture*. His essay, "My Father and I," gives a wonderful sense of both location and generational dislocation; see also his delightful memoir, *My Father and I*.

19. Also see Nye, "The Pacte Civil de Solidarité and the History of Sexuality."

20. For a detailed archival investigation into legally recognized nontraditional unions, especially in fifteenth-century France, see Tulchin, "Same-Sex Couples Creating Households in Old Regime France."

21. Stychin, "Civil Solidarity or Fragmented Identities?," 364.

22. See, in particular, Fassin, "Same Sex, Different Politics."

23. For an update, see Scott Sayare and Maia de la Baum, "In France, Civil Unions Gain Favor over Marriage," *New York Times*, December 16, 2010. The authors reveal that, since 2000, "of the 173,045 civil unions signed in 2009, 95 percent were between heterosexual couples."

24. Fassin, "Same Sex, Different Politics."

25. For this passage and the *Le Monde* citation, see Simo, "Outing in Gay Paree."

26. Jon Henley, "Mayor of Paris Stabbed at Festival," *Guardian*, October 7, 2002. The article also notes that Delanoë is "the first leftwing leader of the city for 130 years," since the Paris Commune.

27. Thanks to YouTube, eternal memory bank of ephemeral culture, you can see the acceptance speech of the film's young star, Romaine Bohringer.

28. This ideal portrait was ruptured the following year by the news that Collard had actually infected (off-screen) a young woman with AIDS who had died of it. See Alan Riding, "Discovering a Film Idol's Feet of Clay," *New York Times*, April 26, 1994. For more details on the death of Erika Prou at age twenty-six, see Rollet and Williams, "Visions of Excess," 208. For the Anglo-American gay community's critical perspective on the film and the homophobia of French society, see Watney, "The French Connection," and opposing it, Nash, "Chronicle(s) of a Death Foretold."

29. For a detailed literary examination of Collard and *Les nuits fauves*, see Hartlen, "Queer across the Atlantic."

30. Ozon once studied with Rohmer in a course on cinema. Interview with author, Ozon's office, Paris, November 2007.

31. Ozon is equally a director of women's films centered on actresses of a certain age (Charlotte Rampling, Catherine Deneuve, Jeanne Moreau, Sophie Ardant) and filled with love, at least of postmenopausal women; younger women who can reproduce occupy a far less positive category. I don't examine them here, but surely there's a queer argument to be made too for *8 Femmes* and *Swimming Pool* (2003).

32. Ozon explained to me that he rewrote the part of the distraught former lover to be a transwoman as an homage to the central character of Fassbinder's later film, *In a Year with 13 Moons* (1978), modifying the character's name from Elvira to Vera in recognition of the change. In *Thirteen Moons*, a young man has become a young woman in a (vain) attempt to hold onto an incestuous father. The film's Oedipal structure is made quite transparent by this reference (personal communication, Paris, November 2007). I wonder whether John Cameron Mitchell's *Hedwig and the Angry Inch* (2001) was inspired by the Fassbinder film too.

33. Gabara, "Screening Autobiography: Cyril Collard's *Nuits Fauves*," 62. Gabara offers an incisive analysis of the film.

34. Maria Schneider died at age fifty-eight on February 3, 2011. Every obituary was focused on *Last Tango in Paris*, though some quoted her complaint that it was the movie that had ruined her life.

35. His best-known films are *Le petit lieutenant* (2005) and *Of Gods and Men* (2010).

GOT MILK?

Gus Van Sant's Encounter with History

27 *November 2008*

In November 2008 a "temporary museum" materialized in a do-nated storefront on the corner of Castro and Eighteenth Streets in San Francisco. Timed to coincide with the opening of the movie *Milk* in the Castro Theatre, the historic movie palace on the same block, the gallery exhibition *Passionate Struggle* traced the history of the gay, lesbian, bisexual, and transgender communities in the city. Despite walls crammed with archi-val photographs and texts, testimony to years of oppression, struggle, and victory parties, the centerpiece was a modest case in the back of the room where a treasure usually kept under wraps in climate-controlled sanctity was now on display: the actual striped suit that Harvey Milk was wearing when he was assassinated. Aged, its fine fabric stained with blood, its tailoring ripped by bullet holes, it lay there in its protective vitrine, a martyr's relic awaiting its pilgrims. Tourists, locals, and moviegoers obliged: motivated by memory or curiosity, they filed in, transforming the hushed storefront into a modern reliquary.

On the thirtieth anniversary of his death, the San Francisco supervisor known as the mayor of Castro Street was receiving a de facto canonization by his public.[1] Simultaneously his canonization by Focus Features and its legend-making apparatus, materialized through the uncanny embodiment of Sean Penn, was taking place up the street, across the country, and around the world.

Spring 1982: The Documentary That Started It All

I was in my second year as a bureaucrat in New York City, serving the public and dispensing its tax dollars as the director of the Film Program for the New York State Council on the Arts (NYSCA). I was also working as a writer, contributing articles on film to the *Village Voice*. What made the day (and night and weekend) job so worthwhile was getting to fund projects I believed in. I considered it important to reset the balance of power so that all those important voices—gay, lesbian, feminist, Latino/a, African American, Asian American—that had been marginalized in mainstream cultural circles could now be heard. The era also marked the start of the "independent" feature film movement. I was excited that NYSCA was newly empowered to fund production projects.[2]

It was with considerable interest, then, that I took a meeting with Richard Schmiechen, a documentary filmmaker who wanted to brief me on an important project he was producing. True, its story and production were both located in San Francisco, while NYSCA, by law, funded only New York State projects. But since he, the producer, was based in New York City and would be doing his work (and thus spending our money) here, wasn't there a way to make it work? He promised this would be a historic film that would present the gay "civil rights" movement for the first time.

The documentary would be centered on a figure who deserved to be better known on the East Coast. His name was Harvey Milk. He was known on the West Coast for spearheading the campaign to defeat California's Proposition 6, or Briggs Initiative, which sought to ban gay and lesbian schoolteachers from California classrooms, and for fighting homophobic forces on the home front that had been unleashed by Anita Bryant, scourge of gays and lesbians everywhere. He was the most visible—though not technically the first—elected gay official.[3] He had been assassinated in 1978, not long after winning election, along with George Moscone, the progressive mayor of San Francisco. Both Milk and Moscone were murdered by Dan White, a crazed homophobe who was their colleague on the Board of Supervisors and who represented white working-class interests, specifically the homophobic police and firemen.[4]

We all knew about Dan White: he was the murderer who got off with only five years in prison for a double murder by claiming the "Twinkie defense." Despite blaming a product whose name was a derogatory term for gays, his defense team had convinced a jury that his consumption of too much sugar-filled junk food had put him into an altered state of diminished capacity for which he should not be held responsible. "Twinkies made me do it" became a legendary line. With White still serving his abhorrently short time in jail, Schmiechen and his director, Rob Epstein, wanted their documentary to get out before he did.

Schmiechen reported on a fundraising event they'd just held in New York City, where the crowd went wild over the film trailer and New York's gay community pledged its support. It was then and there that he had signed on as producer. The sample he submitted to NYSCA was brilliant, eloquently shot and edited.[5] Sure enough, our film-production panelists agreed on its historical significance and artistic quality, and at our next funding round NYSCA granted production monies to Schmiechen and Epstein to complete this documentary, which would be released in 1984 to critical and popular acclaim as *The Times of Harvey Milk*.

Epstein had begun by documenting a campaign waged by Harvey Milk and Sally Gearhart, the lesbian educator and crusader who accompanied him onto television shows and public appearances, debating conservatives with their combination of experience, knowledge, and great sense of humor. Their tireless advocacy and grassroots organizing turned the tide: against the expectation of the state of California's conservative establishment and its Moral Majority supporters, the state's voters rejected the campaign of hatred and hysteria and defeated the measure. Unaware that he was about to become a target of homophobic wrath, Milk must have been on top of the world, his real career finally beginning.

In the aftermath of Milk's death, once the immediate shock had passed, Epstein began interviewing those who had worked with Harvey, known and loved him, helped him get elected, formed alliances with him, and envisioned a truly democratic city, just as he did. The documentary put together an all-star cast of gay men and lesbians from San Francisco's independent documentary film community as director, cinematographer, and editor. Its emotional tone mixed rage and elegy, shock and memory, into a remarkably passionate and emotional document of pride and loss. It's one of the best American documentaries ever made.

It would go on to win the Academy Award for Best Documentary of 1984. Rob and Richard, resplendent in their tuxedos, took the podium, becoming the first "out" award recipients ever to speak openly at the Oscar ceremonies. They acknowledged Harvey and their communities, and Rob even thanked his "life partner" for his support. "History was made that night," wrote one blogger, emphasizing the importance of this coming-out moment at the Oscars. First released theatrically on 16mm, then on television on PBS, then on videocassette, then DVD and Netflix and downloads, popularized through repertory screenings and classroom adoptions, it all started over again with the release in 2008 of Gus Van Sant's movie *Milk*. The documentary *The Times of Harvey Milk* has become the classic that its makers had hoped it would and a legacy that its aesthetic and emotional powers made inevitable.[6] It also became the basis of *Milk*, as Van Sant saw it.

1984–1993: A Film in Search of a Director

Gus Van Sant first started making films half a decade before the New Queer Cinema movement emerged. In some ways, he's a central forefather; in others, he's the kid who's rejoined the party. He admits that he was too busy trying to break into the filmmaking business in L.A. in the 1970s to take time out to move to San Francisco, disco, and meet Harvey Milk when he was still alive and reigning. But Van Sant made up for lost time when he returned in 1986 to present his debut feature *Mala Noche* at the Castro Theatre in that spring's Gay and Lesbian Film Festival.

Mala Noche, a dreamily voyeuristic study of unrequited desire, is still striking today. Wholly original in style and theme, melancholic, tender, and sexy, it details the life of Walt, a shopkeeper on skid row in Van Sant's native Portland, and Walt's obsessive attraction to Johnny, a young undocumented Mexican. It was shot in grainy black and white and based on a story by native son Walt Curtis. It's a luminous film, full of passion and heart, not the kind of niche-marketed comedy that became far too common after NQC caught on and wannabe filmmakers proliferated. No, *Mala Noche* was an uncompromising artist's film that stunned critics like me with its intimacy and nerve when it appeared that year. Cineastes proclaimed a new talent; though his opening base was the gay festival circuit, it was clear Van Sant would go much further. What was unusual was his ongoing willingness to return.

The LGBT festival circuit of 1986 differed in so many ways from today's circuit: people fought over issues within the festival as within all other corners of gay and lesbian life. Were there more gay male programs on offer than lesbian ones? Were ticket prices inching too high, pricing out those in the community without money? Were organizers selling out to corporate sponsors? What about racism? The festivals were a microcosm like any other, and there were battles to be fought, as always. *OutLook*, the first of the important modern journals dedicated to gay and lesbian theories, news, and historical research, was published collectively out of San Francisco at the time. The all-volunteer San Francisco Gay and Lesbian History Project was actively gathering community stories, histories, and images, and then sharing them both locally and nationally. Local rags like the *B.A.R.* covered everything from politics to the bars and the baths, while *OutLook* carried the San Francisco perspective into national literary and academic circles. San Francisco was still a center of LGBT ferment, within the festival as elsewhere.

Van Sant stayed in the living room of the festival's director, Michael Lumpkin, who had seen *Mala Noche* and met Van Sant at the Berlin Film Festival a few months earlier. "That was my introduction," recalls Van Sant of the Frameline experience. "It was when I met everyone."[7] What pleased him the most on that trip to San Francisco, apart from the Castro audience, was his introduction to the filmmaker Rob Epstein. Epstein was fresh off his Academy Award win and, with deep roots in the Castro district, became Van Sant's guide to this world of gay and lesbian filmmaking; after all, back in the 1970s, when Epstein was a fired-up kid, he'd been the youngest member of the collective that made *Word Is Out* (1977), the "first gay documentary." He was the gold standard to which others aspired. That meeting with Epstein was the start of a long friendship, but for Van Sant, it was equally important for the start of his long daydream about someday making a dramatic movie about the life of Harvey Milk.

In 1991 word began to circulate that Oliver Stone was going to make the Harvey Milk story into a movie. It was never clear that he was going to do more than produce, but outrage was immediate. How dare he! Oliver Stone had just come off a string of movies—*The Doors* (1991), *Born on the Fourth of July* (1989), *Wall Street* (1987), *Platoon* (1986)—not likely to burnish his credentials as a gay-friendly director. The gay press teemed with attack-dog columns denouncing Warner Bros., which had bought the rights to Randy Shilts's book *The Mayor of Castro Street*, for allowing Stone to direct the by now sacred story. Then the next round of rumors came: Stone would only produce, while Gus Van Sant would direct and Robin Williams would play Harvey. This was a different prospect altogether, too good to be true. But *The Mayor of Castro Street* was not to be, not yet.

The collaboration didn't work. In early 1993, supposedly over "script differences," Van Sant left the project. He went on to another book and another era, directing *Even Cowgirls Get the Blues* (1993); sadly, it was one of his only critical and commercial misfires, though to this day I remain its fervent champion. He flourished in the mainstream, from *Drugstore Cowboy* (1989) and *To Die For* (1995) to *My Own Private Idaho* (1991) and *Finding Forrester* (2000), until the twenty-first century hit and he began to turn his back on mass-market movies and return to his outsider ethos in Portland. The series of quirky, low-budget films that followed—*Gerry* (2002), *Last Days* (2005), *Elephant* (2003), *Paranoid Park* (2007)—reasserted his originality and returned him to the art school origins of his early imagination.

Along the way, though, Van Sant had never really stopped thinking about the Milk film. At first, post-Shilts, he began to try other approaches to win back the movie. "There was another script I did with two cowriters. It looked like a Charlie Kaufman project, that's how really out there it was. I loved it. But that was back in the early 1990s, and Charlie Kaufman didn't exist yet," at least in movie terms. Van Sant sighed as he detailed the rest to me. He even confessed to a mad scheme to shoot Milk's story as an artistic, low-budget allegory, inspired by the strategies of the Russian director Aleksandr Sokurov, but set in the Castro. The ideas would come and go for more than a decade, without any project coming to fruition, but Van Sant never gave up dreaming or plotting.

2007–2008: The Makings of Milk

As fate would have it, at precisely the moment when Van Sant was comfortably recommitted to low-budget projects of passion, the trades announced that Bryan Singer (*The Usual Suspects*, 1995; *X-Men*, 2000) was going to direct the Harvey Milk project at Warner Independent, the very project originally slated for Van Sant. The screenwriter was Singer's long-time collaborator Chris McQuarrie, and once again, his script would be based on the Shilts book. At least one thing had been simplified: the film's title this time around was shortened to *Castro Street*.[8] However, the curse of the Shilts film hadn't ended: in the typical Hollywood lottery model, only one project can hold the winning ticket, and the Singer–McQuarrie team would be beaten to the punch. Blame Black.

It was then that the young writer Dustin Lance Black (*Big Love*) turned up. He had made his own trek to San Francisco to excavate the story of Harvey Milk and met Cleve Jones, a former Milk disciple who talked with him just as he'd talked with Van Sant a decade and a half earlier. Jones quickly passed Black's script on to Gus, thinking it might be the breakthrough that was needed to bring Harvey to the screen in Van Sant's hands. It was Jones, a rabble-rouser of the Milk era (played by Emile Hirsch in *Milk*), who connected the generations: Van Sant, the once-upon-a-time art kid turned great director, and Black, the upstart gay Mormon kid with a knack for television. Like Van Sant and Jones, Black too dreamed of bringing the life of Harvey Milk to the big screen.

Van Sant read the screenplay and said, basically, Why not? With him on board, and the Black script in hand, Focus Features agreed to produce. After all, the head of Focus, James Schamus, had been one of the earliest producers (with Christine Vachon) in the heyday of New Queer Cinema. Most recently he and Focus had even produced *Brokeback Mountain* with Schamus's longtime collaborator, Ang Lee. Once Sean Penn signed on to play Harvey—with the condition that the film be shot on location in the Castro district—the die was cast. This was going to be as authentic a historical film as they all could muster. They owed Harvey and his community nothing less. So began additional rounds of interviewing many of the people who'd been close to Harvey, going through the Gay and Lesbian History Archives, and scoping out buildings in the area that could be transformed into the 1970s landscape Harvey had inhabited.

San Francisco was buzzing as Van Sant's traveling show came closer to arrival. For the downtown business interests, the film ensured that production monies would be injected into the local economy at a time when productions were more likely to head to Canada or other states. For residents, it meant celebrity sightings more common in the southern half of the state: Sean Penn, James Franco, Diego Luna.

For the city's LGBT community, the arrival of the *Milk* cast and crew and cameras meant much more. This was an unprecedented experience: the legendary past of an LGBT martyr and the city he loved would finally be raised to the level of heroism and tragedy for the big screen. It would be shot on the very streets and in the storefront where Milk himself had lived, loved, and worked to create change. Nobody had ever experienced anything quite like this. The local gay press filled with gossip, sightings, first-person accounts of life as an extra, and on and on, as if San Francisco had suddenly been transformed into a tiny town in the middle of the country going crazy over stars in its midst.

Those of us who care about film, who think about it, write about it, travel to film festivals, and teach film to students can sometimes forget the sheer power of a film to shape consciousness. Not just on the screen, finished, but in

27.1 Harvey Milk's reconstructed office in a scene from
Jenni Olson's *575 Castro Street*, shot on the set of Gus
Van Sant's production of *Milk*. Courtesy of Jenni Olson.

rare cases like this one, in the making too. On a sunny weekday in February,
I decided to walk up Castro to Nineteenth Street, where Van Sant was filming. I was stunned—not by the production but by my experience of entering
a simulacrum.

I found myself unexpectedly mesmerized by a 1970s version of this city.
Real estate offices advertised houses on the market for $40,000. Gas prices
were laughable. The reconfigured Aquarius Record Store had windows packed
with vinyl records and acid rock posters. The Castro Theatre marquee and
neon sign had been restored to full-color brilliance and touted *The Poseidon
Adventure* (1972). Harvey Milk's fabled Castro camera shop was there again,
popping up in the middle of the block like an apparition out of Mary Poppins,
Harry Potter, or some other Brit fabulist's invention. And there it was, the
very office where Milk held court. You can see it, too, thanks to Jenni Olson's
emotional incantation, *575 Castro St.* (2008).[9]

Oddly, amid all the elaborate retooling of shops and façades, what stopped me short was the low-tech image of flyers stapled to the walls. Pre-computer graphics, stark and primitive, their typewriter fonts mixed with hand-drawn headlines and illustrations, churned out by mimeograph and by offset presses on colored stock, a logjam of announcements breathlessly detailed the next gay liberation meeting, the next demonstration, the next gathering of the tribe.

Type font as time machine? Somehow, yes. I walked around the set with a silly grin on my face, duped into inhabiting my own past again, remembering the endless meetings and passions of youth and political action—back then in Chicago and New York City. I returned to that street, day after day, driven to recapture this innocence and hope by jumping through a crack in time. Every flyer was a testimony to an earlier era, before the events, court cases, deaths, and moral crusades assaulted its brief moment of celebration. In the 1980s, when I recounted my experiences of the 1960s and 1970s, I was once told, "You treated life as though it was a feast." Exactly. We gobbled it up, all of us, with vigor. It was a time when people passionately believed the world was changing for the better, and old standards, taboos, and prejudices were being overturned with the power of righteous rebellion. So damn sexy, as I couldn't help but recall. Harvey, of all people, knew that.[10]

The giant crowd scenes, so essential to the re-creation of the time, turned out to involve some hilarious lessons in social history. Websites publicized the need for extras for the marches, the demonstrations, and the infamous "White Night" riot. Volunteering to show up, however, involved agreeing to a list of conditions scripted to avoid fashion faux pas. Websites and flyers reminded a new generation of what did and didn't characterize Castro life thirty years earlier:

> The overall vibe is a sunny day in San Francisco—all sorts of types of clothing looks are encouraged, as in 1978, Gay Freedom Day was a diverse community event and did not only feature any one type of person. 70s appropriate drag and leather is OK.
>
> Shirtless looks for men are encouraged, as it was popular to go shirtless on sunny days in the Castro in the 70s usually with tight Levi's and sneakers. It is important to make sure that not too many tattoos are present, as it was not yet as common in 1978 to have many tattoos.
>
> Shoes: Canvas sneakers such as Converse, leather boots such as Frye, clogs; simple rugged shoes with basic materials such as canvas and leather. Shorts should be worn with sneakers with or without athletic tube socks.

Equally instructive are the kinds of items that were off-limits:

NO overt rainbow themed outfits, as the rainbow flag was not yet the official symbol of the gay community in 1978.
NO "circuit party" clothing or "Rave clothing" that would read as trendy or modern.
NO trendy designer jeans with overt modern finishes. . . .
NO clothing with branding such as Abercrombie, Nike, Gap, etc.
NO overt phrases or logos.

Participants were also warned not to carry water bottles under any circumstances, as people did not drink bottled water in the 1970s. The contemporary crowd had to be reminded that folks back then, shockingly, drank tap water. Other differences surfaced only obliquely, through interactions rather than dress codes. One friend at the recreation of the "White Night" march and riot met an older man, who explained he'd been there for the original. "Was it just like this, back then?" my lesbian friend inquired. "Well," answered the man, choosing his words carefully, "there weren't so many women here back then."

What a diplomatic statement. One of the clearest messages of *Milk*, and to a lesser extent *The Times of Harvey Milk*, is the homosocial nature of LGBT life back in the 1970s. It may not be a deliberate message, but understated evidence of women's absence from Castro goings-on is everywhere apparent. In a time of much closer relationships within and between the LGBT communities, it's easy to forget that lesbians were considered the spoilsports of gay liberation back then. Frowning on public sex, lacking a bathhouse culture, with an insistence on political standards and ethics, antisexism and antiracism, antiobjectification in general, much of the lesbian community was estranged from the gay male life of pleasure and liberation. And vice versa: gay men resented being censured for gentrification, conspicuous consumption, and sexual adventures. This wasn't universally true; lesbians who themselves felt marginalized within the lesbian community for "aberrant" practices like S&M, leather, and bondage play made common cause with gay men against the lesbian-feminist policing of sexual and social practices. Similarly there were politically conscious gay men who made common cause with lesbian feminists on shared social and political issues. Still, in *Milk*, when the actress playing Anne Kronenberg (Alison Pill) comes to the campaign office at Harvey's invitation, she accosts the gang defiantly: "My friends say you guys don't like women. Is that true?" Of course it was, even though the scene was staged to imply the opposite.

As the production continued in San Francisco, spirits from the past continued to stir and swirl around the neighborhood. After all, ghosts abound in San Francisco. I asked Van Sant if anything unusual or out of the ordinary had occurred during the shooting. There was a pause before he answered. Yes, actually. Twice. First came an unexpected visit to the set by Charles White, the grown son of Milk's assassin, Dan White, who had committed suicide not long after his release from jail. Charles contacted Van Sant to say he'd like to stop by the shoot. With supernatural timing, he arrived at the exact moment that the scene of his own christening as an infant was being filmed. The cameras rolled, a priest solemnly declared, "I christen you Charles," and the take was over. Van Sant looked around, but Charles White had already left the set, never to return.

Then there was the night that they were filming in the camera shop, shooting the evening scene when Harvey learned of the *San Francisco Chronicle*'s election endorsement. It was a complicated shot, and Van Sant was completely focused on getting it right. Afterward he was surrounded by the crew, who begged him to explain who the other guy was. What guy? They swore there'd been a stranger in the room, someone they'd never seen before, and that he'd disappeared right after the scene was shot. They couldn't figure out where he'd come in or how he'd left, but they described him in detail. "It sounded just like Harvey," said Van Sant. The visitor, in fact, had been sitting right in Harvey's chair, "but the camera wasn't pointed in that direction."

If there were any doubts that *Milk* had captured the ghosts of the past with any sort of fidelity, they disappeared in the Presidio on October 26, 2008. It was there, in the private George Lucas screening room, that Van Sant welcomed some very important individuals to an advance screening of the film based on their lives and experiences. As the lights dimmed, Anne Kronenberg shared Kleenex with the old gang: Danny Nicoletta, Michael Wong, and Tom Ammiano. All friends of Milk and each other, they'd helped Van Sant and Black with advice, research, even cameos. When the lights rose again, there was plenty of sniffling but also something else: the insistent humor that permeated their shared past, as seen in *Milk*. "What a shame that Scott isn't still alive," one quipped, referring to Milk's lover, Scott Smith. "Can you imagine how thrilled Scott would be to have James Franco playing him? The lucky bastard!"[11] They all congratulated Van Sant on getting it right, on giving Harvey his due.

Film as Simulacrum

Two days later, on October 28, an opening-night party like nothing San Francisco had ever seen came to the Castro and lit up the evening with doppelganger fever: the stars of *Milk* out front, giving interviews on the red carpet, with the veterans whose lives they had embodied standing nearby, giving their own interviews. Only-in-San-Francisco VIPs, from Mayor Gavin Newsom and other politicians to Levi Strauss execs, the mayor of Portland (Van Sant's hometown), film celebrities, and a thousand folks with money not yet lost to the market crash, all turned out for the film's gala, organized specifically to benefit queer youth organizations. They streamed under the Castro Theatre's neon marquee into its palatial interior, gleaming brighter than ever for its cameo, as the ever-present Castro organist played and played until the organ disappeared into the stage, and the crowd roared with excitement. Even the handsome young man sitting behind me drew applause when he stood and announced to all of us, "I'm the one who delivers the pizza." On screen, of course.

When the film began and silence descended, the audience began to realize what a house of mirrors we had entered. As Sean Penn disappeared into the body, voice, and mannerisms of Harvey Milk, it got harder and harder to separate the world on the screen from the one outside the theater. And when the film ended and the credits rolled, there could be no exit: we left the theater only to enter the same streets we'd been watching inside, just moments ago. Harvey and his beautiful boys were gone, though—Harvey Milk to an assassin's bullet, his legions of friends, lovers, and followers to the scourge of AIDS, a disease unknown in his time.

That is one of the many wonders of Van Sant's film: the 1970s were a world before AIDS, a window of time between the wonders of gay liberation and the horrors of the epidemic. Free at last from the fear of exposure (to employer, family, or community) but not yet fearful of exposure to a deadly disease, it was a prelapsarian era of pleasure as politics. That short-lived Shangri-La is central to the attenuated pleasure of the film: nobody knows that Harvey is about to die, though he himself has premonitions. Nor do they know they also will follow, with no assassin to put on trial. It's a world that disappeared, swept away by a medical tidal wave, leaving its trace in the flood of obituaries that filled the papers of the time.

I anticipated the thrill of seeing the film in the Castro, packed with an audience prepared to cheer and weep. Yet I felt as though I'd missed something as the crowd around me cheered. As much as I adore Van Sant's cinematic sensibility, I couldn't find the edgy vigor of his recent movies on screen. Instead the action felt as though it transpired at a distance, once removed; the characters, mere copies of themselves. Perhaps it was because I'd lived through this time, even if not firsthand. I wasn't disappointed in the film so much as in myself. How had I failed?

Perhaps I had watched *The Times of Harvey Milk* documentary so many times in twenty-five years of presenting it in public and in classrooms that I could no longer surrender my memories to these actor imposters. The people around me in the Castro were discovering the story for the first time, and it clearly worked powerfully for them. I, though, had loved the documentary so passionately for its genius at integrating individual stories into the texture of history, for monumentalizing a life. I was thrilled whenever Van Sant mixed it up, stirring a hybrid of fact and fiction, the evidentiary and the imaginary coalescing into a convincing moment of historical revivification.[12] When Sean Penn took an old cassette recorder in hand and intoned Harvey's words—"If a bullet should enter my brain, let that bullet destroy every closet door"—you could hear a pin drop in that house.

But too often I was let down. Was my problem with Black's screenplay, based on secondhand experiences instead of his own and shaped by a television sensibility that was broad-brush and episodic? I was a *Big Love* fan, so that was hard to believe. Was it his reliance on Cleve Jones for so much of the perspective? I sometimes felt that I was watching the Cleve Jones Story, not Harvey's. It's understandable for a witness to history to see himself as the center of the narrative, but when that story is meant to center on someone else entirely, it makes for an awkward prism.

Or was my problem with Sean Penn himself, turning in such a magnificent, gutsy, and, yes, Oscar-worthy performance . . . and yet so fundamentally, so glowingly, remaining Sean Penn? "He was really channeling Harvey," commented one friend who'd known him, "if Harvey had been a movie star." Would I have been more mesmerized by an unknown in the role? Maybe, but would any company have bankrolled it, or allowed it to be shot in San Francisco? Had I turned into a purist who wanted to see a New York Jew, as Harvey was, play the part? I'd never been such a literalist before.

My inner search continued as I carried out a complex forensic inspection of my own psyche. Was it Van Sant's direction, more cautious because he wasn't working from his own script, nor from original material; or perhaps constrained by the need for elegy, the burden of history? Was it the cinematography? Shot by Van Sant's frequent cameraman, Harris Savides, *Milk* felt to me as if viewed at a palpable remove, through a veil or scrim; while I could imagine that being appropriate for an elegy, the right distance for history, what I experienced that night felt wrong. I yearned for closeness and intimacy, I wanted imperfection and improvisation—like the era itself. I knew that Van Sant knew that world. And I knew that there had once been another plan: he had thought about shooting the film like a 1970s documentary with local veterans of those days, wielding 16mm cameras and following the action as if it were live, but Focus supposedly nixed the idea as too improvisational and risky (or costly) for a star-studded movie.[13] A rougher look would have pleased me; it might have catapulted the audience back into the era as successfully as the streets themselves had done, so totally, for me and others, some eight months earlier.

My objections aside, this *Milk* was a biopic, not a documentary, however hybrid its elements aspired to be. The dramatic biopic is one of the most conservative genres in cinema, tied to the fabled exceptionalism of the single heroic (or pathological) individual. As screenwriter, Black had synthesized characters and charted events into a dramatic hierarchy. Van Sant had cast his stars with a knowing eye toward their placement not just in history, but in cinema. I finally concluded that the film was a noble project for which I was not the intended audience. Not yet.

On March 28, as the audience streamed out of the Castro Theatre, we were greeted by a small crowd of enthusiastic protesters with placards, chanting "No on 8! No to hate!" to remind the public what was at stake in the election the following week. Proposition 8, a ballot measure scheduled to come up for a vote, would annul the legality of same-sex marriages in California, passed into law by a California Supreme Court decision only that June. Ironically *Milk* had just traced the battle over Proposition 6 and Harvey's involvement in fighting it through grassroots actions and calls for the gay community to come out. The buttons that Focus handed out at the screening spelled out "Don't Blend In," one of Harvey's political and lifestyle lessons. He was convinced people would only vote on behalf of folks they already knew, thus the importance of coming out, of not "passing." Inside the movie theater, we'd just watched as Harvey, Anne, and their confederates on screen defeated the nefarious proposition. The crowd was eager to cheer, confident that the upcoming election would see history repeat itself, with Californians again voting to defeat prejudice and injustice. How amazing, we thought, that after thirty years *Milk* emerged just in time to mirror another battle over gay legal rights.

It was in that mood that the crowd migrated to City Hall, the same building where Supervisor Harvey Milk and Mayor George Moscone had been shot dead in 1978. But also the building where, in 2008, nearly eighteen thousand gay and lesbian couples had been married since June, often choosing to say their vows in the upstairs rotunda, where a bust of Harvey Milk could preside over the ceremonies. I had made the pilgrimage myself with my girl, Mary, on September 10. So it wasn't at all inappropriate that a celebration rather than any demonstration of grief accompanied *Milk*. Harvey, more than anyone, loved a party.

City Hall's cavernous chambers were transformed for the evening into a high-fashion, Cannes-style premiere party. Sean Penn and Robin Wright Penn were there, along with Diego Luna, James Franco, Emile Hirsch, and Josh Brolin. Also in attendance were Gus Van Sant, of course, Dustin Lance Black, and all the politicians who'd ever passed through the halls in daylight. James Schamus had his New York City contingent in tow, and the top brass from Levi's—the evening's major sponsor—were out in force, reaffirming the brand's ties both to San Francisco history and to its valued 501 gay customers. Harvey Milk could at last be remembered with mirth and celebration instead of mourning. Municipal halls were transformed with bars and buffets, leather sofas, and custom-printed pillows that read, "My name is Harvey Milk, and I'm here to recruit you." The slogan had become a pillow, commemorating the signature line that the canny politician had included with a laugh or a frown in every speech and rally, at least in *Milk*.[14] Some people were shell-shocked from the film and stayed close to the bars, avoiding eye contact and drinking, while others danced as if the big disco ball in the sky was still spinning, spinning, spinning. On the way out, we were handed souvenirs, the obligatory swag of any A-list event: Levi's bags emblazoned with Milk's name and, for the lucky, a pillow to cry on.

The film was wonderful in many ways: in its evocation of a time, its examination of the nitty-gritty of city politics, the summoning of a world too long misremembered in the context of the horrific event and its aftermath. I loved the early scene of cruising in the New York City subway, the audaciousness of Harvey's pickup of Scott, the feel of delirious abandon crossing the country in those days, and the sense of San Francisco's Castro district as the wild west, the land filled with boys, yes, but a land where you might be taking your life in your hands by kissing your boyfriend on the stoop (as the inclusion of the true-story murder by gay-bashing viscerally illustrated). I loved the brief homage to Sylvester, one of the major cultural heroes of the time. I was nonplussed, though, by the film's approach to the sex life of the Castro in the 1970s: not a single mention of the baths where those boys were spending all their time (just one coy mention of a night at the sauna for Scott), no running out to discos every night (only for Harvey's election celebration), and a decidedly chaste version of Harvey's own bedding practices. Still, Van Sant's deft inclusion of so much archival footage along with Black's scripted reconstructions functioned as a sort of architectural collaboration, the classic and the modern molded together into a new statement entirely—a new monument, all of a piece. In spite of my feeling emotionally underwhelmed and dramatically unconvinced that night, very soon, unbeknown to me then, I would be having a change of heart. The movie became so much more than itself. Spilt milk, indeed.

November 4, 2008: History Edits a Film

A week later, I returned to City Hall, this time to vote. Once again, as on the premiere night, we were surrounded by crowds holding up "Obama" and "No on 8" placards, with cars passing by, honking in solidarity. Like that winter day on Castro Street, I once again felt headily empowered. I cast my ballot for Obama in the presidential election and, in the state election, voted against Proposition 8. The addition of Sarah Palin to the Republican ticket gave me another flashback, this time to the culture wars of the 1980s, when conservative forces were easily marshaled by tapping into fear of the unknown, the other, the people "not like us." It felt as if Phyllis Schlafly or Anita Bryant were back on the campaign trail, channeled by the GOP's latest babe.

For months San Francisco seemed to have thrown itself into campaigning for Obama—reviving grassroots efforts, volunteering at phone trees, stumping the state to make sure he'd be the next president. Even Dustin Lance Black, fresh off his press tour for *Milk*, dedicated himself to speaking at rallies across the country to ensure that LGBT communities would turn out on election day to vote for Obama. Dangerously, nobody realized that the Mormon and Catholic Churches were doing exactly the same thing, with Prop. 8 as their target, pouring money into the state, preaching in churches against the godlessness of same-sex marriage, and rallying their troops while the LGBT community leaned on (bad) advertising and uninspiring slogans.

Everyone I knew assumed that Prop. 8 would go down to disgrace. "Everyone" was wrong; it passed. In that very moment, watching the returns in a room of friends buoyed by Obama's win and utterly flattened by Prop. 8's passage, I realized that *Milk* was now a different film.

By the time it opened theatrically, the election had performed a stark re-editing. The conservative formula of its biopic genre was instantly reframed into a commentary on our time. Suddenly all the scenes of Milk amassing grassroots organizers, insisting that gays and lesbians needed to make open appearances to dispel the shadows of prejudice, all that became an op-ed commentary on what had just gone wrong in his beloved state of California. Harvey had understood how to craft coalitions with labor unions and make common cause with other communities and disenfranchised groups, skills sorely needed now. And he understood the kind of smarts, stamina, and shoe leather it took to win campaigns in the hothouse atmospheres of city and state politics. As we carried our gift bags around town, with a denim Levi pocket on the back and a slogan on the front, everything changed. "Your candidate for supervisor Harvey Milk." Their message suddenly felt not only nostalgic but bittersweet. Harvey's legacy had been too narrow: coming out to win acceptance and rights, yes; grassroots organizing to win elections, no.

There was grief in the aftermath of the passage of Prop. 8. No, it wasn't an assassination. And no, unlike Prop. 6 before it, its passage didn't mean that people would lose their jobs or that schools would unleash witch hunts—though loss of children, home, and hospital visiting rights still loomed in people's nightmares. Gay marriage is and was a contested priority for LGBT communities, where many scorned the ritual or the strategy while others desperately coveted the right or urgently needed the legal protection or immigration status. There was a brief moment of hope when Attorney General Jerry Brown filed suit to have the referendum against same-sex marriage ruled unconstitutional for trampling on the rights of minorities.[15] Legal confusion and a spirit of despair filled the air.

Milk opened theatrically around the country after California's antigay ballot measure had already passed. Audiences flocked to see the film: opening weekend grossed nearly $1.5 million in ticket sales. The film became a new pilgrimage for LGBT generations and all those who supported the notion of equality in unions of the heart. Edited by history, *Milk* was no longer the same film that debuted to the gala crowd in October. It had acquired an additional layer of sadness, a renewed sense of loss and betrayal, and a fervid new audience. In San Francisco even weekday shows at 10 A.M. sold out for weeks. In the Castro itself, lines stretched down the block and around the corner. People went to see it as a ritual of shared shock and despair. And more.

With the film as gauge, the soul-searching over Prop. 8 continued. Missteps were called out, strategies berated. Audiences watched the scenes of

Harvey fighting Prop. 6 in his time by defying the *Advocate* magazine's power-brokers, rejecting their call for polite statements and advertising campaigns in favor of in-your-face rhetoric and personalized grassroots campaigning. How did the LGBT community's leadership this time end up taking the exact route that Harvey Milk himself, veteran of so much San Francisco politics, disparaged? *Milk* had turned hideously prophetic now that audiences had hindsight. True, the "Yes on 8" campaign won by developing savvy advertising that preyed on voters' fears and used wording to confuse voters, but it was equally helped by the weaknesses of its opposition. The "No on 8" strategists ran an unconvincing and tone-deaf campaign, further weakened by an underestimation of the strength of the yes vote (and of the church in politics), inadequate grassroots organizing (efforts focused on electing Obama instead), and an inability to counteract still vivid stereotypes and misrepresentations of the measure's plausible results.

The election defeat energized the base—too late, alas, for the vote—and jump-started new campaigns to fight for new legislation all over again, this time with a grassroots presence extending into regional and ethnic communities and with new hope for the future. During the Sundance Film Festival, a special panel convened at the Queer Lounge for the panel "LGBT Civil Rights: Film Activism and Prop. 8," where a number of speakers debated the topic of the media and Prop. 8 to analyze what went on.[16] There had been a call for a boycott of Sundance itself, based on the idea that it was held and (partly) based in Utah, Mormon territory. To me, this was an absurd idea. John Cooper, the gay director of the film festival, pointed out the obvious: the Sundance festival had been outstandingly queer-friendly for most of its existence, playing a catalytic role in fostering the New Queer Cinema flowering of the early 1990s. Also, every year, the LGBT communities of Utah would thank Sundance for being there to provide an alternative. Sure enough, right in that room, an ex-Mormon transwoman spoke up about the massive turnout for the annual Utah Pride Parade in Salt Lake City; a local gay Mormon stood, visibly emotional, to complain about feeling stigmatized in both of his communities; and a handsome young man from rural Idaho came to ask for leadership, only to be told "You're it . . . and we promise to come there to help." As long argued, we were indeed everywhere.

During the discussion, I acknowledged my dismay over the LGBT reaction of blaming the African American community for the proposition's success, even though that community is not characterized by Mormon or Catholic congregations, the troops that had gone to bat, and the bank, for it. I carried a message from one of my oldest friends, a leader in the African American community and one of its many gay-friendly heterosexuals. "Do you really think that the African American community is any more homophobic than the LGBT community is racist?" she had asked me.

Panelists talked about the true meaning of alliances: they have to be reciprocal if they are going to be functional. Where was the LGBT community, for instance, at the time of Prop. 187, which fifteen years earlier had demonized immigrants?[17] Some pointed out that differences on gay marriage had more to do with generation than with race, ethnicity, or religion. Matt Coles of the ACLU declared, "We know that if everyone over sixty were left out of the charts, then gay and lesbian marriage would easily pass and be legal." The mere passage of time might just be the most winning strategy.[18]

March 25, 2009: Aftermath and the Academy Awards

The Oscars. I am always surprised that people care so much about the Academy Awards ceremonies and statues. My own lack of interest in those proceedings is long-standing. The votes have never had much to do with cinematic quality or importance; rather they demonstrate the heft of marketing campaigns and box-office results, the upgrading or downgrading of particular agents, publicists, or studio heads, and a lot of other less savory factors. Then there's the boredom of the interminable show itself. Every year it grinds me down. All around me, however, LGBT communities were holding their breath: Would it be like last time, or would the story this time turn out differently?[19]

When the nominations were announced, Gus Van Sant had acknowledged the respect paid to the film: a total of eight nominations, including himself as best director, Sean Penn for best actor, Josh Brolin for best supporting actor, Dustin Lance Black for best original screenplay, Danny Elfman for best original score, Danny Glicker for best costume design, Elliot Graham for best editing, and *Milk* for best film of the year. And Van Sant's interpretation? "These nominations ensure that Harvey Milk's legacy will live on." Never mind audience, memory, or history. No, it seemed that the Academy members' votes were the measure by which Milk the man and *Milk* the film would claim their place in history. And who can say that Gus was wrong? In the era of Google and Facebook and Twitter and whatever has already come next, movies may be the closest thing to a historical record that our culture possesses.

In the end, two Oscars were awarded to *Milk*, one to Black for best screenplay and one to Penn for best actor. No best director statue for Van Sant:

the *Slumdog Millionaire* juggernaut wiped out all other options. Still, the two important prizes gave *Milk* a respectable showing, commensurate with its nearly $32 million domestic box-office gross and Focus Features' mini-major ambitions. What was important, however, was not the fact of the awards but rather the speech acts that accompanied them.

"You gotta give 'em hope!" That was the message that Harvey Milk had learned from another San Francisco politician, took to heart, and made his own a generation ahead of Obama's presidential campaign. Context is important: Prop. 8 was passed in a moment of turmoil, of political and personal upheaval, with people losing their homes and savings, with cities going broke, hate crimes on the rise, and California on the verge of bankruptcy. All too often such bleak times turn to scapegoats as cheap solutions. Black had brought Harvey Milk back to life at a time when he was needed like never before, for the example of his inspirational leadership and political tactics.

When his name was announced and he sprinted to the stage, Black had a speech ready. Yes, the usual professional courtesies that guarantee the next job were observed: thanks to producers and companies and director. But then Black gave a speech like none in recent memory: "When I was thirteen years old . . . [I] moved from a conservative Mormon home in San Antonio, Texas, to California and I heard the story of Harvey Milk and it gave me hope . . . that one day I could live my life openly as who I am and one day maybe even fall in love and one day maybe even get married." If that had been all, it would have been a historic speech about hope and the great migration from throughout the United States to the dream of California. But Black kept going, and no timer yanked him off the stage or cut his microphone:

> If Harvey had not been taken from us thirty years ago, I think he'd want me to say to all of the gay and lesbian kids out there tonight who have been told that they are "less than" by their churches or by the government or by their families, that you are beautiful, wonderful creatures of value, and that no matter what anyone tells you, God does love you and that very soon, I promise you, you will have equal rights federally across this great nation of ours. And thank you, God, for giving us Harvey Milk.[20]

Sean Penn, who had willed himself into the marrow of Milk's character, who had channeled him down the decades into his very bones and brought him back from the grave in one of the great roles of his career, was there at the Oscars too. While it's a sad truism that straight actors all too easily win an Oscar for playing gay, in this case Penn deserved it.

And we deserved him: Penn interrupted the requisite actor's mantra of thanks to say, forthrightly, to the audience and the camera, "For those who saw the signs of hatred as our cars drove in tonight, I think that it is a good time for those who voted for the ban against gay marriage to sit and reflect and anticipate their great shame and the shame in their grandchildren's eyes if they continue that way of support. We've got to have equal rights for everyone."

Some day, I have no doubt, a kid who heard those speeches by Black and Penn will mount a stage in Hollywood, Washington, or some other place, reflect on their effect on her or him, and credit *Milk* for a change of heart, a change of life. Hope is as essential today as ever, and thus my early ambivalence over the film was transformed by the months and the events of 2008–9 into a wonderment, a sense of destiny that went beyond biopic traditions and NQC expectations, that went to the heart of something that the pioneering film critic and historian Vito Russo (for all our differences) got right: that movies do affect us, our sense of our own identity, our capacity for a different future. Up to a point. I never agreed with *The Celluloid Closet*'s theory of transmission that posited how totally movies mold us, because I think we also fight back and resist them or use them for our own goals. So for that one night in late March, I forgot to disbelieve. I chose to put my faith in movies' magic.

Yes, Harvey Milk's spirit still haunts San Francisco, a city famous for its ghosts. In the public library, an exhibition of his early life was on view for a time in the James C. Hormel Gay and Lesbian Center, named in honor of the gay philanthropist who endowed it. There's a high school, a library, and even a federal building named for Milk, while the Harvey Milk Democratic Club is a force in local politics. The San Francisco press ran multiple articles for the thirtieth anniversary: one on Milk, of course, one on White, one on Mayor George Moscone, and one on the victims of Jonestown—the fervent and hopeful San Franciscan parishioners who had followed the leader of their Peoples' Temple, Jim Jones, to Guyana and drank the Kool-Aid, going to their deaths in the very same week that Dan White murdered Milk and Moscone.

More than a decade after the New Queer Cinema movement, *Milk* the film returned us to a more conventional form and history to recapture a man and a lesson. In doing so, it transcended its own status as a film and became a political fact. In the late autumn and winter of 2008–9, seeing it became a political act. Theaters showing *Milk*—and there were eventually 882 of them across the country—became sanctuaries of a sort, offering retreat and succor for anyone grieving election results: redemption for just the price of a ticket.

History can't always be rewritten: Harvey Milk was as dead and gone at the end of the movie as he was in life, off screen. But *Milk* offered explanations and ideas, provided a scaffold on which to hang new hopes and put to rest old fears.[21] It may not have had the sass and swagger of the early NQC or the flashy pyrotechnics of its early practitioners, but it had its heart in the right place: not gay pride, but something much bigger. Delirium, for instance. And grief and rage and memory.

In retrospect, Van Sant's decision to mix documentary footage and drama was smart: it facilitated the audience's identification of the story with the stuff of history. Its most emotional scenes, for me, were the imported dragnet footage of police busting up gay bars in the 1950s and 1960s, shining spotlights onto the faces of clean-cut men rounded up by the vice squad simply for patronizing a bar, thrown into a police van for having a drink with their kind, criminalized merely for seeking community.

Those self-documented police raids moved me with their harsh lighting and framing straight out of Weegee, the conspicuous shame of the visible, lives ruined right there before our eyes. It was the stuff of documentary, in fact, that was positioned up front by Van Sant, inviting us into the film. *Look back, remember, don't forget*, the footage seemed to signal. *Not all of this is over, you aren't home free yet.* And indeed we aren't. But all these years of all these films have made a difference. We exist in the world now. After the passing fashion of New Queer Cinema, we're still indisputably present, even at the White House, for the Medal of Freedom ceremony, where, in 2009, President Obama presented a posthumous award to Harvey Milk.[22]

Gus Van Sant released *Milk* into the world like a balloon that, let go into the sky, follows the breezes higher and higher until it's out of sight. He made something that was more than a film; it was a trail guide to the way ahead, a treasure box dug up from the dirt of the past, a sign auguring the future. "My name is Harvey Milk and I am here to recruit you," indeed. The exhortation is not easily overlooked, not easily forgotten. Being gay wasn't a lifestyle back then; it was a blood-and-guts battle for existence and recognition. And *Milk* is now here to remind us: while we may not yet have entered the promised land, whatever that may be, there's no turning back.

Notes

Originally published in an abbreviated version in B. Ruby Rich, "Ghosts of a Vanished World," *The Guardian*, January 16, 2009.

1. The phrase was immortalized in *The Mayor of Castro Street*, the book published by the late Randy Shilts in 1988, four years after the Epstein–Schmiechen documentary.

2. Interestingly, production funding was a result of special financing earmarked for the Bicentennial in 1976, when money was funneled to individual artists for the first time to make films for the occasion; thereafter funding to individual film- and video makers continued, although by the 1990s rising production costs made NYSCA's contributions less determinant than they had once been.

3. Already two other gay politicians were in office—in Massachusetts, State Representative Elaine Noble, and in Minnesota, State Senator Allan Spear—but they were less famous and less identified with representing a gay constituency.

4. It is interesting to note that Harvey Milk died in the same year that Proposition 13 passed. Unlike 6 and 8, it was not a proposition that stigmatized California's LGBT citizens. Instead it did more than anyone or anything else to destroy the future of the state's infrastructure, educational system, and legacy by freezing property taxation at original purchase-price levels and increasing to two-thirds the legislative vote needed for all future budget measures, thus ensuring that it could not be undone and that Republican minorities would continue to exercise undue power over state policies.

5. The cinematographer Frances Reid and the editor Deborah Hoffman have had eminently successful careers together as filmmakers. Reid was a cofounder and director of Iris Films, which once distributed lesbian film and video, and codirected *In the Best Interests of the Children* (1977). Hoffman made one of the best Alzheimer films ever, *Complaints of a Dutiful Daughter* (1994). Together they made *Long Night's Journey into Day* (2000), an eloquent tribute to the wisdom and challenges of South Africa's Truth and Reconciliation process. Richard Schmiechen made a second documentary, *Changing Our Minds: The Story of Dr. Evelyn Hooker* (1992). He died of AIDS in 1993.

6. *The Times of Harvey Milk* was reissued in 2011 on DVD and Blu-Ray in a box set by Criterion that includes the testimony of Harvey's gay nephew, Stuart Milk, outtakes, news footage, even an essay on the film by this author.

7. These and all other Van Sant quotations in this chapter are from the author's interview with him by telephone on October 26, 2008.

8. Erik Davis, "Bryan Singer and Gus Van Sant Fight over Spilled Milk," Cinematical .com, April 13, 2007.

9. The film is in cyberspace: http://www.filminfocus.com/video/milk_575_castro _st. Another personal documentary, Jen Gilomen's *Mixed Use* (2008), usefully updates Milk's story by combining the "revived" camera store and Castro footage with present-day interviews with those who knew him.

10. I've criticized the *New York Times* for downplaying Harvey's notorious sex life, but how much more chaste was the movie *Milk*, where even the word *baths* is not uttered. But as anyone involved knows, sex is central to political movements.

11. I met Scott at a San Francisco Public Library event in the early 1990s; he introduced himself as "the widow Milk." He died on February 4, 1995, of AIDS-related pneumonia.

12. Rob Epstein made all his original footage from *The Times of Harvey Milk* available to Van Sant and Black, as well as other materials, all of which became a basis for script details ("adapted screenplay" anyone?). Van Sant had the documentary screened at the Castro for all the extras in the march and rally scenes as an obligatory history lesson.

13. Personal communication from one of the 16mm cinematographers who briefly worked on it, winter 2009; not corroborated by Focus.

14. For the serious purpose behind many a Harvey Milk joke, see Foss, "The Logic of Folly in the Political Campaigns of Harvey Milk."

15. This appeal would go down to defeat, as the state supreme court, ruling now for the third time, acknowledged its inability under California law to rule a proposition illegal. But my partner and I, as one of the approximately eighteen thousand couples who married during the interregnum between May and November, now occupy the peculiar orphan class of those whose marriage has been ruled legal and allowed to stand. At this writing, the legal case is continuing through district and federal courts. The handling of the challenge by the prominent political lawyers Theodore Olsen and David Boies has led many to expect an appeal all the way up to the Supreme Court.

16. Thanks to my fellow participants on the "Film Activism and Prop. 8" panel of January 2009, for their insights: John Cooper, Rob Epstein, Rashad Robinson, Dayna Frank, and, above all, Matt Coles.

17. California's Proposition 187, or "Save Our State," was passed by voters in 1994, while the Republican Pete Wilson was governor. It specified that illegal immigrants be excluded from all access to social services, health care, and education in California. A federal appeals court subsequently ruled it unconstitutional; after the election of Gray Davis, a Democrat, further court action was dropped.

18. A well-organized campaign in Fresno launched a successful gathering in spring 2009, "Meet in the Middle" (of the state of California), attempting to position a different grassroots campaign to win back marriage rights. In the wake of the California defeat, Utah and New Hampshire managed to pass gay marriage legislation.

19. People had still not got over the denial of the Oscar for best film to *Brokeback Mountain* and expressed fear that *Milk* would suffer the same fate.

20. In later remarks at a New York City premiere of *Milk* reported by OurSceneTV on its website, Black added, "I know, my generation didn't do our part, we didn't stand up, we didn't self-represent, we used straight allies . . . and Harvey's message was to stand up for yourself. Walk across the street to the guy who might vote against me, and say: get to know me. And break down some of those stereotypes, and maybe they

won't vote against you on election day. I think there are lessons to be learned from the movie . . . also for the gay community. . . . Go to the video store and pick it up, and say, that's how they did it." Transcribed from interview posted to http://www.ourscenetv .com/posts/45/oscar-s-golden-boy-dustin-lance-black.

21. For more on the film in the context of recent queer cinema as well as recent television culture, see Benshoff, "*Milk* and Gay Political History." Benshoff argues that *Milk* belongs to the "boutique studio neo-queer prestige picture" category in which he also includes *Far from Heaven* (2002), *The Hours* (2002), and *Brokeback Mountain* (2005).

22. On August 12, 2009, President Obama bestowed the Medal of Freedom Award upon Harvey Milk as one of sixteen "agents of change" (others included Sandra Day O'Connor, Desmond Tutu, and Billie Jean King). Rob Epstein attended the ceremony with Harvey's nephew, Stuart Milk.

CONCLUSION

Twenty years after New Queer Cinema's arrival, the terrain for LGBT film-making has radically changed. To an extent, this volume's table of contents maps that history. In the United States by the turn of the millennium, the earlier queer movement had given way to new social landscapes and a new generation of queers. Once again, historical context and political environment played a role. The AIDS retroviral cocktail was discovered in 1996; its accessibility (at least in the United States, where its costs could be sustained) relieved the panic and fatalities of the 1980s and early 1990s. As the death sentences of the past transmuted into longer-term chronic illness with a more benign prognosis for many LGBT communities, longevity allowed for a focus on matters other than survival. The urgency that had fueled the NQC was gone. So was Reagan, replaced by eight years of a Clinton White House (1992–98) that lessened rhetorics of damnation to such an extent that even eight years of George W. Bush couldn't roll back the tide. With President Obama in the White House, even more beach-heads of acceptance could be established.

The marketplace was more crowded now, a legacy of the earlier generation's push for acceptance, though the goal certainly wasn't marketplace acceptability at the time; in capitalism, even queers (with money) get options. Activism gave way to lifestyle, as the old defiance faded into homonormativity.[1] "We're here, we're queer, we're married" is a very different war cry from the 1980s street chant ". . . get used to it." What had transpired? Was this now a postqueer era, as some have suggested? Or had that phase too already passed?

True, the seroconversion of AIDS had changed everything. So, too, did evolutions in societal perception and the changes in status: domestic partner legislation, health insurance availability, gay marriage campaigns, the repeal of Don't Ask Don't Tell policy, corporate targeting of LGBT customer bases. Most important for this volume, New Queer Cinema changed: first it expanded into something, then nothing, and then everything—a relatively rapid transformation from the fringe to the center at the level of subjects and themes. Once taboo or titillating, queers were now the stuff of art films, crossover movies, and television series. Thank you, HBO. Thank you, Focus Features. Or, some might argue, No thanks. As decisively as the outlaw seemed to disappear from LGBT culture, so too did the radical import of NQC disappear from the films that it had made possible. Yes, I'm happy to have more rights, but oh how I miss the outlawry of the old days.

New decades, new platforms, and new debates all arrived. And new technologies, from webcams to social media to iPads. Very likely some will be old news by the time you read these words. As ever, transformation can arrive with lightning speed and no advance notice.

Success, Celebrity, and the End of the Outlaw

The rapidity of change post-1992 may well be an effect of television, though that medium is largely absent from this volume. In a postqueer world in which the marginal can become mainstream in the blink of an eye, Ellen DeGeneres personifies a remarkable cycle of damnation and redemption. She first became an LGBT figure in 1994 with her network appearance as Ellen Morgan, androgynous bookseller, in the eponymous sitcom *Ellen*. Then in 1997, at the height of the show's popularity, she came out in character on a legendary "puppy episode" on April 30, 1997. I remember walking home from the Castro as it aired without missing a single line: every bar and living room along my route had a television tuned to the show with the volume up high. People cheered and laughed. We were in all the homes of America! For a minute, that is. Then came the cancellation of the show by dastardly ABC/Disney, Ellen's very public three-year romance (1997–2000) with the star Anne Heche and their equally public breakup, and Ellen's canonization as LGBT martyr in *The Real Ellen Story* (1997) by the queer chroniclers Fenton Bailey and Randy Barbato. Even her mother, Betty, became a beloved celebrity.

Then times changed again, and fast. By 2002 her name could fuel a popular website (afterellen.com) with no need for explanation. Then *The Ellen*

Show debuted and in 2003, a retooled DeGeneres made a cartoon return as the voice of Dory in *Finding Nemo* (distributed by Disney, no less) and a triumphant television return with *The Ellen DeGeneres Show*, quickly an enormous hit. She hosted the Academy Awards in 2007 and topped it all off by marrying the lovely Portia de Rossi in 2008. By now Ellen DeGeneres is permanently installed as America's lesbian sweetheart.

What happened? Timing and talent, sure, but Ellen became lovable in part because she got some company. On television, gay and lesbian characters showed up all over the remote control. There were hip mainstream shows like *Will and Grace* (1998–2006) and *Buffy the Vampire Slayer* (1997–2003) and *Queer as Folk*, the groundbreaking hit drama of gay men's lives in "Pittsburgh" (2000–2005), the sophisticated moments of gay love and relationships in *Six Feet Under* (2001–5), reality-TV makeover shows like the original *Queer Eye for the Straight Guy* (2003–7), and even the improbably fashionable lesbian series *The L Word* (2004–9), which debuted the year after Ellen's return to the airwaves. However much they merit critique, and they do, oh they do, these shows worked to disrupt and rewrite societal norms and entertain us; they brought LGBT culture out of the shadows and made it audience-friendly.

And there was more. Thom Felicia was starring in *Queer Eye for the Straight Guy* when he was named official designer of the U.S. Pavilion at the 2005 World's Fair in Aichi, Japan. Movement from the edge to the center was becoming downright meteoric in terms of marketing as well as ideology, given Felicia's rhetorical shift from Pier One to patriotism. Sure, we always knew interior designers were gay (or lesbian), but that was an open secret, not a governmental press release.

The price of all that mainstreaming on television was the demise of the boundary-pushing, ideology-challenging New Queer Cinema. Who needed NQC once TV delivered its cuddlier version to networks and cable stations? And anyway, by then who still went to movie theaters?

If this was the downside of so-called progress, there were also upsides. Strand Releasing, the go-to distributor for the early NQC era, prospered and expanded. Marcus Hu and John Gerrans nurtured it beyond queer with a full menu of art films but never abandoned their legacy. Sometimes the two interests coincided, as in Strand's distribution of Fatih Akin's extraordinary crossover film, *The Edge of Heaven* (2007), and a trio of François Ozon movies, and its steadfast distribution of every one of Apichatpong Weerasethakul's queer-friendly films, a loyalty he rewarded by sticking with Strand for his lauded Palme d'Or winner, *Uncle Boonmee Who Can Recall His Past Lives* (2010).

Other key NQC players have followed similar paths, adapting to shifts in filmmaking and society. Christine Vachon had continuing success with the production company Killer Films and a lifelong collaboration with Todd Haynes, including a shared voyage into the wonders of HBO with the *Mildred Pierce* miniseries in 2011. Tom Kalin, John Greyson, and Richard Fung have all gone into academia, kick-starting new classes of queers, and have gone on making films; Greyson has been especially prolific with *Lilies* (1996), *Proteus* (2003), *Fig Trees* (2009), and lots of shorts and television credits that deepen his acerbic brand of camp into increasingly polished treatises.

Rose Troche made two more features, *Bedrooms and Hallways* (1998) and *The Safety of Objects* (2001), and in television, helped to launch *The L Word* and *South of Nowhere* (2005–8); in 2012 she was preparing *Xanadu*, a coming-of-age film about a tomboy. Cheryl Dunye returned to the United States from Amsterdam and teamed up with a coterie of pals to make two low-budget films, *The Owls* (2010) and *Mommy Is Coming* (2012).

James Schamus, meanwhile, was transformed from a collaborator on early NQC films to the cofounder of the Good Machine production company to the CEO of Focus Features, where in 2012 he celebrated his tenth anniversary. There, Schamus has been able to produce or distribute Gus Van Sant's *Milk*, Ang Lee's *Brokeback Mountain*, Dee Rees's *Pariah*, and Lisa Cholodenko's *The Kids Are All Right*. Oh, and he's a professor at Columbia University, where Cholodenko was his student before making *High Art*. Now in L.A., her films slowly moved in the direction of mainstream acceptability. Her fourth feature, *The Kids Are All Right* (2010), a crossover hit with audiences and critics alike, scored a 94 percent rank on the Rotten Tomatoes website and $20 million at the box office. It's Cholodenko's "most approachable" film according to a positive review by the *Denver Post*'s Lisa Kennedy, a member of the Sundance NQC panel in 1992.[2]

But all was not well. If many lesbians were furious at *High Art* for replaying the old formula that dictates a lesbian character must die by the end of the movie, now even more were mad: *Kids* divided the community. Attack central was the Bully Bloggers website, where Judith "Jack" Halberstam took the film apart with surgical finesse for depicting lesbian bed death as a fact of life, neglecting to butch up the Annette Bening character, putting Julianne Moore's character into on-screen sex with a man (Mark Ruffalo) but not Bening and even for assigning a queer motorcycle, an old Beemer, to Ruffalo instead of Bening.[3]

The website's dedicated following mostly agreed with Halberstam. So did lesbian mothers elsewhere on the web: Joan Garry's *Huffington Post* column insisted that Cholodenko (herself a lesbian mom with her partner, the musician Wendy Melvoin, and an anonymous sperm donor) had a sacred obligation because *Kids* was the first hit film to put lesbian families in the public eye. But there was another perspective out there too. The *Nashville Scene's* Jordan Caress laid out a contrarian response:

> Witnessing the whirlwind of baseless accusations forced me to come to terms with some of my own secrets and insecurities. For example, I know plenty . . . who are intrigued by the thought of a male sex partner. One of my closest friends, an astute thinker and confirmed lover of women, commented, "I'm not boycotting shit. I'd sleep with Mark Ruffalo!" . . . A community that supposedly values sexual freedom negates its own philosophy when its members begin judging private sexual behavior. But even with this knowledge, I still instinctively scoff at the stereotype in question. Am I secretly afraid of my future girlfriends escaping lesbian bed death in the arms of a dude? Kind of. Is it partially because I've seen it happen, with unrealistic frequency, on TV and in movies? Probably.[4]

The interplay between lived behavior and behavior as modeled in movies is complex. How to tell the difference between a desire that's organic to the self and one that's implanted by the media? And how to judge a film that stormed movie theaters across the country precisely because it had the conventional elements key to attracting A-list actors, money, and theatrical distribution? As for *The Kids Are All Right*, I loved the lovable parts, cringed at unwelcome truths, frowned at unwelcome falsehoods, and mostly identified with the offspring. Was I happy that queer culture had ended up in a wading pool with mommies and kids and a nuclear family, let alone a sperm-daddy interloper? Hell, no. But enough hit home that I had to clap. As did the overidentifying heterosexual mom in the next seat.

Online and On Guard

Generations of cinema pass quickly. Energies move elsewhere, different locations come into view, and identities mutate rather than disappear. Idioms and communities emerge, grow up, evolve, and atrophy. There's no standing still, however strong the pull of nostalgia may be.

As New Queer Cinema was transformed into an acceptable genre with its own stars and niche audiences, the small market for those films was shrinking: even its movie theaters disappeared. In November 2011 the Laemmle Theatres' Sunset 5 Theatre closed; a mainstay of L.A. exhibition, it had opened the same year NQC debuted and had screened nearly all of its early ground-breaking films. Earlier the same year, Christine Vachon would infuriate an audience in San Francisco by recommending a shift to television and the Internet. "The state of cinema . . . is not necessarily taking place in a cinema" was her tagline.[5] This was not just prophecy; the shift was already happening. The movie industry was desperately turning to 3-D to pull people in to see movies and buy popcorn. New platforms were rising fast, and with them would come new modes of production.

"I just got tired of getting notes from the suits," said Angela Robinson one day in 2007, waiting for a Sundance shuttle. I'd been asking about her next film; I am a rabid fan of *D.E.B.S.* (2003), her lesbian version of James Bond that isn't sci-fi exactly, just posses of female spies, one hot villainess in hot pursuit, and a love story for the ages. Lucy (Jordana Brewster) is the spy girls' arch enemy whose nefarious plots they are sworn to intercept. But Lucy sets her sights on Amy (Sara Foster), pride of the all-girl government spy squad, and turns to staging faux crimes just so Amy can come rushing into battle—and into her arms.

The film was silly and smart and a lot of fun. But after her Disneyfication into *Herbie Fully Loaded* (seriously true) and *The L Word*, I saw Robinson's credits only on TV shows like *True Blood* and *Charlie's Angels* as she failed to get her next film off the ground. Robinson's solution? Give up for a minute on the Hollywood deals and DIY instead. The result was a thrilling series of webisodes known collectively as *Girltrash!* that were released, or rather uploaded, in 2007 on The Chart, a site linked to *The L Word*. The low-budget episodic adventures were turned out on the fly, using television actresses between jobs, scripts scribbled between paying gigs, and sets borrowed from the streets of Los Angeles. They were outrageous action movies, full of gunfire and car chases, but always beginning or ending or both with hot chicks in a clutch. Or in a jam. Or something. Robinson was reveling in scripts that couldn't be blue-penciled or sent back into development hell, while her fans got to revel in Robinson's sublimely sexy, satiric, tongue-in-cheek escapades.

I love serials. They make me imagine the early ones in newspapers, Dickens churning out a cliffhanger every month for eighteen months. We read *Oliver Twist*, but his readers read episodes; same for Armistead Maupin's original *Tales of the City*. Robinson's *Girltrash!* experiment was one of the first of the series produced for the web. It still circulates in the world of the web, but it jumped off-line too, into a yet-to-be-released feature, *Girltrash: All Night Long*, a prequel written by Robinson and directed by Alexandra Kondracke. Robinson herself has a rumored sci-fi film in development. This is a girl who loves her genres.

Low-budget online strategies proliferated as the promise of theatrical distribution companies diminished. It wasn't only fictional fantasies that began to find a home there: political interventions moved online too, as did historical restorations like the ACT UP Oral History Project.[6] Eventually social media would become a powerful organizing tool. In the short term, though, it fed a turning-away from the world as individualism took the place of the group in the political landscape.

Individualism moved beyond *Mad Men* house parties into political manifestations with the website "It Gets Better." On September 22, 2010, a Rutgers University freshman, Tyler Clementi, committed suicide after discovering that his roommate had webcammed his private gay encounter the night before and boasted about it on the Internet. Dan Savage and his partner, Terry Miller, made a YouTube video to assure gay youth, *It gets better*. The idea took off in the wake of the tragedy and the site became a place "to show young LGBT people the levels of happiness, potential, and positivity their lives will reach—if they can just get through their teen years."[7]

Just as *Brokeback Mountain* set off hundreds of thousands of web postings, so did this site. Two years later, the title phrase is trademarked and there are over "50,000 user-created videos viewed more than 50 million times." Celebrities from Suze Orman to President Obama to, yes, Ellen DeGeneres appear on the site. Thus can star-power be harnessed to social service. The IGBP links to an older, more traditional entity: the Trevor Project, founded in 1994 to combat suicide by LGBT youth with the Trevor Lifeline, 866-4-U-TREVOR, a suicide-prevention hotline.[8] Amid the entertainment, misinformation, and hate speech of the web, queer services now appear. And the mainstream-friendly *It Gets Better* keeps racking up celebrity posts.

Screens into Galleries

The Internet is not the only alternative to the big screen. As far back as the 1960s, filmmakers and artists have crossed between worlds. At the end of his life, Derek Jarman returned to painting. He also made *Blue*, the last film shown before his death at age fifty-two. By then he was blind. *Blue* consisted of the color blue and no images, a lyrical spoken text, and a soundtrack by

C.1 Tilda Swinton walks past Derek Jarman's
legendary Prospect Cottage retreat in Isaac Julien's *Derek*.
Screen grab. Courtesy of the filmmaker.

Simon Fisher Turner. The BBC broadcast the film on television with a simul-
cast on radio. The screen beamed International Klein Blue, the color created
by a chemist for artist Yves Klein, into British livingrooms.

The soundtrack was a last will and testament.[9] By 1994 he was gone. In
2008 Isaac Julien and Tilda Swinton made *Derek*, a film in his honor and
memory (fig. C.1). In one scene, Swinton moves through the landscape surrounding Jarman's legendary cottage on the Dungeness coast, as windswept as
the shingled ground, and Julien wanders through an archive of Jarman's work
like a visitor to a bank vault, marveling at the riches. Julien was paying tribute
to Jarman the filmmaker as well as Jarman the artist, and went on to organize
a retrospective of Jarman's art at the Serpentine Gallery in London to coincide
with the release of *Derek*. For Swinton, whose career has now lasted longer
post-Derek than it did with him, it's a return to the source, an opportunity to
plant a stake in the ground and declare what's important in cinema.[10]

Julien himself followed Jarman's model in the years since the NQC panel in
1992; he returned to his roots as an art school kid and became an installation
artist. He began to craft elegant multiscreen installation works that explored
landscapes of desire, such as the impossibly sexy *Long Road to Mazatlan*,
filmed in San Antonio, Texas. It followed Warhol in adopting a western landscape and annexing a gay cowboy ethos into its obsessions. *Long Road to
Mazatlan* restaged desire: how its gaze frames the landscape, how pop culture

frames desire itself, how intoxicating and full of color and light the road to fulfillment can be.[11]

By the time of *Derek*, Julien had made more installations than films. Recent installations have taken up global emergencies, from North African bodies washing up on the shores of Sicily to Fujian Chinese undocumented immigrants dying while harvesting cockles in the tricky waters of England's Morecambe Bay. Julien's interests may have moved beyond narrow questions of sexual identity, yet the embodiment of desire is never far from his thoughts, nor our eyes: bodies foregrounded, desires made flesh, tragedy made manifest.

Like Julien, Sadie Benning has exited the movie theater to enter the museum. First, though, she avoided all the production offers that came her way after *Jollies*. She continued instead to craft miniatures, including the heartbreaker *It Wasn't Love* and the sublime *The Judy Spots*. Benning switched media to take up music but ran into fame again as the media director and founding drummer of a little band she cooked up with Kathleen Hanna called Le Tigre.[12] One encounter with mobs of fans sent Benning back into the studio, where she began sketching, drawing, then animating the characters on the page, inside her head, and outside her window.

Benning emerged in 2007 with an exhibition of her drawings, *Suspended Animation*, at the Wexner Center for the Arts in Columbus, Ohio.[13] The centerpiece of the show was a two-channel digital installation, *Play Pause* (fig. C.2). It's an ode to gritty lust and big-city encounters, to the mixing of classes and races and sexualities once so common in the despised, economically depleted cities of the past, where *flâneurs* and *flâneuses* could mix and mingle

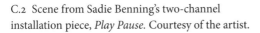

C.2 Scene from Sadie Benning's two-channel installation piece, *Play Pause*. Courtesy of the artist.

and break taboos: the outlawed detritus of proper society, united by the space of a club, a bar, a sanctuary.

Sadie Benning has cut desire off from narrative regimes of sequence to allow free play across wavelengths of minds and bodies shorn of temporality and unconstrained by narrative logics. Benning even reclaimed some of her Le Tigre past, composing and sampling the music and soundtrack. Like Julien, Haynes, and Jarman, her copanelists back in 1992, Benning stayed true to her vision and extended it, burnishing her themes until they shone.

In the universe of *Play Pause*, the full utopian promise of queerness is realized, if only in fleeting moments of longing or connection. This is no romantic idyll. Vacuum cleaners roar, trains thunder overhead, people live paycheck to paycheck; yet the euphoria in the late-night bar when the music's cranked up and pure pleasure rules is incomparable. All those memories, seared into the brain, instantly rush back. Into my mind float the sounds and palpable excitements of The Atomic Lounge, The Bistro, The Baton, Cubby Hole, The Clit Club, The Duchess, Girl Bar, PQs, The Sahara, and all the other beloved joints of my wild years in Boston, New York City, Chicago. "I Will Survive!"

Desire lives in such memories, alongside truths and pleasures and yearning and fulfillment. Benning may live in the same gentrified city of today that many of us inhabit, but she has captured the illicit energies of the old cities, naughty places of possibility and impossibility, miraculous sites where two bodies meeting could transform the world—yours, mine, his, hers, theirs—forever. At least for one night.

Play Pause is a happily-never-after story of urban life that queers the metropolis as thoroughly as Ang Lee queered the landscapes of *Brokeback Mountain* or as Isaac Julien queered those of the prewar Harlem Renaissance and Texas itself. The queerness in *Play Pause* is a brilliant exercise in José Muñoz's "cruising utopia." Its hybrid mash-up of nostalgia and yearning conjures prior eras that threw up fewer boundaries of class, sexuality, race, and vocation against the possibility that corporeal pleasures could mix and match on a whim and a prayer. Its artisan-like appearance, handmade aesthetic, and addictive soundtrack combined to lodge *Play Pause* inside the brain, between the legs, inside the very soul, mainlining desire for a queer nation that is far away from all that today. What city, what gender, what music? Benning's world is void of certainty. She dares us to look as clearly as she does, difference assumed, judgment stowed, heart wide open:

I don't think that gender is one thing—gender is made up of all these different parts and elements. It's stereotypical to think that you can understand somebody's gender just by looking at them. . . . I don't think that I could picture love or romance or sex or the body or gender in a whole picture, where you have a story that goes from beginning to middle to end. . . . The idea of identity is usually based on a marketing concept. . . . It's usually about selling things.[14]

With characteristic acuity, Sadie Benning provides a bridge from past to future and lands precisely in the midst of an important moment in the post-NQC universe.

The New Trans Cinema

By the twenty-first century it was clear: trans was the new queer. Every generation seeks to rebel against, if not obliterate, the one that came before; the queer world is no exception. Just as the queer movement overturned the positive/negative universe of the gay and lesbian past, which had in turn displaced the polite civil rights tactics of its postwar elders, so did the newcomers seek to reclaim and redefine their birthright of rebellion by crossing the boundaries into a redefined outlaw territory, an embodiment of the regendered self. For as much as the NQC did to reposition sexuality in the popular imagination, its agenda never included any such unseating of gender itself, which remained relatively naturalized by comparison.

Now, gender flux was the new standard, as the gender normativity maintained in the NQC days of renegotiated sexualities weakened its grip. Theoretical texts setting out the terms of trans identity and culture had actually appeared around the same time that NQC made its debut, with Leslie Feinberg's and Sandy Stone's early manifestos, but it would take almost another decade before trans texts by Susan Stryker, Paisley Curran, Judith Halberstam, and others would proliferate and trans films begin to arrive in earnest.[15]

The early energy of NQC was reborn as a cinema of transgender and genderqueer identity formations and representations. The New Trans Cinema brought the excitement, uncompromising demands, litany of oppression, new iconic representations, and, yes, the youngsters, all back out in force again. Not only did the NTC stake out new territory; it also overturned the now settled theatrical and televisual norms that had arisen in the wake of NQC. Right on cue for cycles of identity, the new generation complained that the LGBT universe was homonormative, just as my generation tended to see our elders as obsequious homosexuals. What goes around comes around in identity politics, and damn fast.

In 2005 San Francisco Frameline's LGBT film festival made it official with a special program of trans cinema that announced a new presence. The New Trans Cinema carries the same defiant bravado as the NQC once did and just as boldly rejects its inherited expectations. But it is different from the NQC in fundamental ways: its oeuvre so far has been dominated by documentaries, often focused on one character or couple; coming-out stories predominate, albeit in a different register; the filmic style is almost always transparent rather than baroque or disjunctive; and stories inevitably unfold in the present tense without appropriating or accessing histories. It's a film and digital movement devoted to the present tense.

Of course, trans cinema has a complicated backstory with which to contend. Trans characters have long appeared in mainstream and art movies, anchoring comedy or tragedy, from Fassbinder's *In a Year with 13 Moons* (1978, tragic) to Robert Altman's *Come Back to the Five and Dime, Jimmy Dean, Jimmy Dean* (1982, dramatic) to Duncan Tucker's *Transamerica* (2005, comic). Though restricted entirely to M-to-F trans characters, the representation of such figures became incrementally more positive. In the case of *Transamerica*, a Felicity Huffman vehicle, the pre-op transwoman's dilemma is framed entirely in terms of reuniting with a long-lost son, one of the oldest movie tropes in the book, regardless of gender status. More often, the trans characters were positioned in show-biz settings, as if to offer a functional rationale for gender crossing even when narratives were finally tilting in their favor.

The film that brought the transwoman into popular movies was Neil Jordan's *The Crying Game* (1992). Miramax had created an entire Oscar campaign by convincing the press not to reveal the gender identity of Jaye Davidson, the film's mysterious (to some) star. Davidson played Dil, the beautiful, sexy lover of Forest Whitaker's character, Jody, and later an object of lust for Stephen Rea's character, Fergus. Acceptance came at a steep price: the formula for these transitional trans films required the inclusion of a money shot, a reveal that would expose an anatomical gender calculated to contravene (heterosexual) audience expectation. The expected reaction was signaled for the viewer by Fergus, who rushes to vomit at the sight. The scene made for such a voyeuristic ambush that one journalist dubbed *The Crying Game* a heterosexual horror movie. However, despite that initial reaction, Fergus comes around. The money shot could in that sense prove an effective pivot-point to acceptance, by making visible the unspeakable and thus initiating a coming to terms with a new scope of desire and its scopophilic challenges.

Soldier's Girl (2003), a Showtime movie written by a gay screenwriter, Ron Nyswaner (*Philadelphia*), and directed by the veteran Hollywood director Frank Pierson, was based on the true story of Barry Winchell and Calpernia Addams. Winchell was an army private at Fort Campbell murdered in 1999 by fellow soldiers in retaliation for his relationship with Addams, a pre-op transgender woman (and navy veteran) whom he met when she was performing at a bar in Nashville. Winchell was killed while on duty on a Fourth of July weekend, on the very night that Addams won the Miss Tennessee Entertainer of the Year competition.

When *Soldier's Girl* premiered at Sundance, Addams was present to pay homage to Winchell, along with the septuagenarian Pierson and Jane Fonda's son Troy Garity, who played Winchell. After a standing ovation for Addams, there wasn't a dry eye in the house. Transgender tragedy goes down well, especially when it's the bioman who dies. Though *Soldier's Girl* too had a subtle reveal, it reduced shock in favor of humanizing the lovers.[16]

Far more nuanced in its depiction of the challenges of transgender life was Richard Spence's *Different for Girls* (1996), a British comedy starring Rupert Graves and Steven Mackintosh and written by Tony Marchant. Graves plays a motorcycle deliveryman, Paul. Through a far-fetched meet-cute collision, Paul is reunited with his prep school best friend, Karl, who is now a transwoman, Kim (who's not a club performer). The film rejects both comedy and tragedy, tying gender identity to the modes of masculinity and heteronormative prejudices of British society.

Different for Girls also considers seriously the challenges faced by Kim in trying to pass, and her panic over the attention that Paul's laddish behavior is drawing to her. Paul's struggle to recognize, get over, and ultimately accept his attraction to Kim gets plenty of screen time too, of course. While *Different for Girls* succumbs to the same formula of an anatomical shock scene, it complicates matters considerably by firmly rejecting negative consequences. It's probably one of the only transgender films with a happy ending: the guy gets his girl, the girl gets her guy, and nobody gets punished or killed for this love that dares speak its name. Likely made as popular television fare, it merits attention as a precursor to a trans cinema.

When the baton passes from outsider to insider, the terms of cinematic enunciation change abruptly. That was quite clearly the case with the first genderqueer feature *By Hook or by Crook* (2001) by Silas Howard and Harry

Dodge. No money shot, no voyeuristic gaze, no interest in any act of trans-formation whatsoever. While *By Hook or by Crook* adheres to the present-tense conjugations of the New Trans Cinema, it enriches that present with a cultural lineage that's been remapped onto retooled genderqueer coordinates. Howard and Dodge embody references to their own extrafilmic pasts, back when they lived in San Francisco and ran The Bearded Lady Café and Truck-stop. Howard's known as one of the founders of the legendary Queercore band Tribe 8, and Dodge was cast by John Waters as one of a gang of crazed film guerrillas in his *Cecil B. DeMented*. They form their own lineage.

In *Hook* the filmmaker-actors recapture the funky aesthetic and outsider ethos of the early NQC and go further back to claim the be-bop rhythms of beat cinema, like Robert Frank and Alfred Leslie's *Pull My Daisy* (1959). The partnership of Shy (Howard) and Val (Dodge), an oddball pair on the road to adventure, evokes the literary history of Jack Kerouac's *On the Road* and the cinematic history of the Jon Voight and Dustin Hoffman team in John Schlesinger's *Midnight Cowboy* (1969). When they plot a bank robbery, a heist-movie style shadows their activities, and where there are gangsters, there have to be molls, so Billie (Stanya Kahn) and Isabelle (Carina Gia) ap-pear. When plans to travel across the country come into view, so does *Bonnie and Clyde* and every other outlaw film ever made.

Howard and Dodge have no investment in the gender figurations of those predecessors, though; in their universe, gender is held in abeyance or piled on to excess, thrown into confusion or made irrelevant. The unseating of gender rules here gets combined with a fluid, anarchic approach to narrative norms and modes of representation that's rare in the NTC. It's an outlier too as a fiction feature in the NTC. A quixotic masterpiece, *By Hook or by Crook* borrows prized scraps of film history but casts a spell that goes beyond them.

Trans Documentaries, Trans Conflicts

Documentary has been the dominant medium for the New Trans Cinema. In part, that's doubtless due to the ubiquity of new digital cameras that render the personal political in the flash of an eye; the distance between professional and nonprofessional has never been smaller. But that doesn't adequately ex-plain the signal popularity of the trans documentary, which somewhat pre-dates the technological development. The first may have been *Linda/Les and Annie* (1992) by Annie Sprinkle, in which she documented the saga of her love affair with the F-to-M transsexual and intersex Les. But this documentary isn't typical, as it is sexually and anatomically explicit in a way that later trans documentaries would not be, and more seriously, because it ends with abjection in place of celebration. It was released in 1992, contemporaneous with the debut of NQC but with no cohort of its own.

Linda/Les and Annie came out one year after the first Southern Comfort Conference (Atlanta, 1991), an event that would become famous a decade later in the feature documentary that bore its name, *Southern Comfort* (2001), by Kate Davis. An intimate portrayal of Robert Eads, a transman fighting a fatal ovarian cancer diagnosis, *Southern Comfort* won the Grand Jury Prize for best documentary at Sundance and went on to win many more awards. The film served an important function in alerting a broad public to the existence and thinking of transmen, removing misconceptions, and widening the zones of understanding. But it also illuminated issues of great importance for transmen, despite being made by a heterosexual woman director: the importance of kinship, the need for daddies, concern over cancer risk and medical treatment in general, and, of course, the we-are-everywhere impact of its rural southern old-boy setting. *Southern Comfort* was a banner held aloft for F-to-M dignity.

At the same time, the film couldn't help but raise questions for women in the audience: What about *our* ovarian cancer? I had two friends with it at the time I saw the film. Many women get the same bad medical treatment that Eads was detailing, especially in rural areas. While Eads was certainly a victim of a transphobic medical establishment, women were facing odds that weren't very different in battling ovarian cancer. (The question of whether transmen face higher cancer risks due to the injection of testosterone has been raised but not definitively answered; what is clear is that transphobia can increase risk by inhibiting regular screening.)

In the decade after *Southern Comfort*, there was a wave of trans documentaries as well as trans characters in documentaries on other subjects that attracted impassioned audiences at LGBT film festivals. Julie Wyman's *A Boy Named Sue* (2001) tracks the medical and emotional transition of Theo, born intersex, from lesbian to gay male over the course of six years. Wyman is an imaginative filmmaker and her "featurette" documentary is one of the best of the genre, full of aesthetic devices and gestures that make the film even more dynamic than it might otherwise be. On the other hand, the feature documentary *Red without Blue* (2007), a family drama of transition, was made in collaboration with its subjects, twins Benita and Todd Sills, by the filmmaker and family friend Brooke Sebold and is clearly constrained by those ties.

By 2007 the shape of the trans documentary had solidified: straight-forward, chronological, unproblematized except inside the birth family, all elements present in Sebold's film. Most often documentary shorts, NTC films are invariably autobiographical or proximally biographical, often made by a friend or relative. They follow a formula that chronicles a cycle of despair, transition, elation. As though transgressive content forbade formal invention, trans documentaries perpetuate a seeming contradiction of radical content embedded in conservative form.

It's not surprising that the fact of the matter would take precedence for the NTC, as that was true for lesbian and gay work in the 1970s as well. Then too documentaries predominated, driven by a sense of urgency and civil rights motivations. Merely tracking the brave new world was enough—until it wasn't. It took nearly two decades for NQC to tie together aesthetic strategies, political struggle, and the telling of stories. So far, though, transgender theory making has moved much faster and further than trans filmmaking, even on the civil rights front.[17]

Aesthetic strategies are always telling, so it's notable that the straight-forward witnessing of surgical or chemical transition has become the central trope of the New Trans Cinema. Scenes of the medicalized body predomi-nate; double mastectomy surgery and recovery are lovingly detailed along with the obligatory shooting of T and the bodily and emotional changes its administration begins to cause. Exhaustively chronicled, the representations constitute a near-sacred ritual, exceeding their narrative functions within the documentary and representing instead a veritable rite of passage. The oppo-site of the mainstream money shot of horror, they register pride and accom-plishment. They're the NTC's own version of the coming-out story, at least at the current stage when surgery is the marker of status.

Another characteristic of NTC documentaries is their sense of an eternal present, one without a history. Again, that's a stark contrast to the early NQC films that were so intent on claiming a history, but it's very much in accord with AIDS documentaries and public-access cable shows of the early 1980s (the latter of the sort Gregg Bordowitz once lampooned in *Fast Trip, Long Drop*). Perhaps it's the NTC and AIDS documentaries that share an agenda, an urgency, a focus on an unresponsive medical establishment, and an awareness of an inhospitable mainstream society.

The NTC is almost purposefully ahistorical, as though the erasure of past bodies and names, even families, mandates a rejection of precedence in gen-eral.[18] The cost of such a focus on the present, even one under siege, is steep:

stasis and repetition. Films "of transition" tend to stage and restage transformation, each time with a different individual, family, or town. (Recent iterations have begun to include the gay transman as a new identity.) Complexity and historical perspectives will come into play as the genre matures, when NTC's "new normal" settles into place and outlaw images start to emerge.[19] With its development in an early stage and plenty of energy and passion still on offer, time is on its side.

Meanwhile the terrain is fraught. Catherine Crouch's short film *The Gendercator* was the controversy of the LGBT film festival season in 2007. *The Gendercator* was denounced as transphobic by representatives of San Francisco's trans community; more than 130 people signed a petition demanding it not be shown. In a move unprecedented in its thirty-one years of operation, Frameline pulled the film from its LGBT International Film Festival and apologized to the trans community. At that point, members of San Francisco's lesbian community responded, angry over censorship of a lesbian film by a festival that never showed very many.[20]

The Gendercator opens with a sequence shot to look like Super-8, all muted colors and light flare: it's September 20, 1973, and a gang of lesbians are out partying to celebrate Billie Jean King's tennis victory over the misogynist Bobby Riggs in the Battle of the Sexes. Sunshine Sally, an old-fashioned dyke in the lesbian-feminist style, gets so stoned that she passes out and wakes up seventy-five years later. The world is a different place, where anyone attracted to their own kind has to undergo gender-reassignment surgery. After a buddy pastiche of transmen flexing and preening, Sally reunites with an unhappy ex-lesbian transman and tries to escape the surgery regime. A tone of disdain and one dialogue line of "history" explaining that transmen had allied with the religious right to enact gender-reassignment rules were the factors that landed the twenty-minute film in trouble—along with the filmmaker's online comments. The satire has a happy ending (it's just a dream) but clearly not for any transman in the audience.

The controversy pitted trans people who felt attacked by the film against lesbians (particularly older ones) who felt attacked by its censorship. As usual with censorship cases, more was at stake than just a film. Its cancellation brought out long-simmering antagonisms within queer communities that rarely come into view. For the trans community, there was a sense of triumph, of being heard and respected. For the lesbian community, there was a sense of being ignored and disrespected; some pointed to the many misogynist gay films in Frameline's history that had been silently endured.

I weathered my share of censorship battles back at the New York State Council on the Arts: Godard's *Hail Mary*, Spike Lee's *She's Gotta Have It*, Robert Mapplethorpe's photographs, all came under attack. Every era has its censorship flashpoint, its own version of the culture wars. For me, *The Gendercator* was as much a jab at the lesbian feminism of the 1970s as the transmen of 2007. I still believe the answer to outrage is almost always more speech, not less. The result of this controversy was a community's public airing of power disparities long papered over by the faux-equity of the LGBT acronym, raising the question of what became of the old NQC's unifying noun *queer*, or for that matter, the L for lesbian that, with the T for trans, still bookmarks the optimistic acronym of unity.

A New Queer Future: The Films That (Almost) Got Away

As if answering a siren call of necessity, the years 2011–12 have been marked by an unexpected resurgence of lesbian and queer filmmaking set in a plurality of locations—Brooklyn, Iran, San Francisco, Liverpool, even the planet Zots—and a mix of genres, from fiction to documentary and mash-ups of both.

In 2011, three lesbian films debuted at Sundance in one of those seismic concurrences that have surfaced so often in this volume: *Pariah* by Dee Rees, *Circumstance* by Maryam Keshavarz, and *Codependent Lesbian Space Alien Seeks Same* by Madeleine Olnek, as different from one another in shape as in subject.

Pariah is the coming-of-age story of Alike, a butch high school girl struggling to get through school and find a girlfriend while dodging her churchgoing mother's wrath, detective dad's disappointment, and kid sister's snitching. The tone is tragicomic, the execution impeccable. Unlike *Precious,* another film that starts with a P and features an alienated African American young woman, Rees's *Pariah* is stripped down and honest, all about coming into agency, not abjection. Writer/director Rees lets the audience see New York's mean streets the way a young butch might, out for the night with the girls instead of guys. Spike Lee was her mentor, but clearly Rees has Scorsese in her blood.

Maryam Keshavarz sets much of *Circumstance* in Iran's urban club scene, but she locates all the social conflicts inside one family: liberal parents who opposed the shah; a daughter, Atafeh, with a thirst for experience; a son who's a born-again fundamentalist. Atafeh's forbidden love for her best friend

Shireen sets her on a collision course with the morality police.[21] In one scene, the friends dub copies of *Milk* and *Sex in the City* into Persian, transforming their studio for a moment into the wider world they long to join, in a sly ode to the imaginative power of film. Keshavarz transforms the diaspora narrative into a lesbian fantasy, even as we realize it's bound to end badly.

In both *Pariah* and *Circumstance*, protagonists must leave family behind to claim their sexuality: for Alike, there's a bus ride to a new school; for Atafeh, a plane to Dubai. In a galaxy far, far away, though, life might be different. Dispensing with realism and melodrama, Madeleine Olnek created a throwback to old-school sci-fi cheesiness with *Codependent Lesbian Space Alien Seeks Same*, a laugh-out-loud comedy starring three lesbian space aliens exiled from the planet Zots. Gently mocking the pathetic foibles of lesbian dating and romance through the figure of Jane, a sad-sack lesbian everywoman, Olnek employs a George Kuchar–like aesthetic for a retrofitted lesbian fairy tale that thrillingly reinvents lesbian camp.

Later in 2011, the French director Céline Sciamma's *Tomboy* further opened the dialogue on adolescence, passing, and gender identity. The second in her series of films exploring teenage girls' sexuality, it took gender identity for granted. Zoé Héran's pitch-perfect embodiment of her private/public gender binarism as Laure/Michaël make the film's politics of gender dysphoria go down so easy, *Boys Don't Cry* minus the tragedy. *Tomboy* is not a trans film per se, but it suggests new energy for future trans drama.

In 2011 in the United Kingdom, Andrew Haigh updated the early NQC acuity and energy with his brilliant *Weekend*. A longtime editor, Haigh finessed the pace and structure so as to turn a chronicle of a weekend affair into a complex meditation on contemporary queer life. His film's relationship to film history is deliberate: the apartment where the lovers tryst is located on the site of Albert Finney's place in Karel Reisz's *Saturday Night and Sunday Morning* (1960), and the train station ending evokes David Lean's classic, *Brief Encounter* (1945), both films which challenged social norms of love and marriage.[22] In his sense of history, Haigh evokes the early NQC ethos.

History has been on offer in documentary, too, with three features of 2011–12 training their eye on the AIDS years that were the original site of NQC's emergence. *How to Survive a Plague* by a newcomer, David France; *United in Anger: A History of ACT UP* by Jim Hubbard (with Sarah Schulman, who co-organized the ACT UP archive with him); and *We Were Here* by David Weissman all return to the trauma of the AIDS epidemic, with rich archival materials, new interviews, and the long view that witnesses can bring to a history that they've survived but never left behind. The twenty-fifth anniversary of the founding of ACT UP was well recognized.

Weissman gathered a carefully curated band of San Francisco veterans together for in-depth interviews that deliver an emotional punch in their invocation of a lost paradise and the hell that followed, all diagnoses and obituaries, of loves lost and cures found. Hubbard spun *United in Anger* out of an archive's worth of oral histories and camcorder footage. Its visceral sense of those early years, with pride and eros alternating with death and terror, is remarkable. And it puts lesbians back in the ACT UP picture, indelibly and undeniably; many were there in the Castro Theatre the day I saw it, cheering. For *How to Survive a Plague,* France constructed his inside story of AIDS activism from multiple archives, tracking the camera-wielders from frame to frame and tracking them down. One young man's anguished plea was particularly resonant: "Will the last person left in Chelsea please turn out the lights?" With AIDS a fatal killer, he foresaw the entire neighborhood emptying out.

Instead, nearly thirty years later, Chelsea has become a thriving destination for gay men wealthy enough to afford the real estate. *Keep the Lights On,* Ira Sachs's film à clef, which premiered at the 2012 Sundance festival, tracks the life of just such a couple through the dangers of a new era: phone sex, Craigslist hook-ups, and drug addiction. His film's title felt like an answer to the long-ago protagonists of *How to Survive a Plague*'s archival history, an answer echoing down the aisles of history: Keep the lights on, boys. A *Boys in the Band* for a new era, *Keep the Lights On* won the Teddy Award at the Berlin Film Festival, just as its protagonist does for his film-within-a-film. Taken together, this batch of films emerging in 2011–12 provides a benchmark of sorts for this volume, a spiral looping back to the first pages of engagement with the epidemic that would beget a movement.

Ah, but just wait. Enter one Wu Tsang. In New York City in spring 2012, the Museum of Modern Art presented the world premiere of Tsang's hybrid documentary, *Wildness.* Wu Tsang also had a set of gender- and genre-defying installations in town: *Full Body Quotation,* a trans refracturing of *Paris Is Burning,* in the New Museum Triennial and *Green Room* in the Whitney Biennial. Soon Wu Tsang and pals were the toast of film festivals, too, winning awards and making new friends at South by Southwest, Frameline, and OutFest.

Wildness is set in the Silver Platter, a working-class Latino/a drag bar in MacArthur Park, Los Angeles, where Tsang had inaugurated a weekly extravaganza titled Wildness. Culture clash was inevitable when college-educated queer hipsters encountered the lovely *translatinas* who had long called the bar their home, as wildly different notions of performance began to interact, then explode. Tsang and the gang get pulled into activism, set up a legal clinic, take sides, and get their collective asses kicked by forces both predictable and surprising.

Admirably, this is a film that does not take any easy routes into or out of its story. The bar itself is constructed as a character, with a voice imparting the Silver Platter's history in sultry Spanish on the soundtrack, offering context and consolation as the fates conspire for and against it. *Wildness* also pays homage to the dangers that *translatinas* face in daily life: when young Paulina Ibarra is murdered, the film interrupts its celebratory tone to confront life outside the bar. When the bar changes ownership, the conflicts split open the terrain of race, class, inheritance, and homophobia, all set on a collision course. Family and livelihood give no ground, despite all the queer fierceness and generational entitlement thrown their way. The story becomes complex and confusing and rife with pain, just like life itself.

Tsang's willingness, even insistence, on widening the lens to include the full range of queer community across lines of class, race, sexual, and gender identities marks an important new maturity. *Wildness* ushers in a new stage in trans and genderqueer cinema, opening exciting formal directions.[23]

Epilogue

This final chapter has expanded to accommodate new thoughts and new films, over and over, as the time of publication drew near, receded, and finally arrived. A critic's excitement over the discovery of new voices and directions is often in conflict with a scholar's insistence on the careful deliberation and distillation of new material. Consider this last chapter, then, a truce brokered over the course of a lifetime on the front lines.

The next stage will depend on the willingness of queer publics to be both accepting and demanding, for the biggest impediment to the creation of culture is not the imagination of the creator but the receptivity of an audience. Once, a public hungry for change did its part to bring the NQC to life. In the decades since, queer audiences have too often retreated into a comfort zone of familiar faces and cozy narratives. The 2010–12 seasons give me hope that change is afoot, and the harsh economic conditions of our times, the extremity of politics, and the disparity of wealth have created an audience eager to be challenged, and to change. I think it's time for queer publics to broaden their vision once again, not shut it down for legal status, gender definition, or genre formula. The creativity of queer communities ensures that anything happening right now is "just a stage" and that, far from returning to earlier iterations as the phrase used to suggest, instead will continually lead to new beginnings across ever-erased, ever-reconstructed boundaries.

I sympathize deeply with those searching for the outlawry missing from our lives. America has exported its outlaws along with its industries: only terrorists or jihadists qualify. I'd appreciate a little more variety. In the 1950s kids could fantasize a life alongside Zorro, or Robin Hood and his band of Merry Men, or Peter Pan or, when a little bit older, with *Johnny Guitar* or *Rebel without a Cause*. Today Gleeks can watch *Glee* for fun and comfort—but however gleeful Jane Lynch may be, and she is, and however thrilling it is to see queer (though aging) high school kids, the show is still a squeaky-clean sitcom.

Looking instead for something that's dirty, transgressive, and original? That would be *Girls*, Lena Dunham's HBO series, which debuted in 2012. True, Dunham's dystopian show is resolutely hetero (in its first season, anyway) but her unapologetic refusal to come clean and the urban grittiness of both the setting and the sex are reminiscent enough of the early years of NQC to qualify *Girls* as an apt continuation of its lineage.

Now that this volume is coming to an end, be assured that I intend to keep looking. I continue to place my trust in filmmakers near and far, in the neighborhood and the nation and the rest of our world, in those who come to the screen(s) to sort their cultures, tell their stories, and create their own trans, queer, lesbian, or gay genres. I believe there's a resurgent Global Queer Cinema afoot, and we can all be part of it, for queer communities here in the United States and around the globe have always been crucibles of creativity. The discovery of one's own queer sexuality has always been a passport out of town, saving generations from a dead-end job at the factory, back when it was still an option, or a dead-end marriage up or down the social ladder. Getting out of Dodge wasn't just about avoiding danger, it was about embracing something or someone else. There's nothing like not-belonging to get the imagination going, to spur the heart and the brain and the body on to new frontiers.

I am always happy to applaud the new kids in the hall.[24] And I'm forever awaiting with anticipation the generation just coming of age at home, either right there where you're reading or in all the diasporas we inhabit, ready any day now to turn the tables yet again. Perhaps you, dear reader, are one of them: pick up your image-making device and claim your place. When I am asked yet again whether today's films are postqueer, the kind of term usually intended to signal defeat or compromise or at best stasis, I opt for a different formulation altogether. Far from bereft, I remain optimistic, sure that we aren't after the fact at all. Not post-anything. We are surely and absolutely . . . pre-.

Notes

1. See Duggan, *The Twilight of Equality?*

2. Lisa Kennedy, "*Kids* Is Full of Exquisite Family Bumbling," *Denver Post*, July 16, 2010.

3. Jack Halberstam, "The Kids Aren't Alright!," Bully Bloggers, July 15, 2010, http ://bullybloggers.wordpress.com/2010/07/15/the-kids-arent-alright/; Joan Garry, "*The Kids Are All Right? No Way!*," *Huffington Post*, July 26, 2010, http://www.huffington post.com/joan-garry-/the-kids-are-all-right-no_b_659444.html.

4. Jordan Caress, "*The Kids Are All Right* Revives an Old Complaint about Lesbians on Film: Why Are They Always Sleeping with Men?," Nashville Scene, July 22, 2010, http://www.nashvillescene.com/nashville/the-kids-are-all-right-revives-an-old -complaint-about-lesbians-on-film-why-are-they-always-sleeping-with-men /Content?oid=1667693.

5. Public statement, San Francisco International Film Festival, April 24, 2011.

6. See ACT UP Oral History Project, http://www.actuporalhistory.org.

7. This and all subsequent quotes are taken from the website www.itgetsbetter.org.

8. The Trevor Project was founded by the writer James Lecesne, director and producer Peggy Rajski, and producer Randy Stone to accompany the HBO broadcast of their short film *Trevor*, about a gay thirteen-year-old boy who plans to kill himself. See the full history of their starting the hotline on the website www.thetrevorproject .org.

9. The script is online. See, for instance, The Film Stoodle, http://thestoodle .blogspot.com/2010/02/link-to-text-of-derek-jarmans-blue.html.

10. See Andy Kimpton-Nye, "Tilda Swinton on Derek Jarman," *400 Blows*, Sept. 5, 2003, at http://www.400blows.co.uk/inter_swinton.shtml.

11. For a detailed discussion of *Mazatlan*, see Rich, "The Long Road."

12. Their earlier collaboration, *The Judy Spots*, remains one of the best representations of alienated and abused girlhood ever produced, certainly on MTV.

13. See the exhibition catalogue *Sadie Benning: Suspended Animation*, foreword by Sherri Geldin, introduction by Jennifer Lange, texts by Eileen Myles, Aleksandar Hemon, Helen Molesworth, and Amy Sillman (Columbus, Ohio: Wexner Center for the Arts, 2007). Wexner's curator Bill Horrigan deserves a medal for his NQC contributions.

14. Sadie Benning and Solveig Nelson, "A Conversation with Sadie Benning," *Retrospective/Sadie Benning* brochure, Wexner Center for the Arts, The Ohio State University, Feb. 2004, pp.14–15.

15. There are a number of foundational texts. See, for instance, Feinberg, *Transgender Liberation* and *Transgender Warriors*; Stone, "The Empire Strikes Back"; Stryker, "The Transgender Issue"; Stryker and Whittle, *The Transgender Studies Reader*.

16. *A Girl Like Me: The Gwen Araujo Story* (2006), made for Lifetime by the famed filmmaker Agnieszka Holland (an expert on identity and passing), is another film in this tradition.

17. See Currah, Juang, and Minter, *Transgender Rights*. For original rethinking of trans evolutions, see Valentine, *Imagining Transgender*.

18. For a different view of trans genealogies, see Valentine, *Imagining Transgender*.

19. For one of the most stimulating and incisive looks at trans cinema, see Phillips, *Transgender on Screen*.

20. For the history and an exhaustive collection of responses, see Lawless, "The Gendercator, or How I Learned to Stop Worrying and Love the Blogosphere."

21. For more information on the film's gestation, see David Ansen, "Iran's Controversial New Lesbian Film," *Daily Beast*, August 25, 2011; Omid Memarian, "How Lesbians Live in Iran," *Daily Beast*, August 27, 2011.

22. Ernest Hardy, "*Weekend* Director Andrew Haigh Interview," *LA Weekly*, September 29, 2011.

23. Note that Roya Rastegar has cowriter credit for her contributions to the "voice of" the Silver Platter. *Wildness* is very much a collaborative work for a new generation of performance artists, just as the Wildness bar itself was for a generation of *translatinas*. Wu Tsang rejects the straightforward FTM identity tagline in favor of being called "trans feminine but also sometimes . . . a 'trans guy' because I am also that. Or a MUCH more straightforward ID would be: butch queen in heels." For more on Wu Tsang's point of view, see Chris Vargas, "Interview: Wu Tsang" at http://www.originalplumbing.com/2011/02/20/chrisblog-interview-wu-tsang as well as http://www.wildnessmovie.com/class-blog.

24. Missing from this volume entirely has been yet another queer manifestation deserving of revival: the vintage cable television series, *Kids in the Hall*, a brilliant 1980s manifestation of queerness in the key of comedy. Sorry! Too late, I know, but I loved touring the LGBT festivals with my curated show of its greatest cross-dressing hits.

FILMOGRAPHY

All about Eve. Dir. Joseph Mankiewicz. 1950.

All Flowers in Time. Dir. Jonathan Caouette. 2010.

All over Me. Dir. Alex Sichel. 1997.

Amores Perros. Dir. Alejandro González Iñárritu. 2000.

Así se quiere en Jalisco. Dir. Agustín Calderón. 1995.

Audre Lorde—The Berlin Years 1984 to 1992. Dir. Dagmar Schultz. 2012.

Ava and Gabriel. Dir. Felix de Rooy. 1990.

Baise-moi (*Fuck Me*). Dir. Virginie Despentes and Coralie Trinh Thi. 2000.

Basic Instinct. Dir. Paul Verhoeven. 1992.

Beau travail (*Beautiful Work*). Dir. Claire Denis. 1999.

Bedrooms and Hallways. Dir. Rose Troche. 1998.

Before Stonewall. Dir. Greta Schiller and Robert Rosenberg. 1984.

Being John Malkovich. Dir. Spike Jonze. 1999.

Big Eden. Dir. Thomas Bezucha. 2000.

Black and White in Color. Dir. Isaac Julien. 1992.

Blue. Dir. Derek Jarman. 1993.

Borderline. Dir. Kenneth MacPherson. 1930.

Born in Flames. Dir. Lizzie Borden. 1983.

Bound. Dir. Andy Wachowski and Lana Wachowski. 1996.

A Boy Named Sue. Dir. Julie Wyman. 2001.

Boys at Noon. Dir. Apichatpong Weerasethakul. 2000.

Boys Don't Cry. Dir. Kimberly Peirce. 1999.

Boys on the Side. Dir. Herbert Ross. 1995.

Bright Eyes. Dir. Stuart Marshall. 1986.

Brokeback Mountain. Dir. Ang Lee. 2005.

Broken Sky (*El cielo dividido*). Dir. Julián Hernández. 2006.

Buddies. Dir. Arthur Bresson. 1985.

Buffy the Vampire Slayer. Creator Joss Whedon (TV series). 1997–2003.

But I'm a Cheerleader. Dir. Jamie Babbit. 1999.

Butterfly Kiss. Dir. Michael Winterbottom. 1995.

By Hook or by Crook. Dir. Harry Dodge and Silas Howard. 2001.

Capturing the Friedmans. Dir. Andrew Jarecki. 2003.

Caravaggio. Dir. Derek Jarman. 1986.

Cecil B. DeMented. Dir. John Waters. 2000.

Ceux qui m'aiment prendront le train (*Those Who Love Me Can Take the Train*).
    Dir. Patrice Chéreau. 1998.

Chacun cherche son chat (*When the Cat's Away*). Dir. Cédric Klapisch. 1996.

Changing Our Minds: The Story of Dr. Evelyn Hooker. Dir. Richard Schmiechen.
    1992.

Chasing Amy. Dir. Kevin Smith. 1997.

Chicks in White Satin. Dir. Elaine Holliman. 1994.

Chinese Characters. Dir. Richard Fung. 1986.

Chun gwong cha sit (*Happy Together*). Dir. Wong Kar-Wai. 1997.

Circumstance. Dir. Maryam Keshavarz. 2011.

Claire of the Moon. Dir. Nicole Conn. 1992.

Codependent Lesbian Space Alien Seeks Same. Dir. Madeleine Olnek. 2011.

Come Back to the Five and Dime, Jimmy Dean, Jimmy Dean. Dir. Robert Altman.
    1982.

A Comedy in Six Unnatural Acts. Dir. Jan Oxenberg. 1975.

Complaints of a Dutiful Daughter. Dir. Deborah Hoffman. 1994.

Corazón sangrante. Dir. Ximena Cuevas. 1993.

Cosi fan tutte. Dir. Jesusa Rodriguez. 1996.

Crouching Tiger, Hidden Dragon. Dir. Ang Lee. 2000.

Cruising. Dir. William Friedkin. 1980.

Damned If You Don't. Dir. Su Friedrich. 1987.

Danzón. Dir. María Novaro. 1991.

Death in Venice. Dir. Luchino Visconti. 1971.

D.E.B.S. Dir. Angela Robinson. 2003.

Derek. Dir. Isaac Julien. 2008.

Desert Hearts. Dir. Donna Deitch. 1985.

Desperately Seeking Susan. Dir. Susan Seidelman. 1985.

Diabolique. Dir. Henri-Georges Clouzot. 1955.

Diabolique. Dir. Jeremiah S. Chechik. 1996.

Different for Girls. Dir. Richard Spence. 1996.

Dog Day Afternoon. Dir. Sidney Lumet. 1975.

Doña Herlinda y su hijo (Doña Herlinda and Her Son). Dir. Jaime Humberto Hermosillo. 1985.

Dotty Gets Spanked. Dir. Todd Haynes (TV). 1993.

Drôle de Félix (Adventures of Felix). Dir. Olivier Ducastel and Jacques Martineau. 2000.

Drugstore Cowboy. Dir. Gus Van Sant. 1989.

Dry Kisses Only. Dir. Kaucylia Brooke and Jane Cottis. 1990.

Dyketactics. Dir. Barbara Hammer. 1974.

Edward II. Dir. Derek Jarman. 1991.

8 Femmes (8 Women). Dir. François Ozon. 2002.

El lugar sin límites (The Place without Limits). Dir. Arturo Ripstein. 1977.

Elephant. Dir. Gus Van Sant. 2003.

Ellen. Creator Carol Black, Neal Marlens, David S. Rosenthal (TV series). 1994–98.

Emmanuelle. Dir. Just Jaeckin. 1974.

Entre Nous. Dir. Diane Kurys. 1983.

Even Cowgirls Get the Blues. Dir. Gus Van Sant. 1993.

eXXXorcismos. Dir. Jaime Humberto Hermosillo. 2002.

Far from Heaven. Dir. Todd Haynes. 2002.

Fast Trip, Long Drop. Dir. Gregg Bordowitz. 1993.

Faster, Pussycat! Kill! Kill! Dir. Russ Meyer. 1965.

Fig Trees. Dir. John Greyson. 2009.

Fireworks. Dir. Kenneth Anger. 1947.

First Comes Love. Dir. Su Friedrich. 1991.

575 Castro St. Dir. Jenni Olson. 2008.

Flaming Ears. Dir. Ursula Puerrer, Angela Hans Scheirl, Dietmar Schipek. 1991.

Forbidden Love. Dir. Lynne Fernie and Aerlyn Weissman. 1992.

Fox and His Friends. Dir. Rainer Werner Fassbinder. 1975.

Foxfire. Dir. Annette Haywood-Carter. 1996.

Freeway. Dir. Matthew Bright. 1996.

Fresa y chocolate (*Strawberry and Chocolate*). Dir. Tomás Gutiérrez Alea and Juan Carlos Tabío. 1994.

Fresh Kill. Dir. Shu Lea Cheang. 1994.

Frida: Naturaleza Viva (*Frida*). Dir. Paul Leduc. 1983.

Fried Green Tomatoes. Dir. Jon Avnet. 1991.

Frisk. Dir. Todd Verow. 1995.

Fun. Dir. Rafal Zielinski. 1994.

Funeral of Roses. Dir. Toshio Matsumoto. 1969.

Gay USA. Dir. Arthur J. Bressan Jr. 1978.

Gazon maudit (*French Twist*). Dir. Josiane Balasko. 1995.

Gerry. Dir. Gus Van Sant. 2002.

Girlfriends. Dir. Claudia Weill. 1978.

A Girl Like Me: The Gwen Araujo Story. Dir. Agnieszka Holland (TV). 2006.

Girls Town. Dir. Jim McKay. 1996.

Girltrash! Dir. Angela Robinson (web series). 2007.

Glee. Creator Ian Brennan, Ryan Murphy, Brad Falchuk (TV series). 2009–.

Go Fish. Dir. Rose Troche. 1994.

Gods and Monsters. Dir. Bill Condon. 1998.

Going South. Dir. Sébastien Lifshitz. 2009.

Gouttes d'eau sur pierres brûlantes (*Water Drops on Burning Rocks*). Dir. François Ozon. 2000.

Grapefruit. Dir. Cecilia Dougherty. 1989.

Grey Gardens. Dir. Ellen Hovde, Albert Maysles, David Maysles, Muffie Meyer. 1975.

Hairspray. Dir. John Waters. 1988.

Head On. Dir. Ana Kokkinos. 1998.

Heavenly Creatures. Dir. Peter Jackson. 1994.

Hedwig and the Angry Inch. Dir. John Cameron Mitchell. 2001.

High Art. Dir. Lisa Cholodenko. 1998.

How to Survive a Plague. Dir. David France. 2012.

I Shall Not Be Removed: The Life of Marlon Riggs. Dir. Karen Everett. 1996.

I Shot Andy Warhol. Dir. Mary Harron. 1996.

Ich Mochte Kein Mann Sein (*I Don't Want to Be a Man*). Dir. Ernst Lubitsch. 1918.

I.K.U. Dir. Shu Lea Cheang. 2000.

I'm Not There. Dir. Todd Haynes. 2007.

I've Heard the Mermaids Singing. Dir. Patricia Rozema. 1987.

Il conformista (*The Conformist*). Dir. Bernardo Bertolucci. 1970.

Immacolata e Concetta. Dir. Salvatore Piscicelli. 1981.

In and Out. Dir. Frank Oz. 1997.

In a Year with 13 Moons. Dir. Rainer Werner Fassbinder. 1978.

In the Best Interests of the Children. Dir. Frances Reid, Elizabeth Stevens, Cathy Zheutlin. 1977.

It Wasn't Love. Dir. Sadie Benning. 1992.

J'ai pas sommeil (*I Can't Sleep*). Dir. Claire Denis. 1994.

Jeffrey. Dir. Christopher Ashley. 1995.

Johnny Guitar. Dir. Nicholas Ray. 1954.

Jollies. Dir. Sadie Benning. 1990.

Jubilee. Dir. Derek Jarman. 1978.

Keep the Lights On. Dir. Ira Sachs. 2012.

Kids in the Hall (TV series). 1988–94.

Kinsey. Dir. Bill Condon. 2004.

Kiss of the Spider Woman (*El beso de la mujer araña*). Dir. Héctor Babenco. 1985.

L Is for the Way You Look. Dir. Jean Carlomusto. 1991.

L'Auberge español (*Pot Luck*). Dir. Cédric Klapisch. 2002.

La cage aux folles. Dir. Edouard Molinaro. 1979.

La casa vieja (*The Old House*). Dir. Lester Hamlet. 2010.

La cérémonie. Dir. Claude Chabrol. 1995.

La ciénaga (*The Swamp*). Dir. Lucrecia Martel. 2001.

La flor de mis secretos (*The Flower of My Secrets*). Dir. Pedro Almodóvar. 1995.

La haine. Dir. Mathieu Kassovitz. 1995.

La mujer sin cabeza (*The Headless Woman*). Dir. Lucrecia Martel. 2008.

La negra Angustias. Dir. Matilde Landeta. 1949.

La niña santa (*The Holy Girl*). Dir. Lucrecia Martel. 2004.

La petite mort (*Little Death*). Dir. François Ozon. 1995.

La reina de la noche (*The Queen of the Night*). Dir. Arturo Ripstein. 1994.

Last Address. Dir. Ira Sachs. 2010.

Last Tango in Paris. Dir. Bernard Bertolucci. 1972.

La tómbola (*The Raffle*). Dir. Ximena Cuevas. 2001.

Le petit lieutenant. Dir. Xavier Beauvois. 2005.

Le Sang d'un poète (*The Blood of a Poet*). Dir. Jean Cocteau. 1932.

Le temps qui reste (*Time to Leave*). Dir. François Ozon. 2005.

Les amants criminels (*Criminal Lovers*). Dir. François Ozon. 1999.

Les biches. Dir. Claude Chabrol. 1968.

Les innocents (*The Innocents*). Dir. André Téchiné. 1987.

Les levres rouges (*Daughters of Darkness*). Dir. Harry Kumel. 1971.

Les nuits fauves (*Savage Nights*). Dir. Cyril Collard. 1992.

Les roseaux Sauvages (*Wild Reeds*). Dir. André Téchiné. 1994.

Les témoins (*The Witnesses*). Dir. André Téchiné. 2007.

Les voleurs (*Thieves*). Dir. André Téchiné. 1996.

Lilies. Dir. John Greyson. 1996.

Linda's Film on Menstruation. Dir. Linda Feferman. 1974.

Linda/Les and Annie. Dir. Annie Sprinkle. 1992.

A Litany for Survival: The Life and Work of Audre Lorde. Dir. Ada Gay Griffin
    and Michelle Parkerson. 1995.

Living with AIDS. Producer Gregg Bordowitz and Jean Carlomusto (TV series).
    1984–96.

Lonesome Cowboys. Dir. Andy Warhol and Paul Morrissey. 1968.

Long Road to Mazatlan. Artist and creator, Isaac Julien (digital installation). 1999.

Looking for Langston. Dir. Isaac Julien. 1989.

Los olvidados (*The Young and the Damned*). Dir. Luis Buñuel. 1950.

Lot in Sodom. Dir. James Sibley Watson and Melville Webber. 1933.

Love and Death on Long Island. Dir. Richard Kwietniowski. 1997.

Love Is the Devil: Study for a Portrait of Francis Bacon. Dir. John Maybury. 1998.

Ma vie en rose (*My Life in Pink*). Dir. Alain Berliner. 1997.

Ma vraie vie à rouen (*My Life on Ice*). Dir. Olivier Ducastel and Jacques
    Martineau. 2002.

Madame Satã. Dir. Karim Aïnouz. 2002.

Mala Noche. Dir. Gus Van Sant. 1985.

Manila by Night. Dir. Ishmael Bernal. 1980.

Mano Destra. Dir. Cleo Uebelmann. 1986.

Martina: Farewell to a Champion. Dir. Cathy Jones. 1994.

Mauvaise conduite (*Improper Conduct*). Dir. Néstor Almendros and Orlando
    Jiménez Leal. 1984.

Midnight Cowboy. Dir. John Schlesinger. 1969.

Mil nubes de paz cercan el cielo, amor, jamás acabarás de ser amor (*A Thousand*

Clouds of Peace Fence the Sky, Love; Your Being Love Will Never End). Dir. Julián Hernández. 2003.

Mildred Pierce. Dir. Todd Haynes (TV miniseries). 2011.

Milk. Dir. Gus Van Sant. 2008.

Mixed Use. Dir. Jen Gilomen and Sabrina Alonso. 2008.

Monster. Dir. Patty Jenkins. 2003.

Moscow Doesn't Believe in Queers. Dir. John Greyson. 1986.

Mulholland Drive. Dir. David Lynch. 2001.

MURDER and murder. Dir. Yvonne Rainer. 1996.

My Beautiful Laundrette. Dir. Stephen Frears. 1985.

My Best Friend's Wedding. Dir. Paul John Hogan. 1997.

My Own Private Idaho. Dir. Gus Van Sant. 1991.

Mysterious Skin. Dir. Gregg Araki. 2004.

Naked Killer (Chik loh go yeung). Dir. Clarence Fok Yiu-leung. 1992.

Natural Born Killers. Dir. Oliver Stone. 1994.

Nettoyage á Sec (Dry Cleaning). Dir. Anne Fontaine. 1997.

Night Hawks. Dir. Ron Peck. 1978.

N'oublie pas que tu vas mourir (Don't Forget You're Going to Die). Dir. André Téchiné. 1995.

O céu de suely (Love for Sale). Dir. Karim Aïnouz. 2006.

Of Gods and Men. Dir. Xavier Beauvois. 2010.

Orientations: Lesbian and Gay Asians. Dir. Richard Fung. 1984.

Orlando. Sally Potter. 1992.

Pariah. Dir. Dee Rees. 2011.

Paris Is Burning. Dir. Jennie Livingston. 1991.

Parting Glances. Dir. Bill Sherwood. 1986.

Paul Monette: The Brink of Summer's End. Dir. Monte Bramer. 1996.

Personal Best. Dir. Robert Towne. 1982.

Philadelphia. Dir. Jonathan Demme. 1993.

Pink Narcissus. Dir. Jim Bidgood. 1971.

Pixote: A lei do mais fraco (Pixote: The Law of the Weakest). Dir. Héctor Babenco. 1981.

Play Pause. Artist and creator, Sadie Benning (digital installation). 2006.

Poison. Dir. Todd Haynes. 1991.

Portrait d'une jeune fille de la fin des années 60 à Bruxelles (*Portrait of a Young Girl at the End of the 1960s in Brussels*). Dir. Chantal Akerman. 1994.

Postcards from America. Dir. Steve McLean. 1994.

Presque rien (*Come Undone*). Dir. Sébastien Lifshitz. 2000.

Prick Up Your Ears. Dir. Stephen Frears. 1987.

Projecting the Body. Dir. Walter McIntosh. 2008.

Proteus. Dir. John Greyson. 2003.

Public Speaking. Dir. Martin Scorsese. 2010.

Pull My Daisy. Dir. Robert Frank and Alfred Leslie. 1959.

Queer as Folk. Dir. John Greyson, Laurie Lynd, Jeremy Podeswa, Alan Poul, and others (TV series). 2000–2005.

Queer Eye for the Straight Guy. Creator David Collins (TV series). 2003–7.

R.S.V.P. Dir. Laurie Lynd. 1991.

Rabbit Hole. Dir. John Cameron Mitchell. 2011.

Rabioso sol, rabioso cielo (*Raging Sun, Raging Sky*). Dir. Julián Hernández. 2009.

Red without Blue. Dir. Brooke Sebold, Benita Sills, Todd Sills. 2007.

Resonance. Dir. Stephen Cummins. 1993.

Safe. Dir. Todd Haynes. 1995.

Scorpio Rising. Dir. Kenneth Anger. 1964.

Sebastiane. Dir. Derek Jarman. 1976.

Señora de nadie (*Nobody's Wife*). Dir. María Luisa Bemberg. 1982.

Sense and Sensibility. Dir. Ang Lee. 1995.

Set It Off. Dir. F. Gary Gray. 1996.

Sex Bowl. Dir. Shu Lea Cheang. 1994.

Sex Fish. Dir. Shu Lea Cheang. 1993.

She Don't Fade. Dir. Cheryl Dunye. 1991.

She Must Be Seeing Things. Dir. Sheila McLaughlin. 1987.

Short Bus. Dir. John Cameron Mitchell. 2006.

Shulie. Dir. Elizabeth Subrin. 1997.

Sister, My Sister. Dir. Nancy Meckler. 1994.

Sitcom. Dir. François Ozon. 1998.

Six Feet Under. Creator Alan Ball. Dir. Alan Ball, Lisa Cholodenko, Mary Harron, Jeremy Podeswa, Rose Troche, and others (TV series). 2001–5.

Soldier's Girl. Dir. Frank Pierson (TV). 2003.

Sous le sable (*Under the Sand*). Dir. François Ozon. 2000.

South of Nowhere. Creator Tommy Lynch. Dir. Donna Deitch and others.
(TV series). 2005–8.

Southern Comfort. Dir. Kate Davis. 2001.

Sunday Bloody Sunday. Dir. John Schlesinger. 1971.

Superstar: The Karen Carpenter Story. Dir. Todd Haynes. 1987.

Swimming Pool. Dir. François Ozon. 2003.

Swoon. Dir. Tom Kalin. 1992.

Syndromes and a Century. Dir. Apichatpong Weerasethakul. 2006.

Tan de repente (Suddenly). Dir. Diego Lerman. 2002.

Tarnation. Dir. Jonathan Caouette. 2003.

Taxi Zum Klo. Dir. Frank Ripploh. 1980.

Tea and Sympathy. Dir. Vincente Minnelli. 1956.

Ten Cents a Dance. Dir. Midi Onodera. 1985.

Teorema. Dir. Pier Paolo Pasolini. 1968.

The ADS Epidemic. Dir. John Greyson. 1987.

The Adventures of Iron Pussy. Dir. Apichatpong Weerasethakul. 2003.

The Angelic Conversation. Dir. Derek Jarman. 1987.

The Bitter Tears of Petra Von Kant. Dir. Rainer Werner Fassbinder. 1972.

The Blue Angel. Dir. Josef von Sternberg. 1930.

The Body of the Poet. Dir. Sonali Fernando. 1995.

The Brandon Teena Story. Dir. Susan Muska and Gréta Olafsdóttir. 1998.

The Celluloid Closet. Dir. Rob Epstein and Jeffrey Friedman. 1995.

The Cockettes. Dir. David Weissman. 2002.

The Conformist. Dir. Bernardo Bertolucci. 1970.

The Craft. Dir. Andrew Fleming. 1996.

The Crying Game. Dir. Neil Jordan. 1992.

The Delta. Dir. Ira Sachs. 1996.

The Devils. Dir. Ken Russell. 1971.

The Doom Generation. Dir. Gregg Araki. 1995.

The Edge of Each Other's Battles: The Vision of Audre Lorde. Dir. Jennifer Abod.
2010.

The Edge of Heaven. Dir. Fatih Akin. 2007.

The Ellen DeGeneres Show. Dir. Michael Dimich (TV series). 2003–.

The Fall of the House of Usher. Dir. James Sibley Watson and Melville Webber. 1928.

The Garden. Dir. Derek Jarman. 1990.

The Gendercator. Dir. Catherine Crouch. 2007.

The Gold Diggers. Dir. Sally Potter. 1983.

The Hours. Dir. Stephen Daldry. 2002.

The Hours and Times. Dir. Christopher Munch. 1991.

The Hunger. Dir. Tony Scott. 1983.

The Incredibly True Adventure of Two Girls in Love. Dir. Maria Maggenti. 1995.

The Itty Bitty Titty Committee. Dir. Jamie Babbit. 2007.

The Judy Spots. Dir. Sadie Benning. 1995.

The Kids Are All Right. Dir. Lisa Cholodenko. 2010.

The L Word. Creators Michele Abbott, Ilene Chaiken, Kathy Greenberg. Dir. Jamie Babbit, Lisa Cholodenko, Angela Robinson, Rose Troche, and others (TV series). 2004–9.

The Last of England. Dir. Derek Jarman. 1988.

The Leopard. Dir. Luchino Visconti. 1963.

The Living End. Dir. Gregg Araki. 1992.

The Maids. Dir. Christopher Miles. 1975.

The Making of "Monsters." Dir. John Greyson. 1991.

The Meeting of Two Queens (*Encuentro entre dos Reinas*). Dir. Cecilia Barriga. 1991.

The Owls. Dir. Cheryl Dunye. 2010.

The Real Ellen Story. Dir. Fenton Bailey and Randy Barbato (TV). 1997.

The Talented Mr. Ripley. Dir. Anthony Minghella. 1999.

The Times of Harvey Milk. Dir. Rob Epstein. 1984.

The Usual Suspects. Dir. Bryan Singer. 1995.

The Watermelon Woman. Dir. Cheryl Dunye. 1996.

The Wedding Banquet. Dir. Ang Lee. 1993.

Thelma and Louise. Dir. Ridley Scott. 1991.

This Is Not an AIDS Advertisement. Dir. Isaac Julien. 1987.

Thundercrack! Dir. Curt McDowell. 1975.

Tomboy. Dir. Céline Sciamma. 2011.

Tongues Untied. Dir. Marlon Riggs. 1989.

Transamerica. Dir. Duncan Tucker. 2005.

Trevor. Dir. Peggy Rajski. 1994.

Tricia's Wedding. Dir. Milton Miron. 1971.

Tropical Malady. Dir. Apichatpong Weerasethakul. 2004.

Twice a Man. Dir. Gregory Markopoulos. 1963.

Un chant d'amour. Dir. Jean Genet. 1950.

Uncle Boonmee Who Can Recall His Past Lives. Dir. Apichatpong Weerasethakul. 2010.

Undertow. Dir. Javier Fuentes-Leon. 2009.

Une robe d'été (*A Summer Dress*). Dir. François Ozon. 1996.

United in Anger: A History of ACT UP. Dir. Jim Hubbard. 2012.

Urinal. Dir. John Greyson. 1988.

Vanilla Sex. Dir. Cheryl Dunye. 1992.

Velvet Goldmine. Dir. Todd Haynes. 1998.

Velvet Vampire. Dir. Stephanie Rothman. 1971.

Vera. Dir. Sérgio Toledo. 1986.

Video against AIDS. Curators John Greyson and Bill Horrigan. 1989.

Viktor und Viktoria. Dir. Reinhold Schünzel. 1933.

We Were Here. Dir. David Weissman. 2011.

Weekend. Dir. Andrew Haigh. 2011.

Wild Side. Dir. Sébastien Lifshitz. 2004.

Wildness. Dir. Wu Tsang. 2012.

Will and Grace. Creator David Kohan and Max Mutchnick (TV series). 1998–2006.

Without a Trace (*Sin dejar huella*). Dir. María Novaro. 2000.

Wizard of Darkness (*Eko eko azaraku*). Dir. Shimako Sato. 1995.

Word Is Out: Stories of Some of Our Lives. Dir. Mariposa Film Collective (Nancy Adair, Peter Adair, Andrew Brown, Rob Epstein, Lucy Massie Phenix, Veronica Selver). 1977.

Xena: Warrior Princess. Creators John Schulian and Robert G. Tapert (TV series). 1995–2001.

X-Men. Dir. Bryan Singer. 2000.

Y tu mamá también (*And Your Mother Too*). Dir. Alfonso Cuarón. 2001.

Yo, la peor de todas (*I, the Worst of All*). Dir. María Luisa Bemberg. 1990.

Young Soul Rebels. Dir. Isaac Julien. 1991.

Zapata's Bande. Dir. Urban Gad. 1914.

Zero Patience. Dir. John Greyson. 1993.

BIBLIOGRAPHY

Aaron, Michele, ed. *The New Queer Cinema: A Critical Reader*. Edinburgh: Edinburgh University Press, 2004.

Aïnouz, Karim. "Interview with Tania Cypriano." *Bomb* 102 (Winter 2008). Available at http://bombsite.com/issues/102/articles/3046.

Alzate, Gastón. *Teatro de cabaret: Imaginarios disidentes*. Irving, Calif.: Ediciones de Gestos, 2002.

Ardill, Susan, and Sue O'Sullivan. "Sex in the Summer of '88." *Feminist Review* 31 (Spring 1989), 126–34.

Arnzen, Michael A. "Interview with Terry Castle." "The Return of the Uncanny." Special issue of *Paradoxa: Studies in World Literary Genres* 3.3–4 (1997), 521–79.

———, ed. "The Return of the Uncanny." Special issue of *Paradoxa: Studies in World Literary Genres* 3.3–4 (1997).

Asibong, Andrew. "Meat, Murder, Metamorphosis: The Transformational Ethics of François Ozon." *French Studies* 59.2 (2005), 203–15.

Bad Object-Choices Collective, eds. *How Do I Look? Queer Film and Video*. Seattle: Bay Press, 1991.

Bakhtin, M. M. *The Dialogic Imagination: Four Essays*. Trans. Caryl Emerson and Michael Holquist. Austin: University of Texas Press, 1981.

———. *Rabelais and His World*. Trans. Helene Iswolsky. 1968; Bloomington: Indiana University Press, 1984.

Basilio, Miriam. "Corporal Evidence: Representations of Aileen Wuornos." *Art Journal* 55.4 (1996), 56–61.

Beard, William, and Jerry White. *North of Everything: English-Canadian Cinema since 1980*. Alberta: University of Alberta Press, 2002.

Benshoff, Harry M. "*Milk* and Gay Political History." *Jump Cut: A Review of*

Contemporary Media 51 (Spring 2009). Available at http://www.ejumpcut.org
/archive/jc51.2009/Milk/.

Benshoff, Harry M., and Sean Griffin, eds. *Queer Cinema: The Film Reader*. New
York: Routledge, 2004.

Birch, Helen, ed. *Moving Targets: Women, Crime and Representation*. London:
Virago / University of California Press, 1994.

Broumas, Olga. "Sleeping Beauty." *Beginning with O*. New Haven: Yale University
Press, 1977.

Brubaker, Rogers. *Citizenship and Nationhood in France and Germany*. Cambridge:
Harvard University Press, 1992.

Burton-Carvajal, Julianne. *Matilde Landeta, hija de la Revolución*. Mexico City:
CONACULTA and IMCINE, 2003.

Butler, Judith. *Gender Trouble: Feminism and the Subversion of Identity*. New York:
Routledge, 1990.

Caron, David. *AIDS in French Culture: Social Ills, Literary Cures*. Madison: University of Wisconsin Press, 2001.

———. "My Father and I: Jewishness, Queerness, and the Marais." *GLQ: A Journal of
Lesbian and Gay Studies* 11.2 (2005), 265–82.

———. *My Father and I: The Marais and the Queerness of Community*. Ithaca:
Cornell University Press, 2009.

Castle, Terry. *The Female Thermometer: Eighteenth-Century Culture and the Invention of the Uncanny*. New York: Oxford University Press, 1995.

Christ, Ronald. "A Last Interview with Manuel Puig." *World Literature Today* 65.4
(1991), 571–78.

Chua, Lawrence. "I Scream, You Scream: Tomás Gutiérrez Alea's Film 'Strawberry
and Chocolate.'" *Artforum International* 33.4 (1994), 62–65.

———. "Interview with Shu Lea Cheang." *Bomb* 54 (Winter 1996). Available at
http://bombsite.com/issues/54/articles/1915.

Corrigan, Timothy, Patricia White, and Meta Mazaj, eds. *Critical Visions in Film
Theory: Classic and Contemporary Readings*. New York: Bedford / St. Martin's
Press, 2010.

Costantino, Roselyn. "Latin American Performance Studies: Random Acts or Critical Moves?" *Theatre Journal* 56.3 (2004), 459–61.

Creekmur, Corey K. "Brokeback: The Parody." *GLQ: A Journal of Lesbian and Gay
Studies* 13.1 (2007), 105–7.

Currah, Paisley, Richard M. Juang, and Shannon Price Minter, eds. *Transgender
Rights*. Minneapolis: University of Minneapolis Press, 2006.

Curtis, Walt, and Gus Van Sant. *Mala Noche and Other "Illegal" Adventures*. Portland, Ore.: BridgeCity Books, 1997.

Davies, Catherine. "Recent Cuban Fiction Films: Identification, Interpretation,
Disorder." *Bulletin of Latin American Research* 15.2 (1996), 177–92.

de la Mora, Sergio. "Chili in Your Eyes: La Pasión According to Ximena Cuevas." *Senses of Cinema*, January 9, 2000. Available at http://sensesofcinema .com/2000/feature-articles/chilli/.

———. *Cinemachismo: Masculinities and Sexuality in Mexican Film*. Austin: University of Texas Press, 2006.

———. "Fascinating Machismo: Toward an Unmasking of Heterosexual Masculinity in Arturo Ripstein's *El lugar sin límites*." *Journal of Film and Video* 44.3–4 (1992–93), 90.

———. "Mexican Experimental Cinema and Ximena Cuevas." *Jump Cut: A Review of Contemporary Media* 43 (July 2000), 102–5.

———. "*Por un amor*: Lucha Reyes and Queer Mexican Cultural Nationalism." Paper presented at American Studies Association conference, Washington, D.C., 2009.

de Lauretis, Teresa. "Aesthetic and Feminist Theory: Rethinking Women's Cinema." *New German Critique* 34 (Winter 1985), 154–75.

———. "Film and the Visible." *How Do I Look? Queer Film and Video*, ed. Bad Object Choices Collective. Seattle: Bay Press, 1991.

———. "Guerrilla in the Midst: Women's Cinema in the '80s." *Screen* 31 (1990), 6–25.

———, ed. "Queer Theory: Lesbian and Gay Sexualities." Special issue of *Differences* 3.2 (1991).

D'Emilio, John, and Estelle B. Freedman. *Intimate Matters: A History of Sexuality in America*. Chicago: University of Chicago Press, 1988.

Duberman, Martin. *Stonewall*. New York: Plume Books, 1994.

Duggan, Lisa. *Sapphic Slashers: Sex, Violence and American Modernity*. Durham: Duke University Press, 2000.

———. *The Twilight of Equality? Neoliberalism, Cultural Politics, and the Attack on Democracy*. Boston: Beacon Press, 2004.

Dyer, Richard, and Julianne Pidduck. *Now You See It: Studies in Lesbian and Gay Film*. 2nd ed. New York: Routledge, 2003.

Faludi, Susan. *Backlash: The Undeclared War against American Women*. New York: Crown, 1991.

Fassin, Eric. "Same Sex, Different Politics: 'Gay Marriage' Debates in France and the United States." *Public Culture* 13.2 (2001), 215–32.

Favell, Adrian. *Philosophies of Integration: Immigration and the Idea of Citizenship in France and Britain*. New York: St. Martin's Press, 1998.

Feinberg, Leslie. *Transgender Liberation: A Movement Whose Time Has Come*. New York: World View, 1992.

———. *Transgender Warriors: Making History from Joan of Arc to Dennis Rodman*. Boston: Beacon Press, 1997.

Feldman, Eric A. "Blood Justice: Courts, Conflict, and Compensation in Japan, France, and the United States." *Law and Society Review* 34.3 (2000), 651–701.

Foss, Karen. "The Logic of Folly in the Political Campaigns of Harvey Milk." *Queer Words, Queer Images*, ed. Jeffrey Ringer. New York: New York University Press, 1994.

Foster, David William. *Queer Issues in Contemporary Latin American Cinema*. Austin: University of Texas Press, 2003.

Freccero, Carla. "Feminism, Rabelais, and the Hill/Thomas Hearings: Return to a Scene of Reading." *François Rabelais: Critical Assessments*, ed. Jean-Claude Carron. Baltimore: Johns Hopkins University Press, 1995.

———. "They Are All Sodomites!" "Gender and Cultural Memory." Special issue of *Signs: Journal of Women in Culture and Society* 28.1 (2002), 454.

Fuss, Diana. *Inside Out: Lesbian Theories, Gay Theories*. New York: Routledge, 1991.

Gabara, Rachel. "Screening Autobiography: Cyril Collard's *Nuits Fauves*." *French Cultural Studies* 16.1 (2005), 55–72.

Gever, Martha. *Entertaining Lesbians: Celebrity, Sexuality, and Self-Invention*. New York: Routledge, 2003.

———. "Pictures of Sickness: Stuart Marshall's *Bright Eyes*." *Queer Looks: Perspectives on Lesbian and Gay Film and Video*, ed. Martha Gever, Pratibha Parmar, and John Greyson. New York: Routledge, 1993.

Gever, Martha, Pratibha Parmar, and John Greyson. eds. *Queer Looks: Perspectives on Lesbian and Gay Film and Video*. New York: Routledge, 1993.

Gittings, Christopher. "*Zero Patience*, Genre, Difference, and Ideology: Singing and Dancing Queer Nation." *Cinema Journal* 41.1 (2001), 28–39.

Glamuzina, Julie, and Alison J. Laurie, eds. *Parker and Hulme: A Lesbian View*. Ithaca: Firebrand Books, 1995.

Goldie, Terry. *In a Queer Country: Gay and Lesbian Studies in the Canadian Context*. Toronto: Arsenal Pulp Press, 2002.

Gomez, Jewelle. *The Gilda Stories, a Novel*. Ithaca: Firebrand Press, 1991.

Gould, Deborah. *Moving Politics: Emotion and ACT UP's Fight against AIDS*. Chicago: University of Chicago Press, 2009.

Greenberg, Miriam, *Branding New York: How a City in Crisis Was Sold to the World*. New York: Routledge, 2008.

Grémy, Isabelle, and Nathalie Beltzer. "HIV Risk and Condom Use in the Adult Heterosexual Population in France between 1992 and 2001: Return to the Starting Point?" *AIDS* 18.5 (2004), 805–9.

Guerrilla Girls. *Bitches, Bimbos, and Ballbreakers: The Guerrilla Girls' Illustrated Guide to Female Stereotypes*. New York: Penguin, 2003.

———. *The Guerrilla Girls' Bedside Companion to the History of Western Art*. New York: Penguin, 1998.

Gunther, Scott. "Building a More Stately Closet: French Gay Movements Since the Early 1980s." *Journal of the History of Sexuality* 13.3 (2004), 340.

Gutiérrez, Laura G. "Reframing the Retablo: Mexican Feminist Critical Practice in Ximena Cuevas' Corazón Sangrante." *Feminist Media Studies* 1.1 (2001), 73–90.

Halberstam, Judith. *Female Masculinity*. Durham: Duke University Press, 1998.

———. *In a Queer Time and Place: Transgender Bodies, Subcultural Lives*. New York: New York University Press, 2005.

Hammer, Barbara. *HAMMER! Making Movies out of Sex and Life*. New York: The Feminist Press at CUNY, 2010.

Hart, Lynda. "Chloe Liked Olivia: Death, Desire and Detection in the Female Buddy Film." *Fatal Women: Lesbian Sexuality and the Mark of Aggression*. Princeton: Princeton University Press, 1994.

Hartlen, Neil. "Queer across the Atlantic: Homo/sexual Representation in the United States and France, 1977–2001." PhD diss., University of Massachusetts, Amherst, 2006.

Henderson, Lisa. "Simple Pleasures: Lesbian Community and *Go Fish*." *Signs* 25.1 (1999), 37–64.

Horeck, Tanya. "From Documentary to Drama: Capturing Aileen Wuornos." *Screen* 48.2 (2007), 141–59.

Huaco-Nuzum, Carmen. "Matilde Landeta: An Introduction to the Work of a Pioneer Mexican Filmmaker." *Screen* 28.4 (1987), 96–105.

Iglesias Prieto, Norma, and Rosa Linda Fregoso, eds. *Miradas de mujer: Encuentro de cineastas y videoastas Mexicanas y Chicanas*. Tijuana, Mexico: Colegio de la Frontera Norte and Chicana/Latina Research Center, University of California, Davis, 1998.

Indiana, Gary. *Three-Month Fever: The Andrew Cunanan Story*. New York: Harper-Collins, 1999.

Isaak, Jo Anna. *Feminism and Contemporary Art: The Revolutionary Power of Women's Laughter*. New York: Routledge, 1996.

Jarman, Derek. *Modern Nature: The Journals of Derek Jarman*. Woodstock, N.Y.: Overlook Press, 1994.

Jarman, Derek, and Shaun Allen. *Dancing Ledge*. Woodstock, N.Y.: Overlook Press, 1993.

Jarman, Derek, and Michael Christie. *At Your Own Risk: A Saint's Testament*. Woodstock, N.Y.: Overlook Press, 1993.

Jarman, Derek, and Keith Collins. *Smiling in Slow Motion*. London: Century, 2000.

Jarman, Derek, and Howard Sooley. *Derek Jarman's Garden*. Woodstock, N.Y.: Overlook Press, 1996.

Johnston, Sheila. "Death Every Day" (interview with François Ozon). *Sight and Sound* 11.4 (2001), 12–13.

Lawless, Jessica. "The Gendercator, or How I Learned to Stop Worrying and Love the Blogosphere." *GLQ: A Journal of Lesbian and Gay Studies* 15.1 (2009), 131–51.

Leu, Lorraine. *Brazilian Popular Music: Caetano Veloso and the Regeneration of Tradition*. Hampshire, U.K.: Ashgate, 2006.

Leung, Helen Hok-Sze. "New Queer Cinema and Third Cinema." *New Queer Cinema: A Critical Reader*, ed. Michele Aaron. Edinburgh: Edinburgh University Press, 2004.

Longfellow, Brenda, Scott MacKenzie, and Thomas Waugh, eds. *The Perils of Pedagogy: The Works of John Greyson*. Montreal: McGill Queen's University Press, 2013.

Mackenzie, Scott. "*Baise-moi*, Feminist Cinemas and the Censorship Controversy." *Screen* 43.3 (2002), 315–24.

Markham, Jerry W. *A Financial History of the United States*. Armonk, N.Y.: M. E. Sharpe, 2001.

Mayne, Judith. *Directed by Dorothy Arzner*. Bloomington: Indiana University Press, 1994.

McCaughan, Edward J. "Gender, Sexuality, and Nation in the Art of Mexican Social Movements." *Nepantla: Views from South* 3.1 (2002), 99–143.

Meeker, Martin. "Behind the Mask of Respectability: Reconsidering the Mattachine Society and Male Homophile Practice, 1950s–1960s." *Journal of the History of Sexuality* 10.1 (2001), 95–97.

Mendelsohn, Daniel. "An Affair to Remember." *New York Review of Books* 53.3 (2006).

Mitchell, Claudia, and Jacqueline Reid-Walsh, eds. *Girl Culture, an Encyclopedia*. Westport, Conn.: Greenwood Press, 2008.

Mitchell, Tim. *Intoxicated Identities: Alcohol's Power in Mexican History and Culture*. New York: Routledge, 2004.

Moatti, J. P., W. Dab, P. Quenel, N. Beltzer, and M. Pollak. "Social Perception of AIDS in French General Public: 1987–1990 Evolution in Paris Region." *Psychological Health* 9 (1994), 285–96.

Monem, Nadine, ed. *Riot Grrrl: Revolution Girl Style Now!* London: Black Dog, 2007.

Muñoz, José Esteban. "The Autoethnographic Performance: Reading Richard Fung's Queer Hybridity." *Screen* 36.2 (1995), 83–99.

———. *Cruising Utopia: The Then and There of Queer Futurity*. New York: New York University Press, 2009.

———. "Dead White: Notes on the Whiteness of the New Queer Cinema." *GLQ: Journal of Lesbian and Gay Studies* 4.1 (1998), 127–38.

———. *Dis-Identifications: Queers of Color and the Performance of Politics*. Minneapolis: University of Minnesota Press, 1999.

Nájera-Ramírez, Olga. "Unruly Passions: Poetics, Performance and Gender in the *Ranchera* Song." *Chicana Feminisms: A Critical Reader*, ed. Gabriela F. Arredondo, Aida Hurtado, Norma Klahn, Olga Najera-Ramirez, and Patricia Zavella. Durham: Duke University Press, 2003.

Nash, Mark. "Chronicle(s) of a Death Foretold: Notes Apropos of *Les Nuits Fauves*." *Critical Quarterly* 36.1 (1994), 97–104.

Needham, Gary. *Brokeback Mountain*. Edinburgh: Edinburgh University Press, 2000.

Nero, Charles I. "Diva Traffic and Male Bonding in Film: Teaching Opera, Learning Gender, Race, and Nation." *Camera Obscura* 19.56 (2004), 46–73.

Nye, Robert A. "The Pacte Civil de Solidarité and the History of Sexuality." *French Politics, Culture and Society* 21.1 (2003), 87–100.

Onodera, Midi. "Camera Obscura for Dreams." *Practical Dreamers: Conversations with Movie Artists*, ed. Mike Hoolboom. Toronto: Coach House Books, 2004.

Orth, Maureen. *Vulgar Favors: Andrew Cunanan, Gianni Versace, and the Largest Failed Manhunt in U.S. History*. New York: Random House, 1999.

Phillips, John. *Transgender on Screen*. New York: Palgrave Macmillan, 2006.

Proulx, Annie. *Wyoming Stories*. New York: Scribner, 2000.

Rainer, Yvonne. *A Woman Who . . . : Essays, Interviews, Scripts*. Baltimore: Johns Hopkins University Press, 1999.

Rashkin, Elissa. "An Other Cinema." *Women Filmmakers in Mexico: The Country of Which We Dream*. San Antonio: University of Texas Press, 2001.

Reynaud, Berenice. "Le 'hood: 'Hate' and Its Neighbors." *Film Comment* 32.2 (1996), 54–59.

Rich, Adrienne. "Compulsory Heterosexuality and the Lesbian Continuum." *Signs: Journal of Women in Culture and Society* 5 (Summer 1980), 631–60.

Rich, B. Ruby. "An/Other View of New Latin American Cinema." *Iris* 13 (1991), 5–28.

———. "Bay of Pix." *American Film* 9.9 (1984), 57–59.

———. "Feminism and Sexuality in the Eighties." *Chick Flicks: Theories and Memories of the Feminist Film Movement*. Durham: Duke University Press, 1998.

———. "Héctor García Mesa: Man of My Dreams." *Héctor García Mesa*. Exhibition catalogue. Havana: La Cinemateca de Cuba, ICAIC, 2009.

———. "Introduction to U.S. Edition." *Parker and Hulme: A Lesbian View*, ed. Julie Glamuzina and Alison J. Laurie. Ithaca: Firebrand Books, 1995.

———. "Lethal Lesbians." *girlsgangsguns: Zwischen Exploitation-Kino und Underground*, ed. Carla Despineux and Verena Mund. Marburg, Germany: Schüren Verlag, 2000.

———. "Lethal Lesbians." *Village Voice*, April 25, 1995.

———. "The Long Road: Isaac Julien in Conversation with B. Ruby Rich." *Art Journal* 61.2 (2002), 51–64.

———. "Making Argentina Matter Again: Lucrecia Martel's 'La Ciénaga.'" *New York Times*, September 30, 2001.

———. "Manifesto Destiny: Drawing a Bead on Valerie Solanas." *Village Voice Literary Supplement*, October 12, 1993.

———. "Reflections on a Queer Screen." *GLQ: A Journal of Lesbian and Gay Studies* 1.1 (1993), 83–91.

———. "Tough Girls Don't Dance: Sergio Toledo's *Vera.*" *Village Voice,* October 20, 1987.

———. "What's Up, 'Pussycat'?" *Village Voice,* January 17, 1995.

Rich, B. Ruby, and Lourdes Arguelles. "Homosexuality, Homophobia and Revolution: Notes toward an Understanding of the Cuban Lesbian and Gay Male Experience, Part I." *Signs: Journal of Women in Culture and Society* 9.4 (1984), 683–99.

———. "Homosexuality, Homophobia and Revolution: Notes toward an Understanding of the Cuban Lesbian and Gay Male Experience, Part II." *Signs: Journal of Women in Culture and Society* 11.1 (1985), 120–36.

Rollet, Brigitte, and James S. Williams. "Visions of Excess: Filming/Writing the Gay Self in Collard's *Savage Nights.*" *Gay Signatures: Gay and Lesbian Theory, Fiction and Film in France, 1945–1995,* ed. Owen Heathcote, Alex Hughes, and James S. Williams. New York: Berg, 1998.

Román, David, and Alberto Sandoval. "Caught in the Web: Latinidad, AIDS, and Allegory in 'Kiss of the Spider Woman,' the Musical." *American Literature* 67.3 (1995), 553–85.

Rosenberg, Jessica, and Gitana Garofalo. "Riot Grrrl: Revolutions from Within." *Signs* 23.3 (1998), 809–41.

Russo, Mary. *The Female Grotesque: Risk, Excess, and Modernity.* New York: Routledge, 1994.

Salvatore, Armando. "Authority in Question: Secularity, Republicanism and 'Communitarianism' in the Emerging Euro-Islamic Public Sphere." *Theory, Culture and Society* 24.2 (2007), 135–160.

Santí, Enrico Mario. "*Fresa y Chocolate*: The Rhetoric of Cuban Reconciliation." *MLN* 113.2, Hispanic issue (1998), 407–25.

Schor, Naomi. "The Crisis of French Universalism." *Yale French Studies* 100 (2001), 43–64.

Schrobsdorff, Susanna. "Chick Flick Cowboys: *Brokeback Mountain* Has Stolen the Hearts of Women in Middle America." *Newsweek,* January 20, 2006, accessed online August 30, 2006, at www.msnbc.msn.com/id/10930877/site/newsweek.

Scott, Joan Wallach. *Parité: Sexual Equality and the Crisis of French Universalism.* Chicago: University of Chicago Press, 2005.

Sedgwick, Eve Kosofsky. *Epistemology of the Closet.* Durham: Duke University Press, 1990.

Shaw, Deborah. *Contemporary Cinema of Latin America: Ten Key Films.* New York: Continuum, 2003.

Shaw, Lisa. "Afro-Brazilian Identity: Malandragem and Homosexuality in Madame Satã." *Contemporary Latin American Cinema: Breaking into the Global Market,* ed. Deborah Shaw. Lanham, Md.: Rowman and Littlefield, 2007.

Shilts, Randy. *The Mayor of Castro Street.* New York: St. Martin's Griffin, 1988.

Shulman, Alix Kates. "Sex and Power: Sexual Bases of Radical Feminism." *Signs* 5.4 (1980), 590–604.

Simo, Anna. "Outing in Gay Paree." Gully.com, October 30, 2000. Available at http://www.thegully.com/essays/france/001030gay_paris.html.

Sitney, P. Adams. *Visionary Film: The American Avant-Garde*. New York: Oxford University Press, 1974.

Smith, Paul Julian. "*Fresa y chocolate* (*Strawberry and Chocolate*): Cinema as Guided Tour." *Vision Machines: Cinema, Literature, and Sexuality in Spain and Cuba, 1983–93*. London: Verso, 1996.

———. "The Language of Strawberry." *Sight and Sound* 4 (December 1994), 31–32.

Stacey, Jackie. "Desperately Seeking Difference." *Screen* 28.1 (1987), 48–61.

———. *Star-Gazing*. London: Routledge, 1994.

Stacey, Jackie, and Sarah Street, eds. *Queer Screen*. London: Routledge, 2007.

Stam, Robert. *Subversive Pleasures: Bakhtin, Cultural Criticism, and Film*. Baltimore: Johns Hopkins University Press, 1989.

———. *Tropical Multiculturalism: A Comparative History of Race in Brazilian Cinema and Culture*. Durham: Duke University Press, 1997.

Stavans, Ilan. "The Latin Phallus." *Transition* 65 (1995), 48–68.

———. "The Riddle of Cantinflas." *Transition* 67 (1995), 22–46.

Stern, Lesley. "'I Think, Sebastian, Therefore I . . . Somersault': Film and the Uncanny." *Paradoxa* 3, no. 3–4 (1997); reprinted in the *Australian Humanities Review*, November 1997–January 1998.

Stone, Sandy. "The Empire Strikes Back: A Posttranssexual Manifesto." *Body Guards: The Cultural Politics of Sexual Ambiguity*, ed. Kristina Straub and Julia Epstein. New York: Routledge, 1991.

Stryker, Susan. "The Transgender Issue: An Introduction." *GLQ: A Journal of Lesbian and Gay Studies* 4.2 (1998), 145–58.

Stryker, Susan, and Stephen Whittle, eds. *The Transgender Studies Reader*. New York: Routledge, 2006.

Stychin, Carl F. "Civil Solidarity or Fragmented Identities? The Politics of Sexuality and Citizenship in France." *Social and Legal Studies* 10.3 (2001), 347–76.

Suárez, Juan. "The Puerto Rican Lower East Side and the Queer Underground." *Grey Room* 32 (Summer 2008), 1–36.

Subero, Gustavo. "Fear of the Trannies: On Filmic Phobia of Transvestism in the New Latin American Cinema." *Latin American Research Review* 43.2 (2008), 159–79.

Sussler, Betsy. "Lizzie Borden." *Bomb* 7 (Fall 1983). Available at http://bombsite.com /issues/7/articles/333.

Tarr, Carrie. *Reframing Difference: Beur and Banlieue Filmmaking in France*. Manchester, U.K.: Manchester University Press, 2005.

Taylor, Diana, and Roselyn Costantino, eds. *Holy Terrors: Latin American Women Perform*. Durham: Duke University Press, 2003.

Tulchin, Allan A. "Same-Sex Couples Creating Households in Old Regime France: The Uses of the *Affrèrement*." *Journal of Modern History* 79 (September 2007), 613–47.

Valentine, David. *Imagining Transgender: An Ethnography of a Category*. Durham: Duke University Press, 2007.

Vance, Carol S., ed. *Pleasure and Danger: Exploring Female Sexuality*. Boston: Routledge and Kegan Paul, 1984.

Verhoeven, Deb. "Biting the Hand That Breeds: The Trials of Tracey Wigginton." *Moving Targets: Women, Murder, and Representation*, ed. Helen Birch. Berkeley: University of California Press, 1994.

Villarejo, Amy. "The Creature from the Black Lagoon." GLQ: *Journal of Lesbian and Gay Studies* 12.2 (2006), 338–40.

———. "Forbidden Love: Pulp as Lesbian History." *Out Takes: Essays on Queer Theory and Film*, ed. Ellis Hanson. Durham: Duke University Press, 1999.

———. *Lesbian Rule: Cultural Criticism and the Value of Desire*. Durham: Duke University Press, 2003.

Vincendeau, Ginette. *La Haine (French Film Guide)*. Champaign: University of Illinois Press, 2005.

Warner, Michael. *Fear of a Queer Planet: Queer Politics and Social Theory*. Minneapolis: University of Minnesota, 1993.

Watney, Simon. "The French Connection." *Sight and Sound* 3.6 (1993), 24–25.

Weiss, Andrea. *Vampires and Violets: Lesbians in Film*. New York: Penguin, 1993.

West, Dennis. "Strawberry and Chocolate, Ice Cream and Tolerance: Interviews with Tomás Gutiérrez Alea and Juan Carlos Tabío." *Cineaste* 21.1–2 (1995), 16–21.

White, Dave. "The Straight Dude's Guide to 'Brokeback.'" MSNBC, December 8, 2005. Available at http://today.msnbc.msn.com/id/10342237#.UGDUwo5bwdI.

White, Patricia. "Black and White: Mercedes de Acosta's Glorious Enthusiasms." *Camera Obscura* 15.3 (2000), 227–64.

Willis, Ellen. *No More Nice Girls: Countercultural Essays*. Hanover, N.H.: University Press of New England and Wesleyan University Press, 1992.

Ybarra-Frausto, Tomás. "Rasquachismo: A Chicano Sensibility." CARA: *Chicano Art: Resistance and Affirmation 1965–1995*, ed. Richard Griswold de Castillo et al. Los Angeles: Wight Art Gallery, UCLA, 1991.

CREDITS

Chapter 2 was first published in the *Village Voice* of March 24, 1992, under the headline "A Queer Sensation." It was reprinted as the lead article in a special section of *Sight and Sound* 2.5 (1992), 30–34, with the headline "The New Queer Cinema." This version contains the complete original text, not published in either.

Chapter 3 originally appeared as "Collision, Catastrophe, Celebration: The Relationship between Gay and Lesbian Film Festivals and Their Publics," *GLQ: A Journal of Lesbian and Gay Studies* 5.1 (1999), 79–84.

Chapter 4 originally appeared as "What's a Good Gay Film?," *OUT* 60 (November 1998), 58.

Chapter 5 originally appeared as "King of Queer," *SF Weekly*, April 1, 1992.

Chapter 6 originally appeared as "Making Love," *Village Voice*, March 24, 1992.

Chapter 7 originally appeared as "Goings and Comings: *Go Fish*," *Sight and Sound* 4.7 (1994), 14–16.

Chapter 8 originally appeared as "She's Gotta Film It," *San Francisco Bay Guardian*, July 23, 1997.

Chapter 9 originally appeared as "Violence to Glam Rock," *Sight and Sound* 6.12 (1996), 5.

Chapter 10 was originally published as "The I.K.U. EXXXperience: The Shu Lea Cheang Phenomenon," *Cinevue*, Asian Cine Vision Film Festival, July 2000.

Chapter 11 originally appeared as "Tell It to the Camera," *Sight and Sound* 15.4 (2005), 32–34.

Chapter 12 originally appeared as "Tiger by the Tale," *The Advocate*, July 5, 2005, 54. Reprinted courtesy of *The Advocate* / Here Media Inc. © 2005. All rights reserved.

Chapter 13 originally appeared as "Araki Rock (Greg Araki)," *San Francisco Bay Guardian*, May 25, 2005.

Chapter 14 originally appeared as "A Walk in the Clouds (A Thousand Clouds of Peace)," *San Francisco Bay Guardian*, March 31, 2004.

Chapter 15 text derives from original lectures delivered between 1994 and 1999. Elements of this chapter appeared as "Lethal Lesbians," *Village Voice*, April 25, 1995; "Introduction to U.S. Edition," *Parker and Hulme: A Lesbian View*, ed. Julie Glamuzina and Alison J. Laurie (Ithaca: Firebrand Books, 1995), i–xi; and in German, "Lethal Lesbians," *girlsgangsguns: Zwischen Exploitation-Kino und Underground*, ed. Carla Despineux and Verena Mund (Marburg, Germany: Schüren Verlag, 2000), 127–50.

Chapter 16 originally appeared as "When the Saints Come Marching In," *out* 6.2 (1997), 65–67.

Chapter 17 originally appeared as "A Queer and Present Danger," *Sight and Sound* 10.3 (2000), 22–25.

Chapter 24, Part I, was originally published in a shorter version as "Hello Cowboy," *The Guardian*, September 23, 2005, and reprinted as "Queer Eye for the Cowboy," *Sydney Morning Herald*, October 22, 2005, and "How the Western Was Won," *Mail & Guardian*, South Africa, January 24, 2006. Part III was originally published as "Brokering *Brokeback*: Jokes, Backlashes, and Other Anxieties," *Film Quarterly* 60. 3 (winter 2007): 44–48.

Chapter 27 was originally published in an abbreviated version in "Ghosts of a Vanished World," *The Guardian*, January 16, 2009.

INDEX

Proposition 8, 249, 251, 252, 253, 255, 259n15, 259n18
Proposition 13, 258n4
Proposition 187, 254, 259n17
See also San Francisco camcorders, and origins of NQC, xv
Canada:
 early queer films, 10, 16
 See also Forbidden Love (Fernie/Weissman); National Film Board of Canada (NFB); Toronto International Film Festival (TIFF)
Cantinflas (Fortino Mario Alfonso Moreno Reyes), 172–74
Caouette, Jonathan:
 as actor, 87n6
 All Flowers in Time, 87n6
 queering of documentary style, 85–87
 Tarnation, xxi, 81–87
 Walk Away Renée, 87n6
Capturing the Friedmans (Jarecki), 84, 86
Caravaggio (Jarman), 50
Caress, Jordan, 265
Carlomusto, Jean, xxviin5, 10, 30
Caron, David, 220
Carvalho, Walter, 175, 182n15
Casares, Ingrid, 104, 119n6
Castro district, 5, 128, 224–45, 250–51
 See also Castro Theatre
Castro, Fidel, 163, 164
Castro Theatre:
 and Milk, 236, 243, 247–48, 252, 259n12
 and San Francisco film festival, 53, 239, 240
Cavalcanti, Alberto, 143n1
Cecil B. DeMented (Waters), 274
Celluloid Closet (Russo), 6, 32n10, 256
Center for Lesbian and Gay Studies, 44
Chabrol, Claude:
 La Cérémonie, 110, 112, 115
 Les Biches, 5
Chang, William, 43
Chariots of Fire, 50
Charleson, Ian, 50
Chasing Amy (Smith), xxii
Cheang, Shu-Lea:
 Bowling Alley, 77
 Brandon, 77
 Color Schemes, 77
 as director, 77–79, 80n3

Fresh Kill, 78
I.K.U., xxi, 76–77, 78–79
 and New Queer Cinema, 202
 Sex Bowl, 78
 Sex Fish, 78
 Will Be Televised, 77
Chechik, Jeremiah S., 113
Cheney, Dick, 197
Chicago's Video Data Bank, 10
Chicks in White Satin (Holliman), 42
Chinese Characters (Fung), 10
Cholodenko, Lisa:
 crossover success, xxiv, 264
 High Art, xx, 38, 43–44, 133, 264
 The Kids Are Alright, 264–65
Chonin, Neva, 191
Chopra, Joyce, 83
Christie, Julie, 68, 212n6
Cinemien, 21–22
Circumstance (Keshavarz), 278–79
Clarke, Cheryl, 69
Clarkson, Patricia, 133
Clementi, Tyler, xxvi, 267
Clinton, Bill, 75, 135, 261
Close Up (H.D./ Bryher), 4
Clouzot, Henri-Georges, 113
Cocteau, Jean, 214
Codependent Lesbian Space Alien Seeks Same (Olnek), 278
Codikow, Stacy, 202
Colegio de la Frontera Norte (COLEF), 156
Coles, Matt, 254
Collard, Cyril:
 AIDS illness, 224, 234n28
 critical reception, 224
 cultural and political influences, 217–22
 death, 220, 224
 links to Téchiné and Ozon, 215–16, 223–26
 sexuality, 223
 See also Les nuits fauves (Savage Nights)
Collective for Living Cinema, xiv
Come Back to the Five and Dime, Jimmy Dean, Jimmy Dean (Altman), 272
Comedy in Six Unnatural Acts, A (Oxenberg), 5, 60, 68
Condon, Bill:
 Chicago, 136n3
 Dreamgirls, 136n3
 Gods and Monsters, 132–33
 Kinsey, 136n3
Conformist, The (Bertolucci), 5, 155n3

Constantino, Roselyn, 168, 169
Cook, Blanche Wiesen, 114
Cook, Pamela, 31
Cooper, Dennis, 35
Cooper, John, 253
Corbet, Brady, 93
Cottis, Jane, 25–26
Cott, Nancy, 114
Cowan, Noah, 187
Craft, The (Fleming), 112
Crawford, Cindy, 104
Crawford, Joan, 157
Crenshaw, Michelle, 68
Crouch, Catherine, 277–78
Crouching Tiger, Hidden Dragon (Lee), 186, 189
Cruising (Friedkin), 146
Crying Game, The (Jordan), 272–73
Cuarón, Alfonso, 176–77
Cuba:
 gay and lesbian life, xxiii, 159–60, 162, 164, 165
 labor camps, 165
 screening of Word Is Out, 160, 161, 162
 and Soviet economic support, 162
 and U.S. foreign policy, 159–60, 164, 165n2, 166n9
 See also Cuban cinema
Cuban cinema:
 gay themes in, 162–65, 166n7
 See also Alea, Tomás Gutiérrez; Instituto Cubano del Arte y la Industria Cinematográficos (ICAIC)
Cubby Hole, 104
Cuevas, Ximena:
 Corazón sangrante, 170–71
 and Cosi fan tutte, 74
 La tómbola (The Raffle), 172–74
Cukor, George, 4
Cummins, Stephen:
 on Barbed Wire Kisses panel, 17, 29
 death from AIDS, 31n3
 photo, 29
 Resonance, xxviiin12, 17
Cunanan, Andrew, 36, 39n3
Curran, Paisley, 271
Curtis, Walt, 7, 239

Dabney, Sheila, 8
Dahmer, Jeffrey, 28, 32n8
Damned If You Don't (Friedrich), 10
Danzón (Novaro), 153
Daughters of Bilitis, 192
Daughters of Darkness (Kumel), 116